LONE MOTHERHOOD IN
TWENTIETH-CENTURY BRITAIN

Lone Motherhood in Twentieth-Century Britain

From Footnote to Front Page

KATHLEEN KIERNAN
HILARY LAND
JANE LEWIS

CLARENDON PRESS · OXFORD
1998

Oxford University Press, Great Clarendon Street, Oxford OX2 6DP

Oxford New York

Athens Auckland Bangkok Bogota Bombay Buenos Aires
Calcutta Cape Town Dar es Salaam Delhi Florence
Hong Kong Istanbul Karachi Kuala Lumpur Madras
Madrid Melbourne Mexico City Nairobi Paris
Singapore Taipei Tokyo Toronto Warsaw

and associated companies in
Berlin Ibadan

Oxford is a trade mark of Oxford University Press

Published in the United States
by Oxford University Press Inc., New York

British Library Cataloguing in Publication Data

Data available

Library of Congress Cataloging in Publication Data
Lewis, Jane (Jane E.)
Lone motherhood in twentieth-century Britain : from footnote to
front page/Jane Lewis, Kathleen Kiernan, Hilary Land.
Includes bibliographical references.
1. Unmarried mothers–Great Britain–History–20th century.
2. Single mothers–Great Britain–History–20th century. 3. Women
heads of households–Great Britain–History–20th century.
I. Kiernan, Kathleen. II. Land, Hilary. III. Title
HQ759.45.L48 1998 306.874'3'09410904–dc21 97-39267

ISBN 0–19–829070–5
ISBN 0–19–829069–1 (pbk.).

1 3 5 7 9 10 8 6 4 2

Typeset by J&L Composition Ltd, Filey, North Yorkshire
Printed in Great Britain on acid-free paper by
Biddles Ltd, Guildford and King's Lynn

PREFACE

This book represents an attempt to bring together different disciplinary perspectives in order to come to a better understanding of the complicated story of lone motherhood. Each of us has taken the major responsibility for particular chapters, other than the conclusion which was written jointly. Kathleen Kiernan was responsible for Chapters 2 and 5, Hilary Land for Chapters 6, 7, and 8, and Jane Lewis for Chapters 1, 3, and 4.

Kathleen Kiernan would like to acknowledge the support of the Economic and Social Research Council, through Grant No. L315 25 3015 on the Changing Demography of Partnership which forms part of the Population Household Change Programme, and the research assistance of Ganka Mueller. Material from the General Household Survey was made available through the Office for National Statistics and the ESRC Data Archive at Essex University and has been used by permission of the Controller of the Stationery Office. The ESRC Data Archive also supplied the data from the National Survey of Sexual Attitudes and Lifestyles. Hilary Land would like to thank Carol Marks for her speedy and accurate typing. Hilary Land and Jane Lewis would like to acknowledge the support of the Joseph Rowntree Foundation and the research assistance of David Lee and Sophie Sarre. Jane Lewis is also grateful to the European Commission for a Human Capital and Mobility Grant, which brought together a number of European scholars (Franca Bimbi, Pauline Conroy, Ilona Ostner, and Birte Siim) to discuss issues to do with lone motherhood and welfare regimes over a three-year period. Barbara Hobson and Trudie Knijn joined this group part way through its existence and Jane Lewis gained enormously from the group's discussions. She is also grateful to Stephen Cretney and to Janet Fink for reading Chapters 3 and 4, respectively, and offering comments. We are all in debt to Jane Dickson for her expert help with the preparation of the manuscript.

K. K., H. L., J. L.

CONTENTS

LIST OF FIGURES

LIST OF TABLES

ABBREVIATIONS

APA	additional personal allowance
BHPS	British Household Panel Study
CBI	child benefit interim (until 1981, then one parent/lone parent benefit)
CPAG	Child Poverty Action Group
CSA	Child Support Agency
CSO	Central Statistical Office
DEE	Department for Education and Employment
DH	Department of Health
DHSS	Department of Health and Social Security
DSS	Department of Social Security
EOC	Equal Opportunities Commission
FC	family credit
FIS	family income supplement
GMA	guaranteed maintenance allowance
GRO	General Register Office
IS	income support
LCC	London County Council
LEL	lower earnings limit
MCA	married couples allowance
MMA	married man's tax allowance
MSS	Ministry of Social Security
NA	national assistance
NAB	National Assistance Board
NACAB	National Association of Citizen Advice Bureaux
NACSA	Network Against the Child Support Act
NCOPF	National Council for One Parent Families
NCUMC	National Council for the Unmarried Mother and her Child
NIAC	National Insurance Advisory Committee
OPCS	Office of Population Censuses and Surveys
PSID	Panel Study of Income Dynamics
SB	supplementary benefit
SBC	Supplementary Benefit Commission
SMP	statutory maternity pay
SSAC	Social Security Advisory Committee

1

Introduction

During the 1990s the polemical literature on lone mothers, which is often fiercely party political, has been vast. Right-wing 'think tanks' have produced a stream of material deploring the 'end of the family', some of it written by Left-leaning writers, who are equally upset about what they perceive as the end of stable working-class communities. The titles of the pieces that have dominated the debate in the media have stressed above all the cost of lone mother families to the state. Thus the *Sunday Times* ran a piece in mid-1993 entitled: 'A Man—or the State?' (11 July 1993). A BBC TV Panorama programme broadcast in September 1993 went out under the title: 'Babies on Benefit'. The iconography accompanying newspaper discussion of the issue has also been striking. The *Sunday Times* piece showed a mother leading a man with 'state benefits' stamped across his face to the altar, with a number of children following on behind. This lone mother was no hapless victim. The picture suggests strident demands being made of the state by an anti-social citizen. In July 1996, the same newspaper ran another major piece on lone mothers. The accompanying picture was of three generations of women, who appeared to be grandmother, mother, and baby daughter. Both adult women are looking adoringly at the baby. There is almost a Madonna and child look about the mother and child. The women are fatter than most people would wish to be. Are these women comfortable, devoted mothers, or are they idle, overweight spongers? The title of the piece asks: 'Public Enemy or Backbone of Britain? The Truth about Single Mothers' (28 July 1996). These images and the tone of the debate are similar to coverage in 1990s America, but are unique in Europe. The policy response in Britain has also been unique in terms of its confusion. At the beginning of the 1990s, the Government determined to try to stem the flow of benefits to lone mothers by forcing fathers to pay more in respect of their biological children. By the middle of the decade, attention was fixed more firmly on encouraging lone mothers to enter the labour market as a means of reducing their dependence on the state.

During the 1990s, lone mothers have become a social threat as well as a social problem in the minds of many. They are seen primarily as a drain on public expenditure and as a threat to the stability and order associated with the traditional two-parent family. Women are believed increasingly to be choosing lone motherhood, by initiating divorce or by having a child outside marriage, and women with children and without men raise questions about sexual order. The young fathers of children born to young unmarried mothers are feared to be uncommitted and anti-social. The children of lone mother families have been shown to be lower achievers at school and it is also feared that they will reproduce the pattern of lone motherhood in their turn.

This is the popular image of lone motherhood. The light and shade of the academic evidence has largely passed people—and many journalists—by. Academics from many disciplines have contributed to the literature on lone mother families. Demographers have tried to describe and explain the elements of family change—in particular the increases in divorce, cohabitation, and extramarital childbearing—that have resulted in large numbers of lone mothers (Lesthaeghe 1995; van da Kaa 1987; Kiernan 1996a); economists have produced what are probably the most influential theories that purport to explain the behaviour of lone mothers, focusing on the reasons why the rational economic choices made by individuals in respect of marriage, divorce, and childbearing have changed (especially Becker 1981); and other social scientists have explored the everyday reality of lone mothers in terms of employment patterns, length of time spent drawing state benefits, the contributions, or lack of them, made by fathers, and support networks (e.g. Hardy and Crow 1991; Millar 1989; Bradshaw and Millar 1991; Bradshaw et al. 1996; Ford, Marsh, and McKay 1995). Most have drawn attention to the constraints that structure the choices made by the women who become lone mothers, and many have pointed out that not all the children of lone mothers do badly, although the literature on the fate of children, particularly by psychologists and child health experts, has been some of the most influential in the policy debate, first in the United States during the 1980s (Wallerstein and Kelly 1980) and more recently in this country (Cockett and Tripp 1994).

What is missing is an understanding of how we have got to where we are. A more historical approach to the realities of becoming a lone mother, together with scrutiny of their demographic underpinnings, and to the policies adopted towards lone mothers cannot in and of itself explain anything, but we hope that it will give perspective to a debate that has been conspicuously lacking it. There have, after all, always been lone mothers; why has the tenor of debate become so strident in this country in the 1990s? Is there a real problem, or has the problem been re-labelled in some way so that we just see it differently? Most of the significant histories of family change do not cover the last quarter of a century in any detail (e.g. Stone 1995, on divorce), which is when the pace of change quickened dramatically and the number of lone mothers rapidly increased. We therefore lack perspective on change in the twentieth century as a whole, and in particular for the period after the Second World War. There is often a vaguely expressed idea in the polemical literature that the permissiveness of the 1960s is somehow to blame. However, the nature of any relationship between changes in behaviour and the permissive legislation of that decade (on divorce and abortion) is not easy to establish. There is no real understanding of the changing routes into lone motherhood in the post-war period, of the changing context in terms of ideas about marriage, divorce, cohabitation, and unmarried motherhood, or indeed of the precise nature of the policies that so much of the polemical literature blames for the growth in the numbers of lone mothers.

Our approach, which is empirical and inductive and examines what has happened in terms of changing demography, discursive context, and policy, cannot reveal the 'true' explanations for the growth in the number of lone mother families, nor can it produce a definitive statement as to what form policies should take. However, we can show how perceptions of the problem of lone motherhood have often differed significantly from the realities, particularly the demographic reality. We also hope to show how policies developed towards lone mothers have arisen from the way in which the problem has been perceived at a particular historical moment. Given that this is the case, there may be different ways of 'seeing' which would produce different kinds of policies; we return to this point in our conclusion. Ideally, we would like to see similar studies of other European countries, where lone mothers are often not even labelled as a social problem, let alone a social threat. The debate in this country has been overshadowed by the American literature. However, we can do no more than set the comparative scene briefly at the end of this introduction.

Understanding Continuity and Change

Lone motherhood is not a new phenomenon. However, there have been dramatic changes in the composition of the women who are with children and without men.[1] As Michael Anderson (1983) pointed out some years ago, marriages at the beginning of this century were just as likely to be broken as marriages at the beginning of the 1980s, but by death rather than divorce. The great majority of lone mothers were widows at the beginning of the century. Divorce was very uncommon and only available to people of substance, something that did not radically change until after the Second World War, although separation and probably cohabitation were common (Gillis 1985). The illegitimacy rate, on the other hand, has waxed and waned. Prior to the late twentieth century, the last great peak in the illegitimacy rate was in the 1840s, and the reasons are as disputed as those for the huge increase in extramarital births in the last decade. Edward Shorter (1975) has argued that the main reason lay in women's increased independence due to the new possibilities of wage-work in factories. However, John Gillis's (1979) study of the London Foundling Hospital showed that women in the traditional occupation of domestic service were particularly vulnerable to extramarital pregnancy. Intercourse seems not to have taken place until marriage was promised, and unmarried motherhood happened when the marriage failed to take place, often because of employment difficulties on the intended husband's part. Thus in this interpretation, traditional practices fell foul of new economic mobility and uncertainty. Debates about the causes of unmarried motherhood and divorce today continue to revolve around the degree to which they can be attributed to women's increased economic independence. What is certain, is that the changes in the composition of lone mother families, such that never-married and divorced women now predominate, have made the late twentieth-century debate about lone motherhood much more fierce. Widows cannot be held responsible for the deaths of their husbands, but divorced women can be held at least partially responsible, especially when the majority of divorce petitions are initiated by women, and the blame for extramarital births is usually laid almost entirely at the door of the mothers (women have always been accorded the major respon-

---

[1] Readers will find a full demographic analysis with supporting tables in the next chapter.

sibility for reproduction and fertility control (McLaren 1990; Seccombe 1993; Szreter 1996.) The fact that lone motherhood in the late twentieth century is for many women a transitory status, lasting on average three and a half years (Ford, Marsh, and Mackay 1995), is rarely mentioned.

Lone mothers have also become more visible in the late twentieth century. Until the 1970s there was no single term to describe unmarried, divorced, and widowed women.[2] Increased visibility has been due in large part to the increase in numbers as well as to the changes in the nature of lone motherhood. It is also due to changes in where lone mothers are to be found. Until relatively recently, lone mothers were 'hidden away'. To this day, the press reports the odd case of an unmarried mother emerging from the institution to which she had been sent in the early part of the century when pregnancy in an unmarried woman was regarded by many as a mark of deviance so profound that it could only be explained by mental instability. By the mid-twentieth century, single pregnant women no longer ran the risk of incarceration, but they often left their native communities to enter a 'mother and baby' home for the birth. It was then not uncommon for the child to be brought up by the woman's family of origin, the circumstances of its birth remaining unacknowledged. From the point of view of the state, mother and child remained invisible. Only since the 1970s has the majority of never-married mothers joined the dramatically increasing numbers of divorced women living autonomously in the community, often in social housing and often drawing state benefits. Their increased autonomy has made them visible.

Strong elements of continuity in the way in which lone motherhood has been defined by policy-makers as a social problem have paralleled the profound changes in social support that have permitted lone mothers to live autonomously in the late twentieth century. Most twentieth-century welfare states began with a set of ideas about the family that assumed that men would earn and support their female and child dependants, and that women would carry out the unpaid work of caring (Land 1980; Lewis 1992). In this context, the problem of lone mothers was defined as one of women with children and without men.

---

[2] We have used the contemporary term 'lone mothers' in the title of this book, but we use others in their historical context, especially 'one-parent families', which was first used in the early 1970s in an effort to erase the distinction between legitimate and illegitimate children and which is still commonplace, particularly in the literature on social security.

According to this logic, lone mothers could either be defined as 'workers' and be expected to fill the role of breadwinner themselves, or they could be defined as 'mothers', in which case the state had to decide how far and on what terms it would step in to fill the place of the male breadwinner. If the mother is defined as a breadwinner, this begs the question of who is to care for the child.

The nineteenth-century poor law tended to define lone mothers as workers and expected these women to support as many children as they could, the rest would be taken into the workhouse. Early social insurance systems, instituted in Britain in 1911 for sickness and unemployment, offered cover to the male breadwinner and gradually also provided allowances for his dependants. Cover was thus extended to women as wives rather than as mothers. In 1925, widows gained access to insurance-based benefits, but it was never considered possible to make these available to divorced or unmarried women. The fact that unmarried mothers and to a lesser extent separated and divorced women were perceived as a moral problem as well as a social one meant that their treatment was likely to be harsh. The poor law was a needs-based social security system, but operated on the principle of deterrence. The whole process of claiming under the poor law and the conditions of maintenance were not meant to be pleasant. The moral taint adhering to never-married mothers in particular, together with the fear that persisted up to the Second World War that the children might inherit both their mothers' low level of intelligence and their tendency to immoral behaviour made sure that the approach of the authorities was punitive.

The poor law was only abolished in Britain in 1948 and many social policy analysts have pondered the extent to which 'a poor law mentality' persisted in the context of a modern income maintenance system.[3] In particular, in the UK as in the USA, the importance of personal responsibility has always been stressed, although during the 1960s and 1970s more emphasis was placed on the structural causes of poverty. Because lone motherhood is for both divorced women and unmarried mothers an achieved rather than an ascribed status, it is easy to attribute poverty to their status rather than to the particular difficulties these women face in combining work and motherhood, for example. Since 1948, policy towards lone mothers has changed in that they

---

[3] Recent comparative literature has stressed the importance of 'policy inheritance' or 'path dependency' in explaining differences between countries, e.g. Pierson (1994).

have been treated in the same way as other adults claiming assistance-based state benefits, the local discretion over the amount of benefits paid that was exercised by officials under the poor law system having vanished. However, they are still clearly identified as a claimant group, something that is rarely the case in Continental European countries, because benefit systems tend to be more universally directed to children, and because poverty is seen as having more to do with structural issues than with the characteristics of the claimant population. In late twentieth-century Britain and America it is easy for the treatment of lone mothers to become more punitive again.

The approach of government to the problem of lone motherhood changed considerably over time. In 1948, lone mothers were defined as mothers rather than as workers and were permitted to draw national assistance benefits (later supplementary benefit and later still income support) until their children were 16, although as Chapter 8 shows local officials were quite likely to suggest that they enter the labour market during the 1950s and 1960s. Only The Netherlands was similar to Britain among the Northern European countries in making such firm assumptions in the post-war period about lone mothers' main responsibility being motherhood. In France, for example, generous benefits were provided until the child was 3, when the lone mother was redefined as a breadwinner. In the late twentieth century, the pendulum has begun to swing again towards treating lone mothers as workers, first in the United States, but, by the mid-1990s, in some European countries too. In The Netherlands the swing was total in 1996. In Britain it has been partial, but the determination to reduce the role of the state in providing for lone mothers and to increase the contributions from the other two possible sources—men and the labour market—is clear.

We can begin to see that even though there has always been a problem of lone motherhood, the issue of its magnitude and how it has been perceived has changed considerably. We have chosen in this book to look more closely at the changes in the demography of family life since the Second World War that in turn have resulted in the increased numbers of lone mothers. Who lone mothers are and how they become lone mothers is basic to our understanding of the issue. We have also chosen to examine the ideas about marriage, divorce, cohabitation, and unmarried motherhood. It is not our intention to argue that cultural variables are the most important in furthering our understanding of lone motherhood, or that there is any readily accepted relationship between changing ideas and attitudes, on the one hand, and changes in behaviour, on the other. Both the relative importance of cultural as opposed to economic and social variables and the nature of any causal relationship between attitudinal and behavioural change are hotly debated. Our decision to investigate cultural variables further stemmed more from the fact that these tend not to be treated very extensively in the social-science literature and yet they are assumed to occupy a place of considerable importance in the debates over policies towards lone mothers, which is our third main topic. During the 1990s, there has been an abundance of commentary in Parliament, Party Political Conferences, and the press on 'what should be done'. We feel that there is merit in taking a step back and beginning the task of examining how we have come to where we are.

Explaining Family Change

In the post-war period two major shifts altered the composition of the lone mother population. During the 1960s, divorce eclipsed death as the primary cause of lone motherhood and in the 1990s divorce may be set to be eclipsed by the growth in never-married lone motherhood. Different impetuses lie behind the diminishing importance of post-marital lone motherhood (that emanating from divorce and widowhood) and the ascendance of never-married lone motherhood. The recent rise in never-married motherhood is due more than at any time in the past to choice rather than mistake. The traditional nexus between marriage and childbearing has been eroded, a development facilitated by the advent of effective contraception and legal abortion. The contraceptive revolution has also been an important engine behind the rise of cohabitation, while it is the breakdown of cohabiting unions that is the novel and important contributor to the recent increase in never-married lone motherhood. Lone motherhood is the prominent manifestation of the separation of marriage and parenthood to which the rise in cohabitation, extramarital childbearing, and divorce have been major contributors.

Given that the pace of family change has become more dramatic in the 1980s and 1990s, social scientists have devoted considerable attention to where we might look for explanations. It is a fact that the most striking post-war trends—the rise in the divorce rate, the rise in cohabitation and in never married motherhood, and the increase in married women's labour-market participation—all seem to involve and to affect women rather more than men. Gender, then, would appear to be a significant variable and it not surprising that the most popular explanation for the changes in family structure—for demographers and economists—centres on women's increased economic independence.

Certainly, women have to acquire the capacity to live alone with and to support a child, and as we have already pointed out, this is in fact a very recent phenomenon. Until the last quarter of the twentieth century the majority of unmarried mothers found refuge with kin. A century ago, the options facing those whose kin rejected them comprised infanticide, abandonment, informal adoption, or the workhouse. Even in the immediate post-war decades, when lone mothers were entitled to draw social assistance benefits, relatively few were able to gain access to affordable housing. To live independently women with children and without men must have an alternative source of income. In the view of most academic social scientists it is the growth in women's employment, rather than the increased availability of state welfare benefits, that has provided lone mothers with income and that explains the growth in their numbers.[4] The importance attached to women's earning capacity as an explanatory variable is reinforced by influential economic theories of marriage. Gary Becker (1981) has argued that marriage should be understood in terms of the way in which it permits each partner to maximize his or her utility. Given that women desire children, they will look for a good male breadwinner. Men will look for a good housekeeper and carer. According to this theory, a rise in women's employment and an increase in their wages will threaten the stability of marriage, for it will no longer offer women unequivocal gains. As Valerie Kincade Oppenheimer (1994) has pointed out, while there are many academics who do not subscribe to Becker's theory of marriage and family, the idea that women's economic independence has an effect on marital behaviour is widespread, possibly because people with very different politics can buy into it. Feminists are as likely to endorse a theory that stresses the importance of women's economic independence as are neo-classical economists and Right-wing ideologues.

However, there is surely something problematic about an explanation for the increase in lone motherhood that relies on the growth in women's economic independence when the social policy debate about

---

[4] Empirical investigation of this issue has been most intense in the United States, see particularly Garfinkel and McLanahan (1986), and Ellwood and Bane (1985).

lone mothers revolves around their inability to support themselves and
their children. The fact is that only a minority of mothers, married or
solo, can combine the unpaid work of caring for a child with sufficiently remunerative employment to provide the wherewithal for independent living. In most cases the mother must delegate the work of
childcare. This means that we are faced with the paradox that women
who divorce or who have a child outside marriage apparently choose to
make themselves worse off. No single variable can explain such behaviour. The nature of the choices and constraints faced by women who
become lone mothers are much more complicated. In the first place, it
is significant that men's capacity to act as breadwinners has been
conspicuously eroded. William Julius Wilson (1987) was among the
first to suggest that we should pay more attention to the deteriorating
economic position of black men in the United States. In this country
too the proportion of income contributed to married couple families
by men has fallen sharply (Harkness, Machin, and Waldfogel 1996). In
Ann Phoenix's (1991) qualitative study of young unmarried mothers,
the vast majority of the fathers were unemployed. There were certainly
few economic reasons for these women to marry the fathers of their
children. As for the women themselves, waiting a few more years
before having a child would have been unlikely to have improved their
material well-being significantly. To an unemployed girl of 17 or 18
having a baby now or postponing it for a couple of years does not
matter much. Annette Lawson (1993) has drawn attention to the way in
which young teenage mothers will reject what has happened to them
physically, separating the internal experiential self from the bodily
'facts'. Lawson concludes that the child that is born allows for a
wholeness and sense of self that the sex does not. The feelings and
behaviour of the young teenage mother must be differentiated from
the older teenager, who will usually marry or cohabit in due course,
although not necessarily with any greatly increased hope of economic
prosperity (Kiernan 1995). What seems to be central in the case of
unmarried motherhood is the way in which the meaning of marriage
has changed such that parenthood has become detached from it.

In the case of women seeking divorce, research carried out a decade
ago (Graham 1987) showed that women who had suffered violent
treatment in their marriages were also likely to have been mistreated
economically. Divorced and living on state benefits, these women
reported that they were in fact better off. Women seeking divorce
may have already established low expectations of material well-being.

But they may also have high emotional expectations. Arlie Hochschild (1989) has provided a fascinating account of the tension that results from men's refusal to increase their contribution to household work or, more significantly still, to behave supportively, in face of their wives' increased participation in the labour market. This points not to the fact of women's increased employment *per se* as a cause of divorce, but rather to the difficulties couples have in negotiating their domestic roles and, in particular, the problems men have in responding to and coping with change.

The point is that it is unlikely that women abide solely by the dictates of economic rationality in making decisions about marriage, divorce, and motherhood (or indeed as lone mothers, deciding whether to enter the labour market or not). Alternative value systems that give priority to emotional satisfaction and to care may be as important in explaining the rise in lone motherhood as women's increased earning capacity. In which case, Ellwood and Bane's (1985) conclusion from extensive empirical work on US data that, while there is no evidence that state benefits cause women to choose to become lone mothers, they do facilitate independent living after the choice is made is probably correct. Women make choices about becoming lone mothers in widely differing circumstances which may—in the case of many divorcing women—involve prioritizing identity and emotional well-being over material well-being.[5] In the early 1980s Leonore Weitzman's (1985) research in California shocked policy-makers by showing that on divorce women's (and usually children's) income dropped 70 per cent and men's rose 40 per cent.[6] In such circumstances, or in those experienced by the young, ill-educated, and unskilled unmarried mother, the possibility of employment or benefit is not the decisive factor, although the possibility of gaining the means of subsistence— often it is little more than this—from some source is necessary to permit autonomous living. But even if a middle-class mother decides that she

[5] It is well known that a majority of divorces are initiated by women. However, it is not clear that this reflects women's greater desire to end marriage. Women must start legal proceedings in order to sort out their financial support.

[6] Using UK data, Taylor et al. (1994) substantially reduced these figures by taking into account the fact that a significant proportion of women remarried. In the USA, the Weitzman findings were subsequently found also to be an overestimate, see Hoffman and Duncan (1988) and the discussion in Ch. 5. However, the findings played a part in the decisions of the UK, US, and Australian Governments to seek more child support from 'absent fathers'.

would prefer the economic hardship of lone motherhood to an unhappy marriage, she has also to feel that an independent existence is socially and culturally possible. In short, many unhappily married women stayed married in the past because of the stigma of divorce. Similarly, many unmarried mothers sought to keep their pregnancies secret and gave their babies up for adoption Ideas and attitudes have changed and are, we shall argue, a very important part of the story.

Recent academic work has shown more appreciation of the importance of cultural variables, albeit often at the end of empirical work that has considered only economic variables and has found them lacking. Thus Bane and Jargowsky (1988: 246) concluded that 'our hunch is that the real force behind family change has been a profound change in peoples' attitudes about marriage and children'. Karen Oppenheim Mason and An-Magritt Jensen (1995) have offered one of the most thoughtful recent evaluations of the importance of attitudinal change. They have pointed out that the micro-theory of Becker does not recognize or allow for collectively generated or agreed upon norms and sanctions. Yet the meaning that is attached by the majority to marriage may well have changed. For example, if it has become important to maximize income, then high-earning women may be more likely to marry and less likely to divorce, the opposite of Becker's predictions. In addition, women's increased labour-market participation may lead them to prioritize sexual satisfaction and emotional companionship over their husbands' capacity to provide.

At the broadest level, sociologists have grappled with the changing meaning of personal relationships, identifying a shift towards autonomy and individualism. Giddens (1992) has argued that we have seen the emergence of the 'pure relationship', a social relationship entered into for its own sake and for what can be derived by each person from it in terms of material, but more usually, emotional exchange. Love has thus become contingent, rather than 'forever'. Beck and Beck-Gernscheim (1995) have also pointed out that it is no longer possible to say what family, marriage, parenthood, sexuality, and love mean. All vary in substance, exceptions, norms, and morality from individual to individual and from relationship to relationship. The collective norm seems to be that there is no norm. Empirical research into attitudes seems to support the thesis of ever increasing individualization. For example, attitudes towards divorce in marriages where there are children have relaxed considerably in a number of countries since the

1960s (Lesthaeghe 1995; Furstenberg and Cherlin 1991), which many would interpret as the triumph of the pursuit of self-fulfilment on the part of adults over the interests of children.

The evidence regarding an overarching shift in attitudes about personal relationships is persuasive, but the argument is largely speculative. The problem is that there are very real difficulties in showing the nature of the relationship between changing attitudes and behaviour. At the most basic level, we know that it is all too possible for people to say they believe one thing and to do another. V. K. Oppenheimer (1994) has argued that American panel data shows that the experience of divorce or separation is the strongest determinant of attitudinal change, in other words, changes in behaviour precede changes in attitudes. The post-war period seems particularly tangled in this respect. As the next two chapters show, sexual behaviour among young people began to change even before the permissive attitudes of the 1960s took hold. On the other hand, the dramatic rise in the divorce rate certainly did not begin until after the 1960s. The huge increase in never-married motherhood only began in Britain in the mid-1980s, a period not noted for its progressive politics.

In this book we do not attempt to judge the weight that should be given to changes in ideas and attitudes, nor do we attempt the excruciatingly difficult task of relating changes in peoples' behaviour to changes in their attitudes. Rather, we undertake the much more limited task (in Chapters 3 and 4) of investigating how ideas and attitudes changed from above, arguing that changes in ideas about sexual morality in particular were a necessary prerequisite to achieving legislative change and, more importantly still, to reducing stigma. Mason and Jensen (1995: 7) have suggested that it is 'a new *viewpoint*' (their italics) arising from women's increased educational qualifications and employment, rather than actual increases in their earning power, which explains changing family structures. It seems to us that equally changes in ideas as to what the powers-that-be consider acceptable and the kind of construction they have placed upon phenomena such as never-married motherhood provide an extremely important set of parameters within which people make their decisions. For example, the established church has obviously not wholeheartedly endorsed either the rise in the divorce rate or in the extramarital birth rate, but, as Chapter 3 shows, its position on sexual morality has in fact changed significantly since the Second World War.

Understanding Policy Shifts

Our examination of changing ideas and attitudes about lone motherhood and the marriage system more generally among elites forms a
bridge to our consideration of policies towards lone mothers. Many
people have latched onto the idea that individualism has become a
greater force in modern society and have also assumed that it has made
us more selfish at the expense of children in particular. Feminists have
been as ready to see men's 'flight from commitment' as an expression
of selfishness (e.g. Ehrenreich 1983), as Right-wing commentators have
been ready to condemn female selfishness in putting personal fulfilment and career before family (e.g. Gilder 1987). Many academics and
polemicists have also been prepared to condemn government policies for
having exacerbated the trend towards individualism and away from
'familism' (e.g. Murray 1984; Popenoe 1988). The main contention in
the political debates about lone mothers in the USA from the 1980s and
in Britain during the 1990s has been that the provision of state benefits
is a major cause of the growth of lone mother families.

In the United States, academics queued up to comprehensively
demolish Charles Murray's (1984) influential arguments about the
causal relationship between benefits and lone motherhood, while
acknowledging that benefits facilitated independent living. They
pointed out not only that the real value of benefits declined during
the very period that the numbers of lone mothers began steeply to
increase, but that one of the major reasons for the rise in the number of
lone mother families was the decline in the number of two-parent
families, which could have little to do with the supposed incentive
effects of the benefit system (Garfinkel and McLanahan 1986; Ellwood
and Bane 1985; Bane and Jargowsky 1988; Bane and Ellwood 1994).
Similarly, David Popenoe's (1988) argument that extensive social provision in Sweden had the unintended outcome of causing an unprece-
dented decline in the Swedish family[7] looks less robust in comparative
perspective, as extramarital birth rates also rose sharply in Britain and
the USA where government provision was much less generous. The
research of British policy analysts has also supported the view that
'there is no large standing army of never-to-be married, socially
housed, benefit dependent women adding to their families at public

---

[7] Popenoe seems to have focused on the high extramarital birth rate in Sweden, but
to have missed the equally high cohabitation rate and joint registration of births.

expense' (Ford, Marsh, and Mackay 1995: para. 6.10; see also Selman and Glendinning 1996).

An issue that has been missing from the current debate is the fact that beliefs as to the nature of the relationship between government policies and lone motherhood have undergone substantial change over time. In Chapters 6 to 8 we explore the relationship between perceptions of the problem of lone motherhood and legislation in respect of social security, housing, employment, and childcare. The early post-war policy debates took place against a background in which governments assumed responsibility for full-time employment and believed that it was legitimate to pursue re-distributive policies which would reduce inequalities between young and old as well as between different income and household groups. There was still a broad consensus that public expenditure on social provision was not in principle to be deplored. We focus on the way in which lone motherhood became an increasingly important policy issue for central government in the post-war period. (It should be noted that some local authorities, but not all, would have been more aware of lone mothers in the 1950s and 1960s than was central government.) While in the 1970s the focus of government was on structural economic changes with the aim of reducing inequalities, since the 1980s individual 'choice' and 'responsibility' have been emphasized. Thus the reaction to the young unmarried mother, for example, has been either to change what Margaret Thatcher called the 'perverse incentives' which resulted from inappropriate or over-generous welfare provision, or to hold the individual responsible for that 'choice' and let her—and her children—take the consequences. In this climate, the transfer of policy ideas from the USA to Britain about all aspects of social provision became striking.

Lone motherhood would seem to have served as a focus for all sorts of social concerns over the last decade. Sara McLanahan and Karen Booth (1989) have suggested that in the United States it has wrapped up fears about the socialization of children, in terms of low levels of educational attainment and rising levels of criminality; anxieties about the role of women, particularly in terms of whether the mothers of young children should go out to work and suspicion of greater female sexual autonomy; concern about the role of men, who appear to be unwilling to shoulder financial responsibility for their children; and racial anxieties. All except the last have also been powerfully expressed in Britain; the policy debate has not become racialized in the same way as it has in the United States. Anxiety about the work incentives and behaviour of young men who were not tied into families was prevalent at the beginning of the century, but vanished in the wake of the Second World War, only to re-emerge at the end of the 1980s. Lone mothers are by no means wholly responsible for bad behaviour on the part of children, cannot be held responsible for the bad behaviour of young men, and only experience the same sort of problems, albeit in an exacerbated form, as other mothers in combining paid work and caring for children. Yet in the English-speaking countries they have been targeted as a cause of these large social problems. Thus in 1993, the BBC Panorama programme, 'Babies on Benefit', blamed the rootlessness of the young male population on a South Wales housing estate on the refusal of the young lone mothers to marry them, irrespective of the fact that the young men did not appear to the viewer to be a particularly appetizing prospect.

In large measure, the vitriolic condemnation of lone mothers in the 1990s in Britain and the United States, stems from the degree to which they are 'welfare dependent'. Dependence on state benefits in turn is held to sap initiative and weaken character in a manner not dissimilar from the way in which nineteenth-century classical liberals viewed those drawing poor relief. In other words, it is held to be strongly associated with poor achievement on the part of children and anti-social behaviour generally. It is for this reason that Murray (1984) advocated the virtual abolition of welfare benefits for the able-bodied, something that was substantially realized in the legislation passed in the USA in 1996, whereby benefits for lone mothers will be withdrawn after five years (Waldfogel 1996). Murray attached considerable importance to distinguishing the deserving from the undeserving—among lone mothers widows have always been considered inherently more deserving—and to making state benefits as stigmatizing as possible for the undeserving. Less draconian policy solutions have focused on forcing lone mothers into the labour market on the grounds that the example set to children by a working parent is better than no example at all (Mead 1986; Novak and Cogan 1987). In Britain, lone mothers are particularly dependent on state benefits. They have grown increasingly so over the last quarter of a century, although not until the late 1980s was a majority dependent on state benefits. In the late 1980s, the proportion of lone mothers receiving social assistance after four years was 20 per cent in Germany, 34 per cent in the USA, and 83 per cent in the UK (G. R. Duncan et al. 1995). As Chapter 6 shows, the costs of benefits for lone mothers did not become a major political issue until the late 1980s.

There is in all this a fundamental contradiction. In many respects the anxieties about lone motherhood focus on the next generation: what will become of the children, will they in their turn become lone mothers and feckless fathers? However, British social policy shows no sign of focusing on the needs of children despite the fact that child poverty levels have trebled since 1979 (Bradshaw 1990; Hills 1996). In the mid-1970s, at a time when policy-makers were committed to combating poverty, it was fully anticipated that the position of lone mothers would improve. In contrast, the current policy trend is to solve the problem by making life economically tougher for the lone mother. It is in this respect above all that policy in the UK differs from other Northern European countries.

European Comparisons

In terms of the numbers of and growth in lone motherhood, Britain for the most part lies between the USA and the Northern European countries. It has one of the highest divorce rates in Europe, but the rate is lower than for the USA. On the other hand, it has similar levels of extramarital childbearing to the USA, but lower than those found in the Nordic countries. Cohabitation rates are lower in Britain than in other Northern European countries. However, all the Continental European countries have lower rates of teenage childbearing than Britain, which in turn has lower rates than are found in the USA. Teenage motherhood makes a disproportionate contribution to lone motherhood in that these young mothers are more likely to be unmarried than married, and if married are more likely subsequently to become lone mothers. In terms of the debate about lone motherhood, however, the pattern is more clear-cut. Britain has much more in common with the USA in this respect than with its European neighbours.

Lone mothers exist in considerable numbers in other Northern European countries, but they have not become the focus for social anxieties in the same way as in Britain. The problems that lone mothers experience are not attributed to their status in the same way. Thus in Denmark and Sweden, for example, debate centres on the position of one-earner as opposed to two-earner families. Having drawn adult women into the labour force such that their participation rate is virtually the same as that of men, these countries do not have to choose between defining lone mothers as mothers or workers. All adults share a common worker/citizen status. In this context, one-earner families, whether headed by a lone mother or a male bread-winner, are recognized as likely to have financial problems. Further-more, it is recognized that the vast majority of adult women face difficulties in reconciling family and employment responsibilities. The problems of lone mothers will usually be particularly acute in this regard, but policy focuses on the problem rather than on any particular group. In France, where generous benefits are available to mothers with children under 3 years old, lone motherhood is conceptualized as a risk rather than social deviance. In fact French lone mother families rely less on benefits than two-parent families in which the mother is out of the labour market, which is a reflection of the extent to which French social policy has historically redistributed income towards families with children (Lefaucheur 1993).

Continental European Governments have not subscribed to the 'neutral' policy stance adopted by successive British Governments on the issue of reconciling paid and unpaid work (Hantrais and Letablier 1996). In Britain, the problem is viewed as a matter to be solved by individual family members. This in turn has affected the way in which lone mothers package income differently across Northern Europe. Britain is conspicuous for the low labour-market participation of its lone mothers, something that Bradshaw et al.'s (1996) cross-national study has attributed primarily to the lack of affordable childcare. Only in the Netherlands has lone mothers' labour-market participation been historically low, but there the participation rates of married mothers have also been low. Britain is the only country in which married mothers are much more likely to be employed than lone mothers. Indeed, the percentage of lone mothers in employment fluctuated during the 1970s and fell in the 1980s (as we show in Chapter 5). The ability of lone mothers in other European countries to 'package' income[8] from earnings and from state benefits means in turn that they tend to be significantly better off than their British counterparts.

It seems that lone mothers do best where they are allowed to gain income from the state and from the labour market, and where the 'social wage' is high, especially in respect of childcare provision. This casts

---

[8] The term is that of Rainwater, Rein, and Schwartz (1986).

doubt on British studies that see employment as the answer for lone mothers (e.g. Ford, Marsh, and Mackay 1995). In part, such a conclusion results from working within the parameters that have been set for debate in the English-speaking countries, which revolve around an adult work or maintenance perspective, whereas the Continental European emphasis is much more on reconciling care for children with paid employment (see also Lister 1995). 'Family policy' in the sense in which it is used in Continental European countries to refer to the mechanisms for reconciling work and family in the form of childcare provision and parental leave, has been deemed in Britain to be a private rather than a public responsibility. During the 1970s, policies affecting the family were implicit rather than explicit (Land and Parker 1978). This has changed during the 1990s, with the adoption first, of policies explicitly intended to enforce the responsibility of biological fathers to maintain and, more recently, of mothers to enter into paid employment, but unlike the rest of Northern Europe, this responsibility remains a private one.

What has been perhaps most marked in the British welfare state is the extent to which the social security system has been focused on poverty and the operation of a means-tested 'national minimum' level of support for those in need, rather than on work and a social insurance system as has been the case in most Continental European countries. Indeed, British lone mothers are now considerably more long-term dependent on benefits than in other European countries (G. R. Duncan et al. 1995). The reasons for this are complicated, but the heavy reliance on means-tested social security systems such as those in Britain and in the United States makes it more difficult for claimants to enter the labour market (Wong, Garfinkel, and McLanahan 1993). We seem to have witnessed a complicated feedback loop in Britain, whereby the stigma surrounding claiming diminished from the late 1960s as both claimants groups and government began to talk of a 'right' to means-tested as well as insurance benefits, and as the real level of benefits rose in the 1970s, which enabled more lone mothers to live autonomously. But the structure of the benefit system together with the lack of policies to increase women's labour-market skills and to help them combine paid work with childcare has ensured that mothers remain on benefit for longer than in other countries.

In the absence of any firm commitment to integration and social inclusion on the part of Governments in both Britain and the United States, inequalities have grown sharply (Hills 1996) and the position of lone mothers has worsened. Our approach in this book does not lend itself to policy prescription, but it does enable us to see the extent to which the problem of welfare dependency that causes so much anxiety on the part of policy-makers is the result of the choices, or lack of them, that have been created by Government policy. We can also say something about the major policy divide in the debate over lone mothers: whether or not the clock can be put back. If the growth in the numbers of lone mother families has more to do with fundamental changes in attitudes and behaviour whose connection with policy is hard to establish, the prospects for legislating a return to the happy families of the 1950s are not bright. We return to this issue in our conclusion and also make some suggestions for a new focus for policy-making.

2

The Changing Demography of Lone Motherhood

Introduction

Increases in divorce, cohabitation, and childbearing outside marriage have all contributed to the separation of marriage and parenthood, with lone parenthood being the prominent manifestation of this development. Between 1961 and 1994 there was a fourfold increase in the proportion of families headed by a lone mother; from around 5 per cent of all families with dependent children in 1961 to over 20 per cent in 1994. The rise in the proportion of lone mother families that occurred during the 1970s was due in large measure to the rise in the rate of divorce, whereas the more recent increases from the mid-1980s onwards are more associated with the growth in childbearing outside legal marriage. This chapter examines the demographic impetuses behind the growth in lone mother families and the changing character of lone motherhood with particular reference to the last half-century. The routes to lone motherhood are complex and varied. In this chapter as an aid to simplification we divide the lone mother population into two broad groups: never-married lone mothers, those who have never contracted a formal marriage; and post-marital lone mothers, those who become lone mothers after a marriage had broken down. We discuss each in turn. For the group of never-married lone mothers we discuss the pathways to that experience, assessing the role of sexual behaviour, contraceptive practices, abortion, bridal pregnancy, and adoption, as well as changing marriage patterns and the emergence of widespread cohabitation on the incidence of and trends in pre-marital lone motherhood. For the group of post-marital lone mothers we include an examination of the extent to which widowhood or marital separation lie behind trends in lone mother families over the course of the twentieth century; the degree to which children are likely to experience the death of a parent or the divorce of their parents; and the pathways out of lone motherhood. In the final part of the chapter trends in extramarital childbearing, divorce, and lone parenthood in other European countries are examined in order to assess the extent to which trends in Britain are particular or part of a more widespread development.

Routes to Lone Motherhood

There are three main routes to lone motherhood: partnership break-down; death of a husband; and having a child on one's own. The majority of lone mother families emanate from the breakdown of partnerships (either formal ones contracted through marriage or infor-mal ones formed by cohabitation) and the ensuing separation which in the case of married couples is typically followed by divorce. The death of a father remained a prominent cause of lone motherhood until the 1960s but nowadays is a minor cause. Most of the remainder of lone mother families consist of never-married women rearing children on their own. An indication, albeit imperfect, of the routes to lone motherhood can be gleaned from the marital status distribution of lone mothers as portrayed in Table 2.1.

Defining Lone Motherhood

Since the Finer Committee Report on One-Parent Families (Cmnd. 5629 (1974)), British lone mother families have been usually defined as mothers living with their never-married dependent children but with-

TABLE 2.1. *Distribution of lone mother families with dependent children, according to marital status, 1971–1994 (% of all families with dependent children)*

	1971	1974	1981	1984	1991	1994
Single lone mothers	1.2	1.0	2.3	3.0	6.4	8.0
Separated lone mothers	2.5	2.0	2.3	2.0	3.6	5.0
Divorced lone mothers	1.9	2.0	4.4	6.0	6.3	7.0
Widowed lone mothers	1.9	2.0	1.7	1.0	1.2	1.0
All lone mothers	7.5	10.0	10.7	12.0	17.5	21.0

Note: Estimates are based on three-year averages except 1994.

Sources: Haskey 1993; OPCS 1996a. table 4

out a spouse or a cohabitant. Typically, dependent children are taken to be those aged 16 or younger, or aged 19 or younger and in full-time education. Couples where one parent is temporarily absent or working away from home are not classified as lone parent families. A distinction also needs to be drawn between families and households. Lone mother families may form a discrete household or they may be living as part of a larger household, for example a lone mother living in her own parents' household. Lone mother families are frequently classified according to their marital status (as in Table 2.1): single, separated, divorced, and widowed lone mothers. The latter two groups are more readily defined and are formally recognized statuses within our vital registration system whereas the former two categories are more fuzzy. Single as a civil status means never married but in common usage it has come increasingly to mean being without a partner and used by the separated and divorced as well as the never married to describe their partnership status. The rise of cohabitation has further contributed to the murkiness of marital status. For example, a never-married person who has cohabited for a number of years and then separates may not differ substantively speaking from a person who has been married for the same period of time, yet the separated cohabitant will be classified as single and the married person as separated. Whether a separated cohabitant views their situation in the same way as a married person who separates or whether they refer to their status differently is a moot point. In de jure terms the former woman would be classified as single and the latter as separated or divorced, yet de facto their positions are very similar. Most of our information on lone parents comes from data collected in surveys in which self-definition of marital status is more likely than adherence to legal status.

To obviate some of the problems of definition and in an attempt at simplification here we divide lone mothers into two main groups: never-married lone mothers and post-marital lone mothers. The set of never-married lone mothers only encompasses women who have never been legally married and the post-marital, only women who have had a legal marriage. This division has been chosen in recognition that within the law there are still some differences as between the position of children born within and outside marriage. Since the 1987 Family Law Reform Act came into force in 1989, much of the legal stigma associated with being born outside marriage has been removed and the law gives children born within and outside marriage broadly equal rights. For example, the right to claim maintenance and inheritance from the father. But a major difference still remains. If the parents were not married to each other at the time of the birth, then only the mother automatically has the legal rights and duties for the child, which is classed in law as having parental responsibility. If a father wants an equal say in bringing up the child, then he has to acquire parental responsibility through the courts. As well as these legal differences, as we will see in Chapter 5, there are discernible differences in the circumstances and characteristics of lone mother families headed by never and previously married mothers. We will discuss each of these two types of lone motherhood in turn and commence with never-married lone motherhood.

Never-Married Lone Motherhood—Trends

Measures

It is impossible to provide a precise time series of the extent of never-married lone motherhood in Britain but changes in the extent of births outside marriage provide an indication of the potential supply of these mothers. Figure 2.1 shows the trend from 1850 to the present day in the proportion of births outside marriage expressed as a percentage of

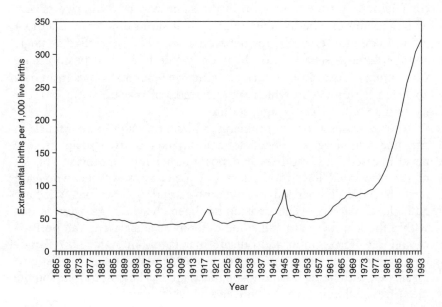

FIGURE 2.1 *Extramarital Birth Ratios, England and Wales, 1865–1993*

all live births in a given year and Figure 2.2 shows the trend in the rate of childbearing amongst the unmarried female population in the reproductive ages, conventionally taken as ages 15–45 years. Prior to the 1988 Family Law Reform Act, these measures were known as the illegitimacy ratio and rate respectively and subsequently have been variously referred to as non-marital or extramarital birth ratios and rates. For consistency we will refer to these measures as extramarital birth ratios and rates.

Prior to examining the trends in extramarital childbearing, it is important to highlight some of the potential deficiencies of these measures. The numerator of the ratio (the number of births to unmarried women) as well as the denominator (the total number of all births) can be affected by independent sets of factors and consequently changes to the ratio can be affected by movements in either the numerator or denominator or both. The number of births outside marriage is affected by the size of the unmarried female population of reproductive age and the prevalence of childbearing outside marriage, whereas the total number of births is also influenced by factors that affect the level of marital fertility; including changes in the proportions of married women, timing of childbearing, completed family size, etc. An alternative measure is the rate which has the same numerator as the ratio, the number of births to unmarried women, but has as its

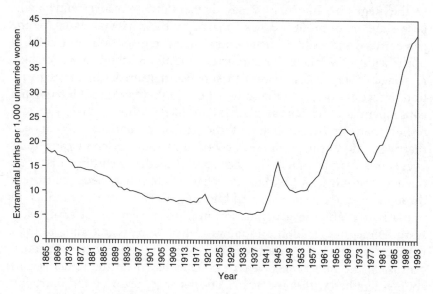

FIGURE 2.2 *Extramarital Birth Rates, England and Wales, 1865–1993*

denominator the total single, widowed, and divorced women in the childbearing ages, in a given year. Compared with the ratio the rate takes better account of the population at risk, which traditionally has been the number of unmarried women. The rate responds to the question, how many women in a given population have a child outside marriage whereas the ratio responds more to the question, what proportion of births to women in the reproductive ages are classifiable as being outside marriage. The rate is a more robust measure of the extent of extramarital childbearing but the ratio, for a number of reasons, is the more frequently cited. Compared with the rate the ratio is easier to understand, more easily calculated, and is often the only available measure when making comparisons across countries or sub-groups of a population.

Historically in England and Wales, for statistical purposes, a child was defined as illegitimate, and more recently born outside marriage, if the mother and putative father were not married to each other when the child was registered. This definition includes not only births to unmarried mothers, that is single, widowed, and divorced women, but also births occurring to parents one or both of whom may be married, although not to each other. The validity of the official statistics on extramarital births is ultimately dependent upon the accuracy of the statements made by the persons reporting the birth to the Registrar. Informants may deliberately or inadvertently make false statements about a date of marriage, their marital status, or the paternity of the child, which results in the registration of a child as born within marriage whose actual status is child born outside marriage. There is less reason to suppose that errors of the registration procedure occur to the same extent in the opposite direction and consequentially the official statistics are likely to be an underestimate rather than an overestimate of the extent of childbearing outside marriage. Moreover, it should be borne in mind in comparing rates over time that it cannot be assumed that the recording of births outside marriage, or within for that matter, has been consistent through time (Nissel 1987). Additionally, calculating the number of unmarried women in a population in a given year is not straightforward. Direct information on the number of women according to their marital status is only measured directly at the time of the decennial census. In the intervening years estimates based on the initial census counts together with information on marriage, divorce, and mortality from vital registration records together with assumptions about migration patterns are used to calculate the number of men and women in different marital status categories. Typically, revised estimates are made at the time of the next census. Revisions are likely to be less if the pace of change has been slow, as is the case with mortality rates at the reproductive ages in recent times, whereas large increases in the divorced population, as occurred during the 1970s, can lead to substantial revisions in population estimates (Sparks 1986). With these caveats in mind we present a brief overview of trends in both extramarital fertility ratios and rates from the last century to the present day, with a more detailed consideration of trends since the 1950s.

Pre-1950s

In 1837 the compulsory civil registration of births, deaths, and marriages came into force. The first assessment of the extent of child-bearing outside marriage was made for the year 1842 when the General Register Office calculated that 6.6 per cent of all births had occurred outside marriage in that year. As can be seen in Figure 2.1, the ratio fell steadily throughout the latter half of the nineteenth century and from the mid-1880s remained relatively stable, apart from the two wartime peaks, until the late 1940s at what now would be considered a very low level of between 4 and 5 per cent of all births. The two wartime peaks arose from the disruptive conditions of war, with spatial separation precluding at least some marriages that would have normally followed a conception. Birth and marriage registration data from the Second World War (OPCS 1987) show that whilst the proportion of extramarital births increased, the percentage of conceptions legitimated by marriage decreased. For example, in 1940 there were 25,633 extramarital births registered as compared with 55,173 in 1944; a 55 per cent increase over the period. In 1940 there were 39,350 births registered that had occurred within 0 to 7 months of first marriage as compared with 27,966 in 1944; a 39 per cent reduction in pre-nuptial conceptions over the period. When the proportions of births outside marriage fell after the war the proportion of pre-nuptial conceptions followed by marriage increased once more. After the Second World War, it looked for some years as though the ratio would fall back to its customary level. From over 9 per cent of births in 1945 the ratio had fallen to 5 per cent of all births by 1949 and it remained at this level for the next decade. With the 1960s came what was described by one contemporary analyst as the 'amazing rise in illegitimacy' (Hartley 1966).

An alternative perspective on trends in childbearing outside marriage is provided in Figure 2.2 which shows the trend in extramarital birth rates from the 1860s to the present time. The picture is one of a gentle decline in the rate of childbearing amongst unmarried women from the middle of the last century until the Second World War. The rate increased during the war but in contrast to the ratio did not return to its pre-war level. The rates continued to rise throughout the 1950s reaching a peak in 1968. As judged by trends in the rate, but not the ratio, the Second World War may have triggered a change in sexual relationships that increased in intensity throughout the 1950s and 1960s.

The 1950s and Later

The proportion of births occurring outside marriage was 6 per cent in 1961 and 8.5 per cent in 1968, a level still somewhat lower than the 9 per cent observed in 1945. The ratio hovered around the 8–9 per cent level until 1977, when it began to rise slowly at first and then much more rapidly throughout the 1980s. In 1980, 12 per cent of births were recorded as being born outside marriage by 1990 the proportion had increased to 28 per cent, and by the mid-1990s had plateaued at one in three of all births. The extramarital birth ratio and rate mapped in Figures 2.1 and 2.2 tell a similar story for the period from the late 1970s onwards but provide different perspectives on the period from 1950 to 1977. It is clear from the distribution of the rates shown in Figure 2.2 that the propensity to have a child outside marriage had been increasing from the mid-1950s. For example, in 1955 the number of extramarital births per 1,000 single, divorced, and widowed women aged between 15 and 44 stood at 10.3 whilst the analogous rate in 1968 was 23.0. After 1968 the rate declined to reach a low point of 16.1 in 1977, paralleling the decline in marital fertility, since when it has increased inexorably to stand at 42.4 per 1,000 in 1994. The initial rise during the 1950s, that continued into the 1960s, was part of a package of changes that included increased sexual activity amongst the young alongside increasingly youthful marriage and parenthood. From the late 1960s and throughout much of the 1970s there were a series of developments that tempered fertility behaviour, within and outside marriage, associated with the contraceptive revolution and the legalization of abortion. Since the beginning of the 1980s, the major engine behind the dramatic rise in extramarital childbearing has been the emergence of widespread cohabitation. Changes in coital behaviour, contraceptive practice, and increased cohabitation are three of the more direct and important forces behind trends in pre-marital motherhood since the 1950s. These forces will be discussed in more detail later in this chapter.

Age and Marital Status

The age and marital status of women who have children outside marriage has varied over the last five decades. From 1950 to 1980 extramarital births were increasingly occurring to younger women, such that in 1980, 67 per cent were to women under age 25 compared with 44 per cent in 1950 and 55 per cent in 1960. From the mid-1980s the proportions of births outside marriage to younger women began to decline such that by 1995 only one in two of these births were to young women (Table 2.2). Data from the General Household Surveys, for the 1970s, also showed that out-of-wedlock births were not confined to young single women. Amongst women who had a child outside marriage during the 1970s, 67 per cent were to never-married women and the remaining one-third were to separated and divorced women, whereas during the 1980s the proportion to single women increased to over 80 per cent (Kiernan 1983; Kiernan and Estaugh 1993). Evidence from earlier studies, some admittedly highly localized, suggests

TABLE 2.2. *Live births outside marriage percentage age distribution of mothers*

Year	Age group				
	Under 20	20–24	25–29	30 and older	Number = 100%
1950	15	29	25	31	35,200
1960	23	32	20	25	42,707
1970	32	27	15	25	64,744
1980	33	34	17	15	77,372
1990	22	37	24	17	199,999
1995	17	32	27	25	219,900

Sources: OPCS 1987; 1996d.

that the extent of out-of-wedlock births to separated and divorced women observed during the 1970s may have pertained since at least the late 1940s. In studies in Leicester in 1949 (McDonald 1956) and Aberdeen over the period 1949–1952 (Thompson 1956) and amongst all British children born in the first week of March 1958 (Crellin, Kellmer Pringle, and West 1971), it was found that about one-third of the out-of-wedlock births had occurred to ever-married women. Furthermore, a study by the General Register Office (GRO 1964) of a sample of births outside marriage that had occurred in 1961, showed that just over one-third (37 per cent) of the births matched with census schedules had occurred to ever-married women and that two out of three of these women were cohabiting, as were one in six of the single women. Altogether one-third of the extramarital births had occurred to women who were cohabiting around the time of the birth. A broadly comparable estimate for 1994 would be 58 per cent, on the assumption that only those couples who jointly registered their child and gave the same address at the time of registration were cohabiting. It is possible that jointly registered births to couples with different addresses and solely registered births also include cohabiting couples. Furthermore, lack of co-residence may not necessarily imply that the mother and putative father are not in a stable relationship and jointly involved in the rearing of their child.

Pathways to Never-Married Lone Motherhood

Amongst the unmarried population the route to lone motherhood involves a series of events and decisions that affect the likelihood of having a child outside marriage. The initial step is engagement in sexual relations and whether contraception is used to prevent pregnancy. If the woman becomes pregnant, either through non-use of contraception or contraceptive failure, some will choose abortion whilst others will choose to have the child. If couples decide to marry before conceiving or having their child, then a non-marital birth is averted. Once the baby is born outside of marriage, the baby may be placed for adoption. With the emergence of cohabitation amongst the never-married population during the 1970s and its subsequent rise, an additional strand has been added to the route to never-married motherhood. In the following sections trends in the alternative strategies on the route to childbearing outside marriage and the potentiality of never-married lone mother-hood are examined.

Sexual Behaviour

Earlier initiation of sexual intercourse and increases in the proportions who have sex prior to marriage have placed an increasing proportion of unmarried people at risk of parenthood. For example, we see from Table 2.3 which contains re-analysed data from the 1991 National Survey of Sexual Attitudes and Lifestyles (NSSAL) (Johnson et al. 1994) that the proportions of women who reported having had sexual intercourse at age 18 or younger has increased from 18 per cent of women born in the early 1930s, who on average were in their late teens in the early 1950s, to over two-thirds of women born since the mid-1950s, who were passing through their late teens from the early 1970s. Men are more likely than women to report having intercourse before age 19, however differences between the two sexes has declined over time and amongst the generation born since the 1950s the differences between men and women are small. Even amongst the oldest cohorts of women in the NSSAL, marriage was not the pre-eminent setting for the initiation of sexual intercourse. Amongst women born in the early 1930s, who typically would have married during the 1950s, only 54 per cent reported that they were married when they first had intercourse, amongst women born during the early 1940s (who typically married in

TABLE 2.3. *Proportion of men and women having sexual intercourse by age 19, by year of birth, age in 1990, and period when age 18*

Year of birth	Age in 1990	Years aged 18	Women (%)	Men (%)	Contraception not used at first sex (unmarried women)
1931–35	55–59	1949–53	18	37	46
1936–40	50–54	1954–58	27	48	45
1941–45	45–49	1959–63	36	51	39
1946–50	40–44	1964–68	43	58	38
1951–55	35–39	1969–73	58	64	35
1956–60	30–34	1974–78	66	72	29
1961–65	25–29	1979–83	68	74	26
1966–70	20–24	1984–88	78	76	29

Source: Analysis of 1991 National Survey of Sexual Attitudes and Lifestyles.

the early to mid-1960s) the proportion had declined to 27 per cent and amongst those born during the early 1950s (who typically married during the early to mid-1970s) the proportion was negligible, 8 per cent.

Contraception

Amongst the sexually active it is a sine qua non that in the absence of effective and consistent use of contraception women are likely to become pregnant. Nowadays, men and women of all ages and marital statuses are entitled to contraceptive advice and supplies as part of the National Health Service. This was a hard-won battle stretching over a century from the Bradlaugh–Besant trial of the 1870s to 1974 when the NHS initiated free family planning services (Soloway 1982; Leathard 1980; Selman 1988). Family planning had not been incorporated into the original National Health Service, which may have been a legacy of the 1930s with its low birth rates and the attending fears about depopulation but perhaps more so because of objections on moral and religious grounds. It was left to non-governmental organizations to continue to be pro-active in this domain. After the war, the Family Planning Association, which had grown out of the amalgamation of voluntary birth control organizations that had developed from the 1920s onwards, expanded its clinic base in response to the increased demand for contraceptive advice from married women. The introduction during the early 1960s of oral contraceptives, or the 'pill' as it came to be known, directly involved the medical profession in the realm of birth control for the first time (Leathard 1980). The advent of the 'pill'; the passing of the 1967 Family Planning Act which allowed local authorities to provide contraceptive advice regardless of marital status on social as well as medical grounds; the introduction of contraceptive advice for the unmarried in 1969; and the provision of free contraception on the NHS in 1974, formed the basis of the 'contraceptive revolution'. Evidence from surveys conducted in the late 1960s (Langford 1976; Woolf 1971) showed that the most popular methods of contraception at that time were the condom and withdrawal, followed by the pill. Other devices such as the diaphragm and intra-uterine devices were less popular methods. National surveys of Family Planning Services in England and Wales conducted in 1970 and 1975 (Bone 1979) showed that during the early 1970s, there was a significant increase in the proportions of married women using the pill. In 1970 one in four married women reporting using contraception took the pill as compared with one in two in 1975. By 1975 the pill had become the most important method of contraception. During the early 1970s, the rise in pill use amongst young single women was even more pronounced; whereas less than one in 10 were using the pill in 1970 the analogous proportion in 1975 was one in three. By the early 1980s it had become normative for sexually active young people to use contraception (Bone 1985) which was in sharp contrast to the early 1960s when the majority of sexually active teenage women used no contraception (Schofield 1965). Whilst contraceptive use has increased markedly, many young people do not use it consistently, a particularly risky occasion is the first time they have intercourse. As can be seen in Table 2.3, the proportions of unmarried women not using contraception at first intercourse has declined over time, but even amongst recent cohorts of young people around one in four unmarried women reported not having used contraception during their first act of sexual intercourse. Unplanned or mistimed pregnancies still occur despite the advent of free and more effective forms of contraception. Over the last few decades pre-marital sexual intercourse has become a free choice zone such that only a minority of the British public, in the main older people, think that pre-marital sex is always or almost always wrong; 19 per cent in 1991 (Kiernan 1992a). Pre-marital sexual behaviour is no longer controversial and nowadays any exhortations to use contraceptive devices tends to be within the context of preventing the spread of sexually transmitted diseases rather than averting unwanted pregnancies.

Abortion

Prior to the 1967 Abortion Act, which became operational in 1968, a legal abortion could only be obtained if it were deemed that a termination was the only way to preserve a woman's life, or to prevent serious injury to her health. The 1967 Act extended the grounds under which a termination could be procured to include injury to the physical or mental health of the pregnant woman, or any existing children of her family. Prior to 1968 it was difficult for women to obtain a legally induced abortion, and although resort to illegal abortion certainly occurred we have no reliable estimates of the extent of the practice. There is also no general agreement on what the figure was likely to have been with published estimates ranging from several hundreds of thousands (Chesser 1950) down to 15 thousand a year (Goodhart 1973). Prior to the passing of the Act, the figure most frequently quoted and used in lobbying for the change in the Law was 100,000 (Simms 1971). Statistics on abortion became available after 1967 which showed the number of legal abortions rising sharply in the ensuing years (OPCS annual: *Abortion Statistics,* table 2). Between 1969 and 1973 the number of legal abortions performed on women resident in England and Wales more than doubled from 50 to 111 thousand, representing to some degree a move away from the illegal to the legal sector. The numbers fell in the next few years, but from 1977 when 103 thousand abortions were recorded the number increased each year, reaching 129 thousand in 1981, and then increased to 174 thousand in 1990 and has since fallen back to 162 thousand in 1995. The rise in abortion rates that occurred during the 1970s was shared by all age groups, although rates were higher and rose proportionately faster amongst younger women. The abortion rate, that is the number of abortions per 1,000 women aged 14–49 years stood at 8.4 in 1971, 10.6 in 1981, and from the mid-1980s has remained in the 12–13 per 1,000 range.

In the years following the Act taking effect the proportions of abortions occurring to never-married and married women were similar. As we see in Table 2.4, in 1971, 47 per cent of the abortions were to single women and 44 per cent to married women, with 8 per cent to divorced and separated women, and 1 per cent to widowed women. The proportion of abortions amongst the separated and divorced has remained relatively steady from the 1970s to the present day, at between 9 and 12 per cent. From the mid-1980s there has been a noticeable change in the marital status distribution of women having

TABLE 2.4. *Percentage distribution of abortions by women's marital status, 1971–1995 (England and Wales residents)*

Marital Status	1971	1976	1981	1986	1991	1995
Single	46.8	49.9	54.4	63.0	66.2	66.8
Married	43.9	39.6	33.0	25.9	22.6	21.0
Other[a]	9.2	10.5	12.5	11.1	11.2	11.3
Number in 000s	94.6	101.9	128.6	147.6	167.4	162.4
Abortion rate per 1,000 (women aged 14–49)	8.4	8.9	10.6	11.7	13.1	12.7

[a] Divorced, widowed, separated, and not stated.

Sources: OPCS 1996c; OPCS annual: *Abortion Statistics,* table 16.

abortions such that the majority of women having an abortion in the 1990s are never-married women, two out of three, and the proportion of married women having an abortion has fallen to one in five. This change is partly explained by changes in marriage patterns, in that over the last two decades there has been a substantial reduction in the married population: in 1971, 27 per cent of women aged between 16 and 44 were never-married compared with 39 per cent in 1992.

Bridal pregnancies

To prevent never-married motherhood, a pregnant woman can have her pregnancy terminated or marry prior to the birth of the child. In Britain, legal abortion has only been an option since 1968 whereas legal marriage has been a popular alternative for centuries (Laslett 1977; Hair 1966; Laslett, Oosterveen, and Smith 1980).

As we see in Table 2.5, there have been changes in the extent to which women are pregnant at marriage. Over the last 40 years, it occurred most frequently during the 1960s when one in five women marrying for the first time were pregnant at their marriage ceremony, compared with one in seven women marrying in the early 1950s, and one in 10 women marrying in the early 1990s. Youthful marriages are the most likely to be preceded by a pregnancy and this was the case for nearly 40 per cent of teenage marriages contracted in the mid-1960s as

TABLE 2.5. *Percentage of first marriages with a pre-maritally conceived live birth—a birth within eight months of marriage (England and Wales), 1951–1994*

Year	All ages under 45	Teenage marriage
1951	14	23
1955	15	24
1960	19	34
1965	22	38
1970	20	35
1975	13	24
1980	14	26
1985	13	27
1990	12	24
1992	10	20

Sources: OPCS 1987; *Birth Statistics* (FM, No. 13); OPCS annual: *Birth Statistics* 1993 (Series FM1, No. 22).

compared with around 20 per cent of those contracted during the 1950s and 1990s. Marriage, the traditionally acceptable response to an out-of-wedlock pregnancy has become, as we discuss in more detail below, the least popular option for an out-of-wedlock pregnancy.

Pregnancy outcomes

The extent of bridal pregnancy following conception could be viewed as an indicator of societal norms concerning the importance of having children within marriage. Abortion may also reflect the same tendency, as well as the extent to which pregnancies are unwanted or mistimed. Proceeding to having a child out of wedlock, where marriage is technically feasible, is likely to be influenced by the importance attached to marital status and the stigma attached to having a child outside marriage. Over the last quarter of a century there have been some dramatic changes in the responses of single women to an extra-marital pregnancy.

Table 2.6 provides information for specified years over the period 1970–1994 on the number of extramarital conceptions which includes: conceptions terminated by abortion, those leading to a live birth outside marriage, and live births occurring within 8 months of marriage. The upper half of the table presents the information for all women and the lower half data for women having a child in their teens. It is apparent that the number of extramarital conceptions and the proportion of conceptions occurring outside marriage has more than doubled over the last two decades. For example, amongst women of all ages the proportion of conceptions that are extramarital has risen from 21 per cent of all conceptions in 1970 to 44 per cent in 1994 and amongst teenage women the analogous proportions have risen from 65 to over 90 per cent. The last four columns in Table 2.6 show the distribution of outcomes for extramarital conceptions which for the purposes of this analysis are: out-of-wedlock births subdivided according to whether the birth was registered solely by the mother or jointly by both parents; births occurring within marriage; and induced abortions.

These data provide interesting insights into the ways that different outcomes have waxed and waned and the processes that may have been at work over the last few decades. Broadly speaking, after the mid-1970s the extent to which women resorted to abortion has remained relatively stable and this is particularly the case amongst teenage women. Marrying before having a child has certainly waned and nowadays is an

TABLE 2.6. *Percentage of conceptions by outcome and age (England and Wales)*

Year	Total number of extramarital conceptions (EMCs) in 000s	EMCs as a percentage of all conceptions	Conceptions outside marriage			
			Out of wedlock birth: Registrations		Pre-marital conception	Induced abortion
			Sole	Joint		
	(1)	(2)	(3)	(4)	(5)	(6)
Conceptions all women						
1970	186.1	21.2	20	16	40	24
1975	160.6	23.2	17	17	26	40
1980	208.6	29.1	16	22	22	40
1985	283.5	35.6	16	32	15	37
1990	377.1	43.0	14	41	9	36
1993	364.3	44.5	13	45	8	33
Conceptions to teenage women						
1970	87.3	64.8	21	9	50	20
1975	76.1	67.9	20	11	31	38
1980	87.6	74.7	19	18	23	40
1985	101.0	84.7	20	20	13	39
1990	103.8	90.2	19	36	6	39
1993	79.1	91.2	19	40	4	38

Source: OPCS annual: *Birth Statistics*, (Series FM1).

insignificant outcome to pregnancy. There are some intriguing indications from this table that pre-nuptial pregnancies may have been substituted by jointly registered out-of-wedlock births, in that the sum of pre-nuptial pregnancies and jointly registered extramarital births (columns four and five) has remained fairly constant for the teenage group from the mid-1970s to the 1990s and for all women up to the late 1980s. The frequency of solely registered births, which are the most likely to represent never-married lone motherhood, has remained almost constant amongst the teenage group, and relatively constant for all women, from the mid-1970s to the latter half of the 1980s. It would appear from these data that there may be a core of women that prefer to have a child on their own and proportionately there has been little change in this group over the last two decades.

The striking increase in joint registrations and its mirror image in the marked decline in bridal pregnancies could be interpreted as a simple re-classification whereby pregnant single women who in times past married nowadays cohabit. This could be interpreted as a positive development in that couples prefer a trial union to a hasty marriage. It also goes some way to explaining why fertile cohabiting unions are more fragile than marital ones. Marriages preceded by pregnancy have been shown to have a higher rate of dissolution than those marriages where children are conceived and born after marriage (Murphy 1985) These vulnerable marriages are now more likely to be included in the cohabiting set and such unions are, other things being equal, more prone to break-up and thus contribute to the pool of never-married lone mothers rather than the pool of post-marital lone mothers. This suggests that some seemingly new developments may well be old situations in new guises.

Adoption

Another option open to unmarried mothers, that is rare nowadays, is to have her child adopted. During the 1950s and 1960s young single pregnant women were encouraged to have their babies in special mother and baby homes, often located outside their own local community, and were also encouraged to have their child adopted. We have no precise statistics on the proportions of unmarried women who placed their child for adoption but we have some indirect information. In 1927 following the enactment of the 1926 Adoption Act, which put adoption on a legal footing for the first time, an Adopted Children's

Register was set up by the Registrar General to record all legal adoptions. Also 1926 saw the passing of the Legitimacy Act which allowed the legitimation of children born to never-married parents who subsequently married. The subsequent 1959 Legitimacy Act extended this right to parents who were married to another at the time of the birth. The recording of legitimations was also made the responsibility of the General Register Office. Prior to 1950 only very basic statistics on the total number of adoptions and re-registrations of illegitimate births under the 1926 Act were published (GRO annual: Registrar General Statistical Reviews, Civil). In 1927 there were just under 3 thousand adoption orders (2,943), in 1940 over 7 thousand (7,775), and in 1949 over 17 thousand (17,317). The number of legitimations in the corresponding years were much less and did not exhibit the same steady upward trend: being 5,495 in 1927, 4,345 in 1940, and 3,028 in 1949.

From 1950 the Registrar General published data on adoption orders for illegitimate and legitimate children and whether the adoption included a natural parent (GRO annual: Registrar General Statistical Review, part 2, table T6). In 1950, 80 per cent of all adoptions were of illegitimate children and the remaining 20 per cent were legitimate children. Table 2.7 shows for selected years the number of illegitimate children adopted and the proportions that were parental and non-parental adoptions. The number of such adoptions were of the order of 10 thousand throughout the 1950s, they increased during the 1960s to peak at over 19,000 in 1968 and then subsequently declined to just over 7,000 in 1977 and had declined further to under 5,000 in 1984 and

TABLE 2.7. *Adoption of children born outside marriage, 1950–1993*

Year	Total	Parental (%)	Non-parental (%)
1950	10,441	30	70
1955	10,341	31	69
1961	12,981	22	78
1968	19,348	23	77
1973	12,993	43	57
1977	7,329	44	56
1982	5,585	—	—
1987	4,092	—	—
1993	4,072	—	—

Sources: 1950–73: GRO annual: table T5; 1977: Leete 1978; 1982–93: OPCS annual: *Marriage and Divorce Statistics*, table 6.1.

in 1993 stood at 4,072 (OPCS 1993a: table 6.1). In 1968, 77 per cent of adoptions of illegitimate children in that year were to non-parents whereas in 1977 the analogous proportion was 56 per cent. It has been estimated (Leete, 1978) that about one in five illegitimate children born during the 1950s and 1960s were adopted by non-parents. Moreover, the great majority of these children were adopted early in life, for example amongst those born during the 1960s, 80 per cent had been adopted by their first birthday.

Changing Marriage Patterns and the Rise of Cohabitation

Undoubtedly, the rise in never-married lone motherhood is being driven by changing marriage patterns. Throughout the twentieth century, marriage had never taken place so frequently or occurred at such young ages as during the 1960s: the culmination of a longer term trend towards near universal and youthful marriage (Kiernan and Eldridge 1987). Since the beginning of the 1970s there have been substantial and continuing declines in marriage rates, exemplified in less marriage and older marriage and associated with the emergence of widespread cohabitation. For example, in 1971 the median age at first marriage amongst women was 21.4 years, by 1980 it had increased slightly to 21.8 but by 1993 it stood at 25.3 years. An even more striking picture emerges when one compares the experiences of different generations of women. For example, amongst women born in 1946, 81 per cent had married by age 25, as compared with 71 per cent of those born in 1956 and 46 per cent of those born in 1966 and amongst the most recent cohort for which we have information, those born in 1970, only 39 per cent were married by this age (OPCS 1993a: table 3.12). These declines in marriage have increased the exposure to the risk of an out-of-wedlock birth by increasing the number of years couples are sexually active outside of marriage. Both the declines in marriage and increased childbearing outside marriage are inextricably linked to the growth of cohabitation.

Cohabitation, whereby couples live together without recourse to the law, is not new (Gillis 1985). Prior to the 1970s, cohabiting unions were largely statistically invisible and probably socially invisible outside of the local community or milieu. There were sub-groups of the population that were probably more prone to cohabitation than others: the very poor; groups ideologically opposed to marriage; and those whose marriages had broken up but were unable to obtain a divorce. Cohabitation in the early decades of the twentieth century was probably most common amongst couples where at least one party had been married before. The restrictive nature of divorce law prior to the 1969 Act such that one partner could prevent the dissolution of a marriage meant that any new union could only be formed via cohabitation. Moreover, for those who could not afford the cost of a divorce, separation followed by cohabitation provided an affordable alternative to divorce and remarriage.

Post-marital cohabitation may not be new but a new type of cohabitation is implicated in the marriage bust that has occurred since the 1970s. This type of cohabitation occurs amongst never-married, young people, predominantly in their twenties and early thirties, who live together either as a prelude to, or as an alternative to marriage. In order to distinguish this new type of cohabitation from earlier forms and particularly cohabiting unions that occur subsequent to a marriage we have labelled it 'nubile cohabitation'; French demographers refer to it as 'cohabitation juvenile' (Roussel 1978). This form of cohabitation came to the fore during the 1970s, escalated during the 1980s, and continues on its upward path during the 1990s. Nowadays, two out of three people cohabiting are never married people under age 35, and living together before marrying has become a majority practice, and well on the way to being the rule rather the exception. In the 1990s, typically 70 per cent of never-married women who marry have cohabited with their husbands compared with 58 per cent of those marrying between 1985 and 1988, 33 per cent marrying between 1975 and 1979, and 6 per cent marrying between 1965 and 1969 (Haskey 1995). The proportion of never-married women who were cohabiting more than trebled between 1979 and 1993, from 7.5 per cent to 23.5 per cent.

Cohabiting unions have tended to be short-lived and childless, but during the 1980s children were increasingly being born within these unions. The changing patterns of birth registration provide some evidence of this (Table 2.8). There has been an increase in the proportion of births that are jointly registered by the mother and father from under 50 per cent at the beginning of the 1970s to over 75 per cent in the mid-1990s. Since 1983, OPCS has provided additional data on whether the mother and father report the same address at the time of registration, which is likely to signify cohabitation. Three out of four joint registrations are to couples giving the same address and this has remained constant over the ten or so years for which data are available.

TABLE 2.8. *Registration of births outside marriage, 1964–1995 (%)*

	1964	1971	1981	1995
Sole registration	60	55	42	22
Joint registration	40	45	58	78
Births outside marriage as a % of all births	7	8	13	34

Sources: OPCS 1987: tables 1.1 and 3.7; OPCS 1996d: table 10.

Cohabiting unions as well as being increasingly likely to include children are also, on average, more fragile than marital unions. From life-history information collected in the British Household Panel Survey, it has been estimated that amongst the most recent generation of women included in the survey that one-fifth of first cohabiting unions were fertile and these cohabiting unions with children have a high rate of dissolution, with about one in two dissolving (Ermisch 1995).

Summary

If one were to summarize the major change that has occurred in recent times in the realm of never-married motherhood, it is that more so than any time in the past it is likely to arise from choice rather than mistake. The traditional nexus between marriage and childbearing has been broken for a significant minority of couples, a development facilitated by the advent of effective contraception, particularly the contraceptive pill, and the legalization of abortion. Moreover, this 'contraceptive revolution' is an important engine behind the rise of cohabitation and it is the breakdown of cohabiting unions that is the novel and important contributor to the recent increase in never-married lone motherhood.

Post-Marital Lone Motherhood

The pathways to post-marital lone motherhood and the demographic impetuses behind them are less complex than those that lead to never-married lone motherhood. Post-marital lone motherhood primarily arises from the break-up of a marriage or the death of a husband. In this section we examine the extent to which widowhood and marital separation have contributed to the formation of lone mother families over the course of the twentieth century, with a particular focus on the period since the Second World War.

The Decline of Widowhood

At the beginning of the twentieth century, the death of a father was probably the major cause of lone motherhood. Motherless families were also much more common in the earlier decades of the century arising from high death rates amongst women at the reproductive ages. We do not have any direct information on the extent of lone parenthood emanating from death but mortality data and information on the marital status of the population provides us with some insights.

Death rates have improved over the course of the twentieth century such that the probability of dying at ages when men are most likely to have dependent children has noticeably declined. For example, as can be seen in Table 2.9 the death rate amongst men aged 35 to 44 years was nearly 10 per 1,000 men in the population at the beginning of the century as compared with 3 per 1,000 in the early 1950s and under 2 per 1,000 in 1995. The rates were somewhat lower amongst women being 8, 2, and 1 per 1,000 women in the analogous time periods. There is also a noticeable excess in male mortality in later middle age

TABLE 2.9. *Death rates per 1,000 population (England and Wales)*

	1901–5	1931–5	1951–5	1971–5	1995
Men					
20–24	4.39	3.15	1.23	0.99	0.84
25–34	5.89	3.31	1.39	0.97	0.97
35–44	9.74	5.40	2.71	2.22	1.69
45–54	17.0	11.2	7.93	7.22	4.14
55–64	34.1	23.6	22.5	20.2	12.2
Women					
20–24	3.66	2.77	0.70	0.43	0.29
25–34	5.04	3.09	1.09	0.57	0.45
34–44	8.05	4.33	2.11	1.56	1.06
45–54	13.1	7.96	4.89	4.37	2.78
55–64	25.4	17.0	11.8	10.2	7.2

Sources: OPCS annual: *Mortality Statistics*; OPCS 1996c: table 13.

(ages 45–54 years). Male mortality at these ages was 30 per cent higher than female mortality at these ages at the beginning of the century, 60 per cent higher in the early 1950s, and 50 per cent higher in 1995. Deaths from infectious diseases were more common at the beginning of the century and such diseases tend to be more gender blind than degenerative diseases.

Table 2.10 provides some further indirect information on the prevalence of lone motherhood. The 1921 census was the first to include divorced as a marital status category and the distributions of widows and divorced women given in Table 2.10 show that from that date there has been an upward trend in the divorced population and a downward one in the widowed population. The estimates only include women in the age range 20 to 54 years as this range covers the period when the women are most likely to have become mothers and to have dependent children. In 1921, 5 per cent of the women in these prime childbearing and rearing ages were widowed at the time of the Census as compared with 2 per cent in 1971, and 1 per cent in 1991. There was only a marked increase in the proportions of divorced women in this population after 1971, and in 1971 the proportions of widows and divorced women were similar.

The Rise of Divorce

Before the middle of the nineteenth century, divorce was an expensive and complicated procedure involving the judiciary, the Church, and Parliament. The 1857 Matrimonial Causes Act simplified the procedure and introduced civil divorce by which a petitioner could seek a termination on the grounds of matrimonial offence. From then until 1971 modifications were made but primarily with respect to the grounds for

TABLE 2.10. *Marital status distribution, women aged 20–54 (Great Britain) (%)*

	1921	1951	1971	1991
Single	33	20	14	25
Married[a]	62	76	81	65
Widowed	5	3	2	1
Divorced	less than 1	1	2	9

[a] Includes women who have been previously widowed or divorced as estimates are based on marital status at the time of the Census.

Sources: OPCS/GRO Scotland (1983): 1991 Census Historical Tables Great Britain.

divorce. From 1857 to 1922, adultery was in effect the sole ground for divorce, in 1938 the grounds were extended to include desertion, cruelty, and insanity, and a major revision to fault-based divorce was initiated in 1971. With the enactment of the 1969 Divorce Law Reform Act 'the irretrievable breakdown of marriage' became the sole ground for divorce. Such a breakdown could be established by the petitioner proving one or more of five 'facts' adultery, unreasonable behaviour and desertion, the erstwhile matrimonial offences, and two new 'facts' separation of two years duration if both parties agreed to the divorce or five years if one party disagreed. Statistics on divorce have always been obtained from information provided by the courts and until 1950 only very basic information on the numbers of divorces were published. The Royal Commission on Population (1949) recommended that the General Registrar's Office as it then was (subsequently renamed the Office of Population Censuses and Surveys, and from 1995 OPCS has been subsumed by the Office of National Statistics) recommended that as divorces now outnumbered deaths as a cause of marital dissolution at ages under 45 that additional statistics should be provided to the GRO by the Divorce Court authorities. This information included date of marriage, and whether the husband and wife had been married before, date of birth of both spouses, occupation of husband at the time of the divorce, and the number of children born during the marriage. National statistics on the ages of the children recorded in broad age groups became available from 1970, and since 1981 the dates of birth of all children in the divorcing couple's family have been collected.

In 1857, in England and Wales 24 couples were granted a divorce the number in 1900 was 512, by 1918 it had surpassed the 1,000 mark, by 1936, 1943, 1960, and 1972 the 5, 10, 50, and 100 thousand marks were passed and in 1995, the most recent year for which data are available at the time of writing, 158 thousand divorces were granted (OPCS 1990: table 4.1 and OPCS 1996c). Whilst civil judicial divorce is the only legal means of bringing a marriage to an end, many couples have and do separate without their separation being recorded or without recourse to the law. The cost of divorce proceedings was prohibitive for much of the population prior to the Second World War and only with the introduction of legal aid in 1950 was it feasible for lower wage-earning groups to initiate formal divorce proceedings (Rowntree and Carrier 1958). Before the Second World War, a common alternative to divorce was to apply for a magistrate's court maintenance or separation order. This type of order, available from 1878, did not end a marriage but allowed a wife a legal claim to financial assistance from an absent husband. In some instances it may have reflected a temporary separation whilst in others a permanent one. As we see in Table 2.11, until the 1930s the magistrate court applications outnumbered divorces by a substantial amount and not until the early 1950s did divorces account for more than one-half of the combined divorces and magistrate applications. These statistics on divorce and magistrate applications may involve an element of double counting as some of those who made magistrate applications may have subsequently applied for a divorce at a later time. But in combination they provide a better indication of the prevalence of marital dissolution than divorce figures alone. During the 1960s magistrate court applications continued at a level of around 26 thousand up to the period 1970–2 when the Finer Committee estimated that one in two of the wives with magistrates' orders went on to be petitioners in the divorce court. Thus, they state that in their evaluation of recent data 'it is probable that the number of marriage breakdowns which leave a legal record are the total number of divorces plus half the matrimonial orders made by magistrate's courts' (Finer Committee 1974: i. 43). They also suggest that a high proportion of matrimonial proceedings in the magistrate courts relate to marriages as dead as those terminated by divorce.

Prior to the 1969 Divorce Law Reform Act, there were in effect two systems of family law dealing with marital breakdown, one for the well-off and one for the rest of the population, since when divorce has become the pre-eminent mechanism for terminating a marriage. It is to the period after 1970 to which we now turn our attention. During the 1970s, three times as many couples experienced a divorce, 1.2 million between 1971 and 1980, compared to the 1960s, 0.4 million, and during the 1980s (1981–90) a further 1.5 million couples divorced. During the early 1990s there has been on average around 160 thousand divorces per year (OPCS 1995c and OPCS 1996d). In 1960 the divorce rate stood at 2.0 per 1,000 members of the married population. By 1970, prior to the 1969 Act taking effect, it had more than doubled to 4.7, the rate increased threefold over the 1980s to stand at 12.0 in 1980 and only increased slightly thereafter to stand at 13.0 in 1990, and in 1995 the rate was 13.1. As divorce became more prevalent it increasingly occurred at an earlier stage in marriage, as is clearly illustrated in Table 2.12 which shows the effect of divorce by duration of marriage on couples who married in different decades. For example, 7 per cent of the those marrying in 1951 had divorced by their 20th wedding

TABLE 2.11. *Matrimonial proceedings in England and Wales, 1900–1954*

| Year | Annual averages of | | | | |
| | High Court petitions for | | Magistrates' Court applications | Total proceedings | Divorces as per cent of total |
	Divorce	Other lesser reliefs[a]			
1900–4	783	126	10,736	11,645	6.7
1905–9	809	139	11,067	12,015	6.7
1910–13	919	182	10,765	11,866	7.7
1920–4	3,150	451	13,603	17,204	18.3
1925–9	3,805	152	14,475	18,432	20.6
1930–4	4,578	169	14,382	19,129	23.9
1950–4	32,451	160	26,835	59,449	54.6

[a] These averages are based on totals of applications by wives for maintenance orders, which are published only for the peace-time years listed here.

Sources: Rowntree and Carrier (1958), based on 1956 Commission *Report*, appendix II, table 1 and *Criminal and Judicial Statistics*, published annually.

TABLE 2.12. *Cumulative percentage of marriages ended in divorce by marriage cohort in England and Wales, 1951–1993*

Marriage cohort	Duration of marriage in completed years				
	3	5	10	15	20
1951	0.3	1.2	3.1	4.9	6.7
1956	0.3	1.3	4.4	7.2	11.4
1961	0.4	2.1	7.1	13.0	17.8
1966	0.7	3.9	12.4	18.9	23.7
1971	2.3	7.1	16.6	22.9	27.5
1976	4.0	10.4	20.3	26.9	
1981	4.7	11.6	22.8		
1986	7.3	13.3			
1991	7.6	—			

anniversary whilst the 1961, 1971, and 1986 marriage cohorts had reached this level by their 10th and 5th and 3rd wedding anniversaries, respectively. Amongst the most recent cohorts to have been married for 20 years almost three out of 10 marriages had ended in divorce.

Children and Divorce

Not all British couples who divorce have dependent children. As can be seen in Table 2.13, in 1991 just over one in two divorced couples had children under age 16, a somewhat lower proportion than observed at the beginning of the 1980s but comparable to that pertaining in 1971. The numbers of children involved in the divorce of their parents were very similar in 1981 and 1991, at around 160,000, which was almost double the figure for 1971. The number of divorcing couples with dependent children hardly changed between 1981 and 1991. Thus, divorce per se is unlikely to have made a major contribution to the growth in lone parent families over the 1980s, whereas it was a major contributor during the 1970s.

There have been, however, important changes in the age distribution of dependent children of divorcees (Table 2.13): with the proportion of divorcing couples with children under age 5 increasing from 25 per cent to 37 per cent in 1981 and increasing still further to 47 per cent in 1991. This increase in couples with young children is a direct conse

TABLE 2.13. *Characteristics of divorcing couples (England and Wales)*

	1971	1981	1991
Divorcing couples			
Children under 16	56%	60%	56%
Children over 16	16%	11%	14%
No child stated	27%	29%	30%
Number of couples in 000s	74	146	159
Divorcing couples with children			
under age 16			
Age: 0–4 years	25%	27%	47%
5–10 years	49%	41%	36%
11–15 years	25%	22%	18%
Number of couples in 000s	42	87	88
Number of children in 000s	81	159	161
Divorce rate per 1,000 married population	5.9	11.9	13.5

Sources: OPCS 1984, 1993a: *Marriage and Divorce Statistics*; GRO annual: Registrar General's Statistical Review 1971.

quence of the move to divorcing sooner in marriage which was high-lighted in Table 2.12 and may well have contributed to the growth in lone parents relying on benefits that has been a prominent feature of the 1980s and 1990s (as discussed in Chapter 6). Given that mothers with young children are less likely to be in the labour market, if divorce occurs they are as a consequence more likely to have to rely on maintenance or state benefits to support themselves and their children.

Children and Lone Motherhood

Undoubtedly, with the increased resort to divorce that has occurred since the 1960s more and more children have been experiencing the break-up of their parents' marriage. Registration data are unable to provide us with direct information on the proportions of children who have ever experienced the break-up of their parents' marriage but survey data provides an alternative source. The information shown in Table 2.14 which comes from our own analysis of the National Sexual Attitudes and Lifestyles Survey is amongst the first that allows us to directly assess this development for generations of children born since the 1930s. However, it should be borne in mind that under-reporting of parental separations may have occurred and this may be particularly

TABLE 2.14. *Family situation at age 16 by birth cohort*

Birth cohort	Lived with both natural parents to age 16 (%)	Parents separated or divorced lived with mother (%)	Father deceased lived with mother (%)	Other situations (%)	Number of cases
1931–35	80	4	4	12	305
1936–40	83	3	5	9	487
1941–45	83	4	3	10	720
1946–50	86	3	3	8	654
1951–55	87	5	4	4	621
1956–60	85	6	3	6	555
1961–65	84	7	2	7	427
1966–70	77	15	2	6	363
1971–74	73	19	1	7	416
TOTAL (per cent)	82.8	6.8	2.9	7.5	100%
Number of cases	3,765	309	133	341	4,548

Source: Analysis of the 1991 Sexual Attitudes and Lifestyles Survey data.

the case if separations had occurred when a child was very young or if people are being asked to recollect (painful) events that occurred many decades ago. Given our interest here is lone motherhood our analysis shows the proportions of respondents, according to their year of birth, who lived with both their natural parents to age 16 and the proportions that had experienced a parental separation or divorce, or a parental death and as far as can be ascertained from the available data subsequently lived primarily with their mother. The other column includes children who were separated from their natural parents for other reasons, including adoption and health reasons as well as those who lived with their father or other relatives after their parents' marriage had broken down or their mother had died. It is apparent from Table 2.14 that living with a lone mother as a result of parental separation is a relatively new feature in children's lives. Amongst the generation born before the mid-1960s, less than 10 per cent had such an experience as compared with 15 per cent of those born in the latter half of the 1960s and 19 per cent of those born during the early years of the 1970s. Only for the generation born since the mid-1950s has marital breakdown become more significant than widowhood in precipitating lone motherhood. One also notes that the proportions of children being reared by both their parents to age 16 was probably at its peak for the generation born during the period between the end of the Second World War and 1960.

Pathways Out of Lone Motherhood

There are two main routes out of lone parenthood: starting to live with a partner in a cohabiting or marital union, and children growing up and becoming independent. There is a paucity of information on the duration of and routes out of lone parenthood and how these elements may have changed over time but data on remarriage provides some insights for the group of post-marital lone mothers, who until recently constituted the majority of lone mother families.

Remarriage

Prior to the Second World War, the majority of remarriages amongst women arose from death rather than divorce, with between 4 and 11 per cent of marriages involving a widowed woman (Table 2.15). After the Second World War up until the 1960s the proportions of

TABLE 2.15. *Marital status at marriage (England and Wales)*

Year	All marriages in 000s	Percentage first marriages	Percentage widows	Percentage divorced women
1900	257.5	93	7	—
1910	267.7	94	6	—
1920	380.0	89	11	—
1930	315.1	94	5	—
1940	470.5	95	4	1
1950	358.5	88	6	6
1960	343.6	91	5	5
1970	415.5	88	4	8
1980	370.0	75	4	21
1990	331.1	74	3	23
1993	299.2	72	3	25

Source: OPCS annual: *Marriage and Divorce Statistics.*

remarriages involving widows and divorced women were broadly similar, thereafter divorced women came to predominate in the remarriage market (see Coleman 1989, for a detailed analysis of remarriage in the post-war period).

Remarriage is more common amongst younger women, be they widowed or divorced, and the available evidence indicates that the chances of remarrying do not differ significantly as between women with and without children (Haskey 1983a; OPCS 1983), although the chances of divorce are much higher amongst childless couples than amongst couples with children. Data from the General Household Survey provides some information on the length of time between separation and remarriage. For example, amongst women who separated from their spouses during the 1970s and the early part of the 1980s, around one in five had remarried within three years of separating, one in three by four years, and one in two within six years of separation. The rate of remarriage amongst the divorced peaked in 1972 following the introduction of more lenient divorce legislation which allowed marriages that had been dead in all but name to be terminated and some long-standing cohabiting unions to be legalized. Remarriage rates have declined dramatically since 1972. For example, the remarriage rate for divorced women was 153 per 1,000 divorced women, had fallen by 30 per cent to 107 by 1980 and in 1993 stood at 48; a 55 per cent decline on the 1980 figure. This marked decline in remarriage is explained in part by the popularity of cohabitation amongst the erstwhile married.

Re-partnering

Cohabiting after a marriage has broken down or prior to remarriage has in fact been more frequent than cohabiting prior to a first marriage. For example, during the 1960s, 40 per cent of remarriages were preceded by a period of cohabitation as compared with 4 per cent of first marriages, in the 1990s the figures were around 80 per cent and 70 per cent, respectively. There have also been increases in the proportions of currently cohabiting, in 1979 when the General Household Survey began collecting information on the extent of cohabitation in the population 18 per cent of the currently separated and divorced women were cohabiting, and these women were as likely to have children as the separated and divorced who were not cohabiting (Brown and Kiernan 1981). In 1995 the proportion of separated and divorced women cohabiting was 27 per cent (Living in Britain, 1996).

Cross-sectional data of the type collected in the General Household Survey provide us with valuable up-to-date information on the women who are currently lone parents, but they do not capture the full extent of lone motherhood. This requires life-history information of the type collected in the British Household Panel Study (BHPS). Using these longitudinal data Ermisch and Francesconi (1996) have provided some life table estimates which suggest that if the rates of entry into and exit from lone motherhood operating during the 1980s were to prevail, then it would be expected that one in three mothers would have experienced a period of lone motherhood by the time they were age 45 and one in four would have exited lone motherhood by entering a cohabiting or marital union. They also estimate that the median duration of lone motherhood for post-marital lone mothers was almost four years whereas the median duration of lone motherhood for never-married lone mothers was less than two years.

Being reared by a lone mother is not necessarily a permanent arrangement as not insignificant proportions of lone mothers re-partner. What of the ex-husbands of lone mothers? The ex-husbands are even more likely than their ex-wives to cohabit and remarry and are also more likely to remarry more quickly after a divorce, with enhanced chances of forming new families in which children are born and reared. Step-families be they created via cohabitation or marriage have high dissolution rates. For example, estimates from the BHPS indicate that one in four step-families dissolve within a year of being formed (Ermisch and Francesconi 1996) and that those formed via cohabitation are almost twice as fragile as those formed via marriage.

Information on the dynamics and further insights into the complexity of the pathways into and out of lone parenthood over the course of the twentieth century is likely to remain a closed book. It is only for the 1990s that follow-up surveys of lone parents have provided the necessary information for the evaluation of the dynamics of lone parenthood (Ford, Marsh, and McKay 1995; Ford, Marsh, and Finlayson 1996). This Department of Social Security and Policy Studies Institute longitudinal survey has followed a group of lone parents (95 per cent of the sample were lone mothers and 5 per cent were lone fathers) over the period 1991 to 1995. As we see from Table 2.16, 43 per cent of the sample were never-married lone parents with almost equal proportions

TABLE 2.16. *Routes out of lone parenthood, 1991–1995*

Route out of lone parenthood	Lone-parent status in 1991 (%)					
	Never partnered	Separated from cohabitation	Separated from marriage	Divorced	Widowed	All
Partnered or re-partnered	23	18	26	14	8	19
Children grew up or left home	7	8	11	14	35	11
Children left and returned	—	1	1	6	—	3
Partnered and then returned to lone parenthood	7	11	8	5	8	7
Continued as lone parent	64	62	56	61	51	60
Number of cases (=100%)	135	132	102	214	37	623
Row per cent	22	21	16	34	6	100

Source: Ford, Marsh, and Finlayson 1996: table 2.6b.

being never-partnered and separated cohabitants. The largest group of post-marital lone parents were the divorced (34 per cent), with lower proportions of separated lone parents (16 per cent) and, as would be expected, a very small proportion of widowed lone parents (6 per cent). The majority of the lone parents, 60 per cent, were still lone parents four years later and of those who had left lone parenthood two-thirds had re-partnered and one-third no longer had dependent children. Amongst those who had departed lone parenthood during the four-year period a noticeable proportion, around one in four, had become lone parents again. Additionally, lone parents who re-partnered tended on average to be younger and that the pace of re-partnering was faster in the early years of lone parenthood and slackened thereafter. With the passage of time children growing up became the more salient reason for exiting from lone parenthood.

Summary

Post-marital motherhood is undoubtedly a declining fraction of the totality of lone mothers; from being the pre-eminent type of lone motherhood during the 1970s and 1980s the signs are that it is likely to be eclipsed by the growth in never-married lone motherhood in the near future, just as divorce eclipsed widowhood as the major cause of lone motherhood during the 1960s. We conclude this chapter with a brief examination of developments in other European countries.

Trends in Other European Countries

The rise of lone motherhood is certainly not confined to Britain. There is a dearth of comparable data on the extent of lone motherhood in other European countries but an examination of extramarital child-bearing and divorce data for a range of European countries provide clues as to the extent of parallel developments in other countries, as well as highlighting the diversity that exists across Europe.

Extramarital Childbearing

Table 2.17 shows the percentage of all live births that were born outside marriage for a range of European countries for the period 1960 to the present time. It is clearly apparent that the rise in

TABLE 2.17. *The proportion of live births outside marriage per 100 live births,*
1960–1995

Country	Year				
	1960	1970	1980	1990	1995[a]
Northern Europe					
Denmark	7.8	11.0	33.2	46.4	46.9 (94)
Finland	4.0	5.8	13.1	25.2	31.3 (94)
Iceland	25.3	29.8	39.7	55.2	59.6 (94)
Ireland	1.6	2.7	5.0	14.6	22.7
Norway	3.7	6.9	14.5	38.6	47.6
Sweden	11.3	18.4	39.7	47.0	52.9
United Kingdom	5.2	8.0	11.5	27.9	33.6
Western Europe					
Austria	13.0	12.8	17.8	23.6	27.4 (94)
Belgium	2.1	2.8	4.1	11.6	13.6 (93)
France	6.1	6.8	11.4	30.1	34.9 (93)
Germany (FDR)	6.1	5.5	7.6	10.5	12.4
Germany (GDR)	11.4	13.3	22.8	35.0	41.4
Luxembourg	3.2	4.0	6.0	12.9	13.1
Netherlands	1.4	2.1	4.1	11.4	14.3
Switzerland	3.8	3.8	4.7	6.1	6.8
Southern Europe					
Greece	1.2	1.1	1.5	2.2	2.9
Italy	2.4	2.2	4.3	6.5	7.7
Portugal	9.5	7.3	9.2	14.7	18.7
Spain	2.3	1.4	3.9	9.6	10.8 (93)

[a] Unless otherwise specified.

Sources: 1970–95: Council of Europe, 1996; 1960: United Nations 1965.

extramarital childbearing is not confined to Britain. Since the 1970s
there have been noticeable increases in the proportion of births outside
marriage in many Northern and Western European countries with
conspicuous increases during the 1980s. As yet signs of stabilization
are only apparent in a few countries: Italy, Switzerland, and Spain, a set
of countries with low levels of extramarital childbearing, and in
Denmark which has a high level. Differences in the extent of extramarital childbearing are very large: at one extreme are Iceland and
Sweden where over 50 per cent of children are born outside marriage.
High ratios are evident in 1994/5 in Denmark (47 per cent), Norway

(48 per cent) and the Eastern part of Germany (42 per cent). At the other extreme are countries like Greece with only 3 per cent of recorded births born outside marriage and Switzerland and Italy with under 10 per cent in 1995. With few exceptions the rise of extramarital childbearing is directly associated with the rise of cohabitation that has occurred across Europe in recent decades (Kiernan 1996a; Prinz 1995).

Divorce in Europe

Table 2.18 shows the crude divorce rate in a range of European countries from the 1970s to the 1990s. In 1994 there was a good deal

TABLE 2.18. *Crude divorce rate: divorces per 1,000 average population, 1970–1994*

Country	Year		
	1970	1980	1994
Northern Europe			
Denmark	1.9	2.7	2.6
Finland	1.3	2.0	2.7
Iceland	1.2	1.9	1.8
Ireland	—	—	—
Norway	0.9	1.6	2.5
Sweden	1.6	2.4	2.5
United Kingdom	1.1	2.8	3.0
Western Europe			
Austria	1.4	1.8	2.1
Belgium	0.7	1.5	2.2
France	0.8	1.5	1.9
Germany (FDR)	1.3	1.6	2.2
Germany (GDR)	1.6	2.7	1.5
Luxembourg	0.6	1.6	1.7
Netherlands	0.8	1.8	2.4
Switzerland	1.0	1.7	2.2
Southern Europe			
Greece	0.4	0.7	0.7
Italy	—	0.2	0.5
Portugal	0.1	0.6	1.4
Spain	—	—	0.8

Source: Council of Europe 1996.

of variation in the level of divorce across European nations with the highest rates to be found in the Northern European countries (Sweden, the United Kingdom, Denmark, and Finland) and very low rates in Southern countries (Italy, Greece, and Spain) with the Western European countries generally holding an intermediate position. One also sees that divorce rates tend to be higher in 1990 than in 1980 particularly in Western and Southern European countries. Divorce rates in several of the Northern European countries have been relatively stable since 1980, the exceptions being Norway and Finland where the rates have increased.

If recent divorce rates were to prevail then in most countries in Europe, the chances of couples divorcing would be around a level of one in three: with Sweden, Denmark, and the United Kingdom leading the league table at around two out of five (which is somewhat lower than the rates for the United States of America and the former USSR with levels of one in two) and some of the Southern European countries lagging behind at the one in 10 level or less (Hopflinger 1990; Council of Europe 1996: table 2.5).

Lone Parent Families

There is only a limited amount of statistical information on the proportions of families with dependent children that are lone parent

TABLE 2.19. *Lone parent families with at least one child of less than 15 years of age in the EC as percentage of all families with dependent children*

Country	1980/1	1990/1
Belgium	9.4	14.6
Denmark	18.1	20.8
Germany	9.8	15.4
Greece	4.4	5.7
Spain	5.4	7.9
France	8.3	10.7
Ireland	7.2	10.8
Italy	7.3	6.4
Luxembourg	9.1	12.2
Netherlands	7.9	12.2
Portugal	11.6	12.5
United Kingdom	13.7	16.0

Source: Eurostat 1994.

families. For example, data published by the European Union Statistical Office (Eurostat 1994) shows the situation in 12 of the Member States at the beginning of the 1980s and 1990s (Table 2.19). As one would expect from our earlier examination of divorce data there is a good deal of variation across these 12 countries, with high proportions of lone parents in Denmark and the United Kingdom, intermediate levels in the Western European countries and low levels in Southern Europe, with the exception of Portugal. The rise in divorce and the breakdown of cohabiting unions lie behind most of the increase in other lone parent families in Europe.

3

The Debate about the Law Affecting Marriage and Divorce In Twentieth-Century Britain

Laslett, Oosterveen, and Smith et al. (1980) have insisted that we can only begin to understand illegitimacy in terms of the changes in courtship and marriage. But there is remarkably little research on the changes in the meaning of marriage and in the marriage system.[1] Attention has usually been drawn to marriage only at its ending—in divorce. This chapter argues that changes in the dominant understanding of marriage, which happened only after extended debate, have been crucial to the construction of a framework within which dramatic changes in behaviour, in terms of the rate of divorce, extramarital births, and cohabitation, have taken place.

As we have seen in the previous chapter, shifts in behaviour in and of themselves are difficult to interpret. It is hard to reach firm conclusions about the timing of the various changes in sexual and marriage behaviour among different groups of people. While popular understandings identify the 1960s as the decade of change, it seems that teenage sex was increasing from the mid-1950s but that the range of behaviours that went to make up the profound change in the marriage system—including the high rate of divorce, of pre-marital sex, and of cohabitation—only become clearly identifiable in the 1970s. The relationship between changes in ideas about marriage and in the law on marriage and divorce, on the one hand, and in behaviour, on the other, is also extremely difficult to establish. It cannot be assumed that legal changes account for changes in behaviour (Finch 1989), even though this has been a very tempting line of interpretation in relation to divorce

---

[1] Gillis (1985) has provided a fascinating account of changes in the marriage ceremony over almost four centuries; and Ross (1993) has probed the meaning of early 20th-cent. working-class marriage. For the late 20th-cent. we must rely on sociological work, where Askam (1984) has been virtually alone in the British literature in enquiring about the meaning of marriage.

reform in particular. While this is something that has been questioned by academics (e.g. Burgoyne, Ormerod, and Richards et al. 1987), lawmakers tend to be firmly convinced as to the effect of law on behaviour. As Baroness Young put it in the course of the debates on the Family Law Bill early in 1996: 'Law influences behaviour and it sends out a very clear message. There would be no point in legislating at all if the law did not influence behaviour' (House of Lords Debates, 29 February 1996, c. 1638).

This chapter explores the changes in ideas about marriage and in particular about sexual morality among the articulate elite in the twentieth century. There was no linear, simple development here either. Ideas that were as radical as those expressed in the 1960s were circulating in the 1920s and 1930s, but it does seem that the 1960s were more of a watershed than they were for behavioural changes. The coalition of opinion favouring a fundamentally different understanding of marriage and sexual morality was sufficiently strong in the 1960s to pave the way for substantial legislative reform. This in and of itself is probably not sufficient to account for behavioural change. In the first place, it is hard to know how far popular opinion on these issues changed, although D. H. J. Morgan (1991) has suggested that there is substantial interplay between elite accounts and everyday constructions. Giddens (1992) has sought to explain a 'separating and divorcing' society in terms of the rise of 'intimacy' changing mentalities rather than changing material circumstances. Late twentieth-century people, he argues, seek 'pure relationships', that is social relationships: 'entered into for their own sake, for what can be derived by each person from a sustained association with another; and which is continued only in so far as it is thought by both parties to deliver enough satisfactions for each individual to stay within it' (p. 58). We would suggest that the shift in ideas about marriage and the legislation that accompanied them is part of the explanation of the growth of what Giddens calls 'confluent love': love that is not, as romantic love was earlier in the century, anchored in marriage, but is rather 'active' and 'contingent' upon providing satisfactions to the parties concerned (p. 61).

However, in any attempt fully to explain changes in sexual and marital behaviour, it would be dangerous to ignore structures. In particular it is necessary to investigate the degree to which the material circumstances encouraging or discouraging marriage have changed. Especially important in this respect have been women's growing capacity for economic independence (although even in the 1990s this can be considerably overstated in view of the substantial male/female earnings differential) and the availability and accessibility of housing for young people. Material changes will also have affected ideas. As families have become more highly 'individuated', to use Bott's (1971) term, the influence of kin on the norms and values of young people may also have changed. Marriage as 'status passage' and a means of allowing young people to occupy new socially legitimate and acceptable roles within their communities is likely to have undergone change more rapidly among some social groups and in some regions than others. But it is also likely that changing ideas about sexual morality will have had an impact on the social status attributed to marriage. The profound changes in understandings of marriage and in the law regulating marriage beginning in the 1960s served rapidly to reduce the stigma attaching to deviant forms of behaviour such as divorce and unmarried motherhood, which in turn may well have promoted a growth in these forms of behaviour.

Any attempt to gain a complete understanding of the changes in the marriage system is beyond the scope of this book. This chapter seeks only to explore one part of the story, the shifts in the understanding of what marriage is about and their relationship to legal change. At the beginning of this century, marriage was constructed in terms of its place as a public institution, carrying with it particular duties, particularly in respect of the support of children. Marriage had 'purposes', which the Archbishop of Canterbury listed in 1956 as the procreation of children, 'natural relations', and mutual comfort. These could be read as profoundly private purposes, but in the first half of the twentieth century the majority view emphasized their importance in maintaining moral order and social stability. During this period few people had access to divorce, although the incidence of separation and cohabitation may have been higher than has often been supposed, and the extramarital birth rate was relatively low. As we have seen in the previous chapter, the dramatic changes in behaviour have been recent. However, the debate over 'marriage reform' has a long history.

Sociologists[2] have argued that over the course of the twentieth century marriage has become less an institution, in terms of both law and popular opinion, and more a relationship. Certainly, more attention has been paid to the quality of the relationship as the defining

[2] Burgess and Locke (1945) are generally credited with first making this distinction. See also Lewis, Clark, and Morgan (1992).

aspect of marriage, but as Richards and Elliott (1991) have pointed out, people continue to want to mark marriage by extravagant ceremony and ritual and obviously continue to regard it as an institution. The 1994 Marriage Act made it possible to hold lavish civil wedding ceremonies in country houses, hotels, or even football grounds. The precise meaning of a shift away from institution to relationship is thus far from clear. We suggest that there has in fact been a shift from an emphasis on the duties deriving from the perceived public purposes of marriage towards seeing marriage as a private arrangement that maximizes individual satisfactions. The former was supported by an externally imposed moral code, which was subject to change as marriage became more companionate and less patriarchal in the early twentieth century, which in turn largely reflected the changes in the status of women. The late twentieth-century view of marriage as a private arrangement sees it as a matter for the individuals involved, who are increasingly assumed to be equals. The quality of a relationship based on romantic love rather than duty can only be decided by the individuals involved. In this context a high divorce rate, while by no means welcomed by policy-makers, becomes difficult to stop. Similarly, there is little means of prohibiting the development of any sexual relationships outside marriage that are meaningful to the men and women concerned.

In Search of a Higher Morality: 1880s–1920s

At the turn of the century, marriage remained a largely patriarchal structure in law. The doctrine of coverture, which stated that husband and wife were as one and that one was the husband, was perceived by lawyers as providing women with a protected status. However, the obverse of protection is usually control and absence of autonomy. While coverture was chipped away, beginning with the married women's property Acts of the 1870s and 1880s, the doctrine was stoutly defended into the twentieth century. In the course of the 1924 parliamentary debate over the Guardianship of Infants Act,[3] which, in the name of child welfare, gave women greater equality in regard to guardianship rights over their children, the Lord Chancellor, Viscount Haldane, declared that 'it is necessary to preserve the family as a unit and if you have a unit you must have a head' (House of Lords Debates

[3] On this piece of legislation, see Cretney (1996).

57, 1924, c. 791). Nevertheless, the great majority of women married, an achievement made more difficult by the surplus of marriageable women during the period 1870–1950.

John Gillis (1985: 259) has concluded pessimistically that 'the long era of mandatory matrimony [from 1850 to 1960] had utterly failed to transform the myth of conjugal love into lived reality as far as ordinary people were concerned'. The marriage system among working people certainly involved clear expectations that men would provide and women would perform their primary task as household managers and child rearers, as well as contributing to the family economy as and when needed. Failure on the part of either to perform might be perceived as the legitimate cause of violence (usually on the part of the man) or separation (Lewis 1986; Ross 1994). However, the meaning of marriage is notoriously hard to get at. José Harris (1993) has pointed out, in the 1900s the marriage rate was highest and the age of marriage lowest in areas where female employment was most prevalent, which casts doubt on the idea of contemporary feminists as well as some historians that women had to marry through lack of any other alter-native. However, in many occupations women's wages were too low to support independent existence. Respectability, status, and indeed affec-tion probably played a larger role than economic calculation in women's decisions to marry. And the same in all probability held true for women of the middle classes. Davidoff and Hall (1987) have shown for the early nineteenth century that it is very difficult to dichotomize motives of material interest and those of affection. Many talented individual women must have agonized about the process of submer-ging their personality in that of their husbands,[4] even though there are many examples of 'affectionate partnerships' in which wives retained substantial autonomy (Jalland, 1986).

The small number of divorces granted under the 1857 Act, which created a court for divorce and established the grounds for procedure, was in large part due to the high cost of the procedure and the limited and unequal grounds that had to be proved (men could petition on grounds of adultery alone, but, until 1923 when the law was equalized, women had to prove a compounding offence such as, cruelty, deser-tion, bigamy, or incest). Nevertheless some 42 per cent of the 17,952 divorces granted between 1859 and 1909 were as a result of petitions by

---

[4] For example, Beatrice Webb's explicitly raised doubts on this score about the possibility of her marriage to Joseph Chamberlain (Lewis 1991).

women, despite the tougher grounds they had to prove and despite the stigma of divorce and the economic problems they were likely to face. Women's preference for freedom from an unhappy marriage was stressed by the Women's Cooperative Guild, a large organization of respectable working-class women, in its evidence to the 1912 Royal Commission on Divorce (Cd. 6481: 149–70), and, despite fears of legislators that women would be divorced against their will, remained a feature of divorce behaviour with each liberalization of the law.[5]

Separation was much more prevalent than divorce and could be either informal, or legalized under the 1878 Matrimonial Causes Act, which provided for separation and maintenance allowances for wives of husbands convicted of aggravated assaults; the legislation of 1886, which extended the power of magistrates to award separation and maintenance orders on the grounds of desertion; and that of 1895, which permitted a wife to apply to the magistrates' courts for separation and maintenance on the grounds of persistent cruelty. The 1912 Royal Commission on Divorce revealed that 6,559 separation and maintenance orders were granted to wives in 1907 alone in England and Wales, and the Commissioners showed that they were very well aware of women's dissatisfactions in particular about the high cost of divorce and the double moral standard embedded in divorce law. In 1888 the *Daily Telegraph* had asked its readers whether marriage was a failure, initiating a correspondence that was abruptly terminated by the editor after some 27,000 letters were received in two months.[6]

The moral code regulating marriage and sexual relationships at the turn of the century was traditional and severe, and was imposed externally by legislation that gave married men the advantage over married women in divorce and in all matters regarding the guardianship and custody of children. Married women had to be 'innocent' in order to secure such redress as was open to them. In contrast, unmarried fathers had no rights. The nineteenth-century poor law ensured that unmarried women bore the brunt of the responsibility for their moral turpitude in the belief that this would act as a deterrent to such behaviour.

The turn-of-the-century debate about the marriage system was primarily a moral debate. Mid-nineteenth-century observations on

---

[5] Although as Goode (1959) pointed out, it is impossible to know how many men manipulate their wives into initiating divorce proceedings.

[6] A selection of the letters was published by Quilter (1888).

sex and marriage had always argued that the family was of central importance and that 'the happiness and goodness of society are always in a very great degree dependent on the purity of domestic life' (Lecky, 1884: 282). However, writers such as the historian of morals, W. E. H. Lecky or Dr William Acton (1875) accepted that men's sexual passions (often referred to as 'lower impulses') were frequent and irregular while women's were not, and that prostitution was therefore inevitable. Indeed, in Lecky's view prostitution became the only way of preserving the purity of the home. While the majority of writers continued to agree that marriage and family was of crucial importance to state and nation, it was no longer possible by the last decade of the nineteenth century either to accept the dominance of the 'lower impulses' as inevitable, or to believe that marital relationships could be built on an impure relationship outside marriage. In other words, the hypocrisy associated with the outwardly strict code of sexual morality was put in question, and because of the superior moral qualities generally accorded women, they assumed an unusual position of authority in the debate. The aim on virtually all sides was to make marriage better: to make it 'a higher relationship'. Very few favoured alternatives to marriage, not least because for women in particular even radicals recognized that alternative 'free unions' carried potentially more risk.[7] Traditionalists could also join in the desire to elevate the marital relationship that was seen as fundamental to the health of the polity, although the means they favoured were inevitably different from other groups seeking reform.

Morality was at the heart of Victorian concerns; indeed, Gertrude Himmelfarb (1986) has suggested that the English made a religion of it. The ideal type of morality consisted of a system of obligations. While human inclination tended towards selfishness, it was believed to be all important to strive to obey the call of duty (Collini 1991). George Eliot was unable to believe in God, but retained her faith in duty (albeit that in her personal life she participated in a 'free union'). The moral and the social were continuously conflated, whether in the search for the cause of social problems such as poverty (as in the categories used by Charles Booth in his social survey of London, which mixed social

---

[7] Bland (1995: 151) has noted that the members of the Men and Women's Club, a group of radical liberal and socialist men and women who met during the 1880s and 1890s to discuss relations between the sexes were convinced that given women's vulnerability and disadvantage, reformed legal marriage was preferable to non-marital relationships.

structural causes such as unemployment with individual failings such as drunkenness), or in the optimistic faith in progress that derived from the use of an evolutionary framework.[8] What made men moral was therefore a matter of crucial concern.

Observers from a wide range of positions saw an important connection between the quality of the relationship between husband and wife and the fulfilment of obligations in the wider society; the married couple was the polis in miniature. The hugely successful novelist, Mrs Humphry Ward, who also opposed votes for women, was typical in believing husband and wife to be the basic unit in society. Such a view was also shared by many feminists, for example, Millicent Garret Fawcett (1894), and crossed Party political lines. Marriage was perceived as a discipline and an order. The institution imposed rational bonds on irrational (sexual) urges. Reckless divorce threatened to destroy an institution that acted as a civilizing force on base human instincts (Ward 1909). There could therefore be no clear public/private divide in the approach to questions of sex and marriage and this showed through clearly in the uncompromising treatment meted out to those cited as co-respondents in divorce cases, most famously in the cases of Charles Dilke and Charles Stewart Parnell, whose political careers were wrecked. The positions adopted by women like Ward and Fawcett have been interpreted as part of their commitment to the contemporary causes of social purity and a single moral standard for men and women (e.g. Rubinstein 1991), but the matter went somewhat deeper than that. At issue was the business of making 'a social ethic of individual morality' (Himmelfarb 1986: 74).

Family relationships were widely believed to give rise to altruistic behaviour. William McDougall's Introduction to Social Psychology (1908) subscribed to the view that it was the parental instinct that gave rise to the 'tender emotion' and that in its impulse lay the root of altruism. Westermarck's Origin and Development of Moral Ideas, published in the same year, also stated that altruism began with maternal filial and conjugal affection and was developed through natural selection. A similar kind of thinking lay behind the importance the majority of turn-of-the-century social reformers attributed to family relationships in the work of forging character, which was, in turn, held to be the only

---

[8] This was most notably characteristic of Herbert Spencer's (1892, 1969) approach to politics and ethics, but was shared by L. T. Hobhouse (1906), who was diametrically opposed to Spencer's view of the state, and by Edward Westermarck (1908).

way of achieving lasting social progress (e.g. Bosanquet 1906). With the growing influence of eugenic ideas, it was additionally possible to see marital and family relationships as the essence of social policy (e.g. Ellis 1912). The search for morality thus led inexorably back to marriage and relations between men and women. Altruism was born in the natural affection between husband and wife, parent and child, and was learned within the family. The basis of intimate relationships between the sexes was therefore a matter of grave public as well as private concern.

Social thinkers, the early sexologists, and 'new women'[9] were all committed to seeking a higher relationship between the sexes. The vast majority of contributors to the debate hoped that the human race was evolving such that the desires of the flesh would be subdued by the spirit. On the one hand, science and morality could be held to be working hand-in-hand to lead men and women beyond mere animal passion. Sex was fundamentally egoistical behaviour and therefore a lower impulse. As Collini (1991: 89) has commented at the end of his essay on the important place of altruism in Victorian social thought: 'it is hard not to hypothesize about the ways it [altruism] may have been related to a kind of distancing of the sexual instincts.' Certainly Comte saw the sex instinct as the most disturbing egoistic propensity and the least capable of being transformed (T. R. Wright 1986). Havelock Ellis, the sexologist, wrote to the feminist Olive Schreiner in 1884: 'I cannot feel anything at all about physical sexual feeling except as a "sacrament"—the outward and visible sign of an inward and spiritual grace. I'm glad you feel that this is so too' (quoted in Grosskurth 1980: 105). Even George Bernard Shaw, while an enemy of the narrower social purity movement, 'looked forward to a time when, in the course of evolution, ecstasy of intellect would replace sexual passion' (Holroyd 1989: 256).

Women writers went furthest in the effort to subjugate the flesh to the spirit as a necessary prerequisite to the creation of higher relationships. Two feminists who took very different views of sexual relationships, Cicely Hamilton (1981), who favoured celibacy, and Maude

---

[9] Lucy Bland (1986: 133) has offered the soundest definition of 'new woman'. While not equivalent to feminist, the 'new woman' at the turn of the century was likely to have held certain feminist convictions: 'she was generally thought of as a young woman of principle, drawn from the upper or middle class, concerned to reject many of the conventions of femininity and to live and work on free and equal terms with the opposite sex. Her hallmark was personal freedom.'

Royden (1922, 1925), the feminist lay preacher, who in the years following the First World War played a major part in laying the foundations for a new sexual morality, both reached the same conclusion that the traditional position adopted by someone like Lecky could only be sustained by a material, rather than a spiritual, conception of honour. He was thus condemned primarily for his failure to invest marriage and sexual relationships with a 'higher impulse'. Women's writing in the early twentieth century was characterized by a biting critique of male sexual behaviour, centred on the incidence of venereal disease and prostitution, and backed up by the strong campaigns for 'social purity' (e.g. Swiney 1908; Re-Bartlett 1911, 1912; Pankhurst 1913).

However, feminist writers were extreme in so strongly privileging the spiritual. Most wanted a proper mixing of the physical and spiritual elements and this resulted in what Peter Gay (1984) has called 'the tender passion', which many contemporaries identified as true love. Ellen Key (1914), the Swedish feminist who so impressed Havelock Ellis, said that love consisted in the harmony between soul and senses and that such harmony was what made relationships between men and women moral and chaste. The perfect melding of soul and senses resulted in a relationship that was invested with considerable moral power. Like Ellis, L. T. Hobhouse, the theorist of New Liberalism, who devoted two of eight chapters of his *Morals in Evolution* (1906) to marriage and the position of women, wrote of marriage as an 'ethical sacrament'. At its best, marriage was characterized by 'perfect love, in which . . . men and women pass beyond themselves and become aware through feeling and direct intuition of a higher order or reality in which self and sense disappear' (p. 231).

Most accepted that higher relationships were by definition also marital relationships, to be characterized by a commitment both to fidelity by the husband as well as the wife, and to loyalty, mutual service, and altruism. Grant Allen's notorious novel *The Woman Who Did* (1895) was condemned by Millicent Fawcett (1895) because it both celebrated sexual passion and denied any sense of 'mutual fidelity, mutual responsibility, mutual duties, mutual rights'. There was nevertheless room for substantial disagreement over how to ensure that marriages became 'higher relationships' and over what to do about an unsatisfactory marriage. It was difficult to decide on what terms less-than-noble behaviour on the part of a spouse, usually the husband, might form the grounds for divorce when so great a premium attached to the institution of marriage as a source of social stability. Commentators had to consider the extent to which the altruism that gave rise to moral relations in the wider society, as well as between the couple, adhered to the relationship independently of the institution. The danger in deciding in favour of the relationship consisted in the logical extension of the argument: that there was nothing then to stop arguments for divorce on the grounds that the moral quality of the relationship was poor, or arguments that higher relationships could be found outside marriage. For example, Mrs Humphry Ward (1894) attacked Sarah Grand's novel *The Heavenly Twins* (1893), which openly addressed the issue of venereal disease in marriage: 'none of these marriages [in *The Heavenly Twins*] were made in heaven; why should they not be dissolved? It must be after all la prudence anglaise which has cut short Mrs Grand's argument in the middle.'

Most of those stressing the importance of achieving a high moral standard in private relationships were censorious of sexual relationships outside marriage, although they differed as to how far they favoured a strict law of marriage and divorce as a means of achieving this. Some of the sexologists felt that a spiritual relationship might be found outside marriage. Havelock Ellis (1910), for example, felt that chastity was a useful means to a desirable end, but that to make it a rigid imperative actually risked overestimating the importance of the sexual instinct. A few were prepared to argue that marriage could constitute an actual impediment to a higher relationship.

Mona Caird presented the most focused attack on marriage as an institution. It was her views that were taken up by the *Daily Telegraph* in 1888 when it invited correspondence on marriage. The heroine of her novel *The Daughters of Danaus* (1894: 129) asked of women who accepted the marriage laws: 'Have they no sense of dignity? If one marries (accepting things on the usual basis of course) one gives to another person rights and powers over one's life that are practically boundless.' Caird took a radical libertarian position and opposed any state interference in marriage: 'The right of private contract is a right very dear to a liberty-loving people; yet in the most important matter of their lives they have consented to forego it!' (Caird 1897: 58). Havelock Ellis (1910) and the socialist, Edward Carpenter (1894), joined Caird in seeking marriage law reform, although they did not believe that it was possible to make marriage a true private contract, a point also made by Shaw in *Getting Married* (1913), in which the protagonists sit down to try to draw up a marriage contract and fail

completely. Like the larger and eminent group of radical reformers of
the inter-war years, which included Bertrand Russell, they favoured
consensual unions when there were no children.[10] Those promoting
what were called at the time 'free unions' were essentially advocating
long-term cohabitation. The 'free love' that was talked about by a few
feminists in journals such as the *Freewoman* in the years before the First
World War was associated with promiscuity and was widely rejected.
Those in favour of consensual or free unions for the most part also
earnestly sought a means of promoting a 'higher relationship' between
men and women, however the social risks of such a decision ran very
high. When Edith Lanchester, a 'new woman', decided to live openly
with a fellow socialist her family had her certified insane (Bland 1995).
Indeed, radical feminists were more likely to advocate chastity and
celibacy than free unions.

Sarah Grand took as dismal a view of marriage as Caird. The heroine
of her novel *Ideala* (1888) asks a bishop at a dinner party whether she is
bound to keep a contract that she has been induced to sign in ignorance. The contract is of course the marriage contract. Yet Grand was
often quoted against Caird because, notwithstanding her jaundiced
view of marriage and her equally bitter indictment of men, she
opposed any reform of the marriage and divorce laws. To this extent
she had more in common with Mrs Humphry Ward, whose novel
Daphne (1909) amounted to a polemic against any reform of the divorce
laws, or Lady Acland (1902), who defended marriage on the grounds
that women would be yet worse off without it. Both Ward and Acland
had a strong sense of the fragility of civilized relations between men
and women and of what might happen if male protection was withdrawn. The treatment meted out to militant suffragettes (see Vicinus
1985) showed that their fears were not without foundation, and that
their assessment of the situation may have been more realistic than that
of the feminists (including Caird) writing in the journal the *Freewoman*
during the early 1910s, who claimed freedom for women to please
themselves without addressing the issue of male power. Ward and
Acland, of course, also wished to avoid anything that might threaten
an institution which they regarded as the basis of nation and empire.

---

[10] This was also the position of Muller-Lyer, who published his book on marriage in
German in 1913. When it was translated into English in 1931 its argument that
marriage was becoming based on personal love and was the union of two independent
personalities influenced many English readers, including William Beveridge.

Reviewing Caird's arguments about marriage, Elizabeth Chapman (1897) most deplored the way in which her critique constituted an attack on the duty of all to uphold marriage. Caird was perceived by most to have crossed what Ellen Key (1914: 34) referred to as the all important 'hair-splitting line between legitimate and illegitimate self-assertion', and (like the suffragettes), to have indulged in egoistical behaviour.

Women writers were divided on whether women should be allowed to leave marriages which obviously failed to come anywhere near the high ideal that they all wished for. Fawcett and Grand permitted their heroines to leave a marriage in which the husband's behaviour was fatally flawed by alcohol or adultery, although neither permitted them to cohabit. However neither favoured extending the grounds for divorce. Fawcett wanted equality for men and women, but by 'levelling up' the grounds for men, rather than 'levelling down' for women (Cd. 6480 (1912): Q.21732). Like Ward and Chapman, she feared that 'facile divorce means licentiousness, disorder, the disintegration of the family, the disruption of the state'. But campaigners for a relaxation in the divorce laws also appealed to the desire for higher relations between the sexes. The influential evidence of the Women's Cooperative Guild to the 1912 Royal Commission on Divorce stressed that women had the right to expect from men the same standard of purity as men demanded from women.

A majority of the members of the Royal Commission on Divorce accepted the arguments in favour of liberalizing the grounds for divorce:

so far from such reforms as we recommend tending to lower the standard of morality and regard for the sanctity of the marriage tie, we consider that reform is necessary in the interests of morality, as well as in the interests of justice, and in the general interests of society and the state. (Cd. 6478 (1912): para. 50)

The majority of the Commissioners, like most contemporaries, wished to strengthen marriage. This, of course, has been the explicit aim of all divorce inquiries and certainly all divorce reformers up to and including the 1969 legislation, and re-emerged as the main concern of many politicians during the 1995–6 debates on the Family Law Act. However, the radical proposals of the 1912 Commission, which Government did not begin to implement until the 1920s, can only be explained in the context of the contemporary debate about marriage. The Commissioners deplored the way in which large numbers of working people, lacking both the money and the grounds necessary to get a divorce, secured a separation order at the hands of a magistrate and then often proceeded to cohabit: 'the remedy of judicial separation is an unnatural and unsatisfactory remedy, leading to evil consequences' (ibid.: para. 234; see also Behlmer 1994). Reform was justified in terms of promoting marriage as an alternative to cohabitation, while it was believed that liberalization would further a higher relationship between men and women.

The Promotion of Radical Sex Reform: the 1920s and 1930s

There was thus no agreement as to the means of achieving a higher relationship between the sexes, but none took the issue of sex and marriage lightly and few were prepared entirely to repudiate marriage. However, Collini (1991) has suggested that by the 1890s the arguments in favour of altruism had been pushed too far, provoking a reaction, although criticism was very much a minority voice and insofar as it affected marriage, was not even especially influential until the inter-war years.

By the early years of the new century, Bertrand Russell and G. E. Moore were in the process of setting out the view that a moral standard and hence an estimation of progress could not be derived from social evolution or the history of morality (as per Herbert Spencer or L. T. Hobhouse), but rather depended upon a judgement grounded independently of them (Collini 1979). Moore (1968) stated clearly that ethics were unable to give rise to a list of duties and in his *Principles of Social Reconstruction* (1916), Russell wrote of all human activity springing from impulse and desire, a far cry from duty. The crucial difference between Russell's conceptualization of sexual morality and that of the vast majority of Edwardian marriage reformers was that he provided the intellectual foundations for the division between public and private morality and indeed for the partial rejection of marriage. Himmelfarb (1986) has noted that in the case of the Bloomsbury Group, rejection of the central importance accorded public duty was paralleled by private promiscuity. In this formulation, the search for a 'higher relationship' between men and women within the framework of marriage was largely redundant.

H. G. Wells, who contributed to the *Freewoman* in the years before the First World War, was closer to the views of Moore and Russell in his determination 'to take sex rather lightly' (Wells 1911: 47). He believed sex to be natural, inevitable, and fun, had no concern about it being a 'lower impulse' and no wish to search for any 'higher impulse' (Lewis 1995). Nor did he show any great commitment to marriage, although he pulled back from advocating free love after both *The Comet* (1906) and his Fabian Society lecture of the same year were roundly attacked for advocating it. In his novel *Ann Veronica* (1909), which was based on his affair with Amber Pember Reeves, the heroine makes the first move, for Wells insisted on women's sexual desires being quite independent of marriage and motherhood. Wells made it clear in his novel *Anticipations* (1902) that the old principles of chastity, purity, self-sacrifice, and sexual sin would no longer do. St Loe Strachey (1909) spoke for many in his review of *Ann Veronica* when he deplored the idea that 'an animal yearning or lust' should be obeyed, and when he denied the possibility of building a self-sustaining and permanent state in the absence of duty, self-sacrifice, self-control, and continence.

Before the First World War, Wells' following was above all young. Both Wilma Meikle (1916) and Margaret Cole (1949) paid tribute to Wells as the prophet of their youth. But the war had a considerable loosening effect on sexual mores, particularly among the middle classes. Chaperonage failed to revive after it, the taboo on public discussion of birth control was lifted (albeit that contraception remained something that Government had no wish to promote for the general population until the 1960s), and moral standards tended to level down rather than up. Indeed, Helena Swanwick (1935: 169) was inclined to trace what she regarded as the 'boring obsession with sex' back to the war. Unmarried mothers enjoyed a brief period of sympathetic consideration during the war as the mothers of the babies of service men who might die for their country, while pragmatic policy-making resulted in the recognition of the 'unmarried wife' for the purposes of separation benefits paid to the wives of service men. The recommendations of the National Relief Fund on the subject were followed by the Government, and unmarried wives with 'an established home' where the service man had been the sole source of financial support were awarded benefits.[11] As the Fund noted, this 'need not prejudice the married state after the war', and indeed by 1927 marriage

---

[11] Markham Papers 1/13 contains the recommendations of the National Relief Fund on relief for unmarried wives, BLPES, LSE, London.

rather than motherhood had been restored as the key determinant of adult women's benefits and unmarried wives had been removed from the list of dependants eligible for benefit (Parker 1990).

During the inter-war years, more radical calls for the reform of marriage and divorce premissed on easy access to artificial contraception (primarily in the form of the sheath and the cap) and including forms of cohabitation came from a number of influential writers, which prompted a rather hard-line response from the leaders of the established church. More moderate clergy and sexologists sought to rework the meaning of marriage, such that the emphasis was less on duty than on personal satisfaction, including sexual satisfaction, and companionship. Thus private morality began to be distanced from public morality in a manner that had only been discussed on the fringes of the pre-war debate and in a way that the majority of contributors to that earlier debate would not have welcomed.

Bertrand Russell's *Marriage and Morals* (1929) was a particularly influential and radical call for reform. Russell (1985: 94) argued that 'love can only flourish as long as it is free and spontaneous; it tends to be killed by the thought that it is duty'. Russell was effectively elaborating his earlier ideas. Where a marriage was childless, he advocated easy divorce. Where there were children, he thought that the parties should stay together, but should not exclude the possibility of other sexual relationships. He was in favour of extending the grounds for divorce to insanity and desertion, but wished to exclude adultery as long as there were no illegitimate children. Like other radical reformers, Russell explicitly recognized that birth control made the distinction between sex and marriage possible; he was a regular attender at the Congresses of the World League for Sexual Reform. Walter Lippman (1929) immediately objected that while it was one thing to recognize the logical implications of birth control, it was quite another to say that convention should be determined by that logic. Like Newsom (1932), the Master of Selwyn College, Cambridge, who replied at length to Russell, Lippman could not accept the idea of the separation of sexual life from parental love, something both he and Newsom found to be essentially egotistical. The critics of Russell clearly understood the extent to which his ideas threatened to undermine the concept of marriage as the nursery of obligations and the microcosm of the polis.

Professor C. E. M. Joad (1946: 46) also insisted that the advent of birth control had 'knocked the bottom out of what is called sexual morality' by giving men and women the wherewithal to conduct any number of sexual liaisons. He predicted that the clear-cut line between married and unmarried unions would become obscured as the number of the latter increased, and the stigma attaching to the 'unmarried mistress' decreased. On the other hand, Norman Haire (1927), the radical proponent of birth control, felt that birth control would permit early marriage, which together with easy divorce, he believed to be more desirable than the only other alternative, large-scale cohabitation. The American, Judge Ben Lindsey (Lindsey and Evans 1929), whose ideas were widely quoted, sought to promote practical legal reform by the creation of something he called 'companionate marriage': marriage with the use of birth control and the right to divorce by mutual consent for the childless. His proposal to make this a legal status was in fact, as Russell recognized, the move of a 'wise conservative' and in the end less threatening than the proposal to ditch large parts of the legal code controlling sexual morality and the marriage system.

Radical reformers were able to draw on the new psychology of Freud and the anthropology of Robert Briffault (who sought to show that the origins of the family centred on mothers and children and that marriage was in origin patriarchal) to legitimize their desire for freedom from repression, pointing in particular (as H. G. Wells had done before the war) to women's need for emancipation from a repressive moral code. In reply, churchmen warned, on the one hand, that the 'new morality' could lead only to a Soviet-style experiment (Newsom 1932), and in support of their case drew on the work of Bronislaw Malinowski, who, unlike Briffault, insisted that there had always been marriage between a single man and woman and that so-called repression was rather much needed self-control (Streeter 1927).[12] On the other hand, somewhat paradoxically, others charged, like a minority of the members of the 1912 Royal Commission on Divorce, that the wish for radical reform was essentially the product of an excess of individualism: 'there is in many quarters a revolt against any view of marriage which emphasises its social aspects and obligations, and an increasing tendency to regard it as a purely individual affair' (Convocations of Canterbury and York 1935).

---

[12] Briffault and Malinowski publicly debated their positions on marriage and the family on the radio in 1931, see the record of their broadcasts in *The Listener*, 7 January 1931, pp. 7–8; 14 January 1931, pp 51–2; 21 January 1931, pp. 92–3; 28 January 1931, pp. 136–7; 4 February 1931, pp. 181–2; 11 February 1931, pp. 230 9.

While no policy-maker would take up the proposals for deregulating childless relationships or even for attaching special regulations to Lindsey's 'companionate marriages', the call for more practical reform of the divorce laws became noticeably more irreverent during the inter-war years. The grounds for divorce between men and women were equalized in 1923, but the lengths to which husbands and wives had to go to get a divorce on the ground of adultery were increasingly pilloried in the 1930s. A. P. Herbert's famous novel, *Holy Deadlock* (1934), was widely perceived as making further liberalization of the divorce law inevitable (in 1937 the grounds for divorce were expanded to include desertion, cruelty, and insanity). Herbert's novel publicized the hypocrisy of carefully staged hotel-scenes designed to provide the evidence needed for a divorce on the grounds of adultery. Mr Boom, the solicitor, pointed out to the couple who wished amicably to part that the judge would say:

Pardon me Mr Adam, but have either of you committed adultery? We are not here, Mr Adam, to secure your happiness, but to preserve the institution of marriage and the purity of the home. And therefore one of you must commit adultery. . . someone has to behave impurely in order to uphold the Christian ideal of purity, someone has to confess in public to a sinful breach of the marriage vows in order that the happily married may point at him or her and feel themselves secure and virtuous. (pp. 23 and 29)

Thus Herbert attacked a morality that privileged the public institution of marriage over the quality of the relationship.

Herbert called his legislative proposal a 'Marriage Bill', and in the tradition of divorce law reformers, argued that the 1937 reform would in fact protect the institution of marriage.[13] However, the call for reform in the 1930s was in many ways more threatening than that of pre-war feminists for measures that would secure a higher standard of behaviour from men, or the equally earnest arguments of divorce law commissioners. Herbert's novel purported to represent the way in which people actually behaved in order to get a divorce and ridiculed the law that made it necessary. The aim may still have been to strengthen marriage, but the tone of the criticism was very different. Some people—how many was a matter of debate—had already begun

---

[13] The long title of the 1937 legislation referred to an Act to amend the law relating to divorce 'for the true support of marriage, the protection of children, the removal of hardship, the reduction of illicit unions and the unseemly litigation, the relief of conscience among the clergy, and the restoration of due respect for the law'.

to 'take sex lightly'. In face of the liberalization achieved by the 1937
legislation, the church dug in its heels. The 1937 Act gave clergy the
freedom to decide whether to solemnize a second marriage, but the
Convocations of Canterbury and York passed a resolution in 1938 to
the effect that remarriage always involved a departure from the true
principles of marriage, a position reaffirmed by a 1957 Act of Convocation (Winnett 1968). Thus the Church establishment determined
against any further erosion of the traditional code governing marriage
and divorce, a position it maintained until the early 1960s.

More moderate religious and sexual reformers began instead to
construct a new basis for marriage in recognition of the threat posed
by radical reformers to the institution of marriage and because they
realized that it was important to offer more than the old code based on
'thou shalt not'. This strand in the inter-war debate did not set out to
'level up' moral standards and was not suspicious of sex as a 'lower
impulse'. The notion of achieving higher personal relationships in
marriage lived on, but the definition of such relationships changed in
significant respects. In particular, sex was acknowledged to be of
central importance to marriage. This alternative to the 'new morality'
offered by Russell, stressed the quality of the personal relationship
between husband and wife. It was therefore ready to drop the emphasis
traditionalists placed on the link between private sexual morality and
public morality, but it retained the emphasis on marriage as the proper
site for sexual relationships, albeit that the love of the couple, something that could only be determined by them, rather than the fear of an
external authority, was to be the moral arbiter.

Marie Stopes (1918) invoked eugenics to legitimize her writing on
birth control, but in mystical and flowery language she also sought to
eroticize 'married love'. Other medical writers on sex in the 1930s and
1940s were quite clear in their prescription for keeping sex inside
marriage, but also in acknowledging the importance of sexual pleasure
for both husbands and wives which could, they advised, be increased by
the freedom from the fear of pregnancy achievable by the use of birth
control (Chesser 1952, 1964; Griffith 1941; Walker 1940). Kenneth
Walker, who began writing on sex and marriage in the 1940s, insisted
that romantic love should be the basis on which all marriage is built
(Walker, 1957). Moderate churchmen such as Herbert Gray, who
worked with the Student Christian Movement in the 1920s and became
recognized as the founding father of the marriage guidance movement
(Lewis, Clark, and Morgan 1992), agreed that sexual passion provided

the driving force for life. It was crucial that sexual expression be the fruit of body, mind, and spirit and it was this that distinguished love from lust. Love in turn was properly unselfish and permanent. Thus Gray arrived at the purpose of sex as an expression of married love. As such it had a procreative function and a baby made love perfectly unselfish, but it also served to express the perfect union of the couple as one flesh (Gray 1923).

In many respects aspects of the pre-war sexologists' views as to the mixing of soul and senses were woven into this new sexual morality. Gray painted a picture of sexual fulfilment, mutual support, and 'comradeship' between husbands and wives. Like prominent social reformers of the 1940s, such as William Beveridge, Gray was anxious to see women's contribution as 'equal but different' and marriage as a harmonious enterprise between male breadwinners and female housewives and carers. Gray made a point of acknowledging the work of Maude Royden, a leading feminist and lay preacher, who like Gray argued that sex outside marriage was motivated by the desire for bodily gratification rather than by love, which was a product of mind, spirit, and body (Royden 1922). But both were bound to admit that the institution of marriage did not necessarily make an immoral relationship, that is one without love, moral. Neither writer was able to deny the possibility of divorce for an impossibly loveless marriage. The idea of morality coming from within as an expression of personality, rather than being imposed and regulated by external institutions was developed by John Mac-Murray (1935) in his influential work of moral philosophy, and it, rather than the radical ideas of Russell, was to prove the Trojan Horse that eventually destroyed traditional sexual morality and paved the way for radical divorce law reform. Even though the moderate reformers of the inter-war years did not advocate any change in sexual behaviour, the new recipe for sexual morality resulted in a new set of concerns. If love was the essence of marriage and marriage was a private relationship, then not only was there no basis for opposing divorce if the partners ceased to love each other, but also there was no basis for denying the morality of relationships in which there was love but no marriage. These problems were to characterize the mid- and late twentieth-century debate on marriage, cohabitation, and divorce.

Conservative Reaction: 1940s–1960s

However, the current favouring reform largely disappeared during the 1940s and 1950s. Unlike the First World War, the Second World War gave rise to a moral panic about family disintegration that strengthened the determination of those opposed to any further reform of the divorce laws. Titles such as *Does Sex Morality Matter?* (Mace 1943), *Morals in the Melting Pot* (Griffith 1948), and *Marriage Crisis* (Mace 1948) drew attention to the rising wartime divorce rate. In 1940, 56 per cent of divorces were granted on the grounds of adultery; by 1947, when the divorce rate peaked, this figure rose to 71 per cent, reflecting the prevalence of long enforced separations and the ease of proof if an absent soldier's wife had a baby. David Mace, the first general secretary of the National Marriage Guidance Council, also looked at the Registrar General's data on premarital conceptions for the period 1938–43 and estimated that one woman in six had abandoned the idea of premarital chastity (Mace 1945). These findings were discussed in the House of Commons in May 1946 (c. 1448). The criticism of what Mace (1943) identified as the unfortunate 'levelling down' of moral standards fell disproportionately on women:

really the woman defeats her own best interests by all this demand for sexual freedom . . . the true woman cheats herself out of her destiny if she is taken in by this sex equality stuff . . . it's only the unnatural masculine woman who can be satisfied for very long with sex alone. (Mace 1948: 42–3)

'Normal' women wanted homes and children, and indeed in the view of social reformers, doctors, and influential psychologists would wish to devote themselves entirely to them (Spence 1946; Winnicott 1958). This reflected the concern of contemporaries to encourage a higher birth rate and better quality mothering. This set of arguments made women the guardians of sexual morality just as effectively as had the late Victorian double moral standard.

While there was no attempt to return to a traditional morality based on fear or to deny the importance of sex in marriage, chastity and fidelity were promoted as ideals necessary for national well-being as well as for healthy personal relationships. The emphasis on the part of the proponents of marriage guidance was in tune with the language of post-war planning with its vision of government and voluntary organizations establishing a network of services for families available at critical periods in the life-course. The real emphasis in the popular literature of the 1940s, especially that emanating from the marriage guidance movement, was on the dangers of sex outside marriage, whether in the form of pre-marital sex or adultery. Having recognized sex as a creative force and as having a purpose beyond procreation, the genie had somehow to be forced back into the bottle, otherwise there was no reason why ideas about morality vesting in the presence or absence of love rather than in the institution of marriage should not take hold. It is therefore not surprising to find the argument that non-marital sex as the selfish expression of bodily lust could only prove destructive of personality (e.g. Griffith 1941: 90).

Divorce was not so much the focus of attention as marriage in the 1940s. Proponents of marriage guidance believed that if more attention were given to marriage preparation and to the quality of married life, particularly in respect of sexual compatibility, there would be less divorce anyway. According to Mace (1948: 111): 'we get the whole thing wrong when we talk as if divorce and separation were the real enemies we're up against. . . . The real trouble lies further back. The true enemy we have to fight is the marriage which has got stuck and stopped growing.' However, he also expressed the view that it was worse for children if their parents parted, no matter how conflict-ridden the marriage, a position that was seriously questioned as early as the 1950s and became a minority view in the 1960s and 1970s, but which has been strongly argued again in the 1990s.

The conservative position on divorce law reform was maintained by the 1956 Report of the Royal Commission on Divorce (Cmd. 9678 (1956)). The Commission was appointed to inquire into the law on divorce and matrimonial causes 'having in mind the need to promote and maintain healthy and happy married life and to safeguard the interests and well-being of children' in the wake of Mrs Eirene White's attempt in 1951 to introduce a Bill to make marriage breakdown a new ground for divorce. Reiterating the concerns of the 1912 Royal Commission, Mrs White wanted to enable those people who had been separated for a number of years to remarry. A majority of the Commissioners were concerned above all to protect marriage as an institution, their concerns echoing those of the majority of Victorian and Edwardian moralists:

it is obvious that life-long marriage is the basis of a secure family life, and that to ensure their well-being children must have that background. We have therefore had in mind throughout our inquiry the importance of seeking ways and means of strengthening the resolution of husbands and wives to realise the idea of a partnership for life. (para. 37)

However, the Royal Commission of the 1950s sat at a time when the dominant call was not for reform as a means of promoting a higher relationship between men and women, as was the case in 1912, but for efforts to rebuild the institution of marriage and the family after wartime disintegration. The Majority Report viewed with great suspicion both the effects of women's emancipation, suggesting that some women did not realize that 'new rights do not release them from the obligations arising out of marriage' (para. 45) and modern psychology, which, in their view, emphasized self-expression rather than self-discipline and overemphazised the importance of sex in marriage (para. 46). The stress on duty and on the need to put marital stability before individual desires and fulfilment was in large measure a reaction to the apparent change in behaviour during the war and was shared by a number of witnesses. Even Helena Normanton, a prominent campaigner for women's legal rights, said that she felt that 'an increase in the grounds for dissolving marriages is not a reform of marriage as an institution' and agreed with the Commissioners that what was needed was education for marriage, together with an improvement in the economic position of wives (Royal Commission on Marriage and Divorce 1956: 864). The Commissioners repeatedly asked witnesses whether they felt that there was an increase in 'divorce-mindedness' and the Report stressed the 'insidious' nature of the tendency to take marriage less seriously.

However, the Commission emphasized that the solution lay in education, pre-marital instruction, marriage guidance and conciliation, rather than a harsher divorce law, although if this strategy failed the majority felt that it might be better to abandon divorce entirely rather than risk the disastrous effects of large-scale marital breakdown on society. The fear, as some witnesses put it, of marriage becoming 'a tenancy at will' (ibid.: 127) made it impossible for the Commission to countenance the idea of extending the grounds for divorce to include marriage breakdown, which rested on the idea of consent rather than on fault. Individuals could not be allowed to decide the fate of their marriages, but rather had to prove some fault against the purposes for which the institution was intended. As a London magistrate put it in his evidence, divorce by consent was wrong because 'the parties are considering their own happiness, not their duties, and their duties involve their children' (ibid.: 382). Even though it became possible to divorce without proving fault after 1969, it is still not possible to divorce by consent because it is maintained that society has a 'vital interest'. When the Archbishop of Canterbury was asked about the moral principles underlying justifiable divorce he said:

I think one would say that the moral principle is that in each ground for divorce there is a frustration of one or more of the purposes of marriage. The purposes of marriage are the procreation of children, natural relations and the comfort that one ought to have of the other. Adultery breaks the union of man and wife. Desertion deprives him of the partner, one of the purposes of marriage. Cruelty frustrates one of them, also insanity, and sodomy and bestiality. I think you could say, could you not, that they all frustrate one or more of the purposes of marriage. (ibid.: 155)

But the idea that love was the true basis for marriage, that only the couple could determine the state of their marriage, and that morality could not be imposed from without in this fashion, was only temporarily stemmed. The idea of marriage as a discipline and an order, and an institution with purposes crucial to the wider world rather than a private relationship, could not be sustained in the face of constructions of marriage that put a premium on the quality of the marital relationship. Large numbers of ordinary people had always sought relief for their marital problems in separation, both legally and informally, and as A. P. Herbert had pointed out in 1934 and as Professor L. C. B. Gower testified to the 1956 Royal Commission, a significant number were prepared to break the law and to 'collude' in order to gain a divorce on the grounds of adultery (50 per cent of undefended divorces were obtained in this manner according to Gower (ibid.: 15)). However, reformers, whether radical or moderate, made no headway in changing the views of establishment opinion until the 1960s. In 1956 leaders of the established church undertook to uphold as far as possible the idea of indissolubility. Yet by 1966 they were prepared to countenance the idea of marriage breakdown as grounds for divorce, even though they ideally wanted the courts to interrogate the couple in order to 'prove' breakdown.

Radical Reform Revisited: the 1960s

During the 1960s the demands for both radical and moderate sex reform were revived against a background of relative stability in sexual behaviour. Cohabitation was probably rarer in the 1950s and 1960s than it was at the turn of the century and the divorce rate remained low. However, teenage pre-marital sexual activity was increasing and considerable concern was expressed in the early 1960s about teenage sexual behaviour, the main issue being the growing incidence of venereal disease among young people and the promiscuity that was believed to be causing it. It was for this reason that the Central Council for Health Education funded Michael Schofield's inquiry into the sexual behaviour of young people. His conclusions proved reassuring, suggesting that promiscuity was not a prominent feature of teenage sexual behaviour. Only 16 per cent of Schofield's whole sample had experienced sexual intercourse, which led him to stress the conservatism of young people's sexual behaviour (Schofield 1965). Similarly, Geoffrey Gorer's study of sex and marriage published in 1971 concluded that England still appeared very chaste; 26 per cent of married men and 63 per cent of married women in the sample reported that they were virgins at marriage. Gorer had carried out a similar survey in 1950 and reported that the main change over the twenty-year period was the increase in the proportion of those who thought sexual experience had a good effect on the person's character.

Ronald Fletcher's 1966 study of marriage and the family in Britain also struck an optimistic note. He concluded that while there was real change, there was no sign of moral decay. Despite the considerable investment in and strain on marriages, he felt that the low divorce rate showed that there was no real instability. Young and Willmott's (1973) study of the family stressed the march of progress and reported that the basis for working-class marriage was more stable in the post-war world. Evidence for this view was provided by Goldthorpe et al.'s (1968) classic study of the 'affluent worker', which concluded that men working in manufacturing industry and their wives were involved in a 'family project', that they were no longer fatalistic, that they were pursuing their goals purposively, and that such a family orientation might be expected to increase given diminishing economic insecurity. Chester (1971) was one of a very small minority to draw attention to the rising divorce rate of the 1960s and to see it as the product of something more than easier access and availability. He insisted on seeing it as part of a new pattern of behaviour which also included rising illegitimacy rates and he predicted that it would continue. Chester attributed these changes to a more permissive approach to personal behaviour. Only an American social scientist emphasized the importance of the 'amazing' increase in the extramarital birth rate, attributing it to a growth in individualism and welfare dependency (she later changed her mind in respect of the latter) (Hartley 1966, 1975).

The optimism of most of these British studies was probably influenced by the strength of the call for sex reform. In their study of adolescents and morality published in 1966, the Eppels accorded considerable importance to the emergence of what was called—as it had been in the inter-war years—the 'new morality', which they traced to the early 1960s. Doctors and birth-control campaigners argued for a radical change of behaviour and greater access to contraception. G. M. Carstairs, a professor of psychological medicine, gave the Reith Lectures in 1962. In his third lecture he spoke of the emergence of a new concept of sexual relations, 'as a source of pleasure but also as a mutual encountering of personalities in which each explores the other and at the same time discovers new depths in himself or herself'. In his view young people were rapidly turning society into one in which pre-marital sex with contraception was an accepted and sensible preliminary to marriage. Just as with those advocating reform in the 1920s and 1930s, sex reformers of the 1960s premissed their arguments on the availability of birth control. Carstairs was optimistic that free access to contraception would solve the problem of unwanted pregnancies. Alex Comfort (1963) argued that pre-marital intercourse was part of the 'normal process of sexual growth', and to be welcomed so long as personal relationships were non-exploitative. Comfort's ideas and the stress he placed on personal growth were resonant of the American 'human potential movement', whose leading proponent, Abraham Maslow (1968), insisted on the importance of self-actualization and the discovery of the 'real me', which, even though Maslow himself did not spell it out, might include any number of sexual adventures.

Campaigners like Comfort were tempted to eschew the whole issue of ethics, preferring to take a pragmatic approach to sexuality and to see sexual relationships as posing emotional rather than ethical problems. This took them beyond the position adopted by Russell at the end of the 1920s. Comfort was determined to treat sex very lightly indeed and denied that any guilt should attach to 'irregular' sexual relationships. Helena Wright (1968) maintained that unrestricted pre-marital sexual experience would give young people the opportunity to exercise judgement and would deepen person-centred relationships. Like Carstairs she was optimistic about the effects of sexual freedom believing that it would lead to less promiscuity and that freer access to birth control would also cause a reduction in the divorce rate.

Churchmen and academic theologians did not on the whole give their approval to extramarital sex, but they nevertheless reformulated ideas about morality such that they could be used to justify more radical, hedonistic, and individualistic behaviour, and they themselves became advocates of further relaxation in the divorce laws. Like MacMurray and Gray in the inter-war years, the contributors to the 1960s debate on sexual morality were united in attacking the notion that morality could be imposed by law. Douglas Rhymes (1964), Canon of Southwark Cathedral, pointed out that Christ had refused a code to which there were no exceptions; the cardinal virtue was charity. The aim was not a more lax code of morality, but 'a higher attitude towards the person, a personal relationship of responsibility and love which will pervade all human relationships' (Rhymes 1964: 27–8). Helen Oppen-heimer (1966: 233) suggested that personal relationships based on duty gave rise to lower level claims than those based on love:

The higher level claims are most usefully described not in terms of obedience but of relationship, a kind of commitment of the personality which makes the claiming of obedience irrelevant. . . . To put it another way, personal relation-ships are relationships of love, swallowing up not invalidating moral obligation.

Thus the efforts of Christians to re-think morality in the 1960s con-tinued to be inspired by the search for a 'higher morality'. At the end of the day, their belief was always that progressive reform, whether in the form of greater access to contraception or easier divorce, would strengthen marriage and personal relationships.

Like religious writers of the inter-war period, the Christian new moralists of the 1960s stressed that love was the only proper basis for personal relationships and they agreed that the morality of sex had nothing to do with marriage; sex could be moral or immoral in or outside marriage. Some felt that the most invidious aspect of the traditional, rule-bound morality was the fact that coercive behaviour inside marriage did not stand condemned (e.g. Barnes 1958). Derrick Sherwin Bailey of the Church of England Moral Welfare Council, whose work played a major part in reorienting the views of the established church towards sex and marriage and in particular to developing a theology of sexual love, confessed honest doubt as to what constituted a 'good' and 'bad' marriage. Bailey (1957) argued strongly that loving relationships were sustained by fidelity and he was also opposed to pre-marital sex, but had to admit that a marriage was over when love failed.

Christian writing on sex, marriage, and divorce became considerably more outspoken in the early 1960s. The Bishop of Woolwich rejected the traditional Christian thinking on marriage and divorce and advocated a position 'based on love', whereby nothing could be labelled as 'wrong'—not divorce, nor pre-marital sex—unless it lacked love (Robinson 1963). A Quaker group, formed to consider the question of homosexuality, also emphasized that sexual morality could only come from within and could only be based on the avoidance of exploitation of another human being. Such a morality would, they argued, prove 'deeper' and more 'creative' and would release love, warmth, and generosity into the world (Heron 1963). These arguments did not go unopposed by traditional Christian moralists (e.g. Demant 1963), but their arguments struck a note that was both old-fashioned and harsh in comparison with the enthusiastic idealism of the new moralists.

The changing views of Christian writers on matters of sexual morality were part of a much broader questioning of the relationship between law and morality. Lord Devlin's Second Maccabean lecture delivered in 1958 after the Wolfenden Committee reported in favour of reform to the law on homosexuality examined the boundary between public and private morality. Devlin's argument that it was possible to identify a common morality and to enforce it aroused a storm of criticism from those who believed that morality in mid-twentieth-century England was necessarily pluralist and that external regulation would effectively impose the behaviour of the majority (see especially H. L. A. Hart 1963). In regard to marriage, Devlin (1965) sought to draw a new line between public institution and private relationship. He argued that only the couple could decide to make and unmake their marriage and it was the job of the state to register this by issuing a separation order. However, divorce was a public issue and required the state to investigate the sincerity of the petitioner in seeking permission to remarry, and to seek an assurance that the children of the first marriage would be provided for. The full implementation of Devlin's proposals would have encouraged a return to a situation in which separation was much more common than divorce, something which had attracted the condemnation of the 1912 Royal Commission on Divorce and interestingly his specific proposals on marriage did not prove influential. Rather, the dominant strand in the 1960s debate stressed the private nature of sexual morality and the need for morality to come from within the individual.

When Leo Abse reintroduced Mrs Eirene White's Bill on divorce in 1963, the Archbishop of Canterbury responded by setting up a group to review the secular law of divorce. Its report, published in 1966, took a radically different line from the position adopted by the church establishment ten years before. The report concluded that the concept of matrimonial offence embodied in the law of divorce committed the courts to a superficial conception of the relationship between husbands and wives and made it impossible for the couple to say honestly that their marriage was at an end. It recommended that the concept of marital breakdown replace that of offence, but, because the church still refused to countenance divorce by consent, it favoured 'breakdown with inquest' (Archbishop of Canterbury 1966). In other words, marriage was still considered a matter for public concern and the interests of the state in determining whether the relationship had broken down were defended in a manner not unlike that proposed by Devlin. However, the Law Commissioners moved swiftly to point out the impracticability of interrogating couples about the state of their marriages. The Law Commission's own proposals, while asserting as ever that the aim was 'to buttress, rather than to undermine, the stability of marriage', were based on the aim of enabling 'the empty shell to be destroyed with the maximum fairness, and the minimum bitterness, distress and humiliation' when a marriage had irretrievably broken down (Cmnd. 3123 (1966): 15). In what was a compromise manoeuvre that avoided the problem of legalizing divorce by consent, marital breakdown was made the sole ground for divorce, but it had to be established by reference to one of five 'facts': adultery, unreasonable behaviour, two years' desertion, two years' separation if both parties agreed, or five years' separation if one party did not. Despite the arguments of traditionalists in the 1950s that women's emancipation was responsible in large part for the privileging of individual desires over duty, the strongest opposition to the legislative reform of divorce in 1969 came from those who feared that if men were permitted to set aside their wives after a five-year period of separation regardless of the wife's wishes, they would do so in order to marry a younger woman. While the economic position of women after divorce was to prove, as it had always been, extremely difficult, the vast majority of divorce petitions (around three-quarters) nevertheless continued to come from women, albeit that the reasons for this have probably had much to do with women's greater need to clarify their financial position which can only happen once divorce proceedings have started.

The 1969 legislation represented a major break. Even though the majority of couples seeking divorce (76 per cent in 1986 (Law Commission 1988)) continued to use adultery or unreasonable behaviour as the proof of marital breakdown,[14] the partial removal of fault significantly changed the role of the state in respect of divorce and hence the regulation of marriage. Prior to 1969 substantial reform had been effected but within the accepted parameters, thus, for example, more equality between the sexes had been introduced into the grounds for divorce. However, this did nothing to change the fact that the grounds for divorce remained fault-based. Fault was determined according to an externally imposed moral code and innocence was a prerequisite for obtaining custody of children and maintenance. This remained the case in the lower courts after the legislation of the late 1960s and early 1970s, although case law in the divorce courts improved the chances of an adulterous wife gaining custody in the 1960s (Smart, 1984) and attempted to improve the claim of women and children to the matrimonial home (Burgoyne, Ormerod, and Richards 1987). After 1969 the interest of the state in the reasons for ending a marriage receded to 'vanishing point' (Davis and Murch, 1988: 13); by 1977 the 'special procedure' introduced in 1973 to enable couples to dispense with legal representation in simple cases had been extended to all undefended cases. Marriage became increasingly a matter for the individuals concerned. The state no longer endeavoured to regulate it using a moral code that was patriarchal in the nineteenth century and more based on partnership in the twentieth, but this in turn raised issues about what had always been considered the duties of marriage, particularly in respect of the maintenance of women and children.

From the Regulation of Marriage to the Regulation of Parenting: 1970s–1990s

In 1965 a commentator on the debate about sexual morality observed that the rather solemn and high-minded personal relationships

[14] Davis and Murch (1988) concluded that unreasonable behaviour, the most popular choice of 'fact' in working-class petitions, remained the real fault-based ground for divorce. Adultery, the most popular 'fact' for middle-class couples, tended to be more collusive.

approach might well in practice be interpreted as sanctioning the kind of behaviour that the sexual radicals frankly accepted (Atkinson 1965: 86–7). While in her study of divorced people in the late 1960s, N. Hart (1976) found that many of her respondents felt stigmatized, stigma rapidly diminished during the 1970s for the divorced and for unmarried mothers (see Chapter 4). Indeed, behaviour changed dramatically after 1970. The divorce rate increased threefold between 1971 and 1991, pre-marital cohabitation rates more than trebled between 1979 and 1993, and the extramarital birth rate increased dramatically after 1985 (see Chapter 2). Whereas in the 1960s, commentators were still speculating on the issue first identified by Russell and Joad—the possibility of separating sex from marriage—by the 1990s the issue had become the possibility that marriage was becoming separated from parenthood.

The degree to which marriage as a personal relationship swiftly became the new orthodoxy was revealed by the 1971 Report of a Commission set up by the Archbishop of Canterbury to look at church marriage. The Report acknowledged that the structure and obligations of the family had changed. Marriage was thought of less in terms of what it is for and more in terms of what it is. In other words, the Commission recognized the significance of the abolition of fault-based divorce. The state had the right to intervene only in respect of children. The Report also recommended that divorced people should be allowed to remarry in church, albeit after investigation to ascertain the circumstances of the divorce, whether men's obligations in respect of the first family were met, and the sincerity of the couple in seeking a new lifelong partnership. However, General Synod refused to go this far. At the end of the decade, the (1979) interdepartmental consultative document on the marital agencies, *Marriage Matters*, set out its understanding of marriage as an interpersonal relationship which allowed for growth (D. H. J. Morgan 1985).

In practice, as Murch (1980: 178) reported after a study of divorcing couples and court welfare officers, the 'shadow' of matrimonial offence lingered on, but it was quickly recognized that with the abolition of fault-based divorce what had hitherto been the 'ancillary matters' of property, maintenance, and arrangements for children became the main concerns of the courts. Furthermore, whereas prior to 1969 the principles regarding the treatment of these had been determined by firm ideas as to the purposes of marriage and who had offended against them, after that date it proved, as Cretney (1985: 53) remarked, very difficult 'to articulate modern principles' especially in respect to the obligation to maintain.

The only clear commitment on the part of the courts was to the principle of child welfare, but this proved subject to negotiation in respect of the norms regarding child rearing and the different interests of mothers, fathers, and the state. For example in regard to custody, the emergence of the child welfare principle during the 1920s alongside pressure from feminist groups challenged the belief of the late nineteenth-century courts in the (married) father's 'natural' rights over the child. During the post-war decades children usually stayed with their mothers after divorce, in line with both the beliefs of psychologists regarding the centrality of the mother/child dyad and the gendered division of unpaid work (Maidment 1984; Brophy 1985; Collier 1995). But by the 1980s the welfare principle had been redefined by psychologists to emphasize the importance of the role of the father to the welfare of children and this, together with the claims of fathers themselves began to override the claims of mothers based on their responsibility for caring (Smart 1991).

In the matter of provision for children after divorce and in regard to the obligation to maintain both women and children, the reconceptualization of marriage ran ahead of the social reality. The transition from the late nineteenth-century patriarchal model of marriage to the early twentieth-century one of partnership, in which women acted as carers and men as breadwinners, was clearly reflected in the shift from men to women as the preferred caretakers for children after divorce, and was adhered to so long as the wife had not been at fault in the circumstances leading to divorce. However, after the 1969 legislation marriage became primarily a personal relationship, the fate of which was decided by the individuals involved. Yet women were not, and are not, fully 'individualized'. The concern expressed during the passage of the 1969 legislation about their economic welfare after divorce was not without foundation as later findings showed (Cmnd. 5629 (1974); Bradshaw and Millar 1991); substantive inequalities remained between men and women in large part because of the unequal gendered division of both paid and unpaid work.

In respect of maintenance, the 1974 Finer Report on One-Parent Families accepted the logic of marriage defined in terms of a personal relationship, stating that while men should pay to support their first families after fair assessment, in the absence of fault-based divorce it was nevertheless inevitable that the state would have to shoulder the main burden of costs. The Committee believed that there was 'no method consistent with the basic tenets of a free society of discharging the community from this responsibility' (Cmnd. 5629 (1974): para. 2.22), because it was impossible to restrict the freedom to divorce, remarry, and reproduce. In practice, the obligation of men to maintain their first families had never been firmly enforced (Eekelaar and Maclean 1986), but the shift towards an individualized, privatized conceptualization of marriage free of any external moral code meant that the 'ought' of maintenance was also no longer entirely clear. The question mark raised over the moral obligation to maintain was revealed most clearly in respect of cohabiting couples during the 1970s. The Supplementary Benefits Commission assumed that if a man and woman were living together in a 'stable relationship', the man would support the woman, who was therefore cut off from benefit. In its 1971 Report on the subject, the DHSS was keen to deny that this involved any moral judgement, but was rather a pragmatic matter of achieving equity between married and cohabiting couples (SBC, 1971).

Individualization reached its apogee in the 1984 Matrimonial and Family Proceedings Act, which favoured a 'clean break' approach to divorce. Eekelaar (1991a) has argued that this legislation paid no attention at all to the inequities in the economic position of wives compared with husbands. Women were assumed to be free-standing, employed individuals (Maclean 1991), and assumptions regarding the equal-but-different partnership of the post-war decades were nowhere evident. However, the main consequence of the legislation was the extent to which it enabled people openly to articulate the possibility of a 'social security divorce', whereby the first wife would rely on social assistance payments, allowing the husband to support a second family (this principle had long been accepted by the social assistance authorities, see Chapter 6). When the Attorney General was asked in the course of the debate on the legislation whether it would strengthen or weaken marriage, he answered that 'it will be a more respectable and cleaner operation' (House of Commons Debates, vol. 54, 16 February 1984, c. 405). For the first time there was no attempt to make the case that marriage would be strengthened.

Increasingly the emphasis was placed on making the divorce process easier. The Law Commission's 1988 discussion paper on the grounds for divorce (HC 479 (1988)) stated that the increase in divorce did not indicate any fundamental weakening of the fabric of society, but it did mean that the process had to be 'consumer friendly' (para. 2.22). Katherine O'Donovan (1993) has contrasted the tone of this document with that of the one preceding the 1969 reform (Cmnd. 3123 (1966)), which talked about ideal standards rather than consumer opinion.

The full acceptance of marriage as something to be controlled by the individuals involved came with the Lord Chancellor, Lord Mackay's 1995 proposals finally to make the breakdown of marriage the sole ground for divorce, without it being necessary to demonstrate breakdown by reference to a 'fact' such as adultery or unreasonable behaviour (Cm. 2799 (1995)). Lord Mackay had announced his intention of introducing measures to cut the rate of divorce. However, the 1995 White Paper proposed instead a collection of measures intended to make divorce less expensive and more amicable. According to *The Independent* (28 April 1995), he had 'recognised an important truth— that the state has limited ability and little right to intervene in the personal relationships of private individuals'.

Significantly, this shift was justified in terms of the desirable effect it was expected to have on negotiations over children in particular. The Law Commission's 1988 paper on divorce said that the continued use of fault after the 1969 legislation had bred conflict and 'ritualized hostility' (para. 3.27). Its 1990 document on the ground for divorce commented that while the objectives for a divorce law set out in 1966 still commanded widespread support, it was necessary to put more emphasis on the amicable resolution of practical issues relating to the discharge of responsibility to each other and the children. It was argued that the further withdrawal of legal intervention from the business of divorce would facilitate conciliation between the parties. Clause 1 of the 1996 Family Law Bill required the court to have regard to three general principles: support for the institution of marriage, the encouragement of 'all practicable steps' to save the marriage, and the ending of marriages with both the minimum distress to the parties and the children and the minimum of cost.

As the state withdrew from the business of regulating marriage, it gave more attention to ways of regulating what had been the duties of marriage, particularly in respect of the parental obligation to maintain and care for children. Mothers and fathers rather than husbands and wives have been the focus of concern in recent legislation. As the nature of marriage changed and as non-marriage became more prevalent, intra-family transfers between men, on the one hand, and women and children, on the other, became more fragile. As Folbre

(1994) has pointed out, with the decline of hierarchical family structures, intra-familial transfers have come to depend more on male altruism. Research during the 1980s drew attention to the poverty of lone mothers and their children.[15]

Academic psychologists also began to insist on children's need to maintain contact with both parents. Research findings on the effects of divorce from the USA reported at the beginning of the decade (especially Hetherington, Cox, and Cox 1978; Wallerstein and Kelly 1980), together with trends in psychological theory that put more emphasis on the importance of the role of fathers (e.g. Lamb 1981) and the activities of the pressure group Families need Fathers (founded in 1974 to press the cause of fathers in custody cases) influenced the direction of research in the 1980s (see Richards 1982, 1993). This was in marked contrast both to 1970s policy-related documents, which, while they always acknowledged that marriage was about children, tended to focus on the couple (e.g. Archbishop of Canterbury 1971), and to the earlier recommendations of psychologists that children would fare best with minimal disruption to their emotional ties to their mothers (Goldstein, Freud, and Solnit 1973). The Law Commission's 1990 document on the ground for divorce stated: 'it is known that the children who suffer least from their parents' breakup are usually those who are able to retain a good relationship with them both. Children who suffer most are those whose parents remain in conflict' (para. 2.19). With the dramatic rise after 1970 in divorce (especially in divorce involving young children), and after 1980 in extramarital births and cohabitation, governments faced the problem of securing traditional family obligations.

The 1987 Family Law Reform Act abolished the status of illegitimacy and enabled an unmarried father to apply for a parental rights order. The Act stopped short of allowing unmarried fathers to share parental functions by private agreement, something that was subsequently granted by the 1989 Children's Act as part of the effort to reinforce the idea that such matters should ideally be private decisions and by so doing to encourage fathers to shoulder responsibility. State concern about parental responsibility has assumed the dual meaning of respon-

---

[15] Weitzman's (1985) American research came up with the startling figure that while men's incomes increased 40 per cent on divorce, women (and children) lost 70 per cent. These figures were substantially modified using British data (Taylor et al. 1994), but a series of British studies documented the poverty of lone mothers (see especially Eekelaar and Maclean 1986; Bradshaw and Millar 1991).

sibility towards children, on the one hand, and a preference for parental responsibility over state responsibility on the other. John Eekelaar (1991b) and Andrew Bainham (1991) have convincingly traced the way in which the second of these came to predominate in the case of the 1989 Children Act. The case is more convincing still when the Children Act and the 1991 Child Support Act are taken together. With these two pieces of legislation, the boundary between the private sphere of family responsibility and that of state responsibility was more tightly drawn, and in addition the responsibility of men to maintain and of women to care—the obligations previously guaranteed by the regulation of marriage—have been reinforced.

The Children Act laid out that parental responsibility is individual responsibility, that it may not be voluntarily surrendered to the state, that it remains undiminished when the care of the child is shared with the state, and that it persists; only adoption ends it. The Child Support Act was intended to impose on all biological fathers a continuing obligation to maintain. In many respects the assumptions regarding the tasks of men and women in the old equal-but-different partnership concept of marriage were written into the new arrangements. While unmarried fathers may share parental responsibility under the Children Act, they have no automatic recognition in regard to care. However, when it comes to maintenance they must provide and indeed this takes precedence. (One aspect of the child support formula that was subjected to severe criticism was the lack of regard for travelling expenses incurred by fathers who maintained contact with their children. (Garnham and Knights 1994a).) The Act also expects fathers to maintain mothers as well as children. This has been justified in terms of the recognition that it gives to the indirect as well as the direct costs of being the parent with care (Maclean 1994a). In this interpretation, the personal allowances for the resident parent is not spousal support, but recognizes instead the cost to the mother of not being able to enter the labour market, or of having to obtain childcare if she does. In practical terms such a personal allowance becomes more necessary in the light of the further deregulation of marriage that follows from the 1996 Family Law Act; there is some indication that mediation may work to the detriment of women in respect of the financial settlement following divorce (Lewis and Maclean 1997). While the proposal is further to deregulate marriage, some effort has been made to moderate the effect of changes in the marriage system by strengthening traditional parental responsibilities and limiting those of the state, although the promise of the Child Support Act to make fathers take financial responsibility for all their biological children and thus to make them think twice about their right to both remarry and procreate has in practice fallen victim to poor formulation and the hazards of implementation.

Conclusion

Early in the twentieth century, Bertrand Russell argued that government should only concern itself with the regulation of relationships between adults when there were children involved. It now seems that the marriage system has changed sufficiently for this to be happening. Early in the century marriage was defined primarily in terms of the obligations arising from it and was perceived as a public institution crucial to the maintenance of social morality and stability. The patriarchal model of marriage and of family law served to uphold this view by imposing a traditional moral code. This externally imposed morality was internalized and expressed in ideas about marital respectability and in the stigma attaching to divorce and unmarried motherhood, which were independently powerful in enforcing traditional sexual morality. Efforts to reform marriage and make it a partnership to reflect changes in the position of women and make it a 'higher relationship', first in terms of subordinating sex and later by elevating the importance of sexual satisfaction, worked within the established parameters of a morality that sought to confine sex to marriage and to bolster marriage. However, the attempt to provide a new basis for sexual morality in terms of the importance of the quality of the personal relationship, first in the inter-war years and then again in the 1960s, contained within it the wherewithal to justify new forms of behaviour.

The importance attached to morality from within and the relational aspects of marriage effectively subordinated the traditional emphasis on the duties of marriage to the quality of the relationship, which came to mean achievement of individual satisfaction. It was this profound shift in the conceptualization of marriage, as much as the change in the law that accompanied it, that helped to promote the change in the marriage system during the late twentieth century whereby both divorce and cohabitation dramatically increased. As Mansfield and Collard (1988) put it in their study of newly-wed marriage, the emphasis shifted from the moral conception of what marriage should be, towards what it could be. We can begin to suggest a possible set of relationships between the profound shift in the understanding of marriage and of sexual morality in the 1960s which underpinned legislative change, and the resulting decline in stigma which promoted new patterns of behaviour. Faced with these changes, government has decided that it is impossible to push back the individualistic tide in respect of marriage and has rather opted to try to enforce sterner regulations in respect of parenthood. This is probably the only sensible course and it is to be regretted that some aspects of this legislative endeavour, especially the Child Support Act, have been so badly implemented; a second bite at this particular cherry will be very difficult. Not only did it become difficult to gainsay the pursuit of individualism and self-interest during the 1980s, but any return to a more duty-based concept of marriage would likely weigh most heavily upon women as the 1912 Royal Commission on Divorce found. Women have paid a heavy economic price for the new freedom to form and dissolve personal relationships. But despite the attempt of the 1996 Family Law Act to put marriage-saving back on the agenda, it will be remarkably difficult to put the clock back in respect of marriage and divorce.

4

Constructions of Unmarried Motherhood in the Post-War Period

Of all the groups of lone mothers, the unmarried have fared worst historically. At the turn of the century the options for single, pregnant women were few. The mortality of children born outside marriage was high, as a result both of natural causes and infanticide (Arnot 1994; Higgenbotham 1989). During the late nineteenth and early twentieth centuries there was also the possibility of informal adoption. Most local newspapers contained numerous advertisements for and by people wanting children to nurse before adoption was made a legal procedure in 1926. The majority of unmarried mothers would have had to resort to the poor law and were usually forced to enter the workhouse, where, because of their moral taint, they were more likely than other women to be employed on the unpleasant task of picking oakum (Thane 1978).

During the First World War, attitudes towards 'war babies' and their mothers briefly relaxed, largely as a result of the efforts of the Council for the Unmarried Mother and her Child (founded in 1917) and the greater concern expressed about the high infant mortality rate among illegitimate children. One Conservative MP was prepared to advocate temporary relaxation of the bastardy laws in order to ease the path of children of men fighting in the war. But between the wars unmarried mothers were more rigorously classified. Voluntary organizations took mainly 'first offenders' and tried to place them in domestic service. The poor law authorities took 'repeaters' and from 1927 had sweeping powers to detain girls who were classified as mentally defective and who were in receipt of poor relief at the time of their child's birth. In the post-war period changing ideas about sexual morality and about the basis of marriage resting more on love than duty eroded the rigid boundary erected between married and unmarried mothers and also, at least temporarily, between unmarried mothers and other groups of lone mothers.

There have been several attempts in the American academic literature to classify the way in which unmarried mothers have been thought
about and the explanations that have been given for their behaviour
over time. In the 1960s Vincent (1961) and Kronick (1966) suggested
that during the early twentieth century the US literature emphasized
moral and inborn sources of behaviour, especially 'mental deficiency';
during the 1930s environmental causes rooted in poverty and social
disorganization held sway; during the late 1930s and 1940s the importance of sub-cultures, particularly among blacks was stressed; while
during the late 1940s and 1950s unmarried mothers were believed to
have psychological problems. Not until the late 1950s did interest in
social and cultural variables revive. There are dangers in such neat
classifications; those described for each period may have been dominant, but they are unlikely to have been exclusive. The significant
trends in the literature are also likely to be perceived differently with
the passing of time. Arney and Bergen's (1984) account of 'the invention of teenage pregnancy' in the USA highlights only one shift, during
the 1960s, from the idea of unmarried mothers as a moral problem
('unwed mothers') to a technical problem ('teenage pregnancy') suitable for study by social scientists and epidemiologists.

The point in tracing such shifts, which will of course be different
for different countries, is not to examine the validity of the understandings expressed. Often, especially in the earlier studies, it is
painfully clear that the selection of the data was likely to prejudice
the findings. However, it may be suggested that the dominant understanding of the whys and wherefores of unmarried mothers' behaviour at any particular point in time does have implications for
policy-making. Stated briefly, policies towards unmarried mothers
that are formulated in a period when the dominant view of their
behaviour stresses the importance of individual psychological variables are likely to be different from those formulated in a period
when the socio-economic characteristics they have in common with
other types of lone mother family are emphasized. Cynics may
suggest that policy-makers do not read and that other pragmatic
issues, for example concern about public expenditure, will be far
more significant at any particular historical moment. Certainly, the
role of ideas in policy-making is controversial and hard to prove;
reference to 'the climate of opinion' has always had an air of vague-
ness, even if the textual analysis that has accompanied latter-day
discourse analysis has given it substance. This chapter claims only

that the dominant construction of unmarried motherhood in any particular period set the parameters within which policy was made.

Compared with the American, the British literature on unmarried motherhood has been slight (Bury 1984). Thus it is not surprising to find in the 1950s and 1960s, and again in the 1980s and 1990s, a heavy reliance on American material. The dominant strand in the US literature of the 1950s was the importance of psychological and psychoanalytical understandings of unmarried motherhood. It was primarily a social work literature, based on observation of the cases comprising American social work practice, which tended to be undertaken among white, middle-class women. It nevertheless achieved wide currency in Britain in the 1960s, where social work writings were also important in the post-war literature because the most visible group of unmarried mothers were those who entered mother and baby homes where they were likely to come into contact with social workers. Indeed, in Britain, the construction of unmarried motherhood in terms of abnormal personality dominated the professional social work literature by the mid-1960s, although not the rather less influential public health literature and not necessarily social work practice.

During the 1950s, the number of lone mothers was relatively small; both extramarital birth and divorce rates were low. It was therefore additionally possible to construct unmarried motherhood as a rather special problem of a deviant few and to focus on the 'internal' dimensions of the problem in terms of the psychological shortcomings of the mothers involved. The attention given to unmarried mothers inevitably ebbed and flowed with the changing demographics of the problem and in particular with the proportion of lone mothers who were unmarried, but it also depended on shifting ideas about sexual morality and the birth status of children. During the 1960s, extramarital birth rates showed a noticeable rise which could not be accounted for by thwarted marriage, as was the case during the Second World War. The 1960s was a period of rising fertility rates within and outside marriage. Thus while psychological understandings of unmarried motherhood continued to achieve a wide currency in the texts of the 1960s, it was becoming more difficult to sustain the idea of unmarried motherhood as the problem of a deviant few.

Extramarital fertility rates fell during the 1970s, paralleling the declines in marital fertility; the increase in the number of lone mother families was produced by the rise in the divorce rate. This change in the composition of lone mother families was accompanied by a shift of focus among researchers and commentators, and, at a time of increasing permissiveness in respect of sexual morality, the lines between the once-married and the never-married lone mother became increasingly blurred to the advantage of unmarried mothers in terms of the way in which they were treated. However, during the 1980s and 1990s, the extramarital birth rate rose sharply, while marital fertility actually fell, with the result that the proportion of births taking place outside marriage rose from 11.8 per cent in 1980 to 28.3 per cent in 1990 and 32.4 per cent in 1994. In a political environment that was also increasingly hostile to 'welfare dependency', unmarried mothers were again singled out from the population of lone mothers for special attention, first in the USA and then in Britain. Thus in the current debate, it has been more the 'external' issues that have attracted attention: the effects on children, the problem of public expenditure, and the effects on communities and on the behaviour of young men of large numbers of women and children living autonomously.

The chapter examines first, the nature of the literature on unmarried mothers in the 1950s and early 1960s and the policy recommendations as to the proper treatment of unmarried mothers and their children to which it gave rise, and seeks briefly to account for the popularity of its psychoanalytical arguments. It then examines the circumstances under which the psychological understanding of unmarried motherhood was abandoned in the late 1960s and 1970s, and the implications of the new construction of unmarried motherhood in which abnormality receded in the face of huge changes in the nature of lone motherhood, ideas about sexual morality in and out of marriage, and the desire to treat all children alike. Finally, it sketches the better known landscape of the 1980s and 1990s, when the constructions of unmarried motherhood were influenced by American social scientists who were self-confessed adherents of the New Right and who elevated lone motherhood, and particularly unmarried mothers, from a social problem into a social threat (Edwards and Duncan 1995), because of the public expenditure burden they represented and because of the broader concerns about the implications of female autonomy for the socialization of children and for the behaviour of young men. With the recent huge rise in extramarital childbearing, the problem of unmarried motherhood has to some extent been constructed for the first time as a problem of men as well as of women.

Abnormal and Victims: The Construction of the 1950s and Early 1960s

Subsequent to the Second World War, the dominant view was that the right place for a child was with his or her parents. The influence of Bowlby's (1951) theory of maternal deprivation has been widely acknowledged and was one factor in the thinking of civil servants in the Department of Health who wished in the late 1940s to close the day care centres set up during the war (Riley 1983), and in the preference of the Curtis Report on the care of children for foster homes as a form of substitute family over institutional care for those children in the care of local authorities (Cmd. 6922 (1946)). However, Bowlby's view of unmarried mothers was rather different: 'The girl who has a socially unacceptable illegitimate baby often comes from an unsatisfactory family background and has developed a neurotic character, the illegitimate baby being in the nature of a symptom of her psychological ill-health' (Bowlby 1977: 112).

In *Maternal Care and Mental Health* (1951), Bowlby cited American research studies that suggested that a high proportion of unmarried mothers were psychologically disturbed, often coming from broken homes, and were unfitted to provide emotional stability for their children. He drew attention to the way in which the American research had resulted in a change in policy in that country, such that more adoptions were being arranged, and he deplored British policy, laid down in a wartime Department of Health Circular (Department of Health 1943), which encouraged social workers to keep the mother and baby together and to try to persuade the mother's parents to take them in.[1]

The main text cited by Bowlby was the one that achieved wide currency in the British literature on unmarried mothers: Leontine Young's *Out of Wedlock* (1954). Based on her work with 350 unmarried mothers and some thousands of case files, Young suggested that the unmarried mother 'wants a baby—but, specifically, an out-of-wedlock baby—without a husband' (p. 28). In her experience, unmarried

---

[1] This Circular represented the first attempt to take unmarried mothers outside the ambit of the Poor Law (Ferguson and Fitzgerald 1954). It was prompted in part by the rising numbers of illegitimate births during the war and the relatively high mortality rate experienced by this group of babies. Concern about the health of the children born to unmarried mothers was especially pronounced before the Second World War (see e.g. the public health journal *Medical Officer*) and remains an issue (see Babb and Bethune 1995), although it is no longer at the forefront of the policy agenda.

mothers were not promiscuous, nor were they mentally deficient, but they did purposefully set out to become mothers, which raised questions about their mental health: 'The serious problem of the unmarried mother is that her urge for a baby has been separated from its normal matrix, love for a mate. The proof of the pathology of her problem lies in this desperately enforced separation and in its compulsive nature' (p. 37). Young attributed this pathological behaviour to the unmarried mother's family background. The majority of cases were, she suggested, 'mother-ridden': 'The mother is basically a woman who has never accepted her own femininity and whose life adjustment is a constant struggle with that fact' (p. 41). The more dominating and rejecting the mother, the more the daughter was bound to her. Having a baby expressed the daughter's feelings of jealousy and revenge. A minority of Young's cases were diagnosed as 'father-ridden'. These unmarried mothers tended to feel only hatred for the putative fathers of their children. In Young's analysis, they had sought to create rivals to their fathers, but they were never able to believe that it would be possible for the child to overcome the father and they therefore did not put it to the test. This group tended to surrender their babies for adoption, whereas the 'mother-ridden' group were as likely to keep the child, surrendering him to their mothers. A final small group of unmarried mothers were observed by Young to have psychopathic personalities.

Young commented that the observations of European social workers were somewhat different in that not all unmarried mothers were said to have personality problems and many more mothers kept their babies, often forming enduring relationships with the fathers. Young attributed this difference to the particularly striking conflict in American culture between the commercial preoccupation with sex and the conviction that sex was nevertheless sinful. Vincent (1961) was also to highlight the cultural disjuncture between the fact that sex before marriage was condoned in the USA, while illicit pregnancy was condemned. However, Young's main concern was with identifying the degree of pathology present in her cases. The higher the unmarried mother's social class the more disturbed she was said to be: 'Almost without exception [a professional woman] . . . is psychologically a sick person.'

In Young's view, the unmarried father was the 'counterpart of the neurotic personality of the unmarried mother'. Like the unmarried mother, he was incapable of combining love and sexual relationships.

Thus any tendency to regard the unmarried mother and father as an unmarried family could only be a 'fallacy'. It was the job of the social worker to understand that she had to help a sick woman to come to a decision about what to do about her baby: 'When a worker can see that, had the unmarried mother wanted a baby for normal reasons, she would have fallen in love, married, and had a child under normal circumstances, the worker's problem begins to resolve itself' (1954: 217). In other words, armed with Young's construction of unmarried motherhood, the social worker would inevitably recommend adoption. Young's view was widely accepted in the United States. As late as 1965, the Executive Director of the Child Welfare League of America was prepared to say: 'the concept that the unmarried mother and her child constitute a family is to me unsupportable. There is no family in any real sense of the word' (Reid 1971: 10).

Such a view would never have been as frankly expressed in public in Britain, where the right of the unmarried mother to keep her child was staunchly defended. However, an understanding of unmarried motherhood in terms of personality problems made substantial inroads. In a review of Young's book, Alexina McWhinnie, the Director of the Edinburgh Guild of Service and a writer on adoption, suggested that British social workers should take note of Young's classification of unmarried mothers, which they 'must admit they sometimes meet' (McWhinnie 1956: 22). Young's ideas permeated the major writings on unmarried mothers in Britain during the 1960s. Based on a study of unmarried mothers in a mother and baby home, Donald Gough, a child psychiatrist trained at the Tavistock Clinic, concluded that: 'a girl in our society who starts a pregnancy with a man whom she is either unwilling or unable to marry has shown herself to be a disturbed personality, and I think that we are entitled to look upon an illegitimate baby as the living proof of his mother's severe emotional difficulties' (Gough 1961: 491).

Gough thus agreed that the pregnancy was symptomatic of deeper psychological problems and this in turn gave social workers the opening to become involved in deciding the fate of the child: 'we may also feel chary of becoming involved in an issue so fundamental as whether a mother should part from or keep her child, unless we believe that, in this group, we are dealing with people who are predominantly expressing unconscious mental problems in terms of reality problems' (ibid.: 490). Gough was invited by the National Council for the Unmarried Mother and her Child (NCUMC) to write a pamphlet on 'understanding unmarried mothers', in which these ideas were repeated (Gough 1966).

In fact, as we saw in Chapter 2, a number of small-scale studies, often conducted by medical officers of health, noted that a not insubstantial proportion of extramarital births were to separated and divorced women (around one third) and that some of these women were cohabiting (Macdonald 1956; Greenland 1957; Wimperis 1960). However, little attention was paid to any but the never-married mothers living alone, probably because, as an Essex medical officer of health commented, the older cohabiting single mother was 'a problem only to the moral susceptibilities of a small part of the population' (Yarrow 1964: 48). It was also the case that the opinion of local authority medical officers of health on such issues was being rapidly subordinated to that of social workers during the 1960s (Lewis 1986). Certainly, in a 1967 House of Lords debate on illegitimacy, Baroness Summerskill referred to unmarried mothers as 'immature' young women. In the major textbook for practitioners published during the 1960s, Jane Rowe acknowledged that there were many types of unmarried mothers, those cohabiting with the father, those who married shortly before or after the birth of the child, those who did not marry but were relatively free of emotional disturbance, and those with personality problems. However, her text focused disproportionately on the last of these groups and relied heavily on the work of Young and Gough (Rowe 1966). Similarly, Jean Pochin's book on casework with unmarried parents, acknowledged that the unmarried mother's motivation was not always unconscious, but leaned heavily towards the view that the pregnancy was 'symptomatic' and that 'the deep sources of unmarried motherhood lie partly in the personality of the mother herself, and partly in the upbringing and home life that have formed her and continue to influence her' (Pochin 1969: 6).

Other more specialized studies of particular aspects of unmarried motherhood also revealed the influence of psychoanalytical theory. At the end of her study of accommodation for unmarried mothers, Izzard (1969) concluded that her research had confirmed the view that illegitimate pregnancy was only a symptom of deeper personality problems, while Nicholson's survey of mother and baby homes emphasized the importance of employing caseworkers 'to resolve the more basic problems of adjustment of which the illegitimate pregnancy may be a symptom' (Nicholson 1968: 134). In addition, Yelloly's (1965) study of adoption confirmed the findings of two prominent American studies

(Vincent 1961; Jones, Meyer, and Borgatta 1966) that the unmarried mothers who decided to keep their children tended to be less emotionally stable than those who gave them up for adoption.

In his study of adoption, Triseliotis (1970) believed that the psychoanalytical view of illicit pregnancy as rarely accidental had gained the most ground, while as late as 1977 Gill reported that conference speakers who used psychiatric terminology and explanations were 'applauded enthusiastically' (Gill 1977: 241). It is noteworthy that while Government Committees of Inquiry did not refer explicitly to the psychoanalytical enthusiasm for adoption, adoption law was investigated and reformed in the 1950s and again at the beginning of the 1970s (Cmd. 9248 (1953); Cmnd. 5107 (1972)). As we saw in Chapter 2 (Table 2.7), there was a notable increase in the number of adoptions of illegitimate babies from the mid-1950s, from 10,000 in 1955 to a peak of over 19,000 in 1968.

There were other available constructions of unmarried motherhood that relied more on socio-cultural explanations. Vincent's work (1961) on a large American sample stressed the importance of the gap between the lack of condemnation of illicit coitus and wholesale condemnation of illicit pregnancy. Vincent also criticized the methodology of studies stressing the importance of psychological variables because they tended to focus only on those unmarried mothers seen by social casework agencies (Vincent, 1971). Some British studies also either played down the significance of personality or elevated the importance of socio-economic variables. M. W. Hamilton (1962) found that there was no significant difference on any count in her sample of 62 adolescents between those who married to legitimize the child and those who did not. Her findings were published in a social work journal, but were not often cited thereafter. (Similar findings also pertained for later generations of adolescents, for example, Kiernan (1995) found that teenage mothers who had a child on their own, or within a cohabiting or marital union did not differ significantly from one another on a wide range of background characteristics.) Epidemiological studies highlighting the importance of occupation and material circumstances (especially Thompson 1956; Greenland 1957, 1958) achieved greater recognition, but did not constitute the mainstream current in the literature as it developed by the mid-1960s. Indeed, articles and letters in the *British Medical Journal* welcomed Young's analysis and agreed that there was 'a neurotic and on occasions, impulsive desire for pregnancy' (Cotter 1967; see also Franklin 1966).

The reasons for the popularity of psychoanalytical constructions of unmarried motherhood require substantial investigation in their own right, but two main lines of enquiry may be suggested. Bernstein (1966) speculated on the links between patterns of explanation and the changing characteristics of the population of unmarried mothers. In the United States, unmarried motherhood became more common among the middle classes during the 1950s, something that did not happen in Britain until the late 1950s and 1960s.[2] In these circumstances, Bernstein believed that 'we find it more comfortable to see the out-of-wedlock mother as a girl whose difficulty stems from underlying, pre-existing personality problems' (p. 109). Thus she suggested that it was easier to avoid the difficult waters of cultural and social variables. Vincent (1961) hinted at similar constraints on academic enquiry when he pointed out that the identification of unmarried mothers as abnormal effectively constituted the major deterrent to unmarried motherhood. Again, it may have been more acceptable to plump for pre-existing personality problems. Furthermore, adoption as a solution served to obscure the illegitimacy of a child and to 'normalize' it, something that a Government Committee of Inquiry objected to in the early 1970s (Cmnd. 5107 (1972)), but which was considered attractive in the 1950s and early 1960s.

The relationship between the formulation of research hypotheses, the changing nature of the characteristics of unmarried mothers, and shifts in societal attitudes has been extremely complicated and particularly significant. As the numbers of unmarried mothers grew and as they became more visible in society so 'the fear that it could happen in our family' (Pochin 1969: 3) became more real. It is highly likely that such profound changes were reflected in the way in which researchers approached the subject.

Second, and more obviously, there is a strong connection between the source of the influential writings—social work—and the way in

---

[2] There is a lack of data on social-class and illegitimacy. Thompson's (1956) study using Scottish data showed a marked social class gradient with illegitimate births increasing downwards from the professional classes to the unskilled. The GRO for England and Wales published similar findings in 1951. After 1951 the only data are for Scotland, where the Registrar General published information on illegitimacy and social class annually. In the early 1950s the highest illegitimacy ratio occurred in social class IV (semi-skilled occupations), which contained a high proportion of agricultural workers in Scotland, and from IV followed a declining trend through social class V, III, II, and I. By the late 1950s, the rank order had changed to become IV, II, III, V, and I (Kiernan 1971).

which psychoanalytical theory was beginning to provide the underpinnings for professionalization in that field of endeavour. This was
already well under way in the United States by the 1940s; in Britain
there was no real evidence of 'the psychological deluge' until the 1950s
(Yelloly 1980). Even then it was strongly opposed. Eileen Younghusband's new generic social work course, set up at the London School of
Economics in 1954, was influential in seeking to unify social work
around the concept of casework, a method hitherto used only by
family caseworkers and psychiatric social workers and defined as a
process that developed personality through consciously effected adjustments between the inner and outer worlds (C. Morris 1954). However,
Richard Titmuss, Professor of Social Administration at the LSE, was
scathing about 'the preoccupation with some of the wastelands of
technique'[3] and Barbara Wootton published a vehement attack on
the new social work in 1959, in which she charged that the 'mal-
adjusted' had 'taken the place formerly reserved for the poor in the
ideology of social work' (Wootton 1959: 269).

Arguably, the psychological 'takeover' of social work was never as
complete in Britain as in the United States. But in Britain, psychological
theory played a particularly important part in the professionalization of
family casework (Lewis 1995) and hence was likely to dominate the
literature on those groups of the population with whom family caseworkers came into contact. Significantly, McWhinnie's 1956 review of
Leontine Young's book on unmarried mothers suggested that Young's
analysis would 'contribute to the professionalization of social work' (p.
22). During the 1950s, the analysis of 'problem families' moved sharply
from an analysis stressing a family's physical and moral incapacity, or
failure to recognize the moral obligation on it to live in accordance
with normal standards, to one which emphasized an inability to form
effective family relationships and the problems of 'immature personalities' (Irvine 1954). Unmarried mothers were another group that came
within the orbit of family casework. The fourth edition of Penelope
Hall's (1959) influential textbook on social services was cautious in its
treatment of Leontine Young's ideas, following the public health studies in pointing out that significant numbers of unmarried mothers
were in fact older women who were cohabiting. But the book never-

---

[3] Titmuss's private papers are most revealing on this score, see 'Social Policy and
Social Work Education', TS, 1957, Titmuss Papers Box 300 C, BLPES, London.

theless went on to make a link between cohabitation and problem families.

However, it is important to note that the trend in the academic literature did not necessarily accurately reflect all social work practice on the ground (Fink, 1997). 'Moral welfare workers' employed in the main by voluntary agencies had traditionally worked with unmarried mothers and continued to do so, often in ignorance of the strictures of psychoanalytical family casework. In her book on moral welfare work in two dioceses, Hall noted that some of the 'more forward looking' moral welfare workers were attaching increasing importance to acquiring 'deeper knowledge of human motivation and behaviour', but she questioned how far it was possible to link Christian doctrine to psychological and psychiatric explanation (Hall and Howes 1965: 247). By the early 1960s, the vast majority of moral welfare workers were women in their fifties and sixties, who were unlikely to take up the newer psychoanalytical ideas. They were as or more likely to be guided by the Government's wartime Circular on the importance of keeping mother and child together than by the newer advocacy of adoption, especially given the evidence from a series of surveys among moral welfare workers and medical officers of health during the 1950s showing that the decision to keep a child did not seem to be a barrier to marriage later on (Macdonald 1956; *Moral Welfare* 1960).

In practice, the construction of unmarried motherhood as a moral problem—in short, as sin—and the task of social work intervention to secure penitence as a necessary step on the road to rehabilitation survived alongside newer efforts to build relationships and develop personality. Nicholson's (1968) study of mother and baby homes found that many still aimed to save souls and all but two held daily prayers. Some still had a rule dating from the pre-war era of moral welfare work, which stated that only women expecting their first illegitimate child, and who therefore might be rehabilitated, would be admitted. Restrictions were usually imposed on visits from boyfriends and on the time the women were allowed to leave the homes. Indeed the line between rehabilitation by the imposition of moral discipline and punishment was often fine. The pre-war rule that mothers should keep their children for three months and breast feed them was designed as much to make the mother aware of her responsibilities as to further the child's health and welfare.

In fact just as the number of mother and baby homes were about to show a steep decline, from 172 in 1968 (Nicholson 1968) to 65 in 1974

(Cmnd. 5629 (1974)): para. 8.178), so both the practice and ideas of moral welfare workers and caseworkers were about to undergo something of an eclipse. Wimperis (1960) reported that just under 40 per cent of unmarried mothers were known to moral welfare workers in a Midlands town in 1950, a figure similar to Hall and Howes's (1965) findings. But by 1972 in London only 25 per cent were receiving help from voluntary organizations (French and Beer 1972). The percentage of children born outside marriage and given up for adoption also declined sharply. The whole construction of unmarried motherhood underwent profound change during the late 1960s and 1970s in response to changes in the composition of lone mother families and shifts in thinking about both sexual morality and about the welfare of children.

Normal but Unfortunate: Constructions of the Late 1960s and 1970s

In her 1964 book on social work and social change, Eileen Young-husband insisted that social workers must be 'neutral' on the question of unmarried motherhood. In a climate where there was 'no clear and consistent code of sex morality', the social worker had to be careful how she approached the issues raised by illegitimate maternity (Young-husband 1964). As early as her 1959 Report on the training of social workers, Younghusband had recommended that unmarried mothers be treated more like 'unsupported mothers', that is widows and divorced or separated women (Ministry of Health and Department of Health for Scotland 1959). Younghusband's motivation in 1959 sprung as much from the desire to promote generic family casework as from the wish to treat unmarried mothers like other lone mothers. But by the late 1960s it is possible to detect a demand that unmarried mothers should no longer be considered 'abnormal', in the manner of both the psycho-analytical and moral welfare approaches. Whereas Hall and Howes (1965) had questioned Younghusband's argument for treating un-married mothers in the same fashion as other lone mother families, on the grounds that their emotional, if not their material, situations were very different, Margaret Wynn's (1968) influential study of 'father-less families', which focused firmly on the economic position of lone mother families, criticized Younghusband for singling out unmarried mothers at all. The ninth edition of Hall's text on social services (edited by Mayes, Forder, and Keedan 1975) only devoted a page to unmarried mothers, noting that society was now more willing to accept them.

During the 1970s, the number of lone mothers increased dramatically again, but mainly as the result of divorce (Chapter 2, Table 2.1). The boundary between once-married motherhood and never-married motherhood became increasingly difficult to sustain. Using the National Child Development Survey's longitudinal data, Ferri (1976) suggested that unmarried mothers who kept their children might offer greater stability to them than could parents who divorced. Lambert and Streather (1980) showed how many of the children in the NCDS data were born legitimate and yet ended up in one-parent families, and stressed the degree of transformation families were likely to experience. Thus a contribution by a social worker in 1980 on single-parent families emphasized the extent to which families moved in and out of lone parenthood (Thorburn 1980); this, rather than legitimacy or illegitimacy had become the dominant focus. As a result, the emphasis was placed on what unmarried mothers had in common with other lone mother families—poverty—rather than anything that might be held to mark them out, such as immature personalities or sinful natures. To the extent that unmarried mothers became integrated into the mainstream of lone motherhood, they ceased to be treated as abnormal. The Finer Report on one-parent families devoted very little space indeed to illegitimacy, stressing instead the 'extra needs' that all one-parent families had in common (Cmnd. 5629 (1974)). The Report advocated a new allowance for all lone mothers (the guaranteed maintenance allowance) because they all had similar needs.

The introduction of the term 'one-parent families' reflected the new preoccupation with the situation of all lone mother families, rather than with the causes of the phenomenon. Wynn's (1968) use of the term 'fatherless families' had signalled the beginning of this trend. In 1973 the National Council for the Unmarried Mother and her Child changed its name to the National Council for One-Parent Families, the motive being the desire to eradicate the distinction between unmarried mothers and other lone mother families (Teichman 1978). The Council also campaigned strongly during the 1970s for the abolition of illegitimacy as a legal status (NCUMC 1968).

During the 1970s, the academic literature on unmarried motherhood was dominated by social scientists rather than social workers and also emphasized the common material needs of all one-parent families.

In part, this concern grew out of the 'rediscovery of poverty' during the 1960s (Abel-Smith and Townsend, 1965), which showed the extent to which children suffered poverty—30 per cent of the persons in low-income households were children—and which led to the setting up of the Child Poverty Action Group. The identification of unmarried mothers as a 'poverty problem', which had its roots in their treatment under Poor Law, had never entirely disappeared. Even Gough, when strongly advocating adoption for illegitimate babies, nevertheless added a rider that would have been quite alien to the thinking of his American contemporaries:

Adoption is very often the best solution for a great many important emotional reasons, but these reasons can scarcely be touched on if there is no real possibility of the mother keeping her baby. We should press the Government to provide accommodation, training and financial support for unmarried mothers who keep their babies . . . it is absurd to suppose that girls in our society will get pregnant to enjoy the service provided for unmarried mothers. (Gough 1971: 17)

The new-found emphasis on poverty and material circumstances meant that no distinction was made between the birth status of children; children were children. This conviction was echoed in other debates over social issues involving children. In 1960 the Ingleby Committee on children and young persons signalled strongly that it was not possible to distinguish between the deprived and the depraved child within the criminal justice system (Cmnd. 1191 (1960)). All were 'children in trouble' (the title given to the 1968 White Paper) and the trouble began as a result of deprivation.

As powerful in forcing a shift in the construction of unmarried motherhood as the determination to treat 'children as children' when it came to their needs, was the profound change in ideas about sexual morality. These were read by defenders of the traditional family in the 1990s as a shift to individualistic hedonism and an autonomous youth culture (Dennis and Erdos 1992), but as Chapter 3 showed, the shift in sexual morality was more complicated and more profound than this. By the early 1960s, the argument that sex was the expression of personality and could only be regulated from within rather than by social institutions was beginning to find acceptance even among churchmen. Particularly influential were the writings of Derrick Sherwin Bailey, of the Church of England Moral Welfare Council, whose progressive opinions were noted but briefly by Hall and Howe (1965) in their account of moral welfare work. Bailey was a friend of David Mace, one of the founders of the marriage guidance movement, and he urged the Church of England to reorientate its attitude towards sex and marriage and in particular to develop a theology of sexual love. He condemned the way in which marriage had been viewed institutionally rather than ontologically. In many respects, Bailey merely developed earlier views that sex was not an expression of sinful desire, but rather of love, and that non-procreative sex could not therefore be condemned. He urged that love be 'considered in terms of personal relation [sic]' (Bailey 1957) and while opposing extramarital sex, he also believed that a loveless marriage was over. Thus while cessation of love would be very difficult to verify, it nonetheless emerged as the fundamental ground for divorce. In 1963 the Bishop of Woolwich concluded that it was possible to justify any sexual relationship so long as it was based on love (Robinson 1963), revealing the full implications of the new thinking about sexual morality and the basis of marriage for non-marital sexual relationships.

While churchmen began to focus on the relational rather than the procreational aspects of marriage, the sex manual writers of the 1960s began to break the link between sex and marriage. In 1960 the British Medical Association published Eustace Chesser's book, *Is Chastity Outmoded?* The outcry was enormous, forcing the BMA to withdraw the book from sale and Chesser resigned from the Association. The book asked bluntly why there was a premium on marital virginity and whether a girl could remain a virgin and yet lose chastity (a reference to the concern about 'heavy petting' which absorbed American, and to a lesser extent British writers on sex in the 1950s (Weeks 1981)). Chesser was not advocating promiscuous sexual relationships among the young, nor extramarital sex, but his matter-of-fact presentation of his position, without any real attempt at a moral defence, caused considerable concern. The reaction to the third of G. M. Carstairs's Reith lectures provoked a similar fuss in 1962. Carstairs, a professor of psychological medicine, also asked whether chastity was the supreme moral virtue and argued that 'our young people are rapidly turning our own society into one in which sexual experience, with precautions against conception, is being accepted as a sensible preliminary to marriage, making marriage more mutually considerate and satisfying' (Carstairs 1962).

The social scientists who conducted surveys of attitudes and behaviour in respect of sex and marriage questioned whether sexual behaviour had changed as much as had attitudes (Schofield 1965, 1973; Gorer 1971). Nevertheless, Schofield's 1973 follow-up report to his mid-1960s survey of the sexual behaviour of young people stressed the variation in sexual behaviour and asked why sex should always be tied to love. Such a position had the potential to transform unmarried motherhood into little more than an unfortunate mistake.

Like churchmen and medical men, social scientists tended to be very optimistic about the changes taking place, acknowledging the existence of real change in behaviour, but denying that there was any sign of moral decay by citing in particular the relatively low divorce rate which indicated the stability of marriage (e.g. Fletcher 1962). Surprisingly little attention in Britain was paid to what Hartley, an American, called 'the amazing rise of illegitimacy' (Hartley 1966). Even though Schofield's (1965) data documented an increase in sexual activity that was paralleled by increases in teenage birth rates, the majority of teenage births occurred within marriage (around seven in ten), notwithstanding that a substantial proportion of teenage marriages were preceded by pregnancy, around four in ten in the 1960s. This made it possible for observers to interpret the changes in terms of an increase in sexual activity without a rejection of marriage. There was a moral panic about teenage behaviour in the early 1960s (for example the *British Medical Journal* carried six articles on aspects of teenage sex between 1961 and 1964), but this centred much more on the increased incidence of venereal disease and crime than on unmarried motherhood (see also Chesser et al. 1961). Carstair's belief that the pill would put an end to fears about any further increase in unmarried motherhood was probably not untypical.

The growing conviction that morality could not be successfully imposed from without provided the framework within which the decision was taken to liberalize the law on birth control, abortion and divorce at the end of the 1960s. The 1967 legislation making contraceptives available under the National Health Service made no mention of marital status, although it remained difficult for unmarried women to get access to birth control until the mid-1970s. In respect of divorce, the reports of both the Archbishop of Canterbury's Group (1966) and the Law Commissioners (Cmnd. 3123 (1966)) agreed that divorce law should focus on the state of the marriage rather than on the errant behaviour of the spouses and gave partial approval to the idea of 'no-fault' divorce. The aim of confining sexual relationships to the institution of marriage remained the same, but the means of securing it had changed. However, once the priority accorded marital stability was abandoned in favour of securing better personal relationships, there was little left by way of defence against sexual relationships outside marriage, so long as they were based on love and mutual respect.

The shift in sexual morality also promoted the blurring of boundaries between unmarried mothers and other lone mothers. The new approach to sexual morality could not provide the grounds for condemning either pre-marital or adulterous sex so long as the relationships were based on love. The Finer Report on one-parent families argued that

today, indissoluble marriage is not compatible with prevalent notions of married love and the right to personal happiness, and so a democratic welfare society issues many thousands of licences to marry again without restriction to all citizens who meet minimal legal requirements. It is therefore unhistorical and socially unrealistic to interpret marriage breakdown merely or exclusively as a concern of social pathology. (Cmnd. 5629 (1974): para. 3.2)

Nor were pathological interpretations of unmarried motherhood possible any more. In her study of illegitimacy published in 1975, Shirley Foster Hartley commented that the strange thing about the psychoanalytical studies of unmarried mothers had been that no unmarried mother had been found to be normal. By the 1970s, none was abnormal, only unfortunate. As Juliet Cheetham (1977: 54) put it in her study of unwanted pregnancy: 'it is inappropriate to treat the young unwed mother as a disturbed person or a moral delinquent.' Cheetham deplored the tendency of the older social work literature to explain unmarried pregnancy in terms of personal pathology, to the neglect of other social factors, foremost among which she placed lack of access to birth control.

In fact there is evidence from research undertaken at the end of the 1970s that some unmarried mothers were refusing to feel stigmatized by their situation. On the basis of a survey of 36 unmarried mothers in south-east England, Page (1984: 127) commented: 'What is interesting to note is the fact that such stigmatization [by situation] did not tend to induce feelings of stigma among the respondents. On the contrary, most mothers stated that the adverse reactions they had received from others had merely caused them to feel resentful.' Similarly, among Macintyre's (1977) sample of 36 single and pregnant Scottish women, of the 22 who could have married, 12 did not. Seven of these believed in marriage but were not sure that they loved the fathers of their children and hence whether there was any true basis for marriage, and five rejected marriage because in their experience it did not live up to their ideal of mutual love and personal development. These responses show first, the extent to which love as the basis for marriage was taken seriously and second, the fact that some single pregnant women felt able to opt for unmarried motherhood rather than marriage. This refusal to feel shame spread rapidly during the 1980s and 1990s, and the increasing visibility that followed from it, for example in the flight from mother and baby homes, fed back into the rejection of feelings of stigma.

Thus, as the number of divorcees increased and the movement in and out of lone parenthood was identified; as attention became focused on the material circumstances of all lone mothers and particularly on their children; and as the ideas about sexual morality became based more upon an 'internal' rather than an 'external' definition of moral behaviour, so unmarried mothers ceased to be abstracted from the general population of lone mothers. Social work practice with unmarried mothers changed considerably during the 1970s. The only time that unmarried mothers were distinguished in the social work literature was in respect of adoption. A 1971 study showed that illegitimate children did better if adopted, irrespective of their mothers' backgrounds, which fuelled social workers' commitment to adoption. But by the end of the decade adoption was no longer advocated for reasons to do with the incapacity of unmarried mothers, but for reasons to do with the child (Tizzard 1977). Indeed, the number of adoptions fell by 33 per cent between 1968 and 1973 chiefly because of the changes in the abortion law, but the further decline in unmarried mothers surrendering their children for adoption during the rest of the 1970s and 1980s also had something to do with the rejection of the 1950s idea that unmarried women were necessarily going to make bad, neurotic mothers. Beyond adoption, unmarried mothers were wrapped up into the designation of lone parents in this as in other literatures. In 1983, an article in the British Journal of Social Work advocated a 'partnership' relationship between the social worker and the lone mother, something that betokened an equality of status undreamt of in the 1950s (Parsons 1983).

Normal and Exercising Choice:
Constructions of the 1980s and 1990s

During the 1970s social assistance benefits (supplementary benefit) rose at a higher rate than real wages (Hills 1995). In addition, the access of lone mothers, particularly unmarried mothers, to council housing improved significantly after the passing of the 1977 Homelessness Act. While only 36 per cent of lone mothers lived independently in 1973–5, some 73 per cent did so by 1986–8 (Haskey 1991). Thus while the more radical recommendations of the 1974 Finer Report for a new one-parent family benefit were not implemented, social policies made it more possible for unmarried mothers to keep their children and live autonomously (thus also making them more visible), while at the same time acting decisively to enforce traditional assumptions regarding men's obligation to maintain via the cohabitation rule (Lister 1973). If a lone mother was found to be cohabiting, it was assumed that the man was supporting the family.

The greater possibility of independent living raised the spectre in the minds of Conservative politicians and New Right theorists in particular that women might be choosing unmarried motherhood. Such a proposition was advanced by Renvoize (1985), a feminist, albeit in respect of middle class, professional women rather than mothers drawing state benefits, and on the basis of a few interviews. But the rise in the extramarital birth rate of young women during the 1980s and 1990s, together with the rapid rise in the extramarital birth ratio after 1985, was enough to confirm the suspicions of the New Right.

Social scientists continued to highlight the poverty of lone mother families and to question whether women deliberately chose unmarried motherhood. According to Bradshaw and Millar (1991) only 8 per cent of their large sample survey said that their pregnancy had been deliberate, while Phoenix (1991) argued from her qualitative study that the main reason for pregnancy was lack of hope of employment. In all probability, the circumstances of the young women in her sample would not have improved even if motherhood had been delayed. However, the dominant understanding of unmarried motherhood in the 1980s and 1990s was not shaped by social scientists who either sought to present their data in a politically neutral fashion, or who declared their sympathies for the plight of unmarried mothers, but by self-confessed American ideologues of the New Right, who were concerned above all about the drain on the public purse and also about the implications of women's sexual as well as economic independence of men. Thus the concerns of the New Right brought back a moral dimension into the debate and, because unmarried mothers were disproportionately reliant on state benefits and were also obviously sexually autonomous, there was a tendency to abstract them again from the population of lone parents and to single them out for special condemnation.

As in the 1950s, dominant understandings of unmarried motherhood were largely imported from the United States during the 1980s and 1990s. The more traditional, authoritarian strand of thinking within the New Right (King 1987) deplored the passing of the two-parent, male breadwinner family model largely because of the adverse effects it was feared that this would have on men. Thus George Gilder spoke out early on against

the benefit levels [that] destroy the father's key role and authority. He can no longer feel manly in his own home. At first he may try to maintain his power by the use of muscle and bluster. But to exert force against a woman is a confession of weakness. Soon after, he turns to the street for his male affirmations. (Gilder 1981: 114)

Thus Gilder argued that by enabling women to live independently, state benefits were also responsible for men acting irresponsibly. (The argument was not dissimilar to dominant views of the working-class family at the turn of the century, when leading social activists suggested that men's obligation to provide for their families was the only sure way of securing labour discipline (e.g. Bosanquet 1906).) Without the 'steadying' effect of family life, Gilder feared that young men would turn eventually to crime. Given the high numbers of young black unmarried mothers drawing welfare benefits in the United States, this argument, centring as it did on the behaviour of young black men, carried particular resonance.[4]

More influential still were the arguments of Charles Murray (1984), who first stressed the extent to which in a society where birth-control techniques were advanced, unmarried motherhood was a question of choice. Whereas most unmarried women exercised their choice not to have children, this was not true of young and particularly black

---

[4] Fatherlessness as a cause of 'sociopathy' continues to exercise American writers, e.g. Blankenhorn (1995).

women. Second, Murray pointed out the drain this behaviour exerted on public funds and, contending that the moral hazard of providing welfare benefits was too great, argued for their abolition. If Murray's prime concern was for the taxpayer, that of Novak and Cogan (1987) was for the children of unmarried mothers, deprived of a breadwinning role model. Murray (1984), Novak and Cogan (1987), and Mead (1986) all emphasized the obligations of citizenship over rights and entitlements and all identified paid work as the primary obligation. Murray pointed out that most married women participated in the labour market in the late twentieth century, and that there was therefore no reason why unmarried mothers should be exempt. Gilder (1987) and Carlson (1987), who saw women's wage earning as part of the problem rather than the solution objected, preferring to focus only on social policy solutions that gave incentives to marriage (for example via the tax system) and forced fathers to maintain their biological children. But the balance of American New Right opinion in the 1980s viewed unmarried mothers as a costly social threat and was therefore also inclined towards social policy solutions such as 'work-fare', whereby all adults, the single mothers of small children included, would be required to train or work in return for benefit (Burghes 1987).

In Britain, concern about lone mothers as a drain on public expenditure gathered force towards the end of the 1980s, when Government reports on lone motherhood focused firmly on the costs of providing benefits for (all) lone mother families, highlighting the extent to which lone mothers were dependent on benefits rather than on wages or on maintenance paid by fathers. The neglect by DSS local offices of the work of pursuing 'liable relatives' (fathers) for maintenance received particular attention and resulted in the passing of the Child Support Act in 1991 (HC 429 (1990)). The increasing emphasis of Government on regulating the responsibility of parents (rather than of husbands and wives) in the face of much greater pluralism in family forms also resulted in attention being directed towards the legal position of unmarried fathers. Historically, the rights of married fathers had been absolute in the nineteenth century and were diluted in the twentieth in order to accommodate the child welfare principle, which forced the recognition of mothers' rights (Brophy 1985; Smart 1991). The price of rights attaching in the first place to married fathers was the complete absence of rights for unmarried fathers, a situation that was unique in Western European countries (Meulders-Klein 1990).

Two Law Commission Reports at the end of the 1970s had raised the possibility of introducing automatic paternal responsibility for unmarried fathers (Law Commission 1979; HC 98 (1982)), prompted in large measure by the growing weight of psychological evidence as to the importance of the role of the father and the lobbying by the pressure group Families Need Fathers in respect of fathers' rights on divorce. However, this proposal encountered strong opposition from the National Council for One Parent Families (1980) and Rights of Women (1980) on the grounds that it might make unmarried mothers more reluctant to acknowledge the father; that it might make mothers more vulnerable to pressure from fathers; and that fathers would have more power *vis-à-vis* third parties such as the local authority. A further Law Commission Report in 1986 recommended legal recognition for unmarried fathers rather than automatic parental rights and this was granted by the 1987 Family Law Reform Act, which abolished the status of illegitimacy while maintaining the distinction between fathers of legitimate and illegitimate children. The unmarried father had to seek parental rights by making an application to the courts, but children whose parents were not married at the time of their birth were given as many claims on their unmarried fathers as legitimate children have on their married fathers. In 1989 the Children Act finally made it possible for unmarried fathers to share parental functions by coming to a private agreement with the mother. Thus while in recent years unmarried mothers have again been singled out for adverse comment, the boundary between married and unmarried fathers has been eroded in order to enforce parental responsibility.

The more polemical political debate only broadened out into a consideration of issues beyond that of public expenditure during the 1990s. English contributions to the debate came from those inclined to the political Left as well as the political Right, from people who were concerned about what they saw as the erosion of decent working-class communities. Dennis and Erdos (1992) sought to trace the rise of the 'obnoxious Englishman' to family breakdown. Similarly, Dench (1994: 17), from a quite different political perspective warned that:

The current attack on patriarchal conventions is surely promoting almost the exact opposite, namely a plague of feckless yobs, who leave all the real work to women and gravitate towards the margins of society where males naturally hang around unless culture gives them a reason to do otherwise. The family maybe a myth, but it is a myth that works to make men tolerably useful.

The chief concern of these writers was the effect of lone motherhood on the behaviour patterns of young men, which meant in turn that they made a firm distinction between the different forms of lone motherhood. Historically, Dennis and Erdos pointed out, the welfare state has 'provided without public controversy least for the single mother and most for the bereaved family [widow]' (1992: 14). By the mid-1970s 'the redundancy of the category of deserving and undeserving had at long last reached the family' (ibid.), something they deplored. In a speech to the Conservative Political Centre in 1993, Michael Howard, the Home Secretary, said: 'If the state will house and pay for their [lone mothers'] children, the duty [young men] to get involved may seem removed from their shoulders. . . . And since the state is educating, housing and feeding their children the nature of parental responsibility may seem less immediate.' Burns and Scott (1994) have emphasized the way in which men and women have adapted rationally to the changing economic climate affecting work and welfare and have become more independent of each other. Whether or not this 'decomplementary theory' is sufficient to explain the changes in behaviour is a matter for debate, but fear of decomplementarity has certainly characterized policy responses in the 1990s.

British writers tended to follow the conservative, authoritarian strand within the American literature, meaning that they had more in common with Gilder and Carlson than with Murray and Mead. Thus Patricia Morgan (1995: 75) saw policies to encourage lone mothers to enter the labour market as 'the solution to the wrong problem' in much the same way as had Gilder in his writing of the early 1980s. Morgan's main concern was to deny that lone mother families had special needs, a view that was accepted by Government in 1995 when it proposed to merge one-parent benefit with child benefit and the lone parent premium with the family premium, freezing both, in order to redress discrimination in favour of one-parent families as compared with two-parent families. Morgan, like Carlson, also argued for more incentives in the form of tax allowances to be given to two-parent families, something that was promised in the Conservative Party's Election Manifesto of 1997. To writers such as Morgan, as well as to politicians (Hansard 1993) and the media (BBC 1993), the main point was to deny that the difference between one- and two-parent families was merely material. They argued that the socialization of children required two parents and in mid-1996 more encouragement was again given to adoption (Department of Health 1996). Individualization and independence were deplored and to the extent that these were deemed to have gone furthest in the behaviour of unmarried mothers, so they were subject to the most condemnation.

Conclusion

Thus in the 1990s, as in the 1950s and early and mid-1960s, the problem of unmarried motherhood was constructed as a moral as well as a social one. Only in the late 1960s, 1970s, and 1980s was unmarried motherhood constructed as a material problem, at first sympathetically and increasingly negatively during the 1980s as the attack on welfare dependency gathered force. During the middle period, unmarried motherhood receded as a social problem in its own right, in part because of the changing composition of lone mother families with the growth in divorce, and in part because of the rhetoric of the permissive moment which deliberately set out to blur the boundaries between the unmarried, the once married, and the married.

The interplay between the changing demographics of lone mother families, attitudes, and the construction of unmarried motherhood has been complicated, but that there has been a set of such relationships is clear. A researcher such as Gill (1977) stated that he began his work with the view that 'unsupported mothers' were adversely affected by existing social policies. It is clear also that he believed, just as had Gough (1971, see above p. 112), that better state support for unmarried mothers would not increase their number. Many commentators in the 1990s have not been so sanguine. But in neither case have the conclusions been based on thorough-going research. Rather, ideas about the proper treatment of unmarried mothers have been as much the result of changes in perception as of real social change.

In the 1950s and most of the 1960s, it was possible to treat unmarried mothers as 'abnormal', either in terms of their immature personalities or, more traditionally, in terms of their 'waywardness'. Rehabilitation via entry into a mother and baby home and, in a large number of cases, adoption followed as the most appropriate solutions to the problem. During the 1970s, the problem of unmarried motherhood was overtaken by the problem of divorce and the distinctions between the two groups were blurred. Both were deemed socially unfortunate, above all in respect of their poverty. During the 1980s and 1990s ideas about the solution to the problem of unmarried motherhood changed dramatically again, and the desirability of meeting the material needs of unmarried mothers was questioned. It may be argued that the increase in the size of the problem of unmarried motherhood is sufficient to explain the changes in approaches to the problem. Certainly, both the extramarital birth rate and ratio have shown a dramatic rise in the more recent period and the reintroduction of the moral dimension of the problem in the 1990s owes much to the parallel decline in two-parenthood. But constructions of unmarried motherhood have also been determined by what has been considered appropriate behaviour for the mothers concerned. In both the 1950s and the 1990s unmarried mothers were deemed inadequate socializers of children, albeit that the push came in the 1950s from those concerned about the immature personalities of the mothers and in the 1990s from those concerned about welfare dependency. It is striking that the problem of unmarried motherhood has, over what is a relatively short period of time, been so completely reconstructed time and again with touching faith that each successive construction constituted truth.

5

Lone Motherhood: Characteristics, Circumstances, and Consequences

Introduction

In the first part of this chapter we examine a range of demographic, social, and economic characteristics of lone mother families, assessing the extent to which the lone mother families differ from one another and from married couple families. We also compare lone mothers of the 1990s with those of the 1980s and 1970s to see whether there have been any changes in the lone mother population over the last two decades. Additionally, we examine the economic circumstances and sources of incomes of women who were lone mothers in the 1990s. This provides a background to the subsequent policy chapters that deal with employment, housing, and social security. In the second part of the chapter we address two issues, namely: who become lone mothers and what are the consequences of family breakdown for children.

Characteristics of Lone Mother Families: 1970s–1990s

Demographic Characteristics

The demographic profiles of lone mothers have implications for the living conditions and circumstances of lone mother families which we discuss later in the chapter. We examined a number of demographic characteristics including: the marital status and age distribution of mothers with dependent children; the ages and numbers of children; the ages at which the women became mothers, as well as assessing the extent to which the profiles of lone mother families have changed over the last twenty years. From the data shown in Table 5.1, which are derived from analysis of the annual rounds of the General Household Survey for the depicted years, we see that the proportion of families with children under age 16 that were lone mother families has

TABLE 5.1. *Demographic characteristics*

	1973–5	1981–3	1991–3
Marital status (%)			
Never-married	18	23	40
Separated and divorced	60	64	55
Widowed	22	13	5
Lone mother families as % of all families with dependent children	8	12	19
Total number of lone mothers	1,073	1,230	1,676
Median age and inter-quartile range in years			
Lone mothers	36 (28–43)	34 (27–41)	31 (26–48)
Never-married	25 (20–30)	25 (21–32)	26 (22–30)
Separated and divorced	35 (28–41)	34 (29–41)	35 (30–40)
Widowed	45 (39–50)	46 (39–51)	41 (37–46)
Married mothers	35 (28–41)	35 (30–40)	35 (30–41)
All mothers	35 (28–41)	35 (29–40)	34 (29–40)
Percentage with child under age 5			
All lone mothers	32	35	48
Never-married	69	64	70
Separated and divorced	30	29	35
Widowed	7	22	(20)[a]
Married mothers	44	40	45
All mothers	43	39	47
Percentage with 2 or more children			
All lone mothers	48	44	48
Never-married	21	19	36
Separated and divorced	57	54	58
Widowed	45	36	43
Married mothers	63	61	62
All mothers	62	58	59
Percentage who became mothers in their teens			
All lone mothers	na	35	38
Never-married	na	40	47
Separated and divorced	na	35	32
Widowed	na	24	25
Married mothers	na	17	14
All mothers	na	20	20
TOTAL NUMBER IN SAMPLE	13,456	10,830	8,684

[a] less than 20 cases.

Source: General Household Survey data for the specified years.

increased over the last twenty years from 8 per cent in the early
1970s, to 12 per cent in the early 1980s, and to 19 per cent in the
early 1990s. In the early parts of the 1970s and 1980s the majority of
lone mother families emanated from marital breakdown, over 60 per
cent, and the proportions of never-married lone mothers were 18 and
23 per cent, respectively. In the early 1970s widowed lone mother
families were the second largest group of lone mother families (22
per cent) but by the 1980s constituted the smallest group (13 per
cent). By the early 1990s there had been more noticeable changes in
the constituent parts of the lone mother population: with 55 per cent
divorced and separated, 40 per cent never-married lone mothers
although not necessarily never-partnered (the evidence from the PSI
survey presented in Table 2.16 in Chapter 2 suggested that one in
two of these single lone mothers may have never been partnered),
and 5 per cent were widowed lone mothers. The median ages and
age distributions, represented by the inter-quartile range, of the
different groups of lone mothers has shown no marked change
over the last two decades. Within the set of lone mothers the
never-married group are noticeably younger than the divorced/sepa-
rated group: some ten years on average, with a median age of around
25 years as compared with around 35 years amongst the divorced and
separated group. The age structure of the divorced and separated
lone mothers is similar to that of married mothers in general,
whereas widowed lone mothers have the highest average age.
Widowed mothers, not surprisingly being on average older, are the
least likely to have children under 5 years of age. There is a marked
contrast in the proportions of separated/divorced lone mothers and
never-married lone mothers with children under age 5. Single lone
mothers are twice as likely as the separated and divorced group to
have a young child and they in turn are less likely to have young
children than married mothers. Given that young children tend to be
an important constraint on being in the labour market, then it would
be expected that single lone mothers are the least likely, other things
being equal, to be self-supporting. We also examined whether different groups of mothers were more or less likely to have two or more
children. As we see in Table 5.1, the married and separated/divorced
lone mothers are more likely than the single lone mothers to have
two or more children. Widowed lone mothers also have smaller
families but this is likely to be due in part to their children being
older and no longer classified as dependent. The noteworthy change

over time with respect to numbers of children is that by the 1990s more of the single lone mothers had more than one child: 36 per cent as compared with around 20 per cent in the early 1970s and 1980s. A plausible explanation for this is that never-married lone mothers, more so than in 1970s and 1980s, include women who have been in cohabiting couple families that have subsequently dissolved. Furthermore, there is evidence that during the 1980s there had been an increase in the number of never-married women progressing to a second or higher order birth (Kiernan and Estaugh 1993). The final demographic characteristic examined here is age at entry into motherhood, in particular the extent to which the different groups of women became mothers in their teenage years. These data were not available for the early 1970s. It is apparent from Table 5.1 that lone mothers, particularly the never-married and separated/divorced lone mothers were more likely to have had their first child in their teens than married mothers. Amongst women included in the 1991–3 surveys nearly one in two of the never-married lone mothers and one in three of the separated/divorced lone mothers had had a child in their teens as compared with one in seven of the married mothers.

Employment Trends

Earnings from employment constitute the major source of income for most families with children. Married fathers tend to be the major earner in two-parent families whereas in lone mother families a mother's earning capacity is the important factor in determining the family's economic well-being. However, on average lone mothers earn less than married fathers which is related to the more general problem of women's low wage rates. Even women who work full-time all year round tend to only earn about 70 per cent of male earnings and this gap is only closing slowly (EOC 1995). However, as we see in Table 5.2 the majority of British lone mothers were not in employment in the early 1990s and compared with the early 1970s the proportion of lone mothers in the labour force has declined. Given that the presence of young children can be an important constraint on whether women are in paid work or not, Table 5.2 shows the proportions of lone mothers and married mothers working according to whether their youngest child was under 5 years of age, age 5–9 years, and age 10–15 years. Over the last two decades the proportions of mothers in employment whose youngest child was aged 5–9 years has hovered around the 60

TABLE 5.2. *Percentage of mothers working or seeking work by age of youngest child*

	1973–5	1981–3	1991–3
All mothers			
All lone mothers	51	41	39
Never-married	43	30	30
Separated and divorced	52	44	45
Widowed	55	43	41
Married mothers	48	49	62
All mothers	48	47	57
Age of youngest child under age 5			
Lone mothers	33	18	23
Never-married	36	17	21
Separated and divorced	30	20	24
Widowed	41	21	25
Married mothers	27	25	50
All mothers	27	24	43
Age of youngest child age 5–9 years			
All lone mothers	56	49	49
Never-married	55	51	48
Separated and divorced	59	49	50
Widowed	49	38	50
Married mothers	61	57	67
All mothers	61	56	63
Age of youngest child age 10–15 years			
All lone mothers	62	55	59
Never-married	65	55	55
Separated and divorced	64	59	62
Widowed	60	47	42
Married mothers	68	69	77
All mothers	67	68	74
TOTAL NUMBER IN SAMPLE	13,456	10,830	8,684

Source: General Household Survey data for the specified years

per cent level. Similarly the proportions working whose youngest child was aged 10–15 years has been fairly stable at around the 70 per cent level. However, this seemingly static picture disguises differences in the trends between married and lone mothers, whereas the direction of change in the propensity to be in paid employment amongst married mothers has been clearly upwards that for lone mothers has tended to be downwards. But the most noteworthy change in the proportions of married mothers in employment as compared with lone mother families is with respect to children under 5 years. For example, in the early 1990s as compared with the early years of the 1970s and 1980s there has been a doubling in the proportions of married mothers with young children who are in the labour force, from around 25 per cent to 50 per cent, but there has been no parallel increase amongst lone mother families. In fact the proportions of all lone mothers with young children who were in employment decreased between the 1970s and 1980s and had not exhibited any increase by the early 1990s.

The information contained in Table 5.2 also allows us to examine whether there are any differences in the employment behaviour of the different groups of lone mothers. Overall, as well as over time, never-married lone mothers have been less likely to be in employment than separated and divorced or widowed lone mothers. For example, in the early 1990s 30 per cent of never-married lone mothers were in the labour market as compared with 45 and 41 per cent, respectively of the separated/divorced and widowed mothers. For the 1990s the difference in the proportions of never-married lone mothers and separated and divorced lone mothers with younger children, under age 10 years, who were in paid employment was not substantial but it was somewhat more marked for mothers with older children, but this difference could have arisen by chance.

In the 1990s most British lone mothers are not in paid work and as a consequence a sizeable proportion of lone mothers have no earnings from employment. Moreover, amongst the lone mothers who were in paid employment 6 out of 10 worked part-time and thus are likely to have to depend on additional sources of income to support themselves and their children. Amongst lone mothers there has been a general movement to relatively fewer of them being in paid employment and amongst those in work for less of them to work full-time. As we see in Table 5.3 in the early 1970s the majority of single and separated/divorced employed lone mothers were in full-time employment whereas in the 1990s more were in part-time than in full-time employment. Working part-time has been typical behaviour amongst married mothers and lone mothers have become more like married mothers in this respect.

TABLE 5.3. *Percentage of mothers working part-time and full-time*

	1973–5		1981–3		1991–3	
	Part-time[a]	Full-time	Part-time	Full-time	Part-time	Full-time
All lone mothers	21	30	22	19	22	17
Never-married	10	33	11	19	17	13
Separated and divorced	20	32	24	20	26	19
Widowed	31	24	28	15	20	20
Married mothers	32	16	35	15	39	23
All mothers	31	17	32	16	35	22

[a] Part-time is under 30 hours a week.

Source: General Household Survey data for the specified years.

Housing Tenure

The long-standing and heavy reliance of lone mother families on public housing is evident from Table 5.4. Lone mother families may be relatively more prominent than two-parent families in the local authority sector in part because people who are most at risk of lone parenthood (e.g. the lower social classes, the less educated, young parents) are more likely to gain entry into the local authority sector in the first place, as well as families who experience marital separation moving out of owner occupation into local authority accommodation, as a result of reduced economic circumstances (Grundy 1989). In the 1990s we see that a majority of the never-married lone mothers were in local authority housing (74 per cent), that widowed lone mothers were the least likely of the lone mothers to be in this type of tenure (35 per cent), and the separated and divorced lone mothers held an intermediate position (53 per cent). In contrast the majority (78 per cent) of married couple families were owner occupiers. As the Finer Committee noted in their recommendations, 'second only to financial difficulties and to a considerable extent exacerbated by them, housing is the largest single problem of one parent families' (Cmnd. 5629 (1974): 501). Whatever the impetus towards local authority housing, selection or contingency, it is evident that public housing is fulfilling an important basic requirement.

TABLE 5.4. *Housing tenure*

	1973–5			1981–3			1991–3		
	Owner-occupier	Local authority	Other	Owner-occupier	Local authority	Other	Owner-occupier	Local authority	Other
All lone mothers (%)	27	57	15	25	69	6	32	61	8
Never-married (%)	19	60	21	12	83	5	17	74	9
Separated and divorced (%)	25	58	16	27	66	6	40	53	7
Widowed (%)	39	53	8	36	57	7	59	35	5
Married mothers (%)	55	34	11	66	28	6	78	17	5
All mothers (%)	53	36	11	60	34	6	67	27	6
NUMBER IN SAMPLE	7,152	4,785	1,519	6,538	3,659	633	5,827	2,317	540

Source: General Household Survey data for the specified years.

Living Arrangements

Whom we live with is a significant aspect of everyday life. Household membership frequently defines a set of primary relationships, a pool of resources, and the persons with whom resources are shared with different arrangements affecting the economic, social, and emotional well-being of individual members. Over the last two decades there have been some noteworthy changes in the living arrangements of lone mother families. In the early part of the 1970s, as shown in Table 5.5, 48 per cent of never-married lone mothers lived with their parents, whereas 35 per cent were doing so in the early 1980s, and only 16 per cent were living at home in the early 1990s. A similar development can be seen for the separated and divorced lone mothers: with 14 per cent living with their parents in the early 1970s as compared with 8 and 5 per cent in the early 1980s and 1990s, respectively. Over time there has been a general movement to living in single family units and away from sharing with others, a movement probably facilitated both by the growth in the availability of housing units and a growing preference for independent living. Some of the reduction in never-married lone mothers living with their parents is also likely to be related to the enactment of the 1977 Housing and Homeless Persons Act, which made local authorities duty-bound to provide accommodation not only for homeless people but for people threatened with homelessness. Before this Act, local authorities only had a duty to provide housing for people who became unforeseeably homeless, and pregnancy did not qualify under this category (Arden 1978).

Are lone mothers living with their parents more likely to be working? It might be a reasonable assumption that care by grandparents is easier to organize if daughters and their children live in three-generation households, although many lone mothers may live in close proximity to their parents which may also facilitate childcare, but we have no information on this. As we see in Table 5.6 in the earliest period, the 1970s, it was not uncommon for never-married lone mothers with young children who were living with their parents to work and to work full-time: in the period 1973–5, 40 per cent were working full-time and 8 per cent part time. Never-married lone mothers living on their own were less likely to be working than those living with their parents (17 per cent worked full-time and 9 per cent worked part-time). These mothers who were living independently had a similar level of overall employment to all separated and divorced lone mothers (30 per cent) as

TABLE 5.5. *Living arrangements*

	1973–5			1981–3			1991–3		
	Alone[a]	With parents	With others	Alone	With parents	With others	Alone	With parents	With others
All lone mothers (%)	72	18	10	80	14	7	86	9	5
Never-married (%)	37	48	15	59	35	6	79	16	5
Separated and divorced (%)	76	14	10	85	8	7	91	5	4
Widowed (%)	87	6	6	88	5	7	92	4	4
Married mothers (%)	93	4	3	95	3	2	96	2	2
All mothers (%)	91	5	4	93	4	3	94	4	2
NUMBER IN SAMPLE	12,290	677	489	10,028	477	325	8,160	323	201

[a] A single adult person household in the case of lone mothers or in the case of cohabiting and married mothers a couple household.

Source: General Household Survey data for the specified years.

TABLE 5.6. *Percentage of mothers with youngest child under age 5 in employment by marital status and living arrangements*

	1973–5		1981–3		1991–3	
	Part-time[a]	Full-time	Part-time	Full-time	Part-time	Full-time
Lone mothers						
Never-married						
living with						
parents	8	40	10	12	10	16
living alone	9	17	19	6	14	6
Separated and	14	16	15	5	17	8
divorced						
Married mothers	20	6	19	6	34	16

[a] Part-time is under 30 hours a week

Source: General Household Survey data for the specified years.

well as their married contemporaries (26 per cent), but proportionately more of the lone mothers than married mothers were working full-time. Higher rates of full-time work amongst lone mothers may be due to the need for higher earnings to support themselves and their children, given that they are the sole earner. Moreover, the opportunities for part-time work may be less if one has to organize formal childcare as opposed to depending on relatives. By the early 1980s (1981–3) amongst the never-married lone mothers who were living with their parents the proportions in employment had declined by over 50 per cent (from 48 to 22 per cent) and amongst those working the proportions working full-time declined from eight out of ten of working lone mothers to just over one in two. In contrast to developments amongst married mothers, particularly the dramatic growth in the labour force participation of those with young children, the labour-market behaviour of lone mothers changed very little between the early 1980s and 1990s. However, it is still the case that never-married lone mothers living with their parents are more likely to be working full-time (16 per cent) than their contemporaries living alone (6 per cent). But we also note that nowadays the majority of lone mothers, over 80 per cent, do not live with their parents. The opportunities for child care by grandmothers is also much less nowadays compared with the early 1970s, as recent generations of grandmothers tend on average to be younger and are themselves more likely to be in the labour market and thus less likely to be available to provide regular child care for their grandchildren.

Educational Qualifications

Since the 1970s more people have been acquiring qualifications either during their school and college careers or later in life. As can be seen in Table 5.7, in the early 1970s only 9 per cent of mothers had A-level qualifications or higher compared with the early 1990s when 25 per cent of mothers had this level of qualification. There was also a concomitant decline in the proportions with no qualifications from 62 per cent in the early 1970s to 28 per cent in the early 1990s. The most noticeable change in the upward movement in the qualification distribution has occurred since the 1980s. All women have benefited from the expansion in educational qualifications but one notes that lone mothers are the least likely to have higher level qualifications and, over time, are proportionately less likely to hold high-level qualifications. There has been a threefold increase in the proportions of married mothers with A-level or higher qualifications between the 1970s and 1990s and a twofold increase amongst the lone mothers. The lower level of qualifications amongst the lone mothers is of some importance in that the more qualified, other things being equal, are more likely to have higher status occupations and higher levels of remuneration. Moreover, as we see in Table 5.8 amongst mothers with young children those with higher qualifications are more likely to be in employment. For example in the 1990s, the proportion of mothers with A-level or higher qualifications who were in the labour market was more than double that of mothers with no qualifications (59 per cent as compared with 24 per cent). Highly qualified married mothers were also more likely to be in employment than lone mothers but lone mothers with qualifications were more likely to be working than their unqualified contemporaries. The greater labour-market participation of lone mothers with some qualifications can also be seen for the early 1980s, but is less clear-cut for the 1970s. One also sees that compared with the early 1970s there has been a threefold decline in proportion of unqualified never-married and separated and divorced lone mothers in employment and a twofold decline amongst the never-married with intermediate level qualifications whereas the proportions of post-marital lone mothers with advanced level qualifications who are in employment has been more stable over time.

TABLE 5.7. *Educational qualifications*

	1973–5		1981–3		1991–3	
	% A-level or higher	% none	% A-level or higher	% none	% A-level or higher	% none
All lone mothers	7	71	10	60	16	38
Never-married	6	70	9	58	12	37
Separated and divorced	7	72	10	60	19	37
Widowed	9	70	10	63	20	44
Married mothers	9	62	14	50	28	26
All mothers	9	62	14	51	25	28
NUMBER IN SAMPLE	1,198	8,394	7,480	5,514	2,183	2,479

Source: General Household Survey data for the specified years.

TABLE 5.8. *Percentage of mothers working with a child under age 5, according to level of highest qualification*

	1973–5			1981–3			1991–3		
	Advanced	Intermediate	None	Advanced	Intermediate	None	Advanced	Intermediate	None
All lone mothers	(41)	45	35	38	34	17	36	28	11
Never-married	(14)	52	43	27	39	20	29	25	12
Separated and divorced	(60)	38	30	42	30	16	40	31	10
Widowed	—	—	46	—	33	9	(50)	(20)	(—)
Married mothers	37	27	29	42	30	26	62	49	31
All mothers	37	28	29	41	31	24	59	44	24
NUMBER IN SAMPLE	576	1,710	3,312	714	1,694	1,795	1,079	2,007	920

( ) Less than 10 cases.

Source: General Household Survey data for the specified years.

The lower level of employment amongst lone mothers with similar qualifications to married mothers suggests that there may be specific factors that curb the employment of lone mothers. An important factor might be their sole responsibility for childcare. The most recent large-scale survey of working mothers' use of childcare (Meltzer, 1994) carried out in 1990 showed that most common forms of child care used by working parents in two-parent families was the father (32 per cent), followed by a grandparent (32 per cent), with playgroups and nurseries used by around 20 per cent of parents, and childminders and other forms used by about 10 per cent or less of parents. In contrast in lone mother families where the mother worked, grandparents were the major providers of childcare (52 per cent), followed by day nurseries (21 per cent), childminders (17 per cent), friends and neighbours (17 per cent), nursery class or school (16 per cent), playgroup (15 per cent), other relatives (13 per cent), parent and toddler group (12 per cent), the father (10 per cent), and other forms of care accounting for under 10 per cent. These figures do not sum to 100 per cent as working parents frequently use multiple forms of childcare. Moreover, the paucity of childcare provision in Britain may be an important part of the explanation for why lone mothers in Britain are less likely to be in employment than their counterparts in other European countries (Bradshaw 1996).

Economic Circumstances of Lone Mother Families

Income

The most striking difference between lone mother families and two-parent families is the disparity in their financial well-being, which arises from the precarious economic position of lone mothers and the diseconomies of scale associated with the maintenance of two households, when fathers live apart from their children. In 1993, 5 per cent of two-parent families with dependent children had a gross weekly household income of under £100 compared with 46 per cent of lone mother families (Table 5.9). Amongst the lone mother families, never-married mothers are amongst the poorest group of all the lone mother families, with 60 per cent of this group having incomes of below £100 in 1993 as compared with around 40 per cent of separated and divorced lone mothers.

The General Household Survey does not allow us to distinguish

TABLE 5.9 *Usual gross weekly household income in £ by family type*

	Under 100	100–150	150–350	350 plus	Base = 100%
Married couples (%)	5	7	31	56	2,268
All lone mothers (%)	46	21	23	9	603
Never-married (%)	60	17	16	6	230
Separated (%)	38	23	34	6	126
Divorced (%)	41	25	21	12	216
Widowed (%)	(13)	(26)	(42)	(19)	31

Sources: OPCS 1995*b*: report table 2.30.

between never-married lone mother families emanating from the breakdown of cohabiting unions as opposed to those arising from solo motherhood. The DSS/PSI studies (Ford, Marsh, and McKay 1995: table 3.2) provide some information for these two groups of women. In the 1993 survey the estimated mean net income for solo mothers was £95, that for those who had previously lived in a cohabiting union was £110, and divorced and separated lone mothers had mean incomes of £141 and £128, respectively. Not all the erstwhile cohabitants in this sample were never married, it is estimated that about one in five had been married but that prior to entry into lone parenthood they were cohabiting (Marsh, Ford, and Finlayson 1997). Net household income does not take into account the fact that needs vary according to family size and ages of children, as do the opportunities for taking paid employment. The use of equivalence scales allows one to control for different circumstances. When Ford and his colleagues (Ford, Marsh, and McKay 1995) used such scales to control for differing family structures they found that the income differentials between different types of lone mother families remained but were narrowed with the mean equivalent incomes for the solo mothers, erstwhile cohabitants, and the divorced and separated lone mother families being £107, £115, £118, and £125, respectively. Thus the erstwhile cohabitants were more similar to their divorced contemporaries than the uneqivalenced data may have led us to believe.

Although some lone mothers are poor before they become lone mothers, undoubtedly many become poor at the time of partnership breakdown. Few studies have prospectively tracked the economic circumstances of families prior to and after divorce. The US Panel Study of Income Dynamics (PSID) is an all too rare and good example of a study that permitted the examination of the economic status of women with children before and after divorce. The general conclusions from this study (G. J. Duncan and Rodgers 1987) were that family income declines steeply after divorce for lone mothers but the decline is less dramatic for men. After divorce men were found to actually have a higher standard of living whilst amongst women, who did not remarry, standards of living changed very little. Furthermore, Hoffman and Duncan (1988) estimated, again using the PSID, that the income of mothers and their children one year after divorce was only 67 per cent of their pre-divorce income, whereas the income of divorced men was about 90 per cent of their pre-divorce income. This study convincingly demonstrated that the widely quoted figures from Weitzman's book, *The Divorce Revolution* (1985), were almost certainly too high, namely that women's standard of living fell by 73 per cent and men's rose by 42 per cent after divorce. Another study (Burkhauser et al. 1991) which compared American and German divorcees (in the PSID and the German Socio-Economic Panel Study) showed that German women experienced even sharper drops in their standard of living after divorce than their American sisters but the men from both countries fared about the same. There is also Australian research which shows that the income situation of children in lone mother families did not bear very much relationship to their level of father's income during the marriage; children with high-earning fathers were as likely to be poor after the divorce as children with low-earning fathers (McDonald and Weston 1986). British women also experience substantial drops in family income following marital separation. It has been calculated by researchers on the British Household Panel Study (BHPS), a longitudinal study of households that has interviewed household members annually since 1990, that almost 50 per cent of the women who experienced marital breakdown between 1990 and 1992 saw their household income fall by two or more deciles whilst for men there was a slight tendency for their household income to increase and only 17 per cent experienced a fall of two or more deciles (Taylor et al. 1994). These disparities in the financial consequences of separation between men and women are hardly surprising given the noticeable differences in the labour-market position of men and women.

Earnings from employment constitute the major source of income for most families with children. However, as we have seen the majority of British lone mothers are not in employment (60 per cent in the early part of the 1990s) and thus a sizeable proportion of lone mothers actually have no earnings from employment, added to this only 17 per cent of all lone mothers in the same period worked full-time. Employed lone mothers as chief economic providers for their families also frequently earn less than married fathers who still tend to be the major earner in two-parent families. The low earnings capacity of lone mothers is obviously related to the more general problem of women's low wage rates. Aside from low wages, a major barrier to employment for most mothers is child care. Whereas in two-parent families the second parent can provide child care or share its cost, the lone mother has no such support. Thus, she is doubly disadvantaged with respect to earnings potential: her wage or salary that she can command is likely to be lower than that of the highest earner in a two-parent family, and her childcare costs are likely to be higher. The financial well-being of lone mother families depends to a large extent on other sources of income than those from earnings with the other two main sources being maintenance payments from the biological father and state support via public transfers. We discuss each in turn.

Child Maintenance Payments

Child support from the father of the child or children is a minor source of income in most lone mother families. In 1993 less than one in three (30 per cent) lone mothers were receiving regular child maintenance (Ford, Marsh, and McKay 1995). Post-marital lone mothers are more likely to be in receipt of maintenance than never-married lone mothers. For example amongst the mothers included in 1993 DSS/PSI survey (ibid: table 5.4), 43 per cent of the divorced, 31 per cent of the separated, and 23 per cent of the never-married lone mothers were in receipt of maintenance. Amongst this latter group there was no difference in the proportions of erstwhile cohabitants and solo mothers who were in receipt of maintenance although in the analogous 1991 survey proportionately more of the cohabitants than the solo mothers had received maintenance (McKay and Marsh 1994). The majority of mothers were not in receipt of maintenance. The most frequent reasons given for why lone mothers had not sought maintenance from their ex-partners were: they thought their ex-partner could not afford to pay it (31 per cent); they did not want to have contact with their ex-partner (27 per cent); and they did not know the whereabouts of their ex-partner (16 per cent) (Ford, Marsh, and McKay 1995: table 5.7). Even when non-residential fathers pay child support, the amount tends to be low and post-marital lone mothers tend to receive higher levels of payment than the never-married lone mothers. In the DSS/PSI 1993 survey the average (mean) amount of weekly maintenance was £33 amongst the divorced, £48 amongst the separated lone mothers, whilst the two groups of never-married mothers had similar levels being £23 amongst the ex-cohabitants and £21 amongst the solo mothers (ibid: table 5.8). Somewhat paradoxically lone mothers in work are more likely to be in receipt of maintenance than those not in work. This reflects compositional factors, namely these lone mothers are more likely to be better educated and to have been married to more educated men with higher levels of remuneration and these men are more likely to be in a position to pay maintenance. Amongst those in part-time and full-time work around 40 per cent were in receipt of maintenance as compared with 25 per cent of those not in paid work (ibid: table 5.5).

There is near unanimity amongst the British public that fathers should be made to make maintenance payments to support their children (Kiernan 1992a). More problematic is determining what share of the cost of raising a child should be borne by the non-residential parent. Before the advent of the Child Support Agency formulae it depended on value judgements with some arguing that child support should depend on the 'needs of the child' and that the father's obligations should vary according to the mother's earnings. For example, analysis of the 1991 British Social Attitudes Survey showed that nine out of ten of the respondents to this survey believed that the level of payment should depend on the father's income but there was less unanimity about whether the level of support should depend on the mother's income, overall 67 per cent thought it should (ibid.).

Since a substantial proportion of divorced people remarry the 1991 survey also enquired whether remarriage should affect the payment of child maintenance. The question was as follows: 'Suppose the mother remarries—should the father go on paying maintenance for the child, should he stop, or should it depend on the new husband's income?'

As we see in Table 5.10, only 16 per cent said that the father should stop paying child maintenance altogether, whilst a further 38 per cent believed that it should depend on the income of the new stepfather. These attitudes to the continuation of maintenance payments on remarriage of the mother suggest that people are less positive about support from the father when the mother forms a new partnership. This perhaps implies that the role of biological father is not seen by everyone as entailing a life-time commitment to the maintenance of children. Rather stepfathers are also expected to and do contribute to the maintenance of

TABLE 5.10. *Remarriage and maintenance*

	All (%)	Men (%)	Women (%)
On mother's remarriage, child maintenance from the father should:			
Continue	42	32	51
Stop	16	20	13
Depend on the new husband's income	38	44	33

Source: 1991 *British Social Attitudes Survey* (Kiernan, 1992).

their stepchildren. However, the centrality and emphasis of biological fatherhood in the terms of reference of the CSA may diminish the role of social fatherhood. People also did not discriminate as between married and cohabiting parents, there was general agreement that fathers should continue to support their children following separation, regardless of whether couples were legally married.

State Support

The major source of income for lone mother families in Britain is public transfers. Research for the Department of Social Security by Bradshaw and Millar (1991) and Marsh and colleagues at the Policy Studies Institute who have monitored the current and changing circumstances of lone mothers since 1990 in the DSS/PSI surveys have consistently shown the dominance of social security benefits in the composition of income amongst lone mothers (Marsh and McKay 1993a; McKay and Marsh 1994; Ford, Marsh, and McKay 1995; Ford, Marsh, and Finlayson 1996). In the 1990s, Income Support, Family Credit, and Child Benefit alone supplied nearly two-thirds of an average lone parent income; about one-quarter came from earnings; 10 per cent from maintenance; and 5 per cent from elsewhere, mainly other benefits. Thus the majority of lone mothers in Britain are dependent on the state to support themselves and their children and the level of that support determines their economic well-being.

Remarriage

Improvements in the economic well-being of lone mothers and their children has been remarkably dependent on remarriage (Duncan and

Rodgers 1987; Bradshaw 1989). Lone mothers who marry or remarry boost their income level and are also the group most likely to move out of poverty (Millar 1989). However, with the growth in cohabitation and unemployment, the benefits of re-partnering have become more nuanced. Ford, Marsh, and Finlayson (1996) observe that entering a new partnership is not necessarily 'a passport to prosperity'. In many cases particularly when the new union is a cohabitation rather than a marriage, it is often the start of further economic difficulties as such partnerships tend to be more fragile, with some new partners not staying very long. The group of lone mothers most likely to prosper in a new partnership are those who are employed and whose new partner is also in employment. The best route out of hardship for all families is undoubtedly to have both partners in employment.

International Comparisons

Research using the Luxembourg Income Study has shown that the extent of financial deprivation in lone mother families varies between countries (Sorensen 1990; Hauser and Fischer 1990). Hauser and Fischer's analyses of the Luxembourg Income Study which used data from six countries (Sweden, West Germany, United Kingdom, Israel, Canada, and the United States) showed that the economic welfare position of lone parent families in all six countries was worse than that of two-parent families (they compared lone parent families with minor children and married couples with minor children). The relative welfare positions showed Sweden to be the most favourable with the discrepancy between one- and two-parent families being rather small (13 per cent). The middle group consisted of West Germany, Israel, and the United Kingdom with a difference of around 20 per cent. In Canada the welfare position of lone parent families was on average about 34 per cent below that of two-parent families, and the USA the difference was over 40 per cent.

   Sweden has come closest to solving the economic problems of lone-mother families. Swedish lone mothers tend to have lower incomes than their married counterparts, but few of them are defined as poor. Generous public benefits and high labour-force participation of Swedish mothers accounted to a large extent for the relatively better position of Swedish lone mothers. The intermediate position of West German and British lone mothers were due to different reasons. West German lone mothers had high labour participation rates (but this was not the case for married mothers in general), but there were less generous public transfers in favour of lone parent families. In Britain lone mothers have lower labour-force participation rates than married mothers, but there is relatively higher levels of state support compared with Germany and the USA.

In a more recent comparative study of the employment of lone parents in 20 industrialized countries, including all the EU countries, the USA, Japan, Norway, Australia, and New Zealand, Bradshaw and colleagues (Bradshaw et al. 1996) showed that the UK has one of the largest gaps between the employment rates of married mothers and lone mothers and that the trend we observed earlier of a decline since the 1970s in the extent to which lone mothers are in employment is the converse of what has occurred in most other industrialized countries. They conclude that the key factor affecting the employment of British lone mothers appears to be the relatively high level of childcare costs in the United Kingdom as compared with most other countries. The United Kingdom has a very limited number of publicly provided child care places and the alternatives in the private sector are unsubsidized. It is estimated that mothers in the United Kingdom pay more for full-time childcare than in any of the other countries.

Who Become Lone Mothers?

Our analysis thus far has largely been confined to the current characteristics and circumstances of lone mother families. Here we take a different perspective and pose the question who become lone mothers? We examine the evidence as to whether there are particular attributes or life experiences that predispose one to lone parenthood or is it more or less a random experience.

Given the recency of the rise in never-married lone motherhood there is as yet only very limited research on this group of mothers (Burghes and Brown 1995). However, we showed earlier that a substantial proportion of the never-married lone mothers become mothers in their teens and one study (Kiernan 1997) has shown that although there are striking variations in the probabilities of becoming a young mother there was little to distinguish between young mothers who have a child within or outside marriage, either on their own or in a cohabiting union. Young mothers, per se, were more likely to come from socially and economically disadvantaged families and to have lower educational attainment but this was largely invariant with respect to the partnership context of teenage motherhood. As yet, there is little information on whether older mothers who have a child outside marriage either on their own or in a cohabiting union differ significantly in their background characteristics from each other or their contemporaries who have a child within marriage.

However, on the question as to who become post-marital lone mothers the literature on the divorced population provides a number of insights. One of the most robust and consistent findings in divorce research is that the earlier a partnership is formed the more likely it is to breakdown and this persists up to high durations of marriage (Murphy 1985; Hoem 1991). In Britain youthful marriages, and its frequent corollary youthful parenthood, occurs most frequently amongst women with the least advantaged family backgrounds, educational and occupational careers (Kiernan 1997). These women are also the most likely to have married men with no or few qualifications and who were in manual occupations (Kiernan 1986). Such backgrounds are the least auspicious for coping with the exigencies and deprivations associated with marital breakdown. The women do not possess the skills and qualifications necessary for obtaining highly paid jobs, which would enable them to support themselves and their children; the parents of the women are unlikely to possess sufficient resources to support their daughters; and their ex-husbands are also the least likely to make a significant contribution to the support of their ex-wives and children. This suggests that lone parenthood as well as reducing the economic situation of mothers and their children may also be selective of women in poorer economic circumstances, which would reinforce the economic plight of lone mothers.

Demographic factors other than age at marriage implicated in marital breakdown include having a pre-marital birth (Kravdal 1988; Bracher et al. 1993) cohabiting prior to marriage (Bennett, Blanc, and Bloom 1988; Haskey 1992), having a spouse who has been previously married (T. C. Martin and Bumpass 1989; Haskey 1983a), and having parents who had themselves divorced (Mueller and Pope 1977; Kiernan 1986; McLanahan and Bumpass 1988). Having a child prior to marriage and cohabiting prior to marriage are independently associated with a higher risk of divorce. This begs the question as to whether this increased risk of disruption is a direct consequence of having a child outside of marriage or whether the act of having a child prior to marrying indicates something about the woman herself. The experience of raising a child on one's own prior to marriage may mean that in the event of an unsatisfactory marriage women may be more confident that they can cope independently and thus be more willing to dissolve the partnership. Alternatively, having a child prior to marriage or cohabiting prior to marriage may reflect a weaker adherence to traditional norms about marriage, particularly the permanence of marriage. The greater fragility of marriages where one partner has been married before may also be due to the willingness of those with a prior experience to be more ready to dissolve an unsatisfactory marriage. Some also argue that attributes (Martin and Bumpass 1989) that increased the chances of a first marriage terminating are also carried into the second marriage whilst others (White and Booth 1985) argue second marriages are more complicated, especially if there are children from a previous marriage. Additionally, a substantial part, but not all, of the association between divorce in childhood and partnership dissolution in adulthood is accounted for by the earlier age at marriage or first partnership amongst children who experienced parental divorce (Glenn and Kramer 1987; Kiernan 1997b).

Economic factors are also related to divorce—the main ones being wives' participation in the labour market (Ermisch 1989) and husbands' unemployment (Haskey 1984), both of which have a positive effect on the risk of separation. There are a number of explanations for the link between women's employment and marital disruption. For example, working outside the home increases the chances of meeting alternative partners; having one's own earnings may lower economic barriers to dissolution; the strains of combining work and family life may also be implicated. Strains, both financial and emotional, may well be implicated in the higher probability of divorce found amongst couples where the husband is unemployed.

This evidence on the relationship between demographic and economic variables and divorce is not matched to the same extent by empirical research in other domains. As White (1990: 907) in her review of research in the 1980s on the determinants of divorce (mainly US studies) notes that 'although we have made substantial progress in the last decade, we still know comparatively little about how divorce is related to relationship quality, family structure or socio-psychological factors'. The prominence of demographic and economic correlates in divorce research may also reflect the absence of appropriate surveys of representative samples of the population for studying family processes. Much of what we know comes from secondary analysis of more

general purpose surveys rather than ones designed to examine family
dynamics, relationships, and processes, and this situation needs to be
rectified.

Consequences of Family Breakdown

As was highlighted in Chapter 1, the growth in lone mother families,
their economic plight, and the consequences for the mothers, fathers,
and children involved has provoked a good deal of discussion in Britain
over recent years. The subject of lone motherhood is politically
charged, as it often involves conflicting values and competing interests
in the allocation of state resources. The poverty of lone mothers
demonstrates the economic vulnerability inherent in women's role as
mothers and highlights the relatively low earning capacity and the
disproportionate responsibility for children that is shared by all
women. Lone mothers being amongst the poorest members of our
society their condition is relevant to debates over inequality between
social groups and particularly the care and support of children. It is to
the consequences of family breakdown for children that we now turn
our attention.

Amongst British children born since the 1950s, divorce has replaced
death as the main cause of family disruption and the rate of divorce has
been increasing such that (as we saw in Chapter 2, Table 2.14) one in
four children born during the 1970s had experienced the break-up of
their parents' marriage by the time they were aged 16 years. This rise
in divorce is one of the most significant developments in family life
over the last 30 years, that brings to the fore fundamental issues about
the care and support of children within society. Given the recency of
the rise in never-married lone motherhood, arising from either solo
motherhood or the break-up of cohabiting unions, we have no robust
research that allows us to examine any effects of this development,
either in the short or more long term, on the lives of the children and
parents involved. Most of the research to date relates to the fallout
from the termination of marriage and it is to this issue that we now
turn our attention.

Divorce can impact on the lives of children both in the short and
long term (Amato and Keith 1991a, 1991b). Following their parent's
separation, children frequently go through a crisis period, when behaviour problems at home and at school are more often reported,

worries become more prevalent and anxiety levels increase. After divorce, families may have to move house through necessity rather than choice, which in turn leads to changes in schools, neighbourhood, and social networks (Symon 1990). Poverty or at least reduced economic circumstances are likely to be a prominent feature of these children's lives.

Later in life, a number of studies from a range of countries have shown, that as a group, children who experience the break-up of their parent's marriage relative to those who do not, have lower educational attainment, lower incomes, are more likely to be unemployed and to be in less prestigious occupations in adult life than their contemporaries brought up by both parents (Dronkers 1995; McLanahan and Sandefur 1994; Elliot and Richards 1991; Maclean and Wadsworth 1988; Greenberg and Wolf 1982). Young women who have experienced parental divorce are more likely than their peers to cohabit or marry at young ages, to bear children in their teens, and to conceive and bear children outside wedlock (Kiernan 1992b; McLanahan and Sandefur 1994), and men and women from disrupted families are in turn more likely to experience the break-up of their own marriage (Mueller and Pope 1977; Kiernan 1986; Glen and Kramer 1987). A small minority of young adults also develop serious mental health problems associated with parental divorce (Chase-Lansdale, Cherlin, and Kiernan 1995), and middle-aged women who experienced parental divorce tend to report higher rates of psychiatric symptoms, with women who experienced parental divorce and then experienced a divorce themselves having noticeably high depression scores (Rogers 1994).

After divorce and particularly after the crisis period has passed, which seems to last typically about two years, many children and families successfully adapt and adjust to their changed circumstances (Chase-Lansdale and Hetherington 1990) whilst others may continue to experience psychosomatic disorders, need extra help at school, experience difficulties with their friends and suffer from low self-esteem (Cockett and Tripp 1994). One would expect that the social, economic, and emotional milieu prior to and after the separation of parents may well affect a child's adjustment, the way they handle the divorce process, and its legacy. British and American studies using longitudinal survey data have shown that long before parents separate, there are observable differences in the behaviour of their children as compared with children in marriages that do not break up (Cherlin et al. 1991;

Elliott and Richards 1991). The results of these studies suggest that divorce should be seen as a long-term process commencing prior to separation, that may include marital conflict and family dysfunction, which regardless of whether or not parents separate are significant factors in children's behaviour problems (Rutter 1981). Moreover, although young adults whose parents divorce compared with those whose parents did not divorce are more likely to experience adverse outcomes in adulthood, it is also the case that within the divorced group the majority do not have such experiences (Kiernan 1994).

For those who do experience adverse outcomes in young adulthood whether this is due to the economic deprivation associated with divorce or other factors has not been satisfactorily unravelled. Statistical adjustments for parental income and social class tend to reduce the effects of growing up in a lone parent family but do not eliminate it. As yet the circumstances and factors that might mediate the effects of parental separation have received scant attention but this is beginning to change. Recent American research that has followed children post-divorce for four years, has shown that a close relationship with the custodial mother, participation by the child in family decisions, and parental behaviour that reduced the chances of a child experiencing loyalty conflicts, as well as being able to see the absent father, were all conducive to better adjustment and made for happier, better functioning children (Buchanan, Dornbusch, and Maccoby 1996). For Britain, in terms of long-term outcomes there is some evidence of the beneficial effects from having had a working lone mother (Kiernan 1996b). Daughters of working lone mothers were as likely to have attained qualifications or become young mothers as their contemporaries from intact families with a working mother and amongst sons, having a working lone mother reflected positively in the economic domain, with men from these families having similar employment levels and dependency on welfare in adulthood as their contemporaries who had lived with two working parents in their teens. Overall the legacy of living with an employed lone mother was somewhat stronger for daughters than sons.

6

Social Security and Lone Mothers

The position of lone mothers in the social security system improved greatly as a result of the post-war welfare reforms. Lone mothers were not required to register for work in order to claim National Assistance (NA) (from 1966 Supplementary Benefit (SB) and from 1988 Income Support (IS)) as long as they had a dependent child of school age living at home. Eligibility rules and levels of benefits were determined by national scale rates and claimants could no longer be required to return to their area or parish of origin in order to claim assistance. Of particular significance to lone mothers was the ending of the household means test (which had occurred with the 1941 Determination of Needs Act and was confirmed in the 1948 National Assistance Act). The obligation on adult children to maintain parents and vice versa and on grandparents to maintain grandchildren ended. This meant that the unmarried mother who returned to her parents' home was entitled to claim benefit for herself and her child(ren) as a non-householder, irrespective of the economic status of her parents. Conversely their benefit status was unaffected.

The committee chaired by William Beveridge had conceived ways of reducing lone mothers' dependence on means-tested benefits by introducing an end-of-marriage allowance along the lines of widows' benefits in their proposed expanded National Insurance Scheme (Cmd. 6404 (1942)). This would, however, have been limited to 'innocent' divorced wives for just as unemployment benefit was restricted to those who had lost their job involuntarily, so only those whose marriage had ended through no fault of their own should be eligible for this proposed new allowance. In the event, the officials and politicians who developed the post-war social security system on the basis of many of the Beveridge Committee's recommendations failed to implement their proposal not least because they did not wish to 'fish in the murky waters of matrimonial disputes'. Lone mothers, with the exception of widows, then remained dependent on means-tested benefits.

Nevertheless, as the authors of one of the official war histories subsequently wrote:

When the great social enactments of the post-war period came into operation, the position of the unmarried mother in society changed beyond recognition. Over a wide area of needs, charity and poor law relief were replaced by social benefits . . .

The psychological and long-term result of this new situation was often as great as its immediate economic effect. The maternity allowance, more than any other principal factor, has changed the position of the unmarried mother within her family. She should no longer be a financial burden while she is unable to go out to work, but can pay her way and preserve her self-respect. She has a greater chance of remaining at home, and the prospects for her own and her child's future are more hopeful than ever before. (Ferguson and Fitzgerald 1954: 140)

During the war unmarried mothers had been encouraged to look first to their parents or other relatives for support. A circular issued by the Ministry of Health (1943) urged welfare workers: 'Whenever possible to persuade the girl to make known her circumstances to her parents and, if the home is likely to be a satisfactory one, to persuade the grandparents to make a home there for the little one.' Adoption was to be considered only if the family would not help and residential employment or nursery care for the child was impossible to arrange. In the disrupted family circumstances of the war, many pregnant women, especially munition workers and service women, needed help and, reluctantly, official schemes had to be developed. In their analysis of the best of them—the scheme for helping pregnant unmarried servicewomen, introduced in 1943—Ferguson and Fitzgerald found that of those using the scheme, one in four were orphans, had been in care or had step-parents or an unhappy home; the parents of one-third had refused to take any responsibility, and one-fifth of the women themselves refused to contact their families (Ferguson and Fitzgerald 1954: 120). However, 30 per cent of the women were made welcome by their families once the baby was born, and others may subsequently have found acceptance and support from their families (Ferguson and Fitzgerald 1954: 126). While the voluntary and statutory services were more likely to be concerned with unmarried mothers for whom family support was not forthcoming, they were almost certainly a minority. A Ministry of Health survey conducted at the end of the war estimated that two out of three mothers of illegitimate children returned either to their families or to the child's father or to their own homes with their babies (cited in PEP 1946). The changes in entitlement to a range of social benefits and services are likely to have made family support more rather than less forthcoming in the following decade.

Stories of the absorption of illegitimate children into the mother's family—sometimes even presenting the mother as the child's older sister—are not infrequent, indeed their 'social history is scattered through fiction and serious work' (PEP 1946: 1). As discussed in chapter xx, Bowlby disapproved of such arrangements which he claimed occurred in 'subcultures, usually among the poorer classes' (Bowlby 1951: 93), for there was some evidence that they often broke down. He deplored the lack of firm evidence and regretted that official statistics relating to illegitimacy failed to distinguish between what he called 'socially accepted' (i.e. children born to couples who were cohabiting or had anticipated marriage) and 'socially unaccepted' types of illegitimacy making them of little use (ibid.). One of the striking aspects of the policy debates about lone motherhood is the extent of the ignorance among policy-makers about the size and nature of the problem. Numbers of illegitimate births were recorded and were readily available, but these revealed little about the circumstances of the mother. Lone mothers were literally 'concealed' in their parents' households where, in addition to accommodation, grandmothers provided childcare for those able to find employment. The degree to which the numbers were underestimated was considerable until, at the end of the 1960s, the Finer Committee reviewed policies towards lone parents. They attempted to get an accurate count of their numbers. However, they found they could not rely on the Census, for the definition of a family for Census purposes only recognizes two-generation families. As the committee later reported:

Census methodology is unsatisfactory for identifying unmarried mothers living with their children . . . if an unmarried mother lives in a household headed by her own parents both she and her child(ren) will be treated as children in a family headed by her father or mother. Both the 1966 and 1971 census analyses understate the probable numbers of unmarried mothers; the figure is clearly too low as it is exceeded in both years by the number of unmarried mothers in receipt of supplementary benefit. (Cmnd. 5629 (1974): ii. 79)

The Committee had found that in 1971 when 61,000 unmarried

mothers were claiming supplementary benefits, the Census had only enumerated 49,000. The General Household Survey, which the Government had commenced on an annual basis in 1970, had estimated a figure of 73,000 of whom 30,000 were in full-time employment. In addition, they found there were 8,000 older widows whose dependent children were in fact grandchildren. They therefore concluded that the numbers of unmarried mothers was probably closer to 90,000, in other words nearly double the number identified in the Census reports.

Opportunities to find out more about illegitimate children and their mothers were not taken. For example, the first national longitudinal study of children based on a cohort of children born at the end of March 1947 excluded all illegitimate children. A study of birth-control practices commissioned by the Royal Commission on the Population in 1946–7 only interviewed 'women whose first marriage at the time of questioning had not been terminated by death, separation or divorce, or whose first marriage had lasted the whole of their reproductive life' (Lewis Fanning 1949). An important part of the background against which social security, housing, or employment policies developed in the post-war years is the growing interest shown by the policy-makers in lone mothers. This was determined in part by their growing visibility, as well as their growing numbers. It was not until unmarried mothers started to leave the parental home and were joined in the 1960s by growing numbers of women leaving the marital home that the policy-makers began to get a measure of them. At the same time, the social taboos which were both a cause of, and a consequence of these changes, and which sustained their invisibility and muted the voice of the women themselves, became weaker.

It was not only lone mothers who were invisible within the parental home, so too were the services provided by their mothers. The exchange of services between the generations and between husband and wife has never been subject to the formal legal regulation to the extent to which the obligation to maintain has been. Nonetheless, it is a powerful social norm. For example, an official involved with one of the wartime schemes for helping unmarried mothers described parents' refusal to help their pregnant daughters as 'a surely deplorable misconception of the *duties* of parenthood' (Ferguson and Fitzgerald 1954: 20, added emphasis). Finch and Mason have shown in their recent work (Finch and Mason 1993) that the extent to which this norm now operated in particular families varies according to the history of relationships within the family as well as being mediated by negotiations between family members. Nevertheless, throughout the period since the Second World War, grandmother has remained a significant provider of childcare—for her married as well as unmarried daughters. This chapter on social security and the following ones on housing and employment show how support within the family or exchanged between friends, like so much of women's unpaid work, is only noticed by the policy-makers when it is no longer forthcoming and demands for the provision of replacement services or the money to purchase them in the market place begin to be made. These chapters will also show, as Barbara Castle argued 20 years ago, that to women the social wage is as important as the cash wage. The demise of 'the social wage' in the 1980s and 1990s is also a very important part of the story behind these policy developments, and the increasing reliance of lone mothers—and fathers—on means-tested benefits.

The 1950s

The social security debates of the 1950s were dominated by concerns about the future costs of retirement pensions. With full employment and growing numbers of mothers taking up part-time paid employment, it was assumed that two-parent families were unlikely to be poor. Family allowances were only increased twice and these increases coincided with the withdrawal of food subsidies in 1952 and 1956. There were even proposals that family allowances should exclude the second as well as the first child of every family (Walley 1972). Benefits for widows and widowed mothers however were reviewed in the middle of the 1950s. There was concern that 30 per cent of widows with children were claiming NA—the highest percentage of any other class of national insurance beneficiary. Moreover, this was only an average—among widows with four or more children the percentage was 75 (Cmd. 9684 (1956): 14). The National Insurance Advisory Committee (NIAC) therefore recommended increasing the rates for all children after the first, thus for the first time treating the children of widows more generously than the children of other insurance beneficiaries. They also argued that these allowances together with the widowed mother's allowance should be paid until the child was 18 not 16, as long as the child was in full-time education or an apprenticeship. This would help widowed mothers to maintain a home for their children for a longer period. In February 1956 the Minister announced an increase of 25 pence for each child for widows (at that time the family allowance was 40 pence for each child except the first, this was increased to 50 pence for third and subsequent children later that year). The average number of children of widows was 1.5 compared with 2 for men claiming sickness benefit and 2.4 for those claiming unemployment benefit (DHSS 1969: table 9). In December 1955 there were 75,000 widows under the age of 60 years (not all with dependent children), receiving NA to supplement their insurance benefit. Two years later this had fallen to 61,000 (Cmnd. 1085 (1960): 44).

NIAC also recommended in their review of benefits for widows that the policy of not recognizing for national insurance purposes marriages contracted abroad if they were potentially polygamous, be changed so that those that were in fact monogamous were recognized. They explained:

We have received representations from a representative of a Muslim community in this country. We have considered the position of persons from various communities of the Commonwealth who today come to this country in increasing numbers to work and become compulsorily insured, and have been married according to their own law which permits polygamy. Experience shows that these marriages are often monogamous in intention and in fact are especially likely to be so when the family has settled here. At present the contributions paid by these men provide nothing for their wives or widows . . . it may happen that the woman, believing her marriage good for National Insurance purposes, may decide not to contribute. That her marriage is not good for these purposes may not come to her knowledge until, possibly, maternity benefit or widows benefit is claimed, or until retirement age is reached. (Cmd. 9684 (1956): 24)

Immigration in the 1950s was a matter of employment policy and was a Ministry of Labour responsibility. When, in the early 1960s, immigration became a matter of controlling numbers, responsibility moved to the Home Office and the context within which claims of immigrants' families were discussed began to shift.

Later in 1956, NIAC considered provisions for dependency in general in the national insurance scheme and under the heading 'Fatherless families' proposed that:

A similar benefit to that provided for the children of widowed mothers should be provided for the child or children of a woman whose marriage has been terminated by divorce, who has not remarried and who has been receiving a substantial contribution for the children's maintenance from her former husband and has lost that contribution as a result of his death. (Cmd. 9855 (1956): 25)

This followed a similar proposal from the Royal Commission on Marriage and Divorce except they would have restricted it to wives who divorced their husbands (i.e. 'innocent' parties). This was never implemented but women divorced over the age of 50 years were able to claim a widow's pension when their ex-husband died.

Separated, divorced, and unmarried mothers had to turn to NA if they were unable to support themselves. Throughout the existence of the National Assistance Board (NAB) only a minority did so. In 1950 the Board commented in their annual report that:

Plainly the great majority of separated wives and unmarried mothers succeed in keeping independent of assistance, either because they receive a sufficiency from the person liable or (probably more often) because they maintain themselves by their own efforts. The Board must be dealing with exceptional cases. (Cmd. 8030 (1950): 21)

The 1951 Census shows that the economic activity rates for widows and divorced women were much higher than those for married women (Table 6.1). It is interesting that the early annual reports of the NAB do not give figures of the numbers of unmarried, divorced, and separated mothers in receipt of benefit in a consistent manner. In 1950 for example there were nearly 98,000 widows under 60 years of age, 35,000 separated or deserted women, and 43,500 'others' receiving benefit. The last category includes unmarried and divorced mothers as well as women not required to register for employment because they were caring either for children or for an elderly relative (Beveridge's 'domestic spinsters'). It is not until the annual report for 1954 that figures are given separately for lone mothers and it is possible to distinguish unmarried mothers (Table 6.2).

The lone mothers claiming NA in the 1950s were only a minority of claimants, but they did present dilemmas for the officials. These arose from the interaction of public and private law which determines the relationship between the claims for maintenance a mother has on the state and those she has on the father of her children. All lone mothers had the right to support from the state-financed social security system without (in theory) suffering the imposition of stigma, as well as a legal right to maintenance from the father of her children. Depending on her legal relationship to him, this included maintenance for herself. Under

TABLE 6.1. *Economic activity rates of widows and divorced women, single women, and married women (1951 Census)*

	Ages 15–19	20–4	25–34	35–44	45–54	55–9	15–59
Widows and divorced women[a]							
Occupied							
Full-time	100	60.0	61.8	57.6	46.7	32.1	45
Part-time	—	4.4	5.8	8.6	7.1	6.1	7
Unoccupied	—	35.6	2.4	33.8	46.2	61.8	48
Single women[b]							
Occupied							
Full-time	80.0	90.4	86.1	77.4	71.3	62.4	80
Part-time	0.2	0.5	1.0	2.3	3.2	4.0	1.2
Unoccupied	19.8	9.1	12.9	20.3	25.5	33.6	18.8
Married women[c]							
Occupied							
Full-time	36.6	33.3	19.0	18.0	17.5	12.1	19
Part-time	1.6	3.8	5.5	7.0	5.9	3.5	8
Unoccupied	61.7	62.9	75.5	75.0	76.6	84.4	73

[a] 100 % = 804.4 (124.2 divorced) (Thousands.)
[b] 100 % = 4,369
[c] 100 % = 10,411

Source: Cmd. 9684 (1956): appendix vi.

TABLE 6.2. *Women recipients of National Assistance, 1955–1965, for whom there was liability to maintain*

	1955	1957	1961	1965
Separated wives[a]	70,800	67,500	84,000	104,000
Unmarried mothers/mothers of illegitimate children	16,000	20,000	26,000	36,000[b]
Divorced women with children	8,000	5,300	8,000	14,000
TOTAL	94,800	92,800	118,000	154,000
Annual expenditure (£ million)	11.1	12.1	20.0	42.7
Value of maintenance received by:				
(a) claimant	0.96	1.2	2.4	4.4
(b) Board	0.9	1.1	1.8	4.0
a + b as % of annual expenditure	16.8	19.0	21.0	17.0

[a] Includes 28,000–29,000 wives each year over the age of 60.
[b] Includes 7,000 widows and divorced women with illegitimate children.

Sources: Cmd. 9531 (1956): NAB Annual Report for 1955; Cmnd. 444 (1958) NAB Annual Report for 1957; Cmnd. 1730 (1962): NAB Annual Report for 1961; Cmnd. 3042 (1966): NAB Annual Report for 1965.

the 1948 National Assistance Act (sections 43a and 44), either the Board or the mother had the right to seek a maintenance or affiliation order against a husband or putative father. (Mothers of illegitimate children had to seek an affiliation order within a year of birth of the child unless the father had already paid some maintenance.) This was then offset in its entirety against the cost of the benefit being paid. Commenting on these responsibilities and rights which were perpetuated in the 1966 Ministry of Social Security Act, Finer and Macgregor later wrote:

Thus one fundamental principle of 43 Elizabeth; namely, the designation in the public assistance legislation of liable relatives, and the right of the public authority granting such assistance to seek reimbursement from the liable relative, still retains its vitality in the social security legislation of today. (Finer and Macgregor 1974: 145)

However, the right to claim maintenance from a husband was not unconditional: it depended on the woman's conduct. Under the poor law, a husband had not been liable to support an adulterous or deserting wife. The Board believed that this was still the position under the National Assistance Act and following a judge's comment on the unreported case of *Aldritt* v. *Aldritt* in 1951 which suggested otherwise, they tested the matter by seeking an order against a husband whose wife had deserted him. The judgment in *National Assistance Board* v. *Wilkinson* ([1952] 2 QB 648):

established that assistance granted to a wife cannot be recovered from her husband without regard to the circumstances which led to his not support-ing her, and that section 42(1) of the National Assistance Act did not deprive husbands of the defences which were open to them before the passing of the Act. The judgement does not, the Board are advised, affect the liability of both husband and wife for the maintenance of their children, nor does it imply that a husband is secure against proceedings for recovery of assistance paid to his wife after a mutual agreement to separate. (Cmd. 8900 (1953): 18)

This remained the position until the 1978 Domestic Proceedings and Magistrates Court Act after which an act of adultery on the part of his spouse did not relieve the husband of the obligation to maintain her. However, as will be discussed below, the distinction drawn between maintenance for a wife and maintenance for children became conten-tious in the late 1960s and 1970s.

Meanwhile in the 1950s, NAB officers found that pursuing liable relatives for the reimbursement of benefits paid out was as time-con-suming and sometimes as fruitless as the Supplementary Benefit Com-mission (SBC) and, more recently, the Child Support Agency (CSA) found. As the NAB stated in their annual report for 1953: 'The amount obtained from husbands is limited first by the difficulty of tracing husbands, and secondly by the inability of many husbands to spare from their resources the full amount necessary for the maintenance of the wives and dependants from whom they are separated' (Cmd. 9210 (1954): 18).

The year before they had analysed the separated wives included in their annual 2½ per cent sample of claimants, using this analysis to supplement an inquiry made in March 1953 into a sample of 57,700 separated wives who had been receiving assistance 2½ years earlier. They concluded that separated wives fell broadly into two groups—those claiming soon after separation and those applying years after. The March inquiry found nearly half the husbands had not been traced and of these in more than half 'the wife had been receiving outdoor relief under the Poor Law before becoming the responsibility of the Board in July 1948, so that the search which has baffled the Board had already baffled the Public Assistance Authority' (ibid 15). They had more success in tracing husbands of applicants newly separated. However, the Board resisted the suggestion that they

should withhold assistance until the rights and wrongs of the matter have been cleared in some way, and possibly longer if there seems any prospect of forcing a reunion by this means. Whether the responsibility for what has happened is hers or her husband's (a matter which may be extremely difficult to determine) a women cannot be left to starve because her marriage is broken, still less her children be left to starve. (ibid. 20)

This, they pointed out, was consistent with private law. The year before the President of the Probate, Admiralty and Divorce Division in (*Wharton* v. *Wharton* [1952] 2 All ER 939) had ruled that an insufficient maintenance order 'was not the proper way to deal with the matter . . . in effect to starve her into reconciliation' (ibid.).

Throughout the 1950s it was Board policy to encourage a lone mother to seek her own affiliation or maintenance order against a putative father or husband, rejecting the criticism that 'legal action in the name of the wife is likely to exacerbate relations between the parties and diminish the chance of reconciliation' (Cmd. 8900 (1953): 18), pointing out that such orders remain enforceable after coming off benefit. At this time newly separated wives were usually on benefit for only a short while so this was important. In addition, the amount a separated wife or lone mother could seek was not limited to the amount received in benefit as was the case if the Board initiated proceedings. The Board could pay for legal representation if she needed it and 'action by the wife has the advantage that she will be able to discuss her case with an experienced official who will take advantage of any opportunities of reconciliation which may be present' (ibid.). The Board's own officers made quarterly home visits to claimants and reviewed 'with particular care the circumstances of women (including widows, deserted wives, and unmarried mothers) bringing up young children single handed so as to make sure that . . . they were getting all the assistance the Board could give them' (Cmnd. 1410 (1961): 22). Throughout the 1950s and 1960s they were assisted with individual cases by members—and sometimes their wives—of the network of Area Sub-Committees (numbering over 400) of the local Advisory Committees established under section 3(1) of the National Assistance Act. The Board's annual reports give illustrations of claimants visited and the positive outcomes particularly in relation to taking up paid employment. As will be discussed in the chapter on lone mothers and employment, some lone mothers regarded these visits less positively and felt very pressured by these home visits to take a job. The reports contain fewer illustrations of women returning to their husbands.

A further difficulty, all too familiar to the CSA, arose not from the process of acquiring a maintenance order but in enforcing it when the liable husband or father had established a second family. 'The Board are then faced with the delicate problem of deciding whether the assistance is to be given to the wife or the paramour' (Cmd. 9530 (1955): 18). Caught between respect for the obligations of marriage, on the one hand, and the practicalities of enforcing the payments, on the other, the Board, as described in the previous chapter, decided 'the paramour' had prior claims to the man's income. At this time there was little or no public concern that either lone mothers or the men who should have been supporting them, were abusing the system. The Board was therefore under little pressure to resolve these principles and instead took a very pragmatic view, paying assistance to the wife and children and recovering from the husband 'as much as he can afford without driving the paramour into seeking assistance' (ibid. 19). When the 1958 Maintenance Order Act came into effect, it became possible to make an attachment of earnings order to reclaim arrears. The maintenance to be paid had to leave sufficient margins above the minimum 'protected earnings rate'. This meant that the man not only had to be left with enough for his own needs but also 'for the needs of any person for whom he must or *may reasonably provide*' (1958 Maintenance Order Act, cited in Cmnd. 1410 (1961): 24, emphasis added). Board policy of balancing the needs of second families against the claims of the first was consistent with private law at the time.

Throughout this period the tax system assisted men in supporting more than one family because tax relief was available for maintenance payments for children and ex-wives and on covenants made in favour of separated wives. Richard Titmuss quotes an estimate that this subsidy from taxpayers to assist mainly surtax payers cost £10 million in 1959 (equivalent to about half the NAB's expenditure on separated wives and lone mothers—see Table 6.2) (Titmuss 1962: 78). He cited Lord Justice Hudson reported in *The Times*, 31 July 1957, as saying:

The odd situation has now come to us in which a man of large means who paid surtax was able to have several wives . . . and to be very little worse off . . . whereas a working man who paid neither surtax nor any considerable amount of income tax found it quite impossible to comply with the law which still in this country enabled divorced wives to obtain maintenance from their husbands and also to provide for an excess of wives. (Titmuss 1962: 77)

This remained the situation until 1988 when, as will be discussed in more detail below, covenants between individuals ceased to attract tax relief and tax relief on maintenance was limited to the value of the married man's allowance.

The 1960s

Changes in private law at the beginning of the 1960s strengthened the claims women could make on the fathers of their children for maintenance. The 1960 Matrimonial Proceedings (Magistrates Courts) Act consolidated and amended the law relating to maintenance proceedings previously contained in statutes going back to 1895. The maximum amounts of maintenance which could be granted were increased from £5 to £7.50 a week for wives and from £1.50 to £2.50 for children. An initial order could be made for children aged between 16 and 21 if they were in full-time education or incapacitated. For the first time a husband could be awarded a maintenance order against his wife, but only if his earning capacity was impaired. Also for the first time a maintenance order could be made against a husband or wife in respect of any child of either (including an illegitimate child) who had been accepted as 'one of the family' by the other. The 1948 National Assistance Act had restricted liability to children under 16 in respect of children of the marriage or adopted children, or illegitimate children of whom he had been adjudged to be the father (i.e. not the legitimate or illegitimate children of his wife of whom he was not the father). The 1959 Legitimacy Act had in any case extended the provision of the 1926 Legitimacy Act which allowed a child to be legitimated by the subsequent marriage of his parents. Following the 1959 Act this included children whose parents were not free to marry at the time of the birth. In 1960 about one-third of illegitimate births were jointly registered. In 1961 the Legal Aid Scheme was extended to cover maintenance and affiliation proceedings in Magistrates Courts in England and Wales.

The number of lone mothers applying for NA increased in the first half of the 1960s and there is evidence from the annual reports that the Board was taking a tougher line. In 1962 there was a 9 per cent increase in the number of women in respect of whom the liability to maintain by the husband or father arose compared with a 5 per cent increase in 1960. The Board's reports give more prominence to 'a type of abuse which again occupied much of the special investigators time . . . the woman who claims to be living on her own and to need assistance on that basis whereas she is living with and being maintained by a man' (Cmnd. 2386 (1964): 47). In 1963 the Board brought 58 prosecutions under section 51 of the National Assistance Act. The following year they reported 98 cases and went on to report that 'in very many more cases circumstances were disclosed which justified the withdrawal of the allowance on the grounds that the woman was not in need although there was not sufficient evidence for prosecution' (Cmnd. 2674 (1965): 49). By this time the NAB was employing 97 special investigators concerned primarily with suspected abuse, compared with 16 in 1954 when the first such appointments were made (Commons Debates, 16 December 1970, c. 179).

The following year, 1965, was the last year of the NAB's existence because the new Labour Government was replacing it with the Supplementary Benefits Commission. The climate was changing: questions were beginning to be asked in Parliament about the cost to the social security system of separated wives whose husbands were failing to maintain them. The Board reported much tougher action and criminal proceedings under section 51 were taken on 525 occasions—a tenfold increase in two years. Nearly half (234) were sent to prison. (This compares with 178 men who were prosecuted for failing to take suitable work to maintain their families, half of whom were also sent to prison.) As this was their final report, the Board had asked the Chairman to review 'some of the more important matters which have occupied the attention of the Board in recent years'. After discussing unemployment, the workshy, the wage-stop (which limited a man's benefit to a level just below his 'normal' earnings) and the unsettled, he discussed abuse

committed by the husband who deserts his wife and children, leaving them to be maintained from public funds. Much of the effort made to ensure that husbands meet their legal liabilities for the maintenance of their dependants is inevitably unproductive; some for instance disappear without trace, others acquire a new family and are then unable to maintain both groups of dependants. *But it is essential to demonstrate that husbands and fathers cannot indulge in this abuse of public funds with impunity, and to reassure the taxpayer that the authorities do not view the matter with complacency.* For these reasons the

Board have resorted to criminal proceedings in appropriate cases. (Cmnd. 3042 (1966): p. ix, emphasis added)

In Parliament the Prime Minister was asked by a Labour Member 'to set up a Royal Commission to investigate the problem of deserted wives and fatherless families' (Commons Debates, 7 December 1965, c. 85). Harold Wilson refused on the grounds that the Government was already engaged in a comprehensive review of the social services. This refers to the committee on the personal social services including local authority Health and Welfare and Children's departments (the Seebohm Committee which reported in 1968 (Cmnd. 3703)). Subsequent questions from Labour Members in 1966 and 1967 were met with a similar response. It was not until 1967 that 'unmarried mothers' appeared for the first time in a separate heading in the Hansard index (Table 6.3).

While deserted wives were attracting more attention from the NAB during the early months of the new Labour Government, the situation of widows was under active consideration in Parliament. The abolition of the widow's earnings rule had been promised in Labour's election manifesto and the 1964 National Insurance Act put this promise into effect at the end of that year. At the time between 70 and 80 thousand widows or widowed mothers had their benefit reduced as a result of this rule. Widowed mothers could earn up to £7 weekly and widows £5 before their benefit was reduced (an unemployed man or his wife could only earn £2 weekly). The Minister, Margaret Herbison, explained during the debates on the Bill, 'We believe, and have often said that the widowed mother who is striving to do her best for her children and who has to be both mother and father to them, ought not to be penalized by an earnings rule' (Commons Debates, 16 November

TABLE 6.3. *Lone mothers receiving National Assistance/Supplementary Benefit 1948–1971*

Women under 60 with dependent children	National Assistance				Supplementary Benefit	
	1948	1951	1961	1965	1966	1971
Number (000s)	32	41	76	108	142	213
% of total claimants	3.8	4.1	4.1	5.4	5.7	7.3
100% =	842	1,011	1,844	2,012	2,495	2,909

Source: Central Statistical Office 1972: table 48, p. 100. (These figures were not obtainable directly from the published Annual Reports.)

1964, c. 1006). Margaret Thatcher, who was a social security spokesperson for the Opposition, argued instead for a continuation of the policy followed since 1956 of increasing dependants' benefits for widows within the National Insurance scheme. (By 1964 widows were receiving £1.75 per child—double the 1956 addition. The unemployed or sick claimant was receiving £1.) The earnings rule has never been reinstated but the cohabitation rule whereby the widow loses her allowance or pension if she cohabits or remarries—a condition introduced in the first contributory widows pensions scheme in 1925 — has remained. Overall, the number of widows under retirement age fell during the 1960s (Table 6.4).

As those concerned with social security policies were becoming more aware of lone mothers and their financial needs, local authority Children's departments and welfare workers in the voluntary sector were also feeling the impact of their growing numbers. The numbers of illegitimate children coming into care because their mother was unable to provide a home for them was growing and by 1966 had increased nearly threefold since 1956 (from 1,040 to 2,933) (National Labour Women's Advisory Committee 1967: 32). As the following chapter shows, Children's departments were also having to deal with the consequences of growing homelessness and lone parents were over-represented among this group. The numbers of children taken into care because of maternal death or desertion had also increased in this period (from 2,716 in 1956 to 5,622 in 1966) (ibid.). As early as 1959 the Working Party on Social Workers in Local Authority Health and Welfare Services (the Younghusband Report) recommended that the needs of unsupported mothers be studied and social workers trained better to assist them. Peter Marris's study of widows was published in

TABLE 6.4. *Number of widows in England and Wales in 1961 and 1971 by age*

Age	Number (000s)	
	1961	1971
Under 45	77	62
45–59	438	400
60 and over	2,012	2,312
TOTAL	2,528	2,773

Source: Central Statistical Office 1976: table 13.

1958 (Marris 1958). Margaret Wynn, drawing on the experience of social workers in both the statutory and voluntary sectors as well as on social researchers, published her book *Fatherless Families* in 1964. Her study started with the question of how many fatherless families there were. She calculated that divorce and separation accounted for 58 per cent of all fatherless children in the country with widowhood and illegitimacy accounting for 33 per cent and 9 per cent, respectively. What, she asked, were the consequences, both economic and social, of fatherlessness? Proposing a new fatherless child allowance she argued that 'the need of the fatherless family for a reasonable income has little connection with the legal description of the mother's marital status' (Wynn 1964: 17).

Lone mothers as a category were thus beginning to surface. Their increased visibility took place, first, against the background of the 'rediscovery' of poverty among families with children. Just before Christmas in 1965, Professors Abel-Smith and Townsend published their re-analysis of Family Expenditure Survey data for 1953 and 1960. They concluded: 'The most novel finding is the extent of poverty among children. For over a decade it has been generally assumed that such poverty as exists is found overwhelmingly among the aged.'

They had estimated that in 1960 there were 2.25 million children in low-income families (defined as an income 140 per cent or less than the National Assistance scale rates). They went on:

Thus quantitatively the problem of poverty among children is more than two thirds of the size of poverty among the aged. This fact has not been given due emphasis in the policies of the political parties. It is also worth observing that there were substantially more children in poverty than adults of working age. (Abel-Smith and Townsend 1965: 65)

Their findings received widespread publicity. The Child Poverty Action Group (CPAG) was formed and poverty among children was placed firmly on the political agenda. The evidence that poor children were found among families in which fathers were in employment as well as among those in which he was sick, unemployed or absent shook the belief that poverty in the post-war welfare state was confined to those at the margins of society whom the benefit system has failed. The question of how the cost of children should be shared between parents and the state and how family income should be adjusted to take account of family size were the subjects of public debate for the first time since the introduction of family allowance at the end of the Second

World War. Because the focus was on children and their needs, concern encompassed both one-parent and two-parent families and was not confined solely to poor families.

Second, the demographic changes and shifting attitudes towards marriage described in early chapters, were having an impact on family law and the rights and obligations within marriage. Reflecting later on this period, the Finer Committee summarized these changes as follows:

The 1950s and 1960s witnessed the cumulative removal of customary and legal restraints upon certain forms of sexual behaviour and upon their public portrayal in print or by the visual arts for commercial purposes. Legal restrictions on the freedom of married people to escape from the bonds which used to be defended as essential safeguards for the integrity of monogamous marriage has been relaxed, and the sexual freedom of men and women has been enlarged. . . . In this climate of opinion compassion for the disadvantages suffered by one-parent families has grown quickly. The old tariff of blame which pitied widows but attached varying degrees of moral delinquency on divorced or separated women or to unmarried mothers is becoming irrelevant in the face of the imperative recognition that what chiefly matters in such situations is to assist and protect dependent children, all of whom ought to be treated alike irrespective of their mother's circumstances. (Cmnd. 5629 (1974): 7)

Third, major aspects of the social security system were under review and proposals for radical restructuring were being considered by the Labour Government. The 1966 National Insurance Act introduced earnings-related supplements to benefits paid during the early months of sickness, unemployment, and widowhood. (An element of earnings-related contributions and benefits limited to pensions had been introduced in the early 1960s.) The 1966 Ministry of Social Security Act gave the functions of the Ministry of Pensions and National Insurance and the administration of the new scheme of Supplementary Benefits (SB) which replaced NA to the new Ministry. The purpose of these changes was 'to introduce a scheme of non-contributory benefits in place of national assistance which will, among other things, provide a form of guaranteed income for those who require such a benefit over a long period' (Cmnd. 2997 (1966): para. 1). Although the changes were aimed mainly at people over pension age, all of whom would receive a long-term addition to their income requirements, others below pension age who had been in receipt of an allowance for at least two years were included. 'Widows and other women with dependent children' would qualify for the addition, but the unemployed could not. By bringing the administration of the different parts of social insurance and assistance schemes together at both national and local level (local offices and advisory committees were to be merged), it was hoped 'in the future there will no longer be the sharp distinction which now exists in the administration of contributory and means-tested benefits' (ibid.: para. 2). In other words, the intention was to reduce the stigma associated with becoming a claimant particularly for pensioners and to place a greater emphasis on the right to claim a means-tested supplement. During the debates on the Bill, Members of all parties demanded more information about the numbers of poor children and the Minister defended the Government by announcing that a national study of families with two or more children was being conducted. It was published the following summer.

The study, *Circumstances of Families*, aimed, in the words of the Minister, Margaret Herbison, 'to concentrate attention on those families having incomes which are below the current level of supplementary benefit as approved by Parliament, and which cannot be brought up to that level, in most cases because of the full-time work disqualification' (MSS 1967: foreword, p. iii). The report estimated that in the summer of 1966 out of nearly 7 million families with children, about half a million families (including one-child families) with about 1.25 million children had resources less than would have then been paid to those on benefit. Of these, 350,000 were receiving NA or would have been eligible to do so. The Minister was particularly concerned about the 160,000 families with half a million children whose fathers were in full-time employment or were subject to the wage-stop and therefore could not have their incomes brought up to a level to meet their requirements. (In 1960, 12,500 unemployed claimants had had the amount of their national assistance benefit reduced under this rule, compared with 2,000 in 1954. By 1967 this had increased to 33,600 (CPAG 1971: 15).) In contrast 'virtually all' the fatherless families were receiving benefit in full (the wage-stop only applied to men and, conversely as explained above, in contrast to lone fathers at this time, women with children were not required to register for employment in order to claim NA or SB). The proportion of families with incomes below their requirements increased with family size: half of all children in these poor families were found in families with at least four children. The problem was therefore perceived to be how to adjust family income to family size when fathers were on low wages without destroying their work incentives.

The Government responded by increasing family allowances for fourth and each subsequent child in the family from 50p to 75p in October. Under the 1967 Family Allowance and National Insurance Act, family allowances were increased the following April to 75p for the second child in the family and to 85p a week for each subsequent child. Adjustments were made to children's allowances payable to widows and other national insurance beneficiaries so that they too benefited from these increases. However, those on SB gained nothing for their benefit was reduced to take account of the increase in family allowance. Fourth and subsequent children in all families irrespective of income received free school meals and welfare milk (school milk was still free for all children at this time), although the Labour Government subsequently withdrew it from secondary school children. However, the increase in cash allowances for children was recovered from fathers who paid income tax at the standard rate by adjusting their tax allowances—a process called 'claw-back'. Recipients of long-term social security benefits (e.g. widowed mothers and recipients of industrial injury benefit) were not subject to 'claw-back'.

In January 1969 the Labour Government published its plans for a more radical earnings-related social security system in the White Paper, *National Superannuation and Social Insurance: Proposals for Earnings-Related Social Security.* Although the focus was on retirement pensions the White Paper contained an announcement to start a further study of the circumstances of families with children 'paying special attention to one-parent families (whether fatherless or motherless)' and to appoint 'a committee to consider the general position of one-parent families in our society and whether there are further methods by which they should be helped' (Cmnd. 3883 (1969): 16). While in no doubt that widows should be included in any reformed social insurance scheme, the Government was yet to be convinced of the need or desirability of including all 'fatherless families' (inverted commas in the original). The terms of reference of the Finer Committee announced later that year went way beyond the consideration of widows' pensions and the social security system. It included aspects of family law and court procedures as well as policies in housing, education, and childcare. Of particular significance for the subsequent debates on support for lone parents the Committee were asked to have regard to, among other things, 'the need to maintain equity as between one-parent families and other families' (Cmnd. 5629 (1974): 1).

The 1970s

The central issues in the social security debates at the beginning of the 1970s were therefore very different from the two previous decades. The relationship between the wages and benefit systems had been called into question by the rediscovery of poverty among children of working fathers and by the growing numbers of two-parent families subject to the wage-stop when fathers were sick or unemployed. (There was evidence that the difference between median male earnings and the lowest 10 per cent of male wage earners was growing despite the Labour Government's attempts in incomes policies to target proportionally higher wage increases on the low paid.) Increases in family allowances had been linked to adjustments in child tax allowances thus raising the issue of the relationship between the tax and social security systems. Evidence of poverty among children, particularly among children of lone parents, was growing. Dennis Marsden's study of lone parents living on what was national assistance at the time of the research was published in 1968. The Government was committed to collecting and publishing. more evidence about the circumstances of lone parents and there was an active lobby monitoring both the extent and nature of poverty among families as well as evaluating policy responses. Claimants were beginning to find a voice and getting informed advice from a growing welfare rights movement and the re-emerging women's movement at the end of the 1960s enabled women, including lone mothers, to speak for themselves.

The reforms of the social security system proposed in Richard Crossman's White Paper in 1969 did not reach the statute book before the Labour Government was replaced by a Conservative Government in 1970. The incoming Government's response to poverty among children in families with working parents was to introduce a means-tested scheme of family support—Family Income Supplement (FIS). They were opposed to across-the-board increases in family allowances, even coupled with an extension of 'claw-back' because this would bring more family men into the tax system and their intention was to reduce tax and the number of taxpayers. At this time the tax threshold was below the SB level for a married man with two children. (Jim Callaghan, Chancellor of the Exchequer when family allowances were increased in 1967 and 1968, and Dennis Healey, Chancellor of the

Exchequer in the 1970s Labour Government, had also favoured a means-tested increase.)

FIS was a new benefit 'for families with small incomes where the breadwinner is in full-time work and there are dependent children' (FIS Bill, clause 1). The amount to be paid was based on half the difference between the family's 'normal gross income' and the 'prescribed amount' which increased with the number of children (£15 for a one-child family and £2 for each additional child). Breadwinners could be a man or single woman—a single woman being defined as 'any woman other than one who is a member of the same household as a man to whom she is married or with whom she is living as his wife' (FIS Bill clause 17). This meant only the man in a married or cohabiting couple could claim FIS. In addition, the resources of a man's wife or cohabitant were taken into account in calculating the family's normal gross income. However, Keith Joseph, Secretary of State for the Social Services, introducing the Bill made it clear that single women who were not householders could claim. 'The Bill will help householders where a single woman with a child or children is living with her parents or relatives' (Commons Debates, 10 November 1970, c. 223). Clause 9 of the Bill was similar to clauses 23 and 24 of the 1966 Ministry of Social Security Act allowing the recovery of the costs of benefits from a liable relative. This however was dropped at the Committee stage because 'it was not our intention in any way to harry the woman whom we seek to help' (Commons Debates, 18 November 1970, c. 1367). It is interesting that clause 9 was not perceived as a measure concerned with harrying fathers. Maintenance payments however were to be offset entirely against FIS. The novel feature of the scheme was the establishment of parity between one- and two-parent families for the first time in Britain in a means-tested benefit. The calculation of the prescribed amounts depended only on the number of children, not on the number of parents.

There was considerable concern that this was a re-run of the nineteenth-century Speenhamland system and some Members from both sides of the House argued for the payments of higher allowances for children. However, all had to admit that increasing family allowances was a blunt instrument for tackling the poverty of many lone parents because of the exclusion of the first child. There was considerable support for the view that 'FIS was the only way of tackling family poverty in the short term' (CPAG 1971: 30 emphasis added). CPAG were subsequently critical of the level of benefits set and the low take-up achieved as well as the increase in the cost of school meals, prescription charges, and the prices of other essentials and the withdrawal of free school milk from primary school children. In its first year nearly 65,000 families claimed FIS, 30 per cent of them lone parents. A study conducted in 1974, by which time half of all recipients were lone parents, found that nearly two-thirds had only one child compared with just under half of lone parents claiming supplementary benefit. Over half of all unmarried mothers claiming FIS were living with their parents (Nixon 1979).

While these improvements in the economic situation of lone parents in employment were being made, the Government had not forgotten those on SB. The cohabitation rule and its application by SB liable relative officers was attracting increasing criticism. In 1967 the new Supplementary Benefits Commission had published a *Report on the Administration of the Wage Stop* because, as discussed above, it was a cause for public concern. In 1971 they published their second report, *Cohabitation*, because 'Although in many cases the provisions cause no difficulty and therefore attract no public attention, there are a minority of cases where difficult problems arise, and where there is sometimes public criticism and much misunderstanding' (SBC 1971: 1).

The SBC rejected criticisms that the cohabitation rule was an example of the failure of legislation 'to take account of changing social developments and as a consequence is no longer generally accepted by society' (ibid. 1971: 4). The abolition of the rule

must produce a situation where married couples would be dealt with less favourably than unmarried couples; where there would be a financial disincentive to subsequent marriage and legitimization of the children; and where common law marriage (accepted for example by some immigrant members of our society) would not be recognized for the purposes of the supplementary benefits scheme. (Cmnd. 5019 (1972): 5)

They did not believe society would regard that as fair. They did however accept that officers must be trained to make enquiries sensitively and that the existence of cohabitation should be determined as much by the stability of the union as by their sleeping arrangements. They also reaffirmed the policy inherited from the NAB of assuming that the man in a cohabiting couple is supporting the woman and her children, including those of a former union, although 'in the last resort' they might use their powers to pay benefit on behalf of the children 'where they would otherwise suffer hardship or where the refusal of benefit might mean the break-up of the household and the detriment, for example, of any children of the current union' (SBC 1971: 11).

Abuse of the social security system in general was concerning the Government at this time and a committee to investigate it was appointed (the Fisher Committee) reporting in 1973. The question of cohabitation was discussed. Although fictitious desertion and cohabitation cases accounted for 14 per cent of prosecutions completed by the SBC, they took up nearly two-fifths of special investigators' time (Fisher Committee 1973: 134). The problem appeared to be a growing one (Table 6.5).

The report described some of the difficulties involved in defining cohabitation and particularly if the man or woman in question had more than one partner. The Committee recognized that:

it can be argued that many of the anomalies would be removed if the women cohabiting with a man, instead of being disentitled to supplementary benefit had merely to give credit for any support actually received from the man. But it is easy to see that the consequence of such a change might be socially damaging and financially unacceptable: *men who are now content to support the women with whom they live would have no incentive to continue to do so.* (ibid. 135, emphasis added)

They recognized that some lone mothers shared with relatives or women friends but did not suggest this should effect their entitlement to benefit (although it would determine whether or not they were treated as a householder and would affect the calculation of their housing costs).

It was clear from the evidence the Committee received that widows were being treated more sympathetically than other categories of lone

TABLE 6.5. *Cases of undisclosed cohabitation and fictitious desertion, 1968–1971*

Year	Number of special investigators	Investigated		Allowances withdrawn or reduced	
		Undisclosed cohabitation	Fictitious desertions	Undisclosed cohabitation	Fictitious desertions
1968	163	4,940	1,233	2,512	682
1969	189	5,981	1,516	2,775	776
1970	248	7,335	2,021	3,406	982
1971	278	8,426	na	3,787	925

Sources: Fisher Committee 1973: 52; CPAG 1971. 7, 23

mothers. They represented only 2 per cent of cases considered for prosecution within the contributory system and none were completed. They accepted that this reflected the greater public sympathy for a widow left with small children and that criticism was likely to be levelled at 'bureaucrats with unworthy suspicion of her morals . . . [who] . . . are attempting to deprive her of the pension for which *her late husband paid by his contributions*' (ibid. 140, emphasis added). Attitudes towards deserted or divorced women or single women with children, on the other hand, while not necessarily hostile were less favourable and 'may also be tinged with the strong disapproval of those who mis-represent their circumstances *in order to live on tax payers money*' (ibid., emphasis added). The Committee recommended that the principles and procedures for instituting investigations into suspected cohabitation in both the contributory and means-tested systems should be the same. They also recommended that enquiries from 'other residents and landlords etc.' should be used as a last resort and order books should never be withdrawn on the spot even if offered. The SBC accepted the former recommendation but rejected the proposed limitations on enquiries in the neighbourhood 'because they would have allowed much serious fraud to have gone undetected' (Cmnd. 5700 (1974): 69).

The creation of a single government department in 1966 to administer the contributory and means-tested social security schemes, had therefore yet to achieve the intended reduction in stigma associated with claiming means-tested assistance. Widows in principle and in practice were more favourably treated than other lone mothers: their husbands had after all, paid for their pensions. The principles underlying the cohabitation rule as well as the ways in which it was applied continued to be contentious. CPAG's journal regularly published articles on the question as well as pamphlets—for example Ruth Lister, *As Man and Wife?* (1973) and Jane Streather and Stuart Weir, *Social Insecurity: Single Mothers on Benefit* (1974). Olive Stevenson's book *Claimant or Client?* also published in 1973 discussed the issues involving unsupported mothers from a perspective more sympathetic to the SBC. The Finer Committee 'had the strong disposition to recommend the abolition of the rule . . . and we would have been glad to make such a recommendation had we been able to discover a reasonable and viable basis for doing so. We spent much time in this endeavour but failed' (Cmnd. 5629 (1974): 340). They could not reject the 'overwhelming argument in its favour. This is that it cannot be right to treat unmarried women who have the support of a partner both as if they had no such support and better than if they were married' (ibid.). They did however recommend improvements in its administration, going further than those of the Fisher Committee.

While abuse of the benefits system was being examined, more radical proposals for reforming the whole benefit system involving merging personal tax allowances with cash benefits, so that any unused personal tax allowances could be recovered in the form of a cash allowance, were being discussed. In 1972 the Green Paper (Cmnd. 5116), *Proposals for a Tax-Credit System* was published. For each child there would be a child credit replacing the child tax allowance, family allowance, FIS, and the child additions in short-term national insurance benefits. This meant that the practice of treating widows (and the industrially injured) more generously, established as discussed above, in 1956, would be continued. The Green Paper left open the question of to whom the child credit would be paid. Any adult in receipt of earnings or a benefit would be members of the scheme. Full-time housewives or separated wives dependent on maintenance were left in an unsatisfactory position. The former would be included in the additional credit married men would receive. Lone parents would benefit from the same additional credit because it was argued 'a parent who has single handed responsibility for a child' (para. 108) should receive the same tax credit as a married couple with the same responsibilities. 'This arrangement would be particularly helpful to women who go out to work to support themselves and their children' (ibid.). In other words the parity between two-parent and one-parent families established in FIS would be carried over into this new scheme.

There was much debate about whether the child benefit should be paid wholly to the father or whether they should be paid, at least in part direct to the mother. As the Inland Revenue Staff Federation in their *Memorandum of Evidence to the Select Committee on Tax Credit System* (HC 341–II (1972/73)) said: 'Until the publication of the "Green Paper" it had clearly escaped public notice that so large a proportion of the total benefit represented by the tax child allowance and the family allowance is received by fathers (para. 7). They, and others, argued that it would therefore be politically impossible to reduce fathers' take-home pay substantially. However, by this time, the women's lobby, encompassing more than those directly involved in the women's liberation movement, together with the poverty lobby had mobilized around the issues and were making it very clear that the only acceptable child credit was one paid directly in cash to mothers. There were local and national demonstrations, including a sit-in in the Post Office in Trafalgar Square which attracted considerable media attention. The arguments which Eleanor Rathbone had used so effectively in the campaign for the introduction of family allowances, surfaced again for the first time since the Second World War. In addition to the feminist argument for recognizing the needs and rights of mothers and children separately from those of fathers, the TUC were wary of putting benefits for their children in the hands of their employers. Pay levels on average were rising well above prices at this time (full-time manual workers' earnings had risen by 13 per cent in 1972 and 14 per cent in 1973) and Edward Heath, the Prime Minister, was making little headway in curbing trade union powers. (For a fuller discussion, see Flemming (1986) and Land (1977).) The Select Committee proposed that child credit should be paid to the mother. In the event the Conservative Government was replaced early in 1974 by a Labour Government committed to increasing 'the social wage' including substantially improved benefits and services for children in return for wage restraint—the Social Contract.

This was the background against which the Finer Committee reported in July 1974. The Finer Committee's central social security proposal was for a guaranteed maintenance allowance (GMA). The GMA would be a substitute for maintenance payments which, under the proposed scheme, would be collected by the authority administering the allowance. This would remove the need for lone mothers to go themselves to court to sue for maintenance. Any maintenance collected would be offset aginst the GMA which would be based on SB rates but together with family allowance (or child benefit) would be sufficient to take lone parents off SB. There would be a cohabitation rule. GMA would consist of a childcare allowance for the adult and a separate allowance for each child (Cmnd. 5629 (1974): 285). Despite the committee's concern to minimize differences between lone parents on the basis of their legal status, they did not adopt the model of the widowed mother's allowance. Instead, the GMA was to be non-contributory and the adult allowance, in contrast to the children's component of the GMA, was to be withdrawn as earnings increased because they 'could not recommend that an allowance of this size, designed for the non-working family, should be paid to all one-parent families, however large their income; to do so would be to put working one-parent families well ahead of the widowed mother's present position and ahead of

many two-parent families, besides being an expensive way of channel-
ling help to the most needy' (ibid. 286).

The GMA was criticized for being too costly by some and by
others for being on a means-tested basis. Frank Field, then director
of CPAG, drew on the experience of FIS with its low take-up (only
half of those eligible), its alleged simplicity which had given rise to
numerous complexities and anomalies and its contribution to the
poverty trap whereby 'a family by increasing its earnings can decrease
its total disposable income' (Field 1975: 20). He warned against more
means-tested benefits. Peter Townsend argued for greater recognition
of the needs of all children, an allowance for the care of children in
the form of a home responsibility allowance similar to the invalid
care allowance the Labour Government was about to introduce and
an allowance for the upkeep of the family home plus a universal
housing allowance.

Greater stress should be placed on the fact that some of the interests of one-
parent families would be served best by measures designed to help two-parent
families as well. . . . While constructing an argument that shows the benefits to
be derived by one-parent families for a new set of measures, that argument will
gain in strength if the needs of other families, and of women generally in society,
are recognized. To press too hard a policy for the separateness of one-parent
families, may be to damage their long-term interests. (Townsend, 1975: 39)

Barbara Castle, as Secretary of State for the Social Services in 1974,
received the Finer Committee's report. She was unable to accept the
proposal for the GMA because of its implications for increasing public
expenditure at a time when, as she wrote in her diary:

the economic situation is hardly propitious for expanding it. My difficulty is
that I am right in the centre of the 'Social Contract' field. Failure to achieve
socially just policies will endanger our whole new approach as a government.
As it is, Treasury wants a meagre child endowment figure which will actually
make some families worse off. . . . I am miserably aware that I shall be able to
do little for the one-parent families during the coming five years—certainly
not Finer's cash payment as of right. (Castle 1980: 169–70)

Later she wrote that she 'certainly did not want to create a new area of
means-testing at the heart of our social policy'. In contrast, child
benefit the new universal benefit payable to the mother for every child
as of right, was one to which women responded enthusiastically.

As a flat rate benefit it was more egalitarian than tax allowances. It also had
the supreme advantage of diverting some money from the husband's pay

packet into the mother's purse, so that she had her own wage at last. Gradually expanded, it could, I believed, play an important part in rolling back dependence on means-testing. (Castle 1993: 469–70)

She did however make some changes aimed specifically at lone parents. There was now substantial evidence of the extent of the poverty of lone parents collected not only by the Finer Committee themselves over their four and a half years of deliberations, but also from the Government's own research. The research conducted in 1970 by the Government's social survey division of OPCS in Dorset, Dundee, Glasgow, Halifax, and Haringay and published in 1973 found that in all five areas 'the mean usual incomes and the mean adjusted incomes (allowing for size of family) of fatherless families are less than half those of two-parent families' (Hunt, Fox, and Morgan 1973: 31). The Finer Committee estimated that in 1971 about 280,000 or 45 per cent of all lone parents were either living on SB or had incomes below or within £2 of that standard (Cmnd. 5629 (1974): 254). Such evidence could not be ignored. In order to assist lone parents on benefit to supplement their incomes themselves, the earnings disregard was increased to £6 in 1975 (compared with £2 for unemployed claimants and £4 for their partners). The 1975 Child Benefit Act made provision for introducing child benefit for the first child of all lone parents a year in advance (1976/7) of the main child benefit scheme. In 1981 child benefit interim (CBI), as this was called, was renamed one-parent benefit and it remained a tax-free benefit paid irrespective of the lone parent's employment or income status throughout the 1980s only being called into question in the mid-1990s. In the Budget of 1975 the Chancellor of Exchequer equalized the additional personal allowance (APA) for lone parents with that of the married man's tax allowance. By the end of the 1970s it was estimated that 425,000 lone parents out of 825,000 benefited from the APA (Cmnd. 8093 (1980): 41).

Lone parents had a lower profile in the second half of the 1970s. In 1975, in addition to the Child Benefit Act, Barbara Castle successfully steered the Social Security Act and Pension Act through Parliament. Both improved the position of women within the national insurance system, reduced the extent to which their claims to benefit depended on their marital status and began to recognize the contribution women made as carers. The presumption that Beveridge had made that women were, and ought to be, financially dependent on their husbands was becoming weaker, although the attempts to delay and undermine the child benefit scheme after Barbara Castle left the DHSS when Callaghan became Prime Minister in 1976, demonstrated how deeply rooted that presumption was. (For a fuller discussion of the introduction of child benefit see Land 1977; *New Society* 1976; CPAG, 1976.) The cohabitation rule remained contentious and within private law the extent to which maintenance for children could and should be treated as distinct from maintenance for their mothers, became an issue in a number of ways.

The 1968 Maintenance Order Act had removed the limits of the maintenance which could be paid under the 1960 Matrimonial Proceedings and Magistrates Courts Act. Just before this Act, in a case *Northrop* v. *Northrop* ([1967] 3 WLR 907), it was held that whether or not the husband and wife had agreed to part or whether or not one had deserted the other, the husband by paying maintenance for a young child had implicitly undertaken to maintain his wife because the care of the child impairs the wife's earning capacity so that she could not support herself. In other words, the child's and the care giver's needs were inextricably linked. The SBC like its predecessor the NAB, treated maintenance as a resource and if a child's maintenance exceeded the amount of the child's scale rate, this was offset against the mother's benefits. (Until the limits on maintenance were removed in the 1968 Act, this was unlikely to happen because the scale rates, particularly for older children were close to the maximum.) As the 1966 Ministry of Social Security Act stated 'where a person has to provide for the requirements of another person their requirements and resources should be aggregated'.

In 1976 this was challenged as a result of a case in the Court of Appeal in 1974 concerning the treatment of the award of damages to illegitimate children whose father had died in an accident. The amount awarded to the children far exceeded the level of SB allowance each child would attract, but the court ruled that the children's resources should not be aggregated with those of their mothers, thereby removing the mother's entitlement to SB, on the grounds that she was no longer a person who 'has to provide for the requirements' of the children. The Commission did not think the ruling applied to maintenance payments until an SB Appeal Tribunal reached an opposite conclusion in 1976. At this time there were so few cases involving maintenance paid to children rather than to the parent with whom they were living, the Commission accepted the ruling. However it received wide publicity and welfare rights officers and lawyers advised their clients to arrange for maintenance to be paid to children in growing numbers. Believing this to be contrary to Parliament's intention and frustrating 'the long established legal principle that a man is liable to maintain his wife and children' (Cmnd. 8033 (1980): 90), the SBC proceeded to aggregate all maintenance payments when assessing SB. This was challenged in 1979 when an SB Appeal Tribunal, relying heavily on *K v. JMP,* decided in favour of Susan Jull and against the SBC. Their appeal in the High Court in 1980 failed as did an appeal involving Mrs Y a month later. She won on the grounds that maintenance paid to the mother for the child were not the mother's resources either (*Supplementary Benefit Commission v. Jull, Y v. Supplementary Benefit Commission* [1981] AC 1025, [1980] 2 All ER 65 (HL)). By this time the 1980 Social Security Act was going through Parliament and an amendment was introduced in the House of Lords at the Committee stage confirming the practice of aggregating maintenance payments. The same Act abolished the SBC.

The treatment of maintenance payments in the taxation system throughout this period encouraged the payment of maintenance to children in that, provided there was a court order to pay maintenance to the child, the income was treated as that of the child against which a full personal tax allowance could be offset. This was important because as described earlier, provided maintenance payments were in a legally binding form and were capable of lasting more than six years they attracted tax relief at both basic and higher rates for the payer (1980 Income and Corporation Taxes Act, s. 434). Maintenance payments counted as the recipients' taxable income. Under the 1980 Magistrates' Courts Act, s. 62, maintenance payable to the child and registered in the magistrates courts could be directly paid to the person with whom the child was living but still regarded for tax purposes as the child's allowance. If a man remarried he was able to claim the married man's tax allowance in addition to receiving tax relief on maintenance for his ex-wife and children. As John Eekalaar wrote in 1978 'It is not only where social security payments are made that public funds support a man who has to support two families' (Eekalaar 1978: 191).

In addition to these different assumptions and practices in the tax and social security systems concerning the aggregation on resources within the family, there were also different practices adopted by the courts and the SBC concerning the allocation of a man's resources between his first and second families. As already described, in the 1950s, the numbers of divorced mothers on benefit were small and the NAB took a pragmatic view. The numbers of divorced lone mothers dependent on SB grew in the 1960s and 1970s doubling between 1970 and 1975 (see Table 6.6), so the Commission developed some guidelines for negotiating with liable relatives. The Finer Committee noted that these were different from the principle and practices in the Magistrates Courts which in turn were different from those of the Divorce Courts. If there was insufficient income to go round, the courts aimed at producing equality at the SB level. The SBC, on the other hand, used a formula which left the liable relative above SB level, while the lone mother was supported at SB level. (It was revealed publicly for the first time in their evidence to the Finer Committee that the liable relative was allowed to keep for himself and his second family the amount they would be eligible for on SB plus housing costs, plus a quarter of his earnings net of tax and national insurance (but not of work expenses), or £5 which ever was higher.) However, there was evidence that in practice the courts were also likely to be more lenient with the ex-husband with a second family because of the risk of non-compliance. John Eekalaar quotes a registrar as saying: 'I have been tempted in some cases to make an order leaving both sides on social security, but (the husband) won't pay. His bread is buttered on the side of the women he is sleeping with' (Eekalaar, 1978: 191).

The Finer Committee had proposed a unified family court system to replace divorce courts and the matrimonial jurisdiction of the magis-

TABLE 6.6. *Lone mothers on Supplementary Benefit, 1970–1980*

Year	Single	Widowed	Divorced	Separated	Prisoner's wife	Total	
						N (000s)	% claimants
1970	57	25	35	88	8	212	7.7
1971	61	26	42	103	6	238	8.01
1976	82	12	92	120	5	311	10.5
1980	100	7	109	100	4	320	10.2

Sources: Cmnd. 4714 (1971) and Cmnd. 5019 (1972): Annual Reports of the DHSS for the years 1970 and 1971; Cmnd. 6910 (1977) Annual Report of SBC for 1976; and DHSS (1981) for 1980.

trates courts. This was not accepted by the Government. They did however, support developments to bring Magistrates Courts more into line with Divorce Courts in the matter of making financial orders. In 1976 the Law Commission proposed that the legislation should be based on the principles that both parties had an absolute obligation to maintain their dependent children, irrespective of how they behaved towards one another and that the obligation to maintain each other was fully reciprocal. A single act of adultery or desertion on the part of the wife should no longer debar her from seeking maintenance for herself from her husband. Since 1971 the Divorce Courts' practice was to ignore the parties, conduct when considering maintenance unless it had been 'obvious and gross'. Their proposals were incorporated in the 1978 Domestic Proceedings and Magistrates Courts Acts and implemented in 1981.

The numbers of lone parents claiming SB or FIS continued to grow through the second half of the 1970s until 1979. The cohabitation rule remained an issue. In 1976 the SBC produced another report on the subject called *Living Together as Husband and Wife*. Reiterating the need for a cohabitation rule, especially as single-parent families were now receiving more generous help, they reviewed their guidelines and officers were instructed to allow couples time to decide whether or not they wished to remain together rather than withdraw benefit before establishing that the relationship was a stable one. The 1976 Social Security (Miscellaneous Provisions) Act, substituted the phrase 'living together as husband and wife' for 'cohabitation'.

Appeals against the operation of the rule increased in numbers suggesting that claimants were still unhappy about its application. Moreover a growing proportion of appeals succeeded (see Table 6.7). Nevertheless as Jo Richardson said during the committee stage of the Social Security Bill in 1980: 'As a result of the SBC's action, we have disposed of some of the worst difficulties—perhaps not all—and we

TABLE 6.7. *Appeal against living together decisions*

Year	Appeals	Heard by Tribunals	Revised by Tribunals (%)
1974	474	340	16
1976	745	573	16
1978	1,031	747	22

Source: Cmnd. 8033 (1980).

hear less now of the kind of case which was not uncommon in the mid 1970s' (quoted Cmnd. 8033 (1980): 87).

The final report of the SBC published the year following the election of the Conservative Government devoted few pages to lone parents. As is discussed in Chapter 8 in more detail, it had come as an 'agreeable surprise' that in 1979 the numbers on benefit had fallen from 322,000 to 306,000, although with rising unemployment levels they expected the numbers to increase again.

In 1980 the Commission welcomed the Government's decision to reduce the qualifying period for the receipt of the long-term addition from two years to one although they regretted the exclusion of the unemployed. The case for the long-term addition did not rest on the characteristics of the claimants as such, but on the fact that those who were dependent on benefit for longer periods became poorer. Throughout the 1970s the average length of time a lone parent was on benefit was double that of two-parent families on benefit.

In 1976 the Commission's Policy Inspectorate had carried out an inquiry into the circumstances of one-parent and two-parent families because of 'the continuing public interest in the problems of lone parents' (Cmnd. 7725 (1979): 42). They had made careful comparisons of their needs and the extent to which they were being met by exceptional needs payments, etc. They reported that

No evidence was found that one-parent families on supplementary benefit have any special expenses or greater needs than comparable two-parent families on benefits. . . . In general many more lone parents receive supplementary benefit for much longer periods than two-parent families, including those who are unemployed. This evidence suggests that if there is a case for paying higher rates of benefit for one-parent families, it should be based on the argument *that they are more numerous and depend on benefit for longer periods, not on the arguments that they have greater financial needs*. The unemployed two-parent families with children who have been living on benefit for a year or more, although smaller in numbers, are the hardest pressed group of claimants. (ibid. 45, emphasis added)

The Commission concluded this section in their 1978 report with a plea for larger child benefits, improved SB payments for claimants with children, especially the unemployed whose numbers had doubled since the 1970s, giving mothers a real choice whether to take paid work or not, and more cooperation between the services with responsibilities for children. Recognizing the need to preserve man's work incentives, along with policies to reduce unemployment, increased child benefits 'should be the first priority for any additional expenditure on the whole system of social security' (ibid. 4). Within the SB scheme itself their priority would be to extend the higher long-term rate to unemployed claimants.

Within the Labour Government the policies of the latter half of the 1970s placed an emphasis on the extent to which the needs of lone parent families on benefit were similar to those of two-parent families, and could therefore be better met by improvements in benefits and services for all children. All fathers needed jobs and lone mothers needed to be able to choose whether to take up paid work. The Conservative Government elected in the summer of 1979 had very different priorities and perspectives.

The 1980s

Social security in general was high on the Conservative Government's agenda throughout this decade because of their commitment to curb public expenditure and to shift the emphasis from universal or contributory systems of income maintenance to selective schemes 'targeted' on the needy. The move away from dependence on means-tested benefits which Barbara Castle had wanted was quickly reversed. The 1980 Social Security Act cut the value of short-term insurance benefits by 5 per cent in real terms, removed the earnings-related additions, began to phase out the child dependant's additions (but not for widows) and made them all taxable. The link between benefit upratings and the greater of earnings or price increases, established by Barbara Castle in the 1975 legislation, was broken and henceforth all benefit increases were linked at most to price increases. (Child benefit and unemployment benefit were not even price indexed.) Equal treatment between men and women required by the EC Directive on Equal Treatment for Men and Women in Social Security (19 December 1978) was achieved by levelling men's benefits down rather than levelling women's benefits up. The same Act abolished the Supplementary Benefit Commission and the National Insurance Advisory Committee and replaced them with the Social Security Advisory Committee, which as the name implies, had none of the executive powers enjoyed by the SBC. Thus lay influence on the development and implementation of social security policies going back via local assistance and insurance advisory committees (which had survived until 1972 when they were abolished by Keith Joseph) to the nineteenth-century Boards of Guardians, was reduced to four national committees which could only advise Ministers. Ministers were free both to ignore their advice and not even to seek it in the first place. Subsequently much of the detail of social security legislation was not revealed at the time Bills were debated in Parliament, being left instead to be settled by Regulations. This reduced the opportunity for Parliament to scrutinize and debate proposed changes and analyse their impact. Social security policies and practices were in the future to be determined by national priorities and politics as interpreted by Ministers modified occasionally by various European directives. This, as will be discussed below, is a very important part of the background to the 1991 Child Support Act.

In the early 1980s the Government was preoccupied with the unemployed and particularly the young unemployed whose numbers grew dramatically because the recession coincided with record numbers of school leavers entering the labour market (the numbers of births in the UK had peaked in 1964). Young people had their benefits reduced even before the social security system was the subject of a major review in the mid-1980s. The escalating costs to the social security system of residential care for elderly people drew Government attention to the respective responsibilities of local and central government for funding and providing residential community care. The strikes of the early 1980s, in particular the miners' strike, focused Government concern on the relationship between benefits and services for children and their fathers' work incentives and the propensity to take and continue strike action. The discussion about the ways in which some local authorities were using the free school meals system, for which at that time they were still responsible, to 'subsidize' striking miners families were reminiscent of the debates over the same issue in the early 1920s.

Against this background, lone parents did not attract a great deal of attention and the changes made to their benefits in the early 1980s were on the whole, improvements. For example, the maternity grant (small though it was, for it had not been increased since 1965) was made non-contributory from 1982 benefiting in particular young teenage lone mothers, the wives of students, and of prisoners. In the 1980 Social Security Act, the qualifying period for the long-term addition as announced by the Labour Government in 1979 just prior to the election was reduced to one year, except for unemployed claimants. A tapered disregard for earnings was introduced for lone parents on SB which was more generous than for unemployed claimants or their partners. The child's supplementary benefit scale rates were reduced from five to three benefiting families with children under 5 (as well as the 11 to 12 year age group). Single lone mothers were twice as likely to have a child under 5 years either than any other group of lone mothers or than two-parent families. The lone parent's child benefit was increased from £2 to £2.50 and again to £3 from November 1980, in contrast to child benefit which was increased only by 75p. Personal tax allowances, including the APA maintained their real value. Much emphasis was placed in debates on social policy on the need to strengthen family responsibilities and tackle 'the dependency culture'. At that time it was the responsibilities of parents for older teenage children, and adult children for their elderly parents, which attracted the most attention. Carol Smart summarizing these changes, wrote that the family was becoming 'the main welfare agency of the 1980s' (Smart 1989).

The move away from discretion in the SB scheme towards a codified set of entitlements, together with cuts in the numbers of civil servants, including supplementary benefits officers, resulted in the cohabitation rule being less of an issue. The home visits, regarded as so essential by the NAB and SBC in establishing the needs and legitimacy of lone mothers' claims and in chasing liable relatives, began to be replaced by impersonal administrative procedures. When, at the end of the decade both the National Audit Office and the Committee of Public Accounts looked at the cost of support for lone parents, they attributed the decline in maintenance payments made to lone parents in part to the reduction in resources the DHSS was spending in recovering such payments (HC 153 (1990/1): 7 and HC 429 (1990/1): 11). The amount of staff time devoted to liable relative work had fallen by one-third between 1981 and 1988. In 1981/2 half of all lone parents on benefit received some maintenance but by 1988/9, this proportion had fallen to less than one-quarter (Cm. 1264 (1990) vol. ii).

In November 1983 an inquiry into provision for retirement was set up followed by a housing benefit review the following February. In April, the Secretary of State for Social Services announced three further reviews—one concerning benefits for children and young people, another to examine disablement benefits, and the third to study the structure and administration of the supplementary benefit scheme. This, the House of Commons was told would 'constitute the most substantial examination of the social security system since the Beveridge report 40 years ago' (Commons Debates, 2 April 1984, c. 660). A Green Paper in three volumes *Reform of Social Security* (Cmnd. 9517, 9518, and 9519 (1985)) was published in June 1985 followed by a White Paper *Reform of Social Security: Programme for Action* (Cmnd. 9691 (1985)) six months later. The 1986 Social Security Act reached the statute book the following summer.

Lone mothers attracted little attention in the Green and White Papers. Indeed women and children as a whole were conspicuous by their absence in these documents compared with the Beveridge Report. The focus was on men and their responsibilities (see Land 1986, for further discussion). Also in contrast to the Beveridge proposals, the focus was on means-tested benefits more than contributory benefits which were further downgraded, this time affecting long-term as well as short-term beneficiaries. The most important change for lone parents was the proposed replacement of SB with Income Support (IS). In order to reduce the complexity of the system and to reduce discretion to a minimum, the SB scale rates, long-term additions, exceptional needs payments and additional allowances for special circumstances were replaced with scale rates and premiums depending on the age and household circumstances of the claimant, plus loans from a new social fund. All families with children would receive a family premium representing 'an important step forward in support for families with children, especially for those unemployed families and lone parents at present on the short-term rate' (Cmnd. 9691 (1985): 23). Lone parents would in addition immediately qualify for a separate premium which like the long-term addition was 'in recognition of the extra pressures faced by lone parents' and the controversial lower scale rate for under 25 year olds would not apply to lone parents over 18 years. In addition the lone parent premium would continue as long as the child remained in full-time non-advanced education in contrast to the long-term addition in SB which had ended when the youngest child reached 16 years. However, widows would no longer be entitled to the contributory widowed mother's allowance while they had other teenage children living at home unless these children were in full-time education, thus reversing one of the improvements made to widows benefits in 1956. Thirty years on the Government believed that 'the needs of widows and their ability to provide for themselves have changed remarkably over the last forty years. The greatest needs now are to help with the immediate impact of bereavement and to provide continuing help for those who are least able to help themselves.' All lone parents on IS would immediately qualify for the higher disregard based on gross earnings not net of work expenses such as travel or childcare expenses. Unemployed couples would have to wait for two years to quality for these. In other words, lone parents were still being treated differently from two-parent families, not least because the Government was still preoccupied with preserving unemployed and low paid father's work incentives.

This was very clear from the controversial proposals made to pay family credit (FC) which replaced FIS, in father's pay packets rather than via a benefit book sent to the mother but cashable by either parent at the post office. Ideally, FC would have replaced child benefit but even their own surveys, as well as those of the poverty and women's lobbies, showed how unpopular this would have been. Again the question to whom benefits for children should be paid—the mother or the father—surfaced again. The campaign to save child benefit together with peers in the House of Lords, the National Farmers' Union, and the Federation of Small Businesses, succeeded in amending the Social Security Bill and FC, like FIS, is paid to the mother. All claimants of FC qualified by working a minimum of 24 hours. However earnings were to be assessed net of tax and national insurance. There were still no disregards for maintenance payments, travel costs, or childcare expenses which was of particular significance to lone parents. Unlike FIS claimants, the children of FC recipients would not be eligible for free school meals and welfare foods and owner-occupiers would not be eligible for housing benefit. The poverty trap was therefore still significant. The basic rates of FC preserved the parity between one- and two-parent families introduced 15 years earlier.

It was also clear from the Government's projection of expenditure on national programmes and numbers of claimants published in the Green Paper that they were *not* anticipating either a large growth in the numbers of lone parents or in the cost of means-tested benefits received by them. It was the anticipated cost of retirement pensions which accounted for most of the increase in the social security bill. The cost of SB for lone parents would amount to between £1 billion and £1.2 billion by 1995/6 (in 1984/5 prices) depending on whether unemployment rates were 6 per cent or 10 per cent. This compared with £1 billion in 1984/5 (Cmnd. 9519 (1985): 39). The assumption was that numbers of lone parents receiving SB would fall from 500,000 to 400,000 in 1995/6 unless unemployment rates were 10 per cent in which case the numbers would increase to 600,000. (ibid. 42). FIS claimants were expected to fall by half to 100,000 if rates were only indexed to prices and to remain the same if indexed to earnings (Table 6.8).

While the social security system was being revised with a greater emphasis on family responsibility and private provision, family law was also under review. In particular there was some concern that the interests of children were being overlooked in the process of arriving at a divorce settlement (see e.g. Wadsworth and Maclean 1986). These were therefore moves to shift the emphasis from the issue of spousal support, the determination of which still retained a consideration of the behaviour of the parties, to the question of child support. A study of the financial consequences of divorce conducted in the early 1980s (Eekalaar and Maclean 1986) showed that periodical payments after divorce almost always existed only where there were, or had been, children of the marriage. They were thought of as due to the wife but in practice the payments were a recognition of the detrimental impact which caring responsibilities have on a carer's earning capacity. Moreover, the awards were usually low. For example a national study sponsored by the Lord Chancellor's Department in 1984 found that on average a divorced mother received £10 per child (compared with SB scale rates of £14.35 for an 11–12 year-old and nearly £20 for a teenager in 1984) and that a divorced mother with two children was receiving in total £40 weekly. Earlier studies had also revealed low payments for children, which all too often were not paid (see Gibson 1994: 194). Reflecting on this period Mavis Maclean

TABLE 6.8. *Increases in lone mothers on Supplementary Benefit/Income Support, 1980–1993*

Year	Single	Widowed	Divorced	Separated	Prisoner's wife	Total	
						N (000s)	% claimants
1980	100	7	109	100	4	320	10.2
1986	213	9	172	180	4	578	11.7
1988	288	13	194	194	5	694	15.9
1990	347	13	192	220	3	774	18.5
1993	464	16	192	315	3	989	17.4

Sources: DHSS (1981), DHSS (1987), DHSS (1989), DHSS (1991), and DSS (1994) Annual Reports of DHSS for 1980, 1986, 1988, 1990; and DSS for 1993.

later wrote: 'Financial arrangements on divorce until the mid-1980s had an appearance of a hang-over from the pre-1969 fault-based divorce, incorporating an extension of the marital dispute between the parties' (Maclean 1994b: 149).

The 1984 Matrimonial and Family Proceeding Act was an attempt to improve the court-based maintenance system. Courts were instructed to put the children of the family first when making financial arrangements, but their interests were not necessarily paramount. 'This means that other considerations should be taken into account and in some circumstances could be overriding. The new enjoinder does not mean, for instance, that the husband's moral obligation towards his second family should be ignored' (Bromley and Lowe 1987: 618).

Thus, the courts were still left with the problem of reconciling the interests of a husband's first and second family and deciding what was fair and just. Although it was not the intention of Parliament, the new legislation, particularly in the changed economic climate at the end of the 1980s, encouraged the courts to continue to put the divorcing father's responsibilities to his second family before those of his first family.

First, the greater emphasis placed on both parties becoming self-sufficient and the ending of the principle (rarely put in practice following divorce) of life-long support for the wife, attracted much attention and was, as a previous chapter shows, summed up as a 'clean break'. Although the Information Pamphlet issued by the Lord Chancellor's Department suggested that a clean-break order was not appropriate where there were dependent children, in practice that often was achieved by trading the equity in, or the right to remain in the matrimonial home against future maintenance payments from the absent spouse (usually the father). With the sale of council housing in the early 1980s home ownership had extended further down the income scale and this was a more common situation. However in the recession following the housing boom in 1988:

High interest rates, falling property values and increased unemployment, have resulted in a number of cases where the equity in a family home is negative, the house cannot be sold, and the owner is on benefit. In these cases the present practice is for the absent parent to walk away from the house and mortgage which simply represents a millstone around his neck, and to leave the wife and children in the home, while, if she is on Income Support, the DSS will, for a time [sic], meet the mortgage interest repayments. (Maclean 1994b: 159—this should read 'after a time')

When FC replaced FIS in 1988, housing benefit for owner-occupiers was confined to those on IS, thus possibly acting as a disincentive to move off IS into paid work. Second, although the courts had sometimes used supplementary benefit rates as a benchmark for establishing what would be a reasonable level of maintenance, as already discussed, the availability of state benefits was not supposed to be used to reduce the absent parent's liability. However by the end of the 1980s there were cases (e.g. *Delaney* v. *Delaney* [1990] 2 TLR 457) where the courts were explicitly doing so. So quite apart from the demographic changes described in the early chapters and rising unemployment affecting women as well as men, it is not surprising that the cost of supporting lone parents on IS, which replaced SB in April 1988, increased. What shocked the Government was the rate and size of the increase.

While changes were being introduced in the social security system and in the courts, the reform of the income tax system was also on the agenda. The personal tax system which treated married women as dependants of their husband had been the subject of criticism during the 1970s, both from the women's movement and the poverty lobby which argued that the forgone revenue could be used to improve child benefit and to redistribute resources to families with caring responsibilities. When Chancellor of the Exchequer, Geoffrey Howe had wanted to reform the system for taxing married couples and in 1980 had published a Green Paper—*The Taxation of Husband and Wife*. This had a mixed reception and Margaret Thatcher was not convinced of the need for reform because, Nigel Lawson suggests, she identified with the two-earner couple who did rather well under the existing system and thought that if families were to be helped, the reintroduction of the child tax allowance was preferable (see Thatcher 1995: 631). When Nigel Lawson became Chancellor of the Exchequer he pursued the matter for, in addition to reforming company taxation, reducing tax rates, and raising the tax threshold, he was determined to reform the personal tax system.

A good tax system should be broadly based, with low tax rates and few tax breaks . . . tax breaks are inevitably abused as methods of tax avoidance, which means the general level of taxation has to be still higher to bring in the required revenue. Moreover the practice of the tax break always increases the political pressure for others. (N. Lawson 1992: 341)

He finally persuaded Margaret Thatcher to publish a Green Paper in 1986, proposing independent taxation with a fully transferable tax allowance between spouses. This met rather more criticism than he had anticipated and it involved technical issues the Board of Inland Revenue was not then equipped to deal with, so in his 1988 Budget he announced the introduction in 1990, of independent taxation, retaining the married man's allowance (renamed married couples allowance). In keeping with the Conservative Government philosophy of interfering as little as possible within the family, he took the opportunity in the same budget to abolish or reduce a range of tax reliefs which had recognized various family responsibilities, including those which had benefited cohabiting couples and men paying maintenance to former wives and children.

It is clear from his budget speech that he was concerned about the growing lack of parity between married couples and cohabiting couples, which favoured the latter. The additional personal allowance (APA) which lone parents could claim took no account of their household circumstances so a cohabiting couple with at least two children could each claim APA, thus getting, in effect, double the married man's allowance. In addition each member of a cohabiting couple could claim mortgage interest relief against their share of the home loan. Only the husband of a married couple could claim mortgage interest relief (he could agree to *share* it with his wife) for their incomes were aggregated and deemed to belong to him. This meant the cohabiting couple could claim tax relief up to a ceiling of £60,000 compared with £30,000 for the married pair. When the ceiling on the relief was close to average house prices this did not matter but when house prices took off in 1987, what was perceived as a tax penalty on marriage became more widely visible. This did not accord with the Conservative Government's aim of supporting the 'traditional' family and it was a costly loophole. Nigel Lawson therefore not only announced the introduction of independent taxation in this Budget, but restricted mortgage interest relief to the house or flat irrespective of the number of borrowers. He also limited unmarried couples to one APA between them, thus restoring parity with married couples. (Although announced in the Budget speech in March it did not take effect until August. This, as Margaret Thatcher wrote later, 'gave a huge immediate boost to the housing market as people took out mortgages before the loophole ended, and it happened at just the wrong time when the housing market was already overheating' (Thatcher 1995: 674).) He also reformed the tax treatment of maintenance removing what he called 'one of the less known tax penalties on marriage' (Commons Debates, 15 March 1988, c. 1002).

Unmarried couples he explained could use the covenant system to make 'large payments either between themselves or to their children, and get tax relief that would not have been available had they been married' (N. Lawson 1992).

Covenants between individuals were abolished (affecting mainly students and their parents). He also restricted the amount of tax relief on payments to ex-spouses. 'The present rules can be complex and confusing for people going through separation and divorce. The tax-system ought to intrude as little as possible, though it is reasonable that there should be some recognition of the fact that an ex-husband is continuing to support his ex-wife, or indeed vice versa' (ibid.). Main-tenance payments were henceforth to be tax free for the recipient and the relief to the payer was restricted up to the difference between the married and single allowances. He argued that not only would the new system be simpler but 'it will reduce the tax relief that can be obtained by the better-off payers of large amounts of maintenance, but for most couples the ex-husband will continue to enjoy full tax relief while the ex-wife will not be taxed' (ibid.). As tax rates had fallen in the 1980s, the value of tax relief on maintenance payments was worth less than during the 1970s when tax rates were much higher. However, since the early 1980s, a Practise Direction had been devised which facilitated the payment of school fees direct to the school while still attracting tax relief for the payer (see Bromley and Lowe 1987: 657). In 1987 a father with custody of the children took advantage of this by applying an order against himself (*Sherdley* v. *Sherdley* [1987] All ER 54). As Lord Meston said during the debate in the House of Lords on the Family Law Bill nearly ten years later:

It was a tax regime which lasted until 1988. If ever there were a time for cynical millionaires to try to get bogus divorces it was then. As a practitioner at the time, I was pretty irritated to see some of my clients receiving that level of tax relief, but I was never tempted to go through a divorce to get the housekeeping set against tax (Lords Debates, 29 February 1996, c. 1526).

Since the introduction of independent taxation the married couples' allowance has declined in real value and currently can only be set against the lowest rate of tax. The APA has been similarly reduced. What is interesting about the 1988 Budget is that it marked a shift in the debate about parity between one- and two-parent families to that between married and cohabiting couples. For the first time it was argued that parity required a reduction in the benefits enjoyed by lone parents, moreover benefits usually enjoyed by lone fathers. With the advantage of hindsight, it was a sign of things to come (Table 6.9).

By the end of the 1980s the numbers of lone parents and the cost to the social security system of their benefits were increasing rapidly. In 1979 families headed by lone mothers were 10 per cent of all families. By 1990, this had nearly doubled to 18 per cent. Expenditure on their benefits had also doubled in real terms. Moreover the biggest increase was among mothers who were single and had never married (from 2 per cent to 6 per cent). The children of lone parents accounted for three-fifths of all children of IS claimants in 1989, compared with under half in 1986 (see Table 6.10). It was estimated that the UK had the highest proportion of lone parent families in the EC (Roll 1992). Both the main parties had claimed to be the party of the family (meaning the traditional married family) in the 1979 election, and as the 1980s drew to a close Margaret Thatcher took a growing interest in these demographic trends and their consequences not only for public expenditure but also for society as a whole. She wrote later:

I became increasingly convinced during the last two or three years of my time in office that, although there were crucially important limits to what politicians could do in this area, we could only get to the roots of crime and much else besides by concentrating on strengthening the traditional family . . . all the evidence, statistical and anecdotal, pointed to the breakdown of families as the starting point for a range of social ills. (Thatcher, 1995: 628–9)

Lone parents had been moved into the political spotlight and for the first time, influenced by the US New Right theorists such as Charles Murray, absent fathers were caught in its beam. As the earlier discussion in this

TABLE 6.9. *Expenditure on benefits for lone parents, 1978–1993*

Year	£ million (1992/3 prices)	£ million Cash terms
1978/9	2,448	877
1984/5	3,100	1,980
1986/7	3,759	2,614
1988/9	4,614	3,631
1990/1	5,358	4,853
1992/3	6,631	6,631

Source: DSS 1993a: 23.

TABLE 6.10. *Number (000s) of children in lone parent families as a per cent of children in all families on Supplementary Benefit/Income Support, 1979–1993*

Age of children	1979			1986			1989			1993		
	N=	%	Total all families	N=	%	Total all families	N=	%	Total all families	N=	%	Total all families
Under 11	378	52	724	694	49	1,427	989	63	1,558	1,377	61	2,251
11–16	170	60	284	266	45	590	261	58	451	389	56	688
16–17	19	65	29	45	44	102	45	50	90	84	52	161
TOTAL	567	55	1,037	1,005	47	2,119	1,295	61	2,099	1,850	60	3,100

Sources: DHSS (1980): *Social Security Statistics for 1979*, table 34.31 p. 160; DHSS (1987): *Social Security Statistics for 1986*, table 34.82 p. 211; DSS (1990): *Social Security Statistics 1989*, table A2.12 p.27; DSS (1994): *Social Security Statistics for 1993*, table A2.09 p. 21.

chapter has shown, sustaining men's incentives to take and to keep paid employment has always been a preoccupation of those responsible for the benefit system, but now their willingness to support their children outside, as well as within marriage, was under scrutiny. The image of the lone parent behind many of the reforms between the mid-1960s and mid-1980s had been the parent (often a widow or widower) struggling 'single-handed' to bring up her (his) children. By the end of the 1980s the image had shifted to the young never-married mother entirely dependent upon the benefit system, freeing the 'feckless father' of all responsibilities, or of the divorced mother whose ex-husband had walked out to create a second family, leaving his first dependent on the state.

The 1990s

The decade started with a recession. Between March 1990 and September 1993, nearly 440,000 female full-time jobs and 1.4 million male full-time jobs were lost. Part-time employment grew by 120,000 for women and 90,000 for men (HC 227–iii (1994/95): 421). The ability of men and women to support their families single-handed was diminished. Margaret Thatcher lost little time in putting a change in the direction of family policies high on the Government's agenda. In a widely reported speech to the National Children's Homes in January 1990 she announced her determination that separated fathers should pay more towards the maintenance of their children. She recalled in her memoirs that she

was appalled by the way in which men fathered a child and then absconded, leaving the single mother—and the tax payer—to foot the bill for their irresponsibility and condemning the child to a lower standard of living. I thought it scandalous that only one in three children entitled to receive maintenance actually benefited from regular payments. So—against considerable opposition from Tony Newton, the Social Security Secretary and from the Lord Chancellor's Department—I insisted that a new Child Support Agency be set up and that maintenance be based not just on the cost of bringing up a child but on that child's right to share in its parents' rising living standards. This was the background to the 1991 Child Support Act. (Thatcher 1995: 630)

An interdepartmental working party was established and in October 1990 the White Paper, *Children Come First* was published. Meanwhile, without waiting for the legislation which established the Child Support Agency, changes were included in the 1990 Social Security Act to strengthen the liable relative procedures. These allowed the DSS to recover IS paid from a wider range of relationships. As already discussed, prior to 1990 a spouse was liable in respect of IS paid to his or her spouse and a parent was liable in respect of IS paid for his or her children, irrespective of whether the child was born within marriage. Former spouses were not liable except insofar as it was paid to an ex-spouse for their children.

The 1990 Social Security Act inserted a new section 24a into the 1986 Social Security Act which meant that a former spouse could be liable not only for the IS paid for the children but also for the IS paid for the maintenance of the parent with the care of the children. It also applied to unmarried parents if a maintenance order was in force in favour of one or more of the children or the parent (an unlikely situation). However, there were circumstances in which a mother had allowed a maintenance order to lapse because, for example, attempts to enforce it had created difficulties over the arrangements for access to the children. So although the 1990 Social Security Act did not give the Secretary of State the power to initiate an application for a maintenance order, it gave considerable discretion to the DSS officers to reactivate orders.

These changes, together with more emphasis placed on liable relative work following the criticisms of the Public Accounts Committee and the National Audit Office already mentioned, had an impact on IS claimants as measured by the increased numbers who ceased claiming shortly after contact with the liable relative's unit, as Table 6.11 shows.

The 1991 Child Support Act has much wider powers than any

TABLE 6.11. *Income Support claims which ceased within four weeks of liable relative action*

Year	Numbers of claims ceasing	£ million	
		Savings (A)	Savings (B)
1989/90	47,122	207	270
1990/1	60,056	232	315
1991/2	80,261	283	400

(A) assumes benefit saved for 21 weeks; (B) 51 weeks.

Sources: HC 69 (1993/4): 44; HC 440 (1995/6): 81.

previous social security legislation and, as discussed in earlier chapters, responsibility for the maintenance of children and their mother in her capacity as their carer, rests with the biological father irrespective of any past or present marital relationship. It was clear from the formula that the needs of first families were to take precedence over the needs of second families, thus reversing the former pragmatic policies of the NAB, SBC, and the DHSS. The Secretary of State's powers to initiate an application for a maintenance order even if the claimant wishes to have no further contact with the absent parent are much stronger than in any previous legislation and the refusal of a mother to name the father without 'good cause' can lead to a reduction in her allowance. In the White Paper, the Government only envisaged allowing a mother to refuse to name the father of her child(ren) if 'the child had been conceived as the result of rape, or where there has been incest' (Cmd. 1264 (1990): vol. i, para. 5.36). Otherwise her refusal to cooperate in the enforcement of a maintenance order against the father would incur a penalty of a reduction of 20 per cent in her benefit. The House of Lords removed the penalty in the passage of the Bill through the House, but the House of Commons reinserted it but such was the opposition to the narrow range of circumstances in which it was legitimate for a mother to refuse to be forced into dependence on the father of her children, the Act recognized a slightly wider range of circumstances. The Act states that the Secretary of State will not take action to recover child support maintenance from the absent parent where there are reasonable grounds for believing that if she gave or was required to give authorization 'there would be a risk of her, or of any child living with her, suffering harm or undue distress as a result' (s. 62).

Similarly s. 46(3) of the Act states that the child support officer, before serving notice requiring compliance, must consider these risks when the mother has failed to comply even though the Secretary of State has required action to be taken. Bradshaw and Millar's study found that one in six of divorced and one in ten of single and separated mothers on benefit gave violence as the main reason for leaving the father of their children (Bradshaw and Millar 1991) so the penalties incurred by the mothers—and their children—if the child support officers interpret section 6 too narrowly, go far beyond the financial ones.

During its passage through Parliament, there was concern about the possible negative impact on the welfare of lone mothers and their children, in particular the requirement that they name the fathers of their children and penalizing them with a cut in benefit if they refused without a 'good cause'. There was also concern that payment of maintenance would leave parents and children on IS no better off because any increase in maintenance paid would result in an equivalent reduction in benefit. Amendments to include a maintenance disregard in IS, as there would be for Family Credit, failed. Nevertheless, there seemed to be widespread public acceptance of the principle that parents should provide realistic financial support for their children whenever possible. While lawyers, particularly those in the House of Lords, were concerned about splitting the determination of maintenance from the system dealing with other financial aspects of divorce into an administrative agency with an extremely limited appeals mechanism, they welcomed the reduction of uncertainty which the application of the formula would bring to their clients. Parliamentary scrutiny of the proposals was limited by the fact that the Bill gave the Secretary of State for Social Security over 100 regulation-making powers. In other words, crucial details would be settled after the Bill had reached the statute books. Lord Mishcon called the Bill 'a legislative skeleton' (Lords Debates, 25 February 1991, c. 780).

In its first year the Child Support Agency (CSA) attracted enormous media attention, featuring in front-page headlines and much of it highly critical. Hate mail and death threats led to round-the-clock security at its regional offices. On the day of the Agency's first anniversary, wreaths were laid outside the home of the Chief Executive, Ros Hepplewhite, because six suicides had, unofficially at least, been attributed in part to the Agency's dealing with fathers faced with increased bills for maintenance. An active and vocal campaign against the Child Support Act was quickly established. Within six months of its implementation there was sufficient concern for the House of Commons' Social Security Committee to examine its operations.

The complaints arising from the application of the formula for calculating maintenance which received most media attention came predominantly from fathers already paying some maintenance and/or still in contact with their children. There were several reasons for this. As Ros Hepplewhite told the Social Security Select Committee in their first examination of the Act:

I think there was a lack of awareness about the nature of the new arrangements. Certainly we had a great deal of coverage about the concerns of parents with care. We also had a great deal of coverage . . . about 'full away fathers'. In reality, the new arrangements affect *all* fathers. (HC 470 (1993/4): 19; emphasis added)

Those fathers who did not see themselves as 'runaway' or 'absent' did not expect to attract the attention of the CSA. When they did, they were very angry at having to pay substantially increased levels of maintenance, particularly as they felt the formula was far too crude in a number of respects.

There was resentment that the legislation was being applied retrospectively and thus overturning agreements made in court. 'Clean-break' settlements were ignored and fathers who had given up their share in the equity in the matrimonial home or had borrowed money in order to secure a home for their former wife and children in return for reduced maintenance payments were outraged to be faced with large assessments. Those who saw their children regularly were angry that expenses connected with visiting children or having children visit were ignored by the formula and some decided they could no longer afford to maintain contact with their children. Those with second families found that their standard of living was sharply reduced because the cost of maintaining stepchildren and a second wife were ignored in the formula whether or not the absent father was actually maintaining his second family. They and their new partners felt second families were being treated unfairly compared with first families. There was particular resentment at having to pay £44 (the value of the IS allowance for an adult) to 'the parent as carer', particularly as this continued until the youngest child was 16 years—an age well beyond that which prevents a mother from taking paid employment.

The anger of this group of fathers was fuelled by the belief that they were 'soft targets'. The Government had set the CSA the task of saving £530 million in their first year by increasing the amount of maintenance paid to lone parents on benefit and thus reducing the benefit paid. Moreover, Ros Hepplewhite was on performance-related pay and it was widely believed that CSA staff received bonuses on the basis of the amount of maintenance recovered. In her evidence to the Select Committee Ros Hepplewhite admitted that a year before the CSA began its work, it was agreed 'that the absent parent who currently paid should be given priority' (HC 470 (1993/4): 8) because they were taking over responsibility for this group from the liable relatives unit. However, she went on to say that they were only one-quarter of the group the CSA was dealing with in their first year because the majority of cases being dealt with were people newly claiming IS or Family Credit. By the end of their first year the CSA was aiming to have one million cases and in 750,000 of those maintenance would be payable although some of the assessments would not be made until 1994/5.

The Social Security Committee's first report in the parliamentary session 1993/4 was devoted to an analysis of these complaints in the context of a review of the overall operation on the CSA. They recorded their approval of Government statements that 'it will listen carefully to detailed criticisms of how the new Act is functioning' because the Committee believed that 'the Child Support Act represents the most fundamental change in social policies for 40 years or more' (HC 69 (1993/4): p. vii). They recommended making adjustments to the formula in order to 'maintain and increase public support' (ibid., p. xv). The 'intensity of feeling which has been expressed in correspondence to the Committee' was noted, adding that the CSA 'is, after all, dealing with one of the most sensitive areas in which any government can intervene' (ibid., p. xvii).

They recommended that adjustments should be made to the formula. In particular, the income below which the absent parent's income should not be pushed should not be less than £20, or even £40, above IS levels, compared with the existing £8. Payment of assessments should be phased in over a period of two years, an allowance for the cost of the care of stepchildren should be made and some consideration should be made to reducing the care component of the maintenance assessment once children reached 11 years of age because the carer was more likely to be able to take up paid employment herself (or himself) at that stage. Although they had some sympathy for absent parents who had thought that in making a capital settlement they would not be asked to pay high levels of maintenance, the Committee could not see how past settlements could be valued in order to give some historical figure for current income. In any case they accepted the Government's view that in principle the law had never allowed fathers to be completely absolved from paying maintenance for their children; even after 'clean-break' settlements it was still open to the ex-spouse to return to court and seek higher maintenance.

The Committee questioned Ros Hepplewhite about the CSA's operational problems for they—and the Press—had received numerous complaints about the length of time assessments were taking, delays in responding to letters, mistakes in assessments, etc. In the first six months, the CSA had taken on 527,000 cases (all but 20,000 on IS) and calculated benefit savings were £100 million, well short of £530 million. The average maintenance assessment was £50, double that of the average court payment. By November the Agency had processed 56,000 cases of which 36,000 actually involved making a maintenance assessment. Individual assessments were taking between 6 and 14 weeks even in straightforward cases and during that time absent parents were building up arrears amounting to hundreds of pounds. This, as the Committee said, was 'simply too long'. As the acting Chief Executive of the DSS Information Technology Services Agency told the Social Security Committee in a later inquiry on the work of the DSS and its agencies (HC 382 1994/5)), some of the CSA's difficulties arose from the fact that:

The CSA was a new business [sic] for UK social security. It was staffed by a set of people who in the main had come from other bits of the DSS and were creating a new set of legislation, a new approach and a new operation. Those people who were creating that were also defining the requirements for a computer system.

He continued:

The system was produced in a very short and very aggressive timetable (HC 382 (1994/5): 80)

These views echoed those of the Ombudsman who, in his third report for the session 1994/5, was disappointed that so little had been learned from the teething problems of the introduction of the Disability Living Allowance (HC 199 (1994/5)).

The adjustments made to the formula in February 1994 in the light of the Social Security Committee's proposals added to the Agency's workload in the short run and the Secretary of State for Social Security had to admit 'operational experience is showing that the assessment process is more time consuming than expected . . . it is clear that both staff and clients are taking longer than expected to get to know the new procedures' (cited by NACAB 1994: 64).

Criticism of the CSA continued throughout 1994. The organizations in the voluntary sector who worked with and advised social security claimants published a number of critical reports (Garnham and Knights, 1994b; NACAB 1994; NCOPF 1994). Unlike the press, which had focused on absent fathers and their second families, they drew attention to the difficulties lone mothers were having and were critical of Ministers who:

have sought to characterize the present debate about the merits of the child support scheme as a conflict between the interests of parents with care and those of absent parents. Concessions to one lobby would mean losses to the other. . . . Crucially, the scenario presented by ministers ignores the interests of children and the role the government has in ensuring their welfare. (NACAB 1994: 107)

The press was also monitoring the progress of the CSA. Campaign groups like Families Need Fathers and the new Network Against the Child Support Act (NACSA) lobbied politicians and journalists. On Father's Day they had attempted to hold a rally in Trafalgar Square but the Heritage Commission banned it.

'Child Agency Says Sorry' was the headline in the *Evening Standard*, 4 July 1994, announcing that Ros Hepplewhite had admitted and regretted in the CSA's first annual report that the CSA was falling short of its £530 million target by £112 million, was arranging maintenance in fewer than one-third of eligible applications against a target of three-fifths, was still taking too long in making assessments and replying to letters and so on. On that day the House of Commons debated an Opposition motion on the CSA calling attention to 'the collapse of public confidence in the system and ever-increasing administrative problems besetting the Agency' and calling for 'an urgent and funda-mental review to eliminate injustice by tackling key areas of concern' (Commons Debates, 4 July 1994, c. 23). The debate lasted over six hours and focused on the inflexibility of the formula, the lack of a maintenance disregard for IS claimants, the failure to recognize clean-break settlements and the lack of an independent appeal procedure. The Minister of Social Security noted that 'more voices were raised on behalf of women than we have heard in past debates on this subject . . . much of the debate and newspaper coverage had focused on men's problems' (Commons Debates, 4 July 1994, c. 111/112).

Official reviews of the CSA's performance were also critical. The Chief Child Support Officer's first annual report (HC 596 (1994/5)) found a very poor standard of adjudication even allowing for a difficult first year. In a sample of 1,380 maintenance assessments, 39 per cent were found to be incorrect, 11 per cent were correct but wrongly adjudicated, and in 35 per cent of cases there was insufficient evidence to judge. Only 14 per cent were completely correct. Earnings and

housing costs were the most problematic items (cited in *Benefits* (April/
May 1995): 43). The backlog of assessments was getting worse. Just
before Parliament rose for the Christmas recess, the Social Security
Minister announced that one-third of all the cases identified by the CSA
would be put aside until a more efficient way of processing new cases
had been developed. 'Child Agency Shelves a Third of its Cases' was
the headline in the *Daily Telegraph*, 21 December 1994, explaining that
this meant 'hunt for 350,000 fathers called off'. By this time, Ros
Hepplewhite had resigned.

Further changes were introduced in 1995 following the Social Security Committee's second report on the CSA (HC 303 (1994/5)). Some
changes to the formula were introduced quickly in April following the
publication of the White Paper, *Improving Child Support*, in February,
for these only required a change in regulations. These included making a
'broad brush' allowance for property transfers made before April 1993,
making an allowance for travel to work costs, allowing an absent parent
to deduct all reasonable costs of housing his new partner and stepchildren and setting a ceiling of assessments of 30 per cent of net income.
Other changes required primary legislation. The 1995 Child Support
Act reached the statute books in the summer. This introduced a
limitation to the arrears in maintenance which could accrue due to
the Agency's delays, deferred indefinitely the take-on of non-benefit
cases, introduced a child maintenance bonus, and provided for com-
pensation for parents on Family Credit or disability working allowance
whose maintenance was cut because of other policy changes. The child
maintenance bonus worth £5 a week could be accumulated by lone
parents on IS up to £1,000, cashable when they returned to work. This
was offered instead of a straightforward maintenance disregard. Once
an assessment had been made it would be possible for either parent to
apply for a 'departure' from the assessment. It was claimed that these
would be under 'tightly defined circumstances' and included circumstances in which the absent parent had presented a false or misleading
picture of his (or her) circumstances. Overall, these changes addressed
some of the most pressing problems and in the longer term 'may not
be exactly a "Prague Spring" but they do seem to constitute an
admission that the original, somewhat ideological system was bound
to achieve injustice in some cases. For this one must be grateful'
(District Judge Roger Bird (1995): 1114).

While the Government was responding to absent fathers' concerns
more positively, there was still concern about the growing numbers of

never-married mothers and the rising cost of social security benefits. 'Lilley Targets Benefits of Lone Mothers' was the headline in the *Daily Telegraph*, 31 March 1995. It was reported that:

Mr Lilley has decided to revive controversial proposals to limit benefits for lone parent families which were abandoned after the 'back to basics' fiasco last year. . . . The decision to return to the issue of unmarried mothers follows growing concern in Whitehall over figures suggesting that the numbers of lone-parent families claiming income support will grow by 50,000 a year to the end of the century. . . . Two-parent families face a notional bill of £1,700 per household to meet the costs of lone parenthood.

Here the interests of lone parents were being presented as being in conflict with the interests of two-parent families. While the CSA continued to be criticized despite the 1995 Child Support Act, for there were many both inside and outside Parliament who were convinced that it should be abolished rather than reformed, the debates about lone mothers took place against the background of growing concern about the alleged lack of support for the 'traditional' two-parent family. As discussed in earlier chapters, this was also an important feature of the controversies facing the passage of the 1996 Family Law Act through Parliament. As the following chapter shows, these concerns also had an impact on the measures contained in the 1996 Housing Act. Parity between one- and two-parent families was high on the agenda again but, unlike the 1970s, the search was for measures which would reduce benefits paid to lone parents in general and lone mothers in particular. This combined with growing concern about social security fraud—a concern which also exercised those responsible for housing benefit—resulted in changes in benefit rules which were more punitive than previous measures.

In November 1995 when there were 1,056,000 (64 per cent) lone parents claiming IS, Peter Lilley made it clear that:

it was the government's intention, over time, to narrow the existing gap between benefits which go to lone parents and those which go to couples. . . . As a first step towards narrowing the gaps. . . . One Parent Benefit and the lone parent premiums in the income-related benefits would not be increased at the April 1996 uprating. (Cm. 3926 (1996): 11)

The question of parity between one- and two-parent families was raised again in 1996 when it was announced that after April 1998 no new claims for one-parent benefits would be accepted and those newly claiming IS would no longer qualify for the one-parent premium. In the 1996 Budget the MCA was increased (along with the APA) although its use was still restricted to the lowest tax-rate. The Conservative Party's ambivalence about phasing out the MCA altogether was reflected in the announcement during the 1997 Election Campaign that the spouse at home looking after children or a sick or elderly person would be allowed to transfer their unused personal tax allowance to the bread-winner. This is similar to the proposed transferable allowance in both the Green Papers on reforming the tax system in the 1980s already discussed. Overall these measures will reduce the incomes of the poorest lone mothers and their children and will do little to help either two- or one-parent families earn sufficient income to support them-selves and their children. They do indicate a determination to reward the 'traditional' married two-parent family and a belief that making life harsher for lone mothers will make them 'choose' married parenthood. The impact on the children appears to have been little considered.

Escalating expenditure on IS also intensified the search for fraud and attention turned, as opponents to the original Child Support Act had predicted, to those lone mothers who were pleading that they had 'good cause' in not naming the fathers of their children.

The Social Security Committee had looked at how the good cause provisions were working in their Fifth Report of 1993/4 (HC 470 (1993/4)). The CSA figures showed in the first year that 8 per cent (65,000 cases) of the application forms issued needed investigation into whether or not there was a good cause. In nearly half these cases 'good cause' was accepted and only in 700 cases was benefit reduced. A further review was conducted and published in April 1996 (Analy-tical Services Division 1996) and found that good cause had become an issue in about 15 per cent of cases. In a total of 112,378 cases, good cause had been accepted and about 50,000 reduced benefit directives issued in the first three years of the Agency's work. The Social Security Committee looked at the issue again in the summer of 1996; for the DSS was concerned that the proportion of parents accepting a reduced benefit direction had doubled in a year from 4.3 per cent to 9 per cent. 'There is a real danger that co-operation with the Child Support Agency could be seen as voluntary' (HC 440 (1995/6): p. vii). Given that the first year or so had included a higher proportion of lone mothers in contact with fathers who were paying maintenance (the soft targets already discussed), it is not surprising that this proportion had increased.

Fear of violence was the main reason given (in 73 per cent of cases) for not naming the father, followed by concern for the interests of the welfare of the child. In 1990 the DSS told the Committee that only 4 per cent of lone mothers were refusing to name the father because of fear of violence. (This is hardly a fair comparison as the legal framework then was rather different for the father of an illegitimate child then had no responsibility to maintain the mother, as already discussed.) The Social Security Committee was concerned that fear of violence was only corroborated in 4 per cent of cases and, citing practice in New Zealand, recommended that mothers notify the police in all cases involving fear of violence. They also drew attention to the lack of personal contact with the CSA compared with the former liable relative system. Under that system all parents with care were interviewed unless it was already clear that it would not be 'cost-effective' in terms of the public purse to pursue maintenance. In other words, they worked pragmatically and if the liable relative was in low-paid employment or there had been no contact within a given period, the matter was not pursued. The process of arranging maintenance went alongside the process of awarding benefit and usually involved personal contact. This had been lost in the lengthy CSA procedures averaging 37 weeks and conducted mainly by letter and telephone. (The results would have come as no surprise to former NAB or SBC liable relative officers for as already discussed these were recognized to be very sensitive issues requiring delicate handling, even if in some cases this was not forthcoming.)

In their evidence to the Social Security Committee and subsequently to the House of Commons Standing Committee on Delegated Legislation, in July (on the day Members of Parliament voted themselves a 28 per cent pay rise) the Government made much of a study based on the detailed examination of just 72 cases drawn, it was not revealed how, from a bigger study of 3,000 cases. It was reported that in nearly half the cases fraud was established or suspected. Moreover, in 45 per cent of cases where a reduced benefit direction had been issued, the parent with care failed to make contact with the Agency. They concluded that current penalties were inadequate: 'The level of the reduction—less than £10 for the first six months, half that amount for another year and then no penalty at all—provides insufficient incentive for those minded to abuse the child support system' (Sixth Standing Committee on Delegated Legislation, 10 July 1996, p. 4).

The penalty was increased to 40 per cent (nearly £20) of the parent's allowance for three years with the possibility of renewal. As Mildred Gordon, opposing the regulation, said:

Given the changing relationships between men and women, we have a serious problem with finding a good system of child maintenance and we have a serious problem of child poverty. Giving more draconian powers to the Child Support Agency will not solve these problems, it can only harm the children whom we want to help. (ibid. 14)

Conclusion

In less than ten years, lone mothers had moved to centre-stage in the debates about rising expenditure on social security, fraud, and abuse. Their increased visibility in the social policy debates was not, as the debates in the late 1960s and 1970s had been, primarily due to either concern about the welfare of children in general and poor children in particular, or to an acceptance of the desirability of reducing inequalities between men and women. These concerns involved a debate about the collective responsibility which wider society should have for its children as well as about the responsibilities which all parents have to maintain and care for their children and each other. From the mid-1980s the debates were more narrowly framed within a discussion about the ways in which responsibilities for children should be shared between individual mothers and fathers in order to reduce the cost of children in general and by lone mothers in particular to the state and therefore to 'the taxpayer'. As a result the interests of mothers and fathers and of first and second families were pitted against each other. In the process the needs and rights of children, particularly the growing number of poor children, were lost. As it became clear that many fathers were either unable or unwilling to contribute more to the cost of their children, policies switched away from trying to change the behaviour of fathers to changing that of lone mothers. As Chapter 8 shows, emphasis on improving mothers' abilities to support themselves and their children by taking paid employment grew in the latter half of the 1990s. However, these policy initiatives failed to address the structural factors driving the shocking increase in child poverty in the 1980s and 1990s, and lone mothers' vulnerability to poverty. The focus instead was on altering the behaviour of lone mothers, if necessary by withdrawing benefits from them. Lone mothers and their children have always been vulnerable to poverty but changes in family and labour-market structures during the 1980s and 1990s at the same time as reduced access to alternative forms of support, particularly from within the family, as the next chapter will show, had increased their vulnerability.

7

Housing and Lone Mothers

In the immediate post-war years priorities and public subsidies affecting both the public and private housing sectors were determined nationally. Local government remained responsible for the provision and administration of social housing. The provision of public-sector housing had not undergone the major restructuring which had occurred within the social security system. Enormous scope for local variations with respect to both allocation policies and rent levels remained. Moreover, while applicants for local authority accommodation did not have to have been born in the area, it was common policy to require them to prove 'a local connection'. The old laws of settlement going back to the fourteenth century no longer cast their shadow on the social assistance system after 1948 but continued to do so on post-war housing policies. This lingered on into the 1970s and, as the discussion on the debates leading up to the 1996 Housing Act will show, concern about the perceived priority homeless families had over local families on the waiting list in the allocation of social housing, was one of the considerations in the removal of a local authority's duty established in the 1977 Housing (Homeless) Act to offer such families permanent housing. The fact that a disproportionate number of homeless families were lone mothers, albeit mainly with a local connection, added to the sense that priorities within the social housing sector were both unfair and wrong.

The 1950s and 1960s

In the 1950s and 1960s however, lone parents were of no particular concern to those responsible for housing policies. In 1950 nearly half of all households were in privately rented accommodation and property owners were free to select tenants on whatever basis they liked. Until the early 1970s, maybe as many as half of all unmarried mothers were 'concealed' in their parents' households. Those who could find no room in the private sector or within the family home could easily be ignored by local authority housing departments. Although local authority housing was for families, this meant two-parent families. Few housing departments were responsible for housing homeless families throughout this period, so it was left to welfare departments and children's departments to deal with the consequences of the failure of both public and private sectors to provide affordable accommodation for all who needed it. Not surprisingly, the response to the needs of lone mothers when they did make demands on local services was often inconsistent and contradictory. The changing structure of, and division of responsibilities between, local government departments in the 1970s as well as the shift in the 1980s and 1990s from subsidising 'bricks and mortar' to subsidizing individuals through means-tested benefits and taxation policies determined nationally, is the context in which housing policies have affected, and been affected by, perceptions of lone mothers and their problems.

The focus of debates on housing in the 1950s and 1960s did not encompass lone parents per se at all. Insofar as they were seen, their existence as well as their problems were seen to be the result of inadequate responses at all levels of government to the housing and demographic changes of this period. At the beginning of the 1950s both Labour and Conservative Governments were committed to building large numbers of dwellings despite the shortage of materials. There had been two million wartime marriages and families wanted and expected a home of their own. At the same time, nearly half a million homes had been destroyed or rendered permanently uninhabitable and there were still half a million slums waiting to be cleared from 1939. The Labour Government gave high priority to building new homes, particularly in the local authority sector and by 1951 had built 900,000. The Conservative Government's 1952 Housing Act increased the subsidy to local authorities to build but at the same time increased the number of licences granted to private builders. In 1954, a year in which 348,000 dwellings were built, the Housing and Repairs Act was passed. This reduced the subsidies to 'general needs' housing which enabled local authorities to house families from the waiting list. Subsidies for slum clearance were retained. Three years later all subsidies for general needs housing ended and were only available for slum clearance and special needs housing, in particular one-bedroom dwellings for elderly people. By then local authority building had fallen by half, some local authorities, for example London had in effect closed their waiting lists.

Between 1956 and 1960, the LCC rehoused only 5,000 of the 160,000 on the waiting list (Donnison and Chapman 1965). Housing policies were aimed primarily at private building and improving the existing housing stock. Altogether during the 1950s, two and a half million dwellings were built in England and Wales, two-thirds in the local authority sector.

The pattern of tenure was changing. As Table 7.1 shows, the local authority sector grew significantly during the 1950s. However, there is evidence that lone parents were less likely than two-parent families to become tenants of local authorities. The Central Housing Advisory Committee published a report on unsatisfactory tenants in 1955. They wrote of 'one special group of families to whom we wish to draw attention' and continued:

These are the families which consist of unsupported mothers with children: the mothers may be widowed, divorced or separated from their husbands or deserted by them, or they may be unmarried. Whatever their situation, these women generally have very great difficulty in finding homes for themselves and their children. Yet it would appear at least as desirable that children deprived of a father should be given the advantage of a home background as children with both parents. . . . We should like to support the suggestion of the County Councils' Association that in the interests of the children housing authorities should in appropriate cases, offer such families some of their lower rented houses. (Central Housing Advisory Committee 1955: 19)

The committee had found that in the first four months of 1954 there were 401 unsupported mothers in temporary accommodation provided

TABLE 7.1. *Proportion of households in different housing tenures by year*

Year	Owner-occupier		Public-sector rented		Private-sector/ housing association dwellings rented and other		Total
	000s	%	000s	%	000s	%	
1950	4,100	30	2,500	18	6,200	53[a]	13,900
1961	6,885	42	4,201	26	5,187	32	16,273
1971	9,610	51	5,811	31	3,578	18	19,000
1981	11,936	57	6,387	30	2,755	13	21,078
1991	15,517	67	5,049	22	2,418	11	22,983

[a] includes 8% 'other'.

Sources: Cm. 2207 (1993); CSO 1970: 136.

under part III of the 1948 National Assistance Act with a total of 1,094 children among them. The majority of the children were with their mothers but 144 were in the care of children's departments. Only 116 of these families had their names on a local authority waiting list. 'This may be partly due to a belief that they stood little chance of success' (ibid.). Lone parents, with the exception of widows, were also less likely to be rehoused as a result of slum clearance because they were more likely to be newcomers to the area and most local authorities did not accept responsibility for households who had lived in their accommodation for a short period.

Slum clearance was also reducing the private rented sector. The 1957 Rent Act, which attempted to reinvigorate the private sector by decontrolling rents, failed to reverse this trend (see Table 7.1), although within a year nearly one-fifth of rents had become decontrolled and by 1962, nearly one-third. Altogether in the three years 1957 to 1960, nearly one and a half million tenancies in the private sector were decontrolled (two-thirds because the tenants moved out). This left 2.9 million controlled tenancies.

At the same time house prices as well as rents were rising, particularly in the lower end of the market. Between 1958 and 1963 average house prices in London and the south-east rose by 60 per cent compared with 25 per cent in the north-east. The demand for more housing was increasing not just because the population was increasing overall (the population of England and Wales increased by 5 per cent between 1951 and 1961) but because the number of households was increasing at a faster rate (12 per cent during the 1950s). This was due both to the growing number of elderly people who expected to remain living in separate households and partly due to growing numbers of young married couples who, because of higher standards of living, expected to have their own home. Large conurbations and Greater London where job opportunities were growing attracted newcomers who added to the pressures on the housing market.

By the early 1960s homelessness and the shortcomings of the private rented sector were becoming issues of public concern. Jeremy Sandford's play Cathy Come Home was not televised until 1967 but his first article on the subject of homelessness was published in The Observer in 1961 and attracted much correspondence. The scandals surrounding the activities of the London landlord Perec Rachman vividly portrayed how poorer tenants and newcomers including recent black immigrants were open to appalling abuse in the overcrowded market for rented accommodation. This added to the pressure on the then Conservative Government to set up a committee of inquiry into the operation of the private rented sector in London, for it was clear that their policies were not working. The committee, chaired by Sir Milner Holland QC, was appointed in 1963 by Sir Keith Joseph and reported two years later. By this time there was a Labour Government. The committee concluded that:

Those who suffer most from the lack of security of tenure are probably families with young children, particularly those with low incomes and those who have not lived in London very long. In present conditions they are the people who have greatest difficulty in finding alternative accommodation. (Cmd. 2605 (1965): 187)

In their analysis of different household types and their housing situations the committee did not categorize lone parent families separately. Instead they distinguished between large families (three or more children) and small families.

Between 1960 and 1964 another half a million local authority dwellings were built and local authorities were encouraged by subsidies to build high-rise flats using system-build methods. The 1964 Housing Act, passed by the incoming Labour Government, strengthened local authorities' powers to enforce minimum standards on privately owned housing and encouraged housing societies to build for low rent and for co-ownership by establishing a Housing Corporation which had powers to borrow from the Exchequer (£50 million in the first instance) for this purpose. The Corporation had powers to acquire land for societies and to make loans to enable them to develop their work. It was seen as a compromise between owner-occupation and private renting. After five years renting, a member became a part owner of the development in which he (or she) lived. The Finer Committee ten years later could find no evidence that this measure, which in any case had developed very slowly, had been of particular value to lone parents.

The 1965 Rent Act introduced 'fair rents' for unfurnished accommodation and gave private tenants in unfurnished, but not in furnished lettings a greater measure of security of tenure which if necessary could be enforced by the courts. (Legal aid was not available for this purpose.) Audrey Harvey, in a Fabian pamphlet *Casualties of the Welfare State* (first published in 1960 and reprinted four times between 1960 and 1968) quoted David Donnison as saying that the Act 'is in the longer run a measure for the raising rather than the lowering of rents'

(Harvey 1960: 63). In the following three years 52 per cent of rents went up and 10 per cent remained unchanged. She also pointed out that it had been used more by middle-class tenants and property companies than by poor tenants (ibid.). The Supplementary Benefit Commission paid the rents of those claiming benefit but not in full if the rent was deemed 'unreasonable'. Only 1 per cent of claimants did not have their rents paid in full but: 'this represents many thousands of under-assisted tenants nearly three-quarters of whom live in the worst type of furnished rooms in the most overcrowded parts of industrial cities, those of London, Birmingham, Manchester and Liverpool particularly' (ibid. 67).

The debate about how best to assist householders to meet the cost of the accommodation they needed whether it was found in the public or the private sector and whether or not they were claimants developed during the latter half of the 1960s. The National Prices and Incomes Board recommended rebates for private tenants and Birmingham Corporation put forward its own Bill. A national housing allowance scheme was being debated within the Labour Party during the second part of the 1960s (Nevitt 1967). A mandatory national scheme of rate rebates was introduced by the 1966 Rating Act, following an inquiry into the impact of rates on households (Cmd. 2582 (1965)).

Local authorities had had rent rebate schemes for their own tenants since the 1930s but the 1,450 local housing authorities were free to determine their own schemes and there was much variation in methods of subsidizing rents. The Ministry of Housing issued a 'model' rebate scheme for council tenants (Circular 46/67) in an attempt to encourage some uniformity. This had little immediate impact. The Cullingworth Committee, appointed early in 1968, found that in their sample of local authorities

nearly one-third do not operate a rent rebate scheme. But rent rebate schemes vary enormously and some are very limited in scope. For instance, one northern county borough has a scheme which applies only to houses built since January 1968 and provides for a minimum weekly rent of 53s 9d (£2.65). At the other extreme are schemes where the minimum net rent is purely nominal (e.g. one shilling (5p)) or even nil. (Central Housing Advisory Committee 1969: 17)

There is one interesting feature of the illustrative rent rebate scheme contained in this Circular, however, which marks the beginning of policies to treat lone parent families on a par with two-parent families.

This was not controversial at the time for the lone parent referred to was a widow(er). In calculating the allowances to be deducted from a tenant's gross income in order to arrive at the 'assessed income', reference was made to 'married person (or widow(er)) with one or more dependent children - £8' (Circular 46/67, p. 7). It would after all have been unreasonable to expect a widow to pay an increased rent after her husband died. This image of the lone parent at this time was respectable and beyond reproach.

Homelessness continued to be a problem as the housing markets in big cities, and especially London, became more difficult for poorer families. More families were losing rented accommodation either because their landlords wanted it or because more landlords refused to take families with children. These became the largest single causes of homelessness. Few housing departments had taken responsibility for homeless families, so it was left to welfare departments and children's departments to deal with the consequences of this growing problem. The association between homelessness and family breakdown was becoming more apparent and more openly discussed both in the media and by policy-makers and advisers.

Research on homeless families was undertaken. As David Donnison explained in the preface to the first of John Greve's studies for the London County Council (LCC):

In 1961, the LCC was faced with a growing number of homeless people who sought the help of its Housing, Welfare and Children's Departments. This problem could not be disregarded: a large number of children were already coming into the Council's care for no reason but the homelessness of their parents, and it was clear that considerable resources would have to be devoted to helping such families through the medium of one service or another. The happiness of children, the survival of families and large sums of public money were at stake and policy decisions were called for. (Donnison, preface to Greve 1964)

In this study, repeated in 1969, Greve showed that in large cities at least, homelessness was a growing problem ensnaring more and more two-parent families. In London in 1961, two-thirds of applicants for temporary accommodation were married compared with fewer than half two years earlier. Conversely, the proportion of separated women had nearly halved to one in six. Nevertheless one-third of mothers entering reception centres for homeless families were either not legally married or had separated from their husbands. He also found that between 1959 and 1961 'domestic friction' accounted for 26 per cent of instances of homelessness. He defined 'domestic friction' as covering: 'nagging, persistent complaining, arguments, quarrelling and other kinds of disagreements or incompatible relationships which sometimes exist between members of a household, or with others (such as in-laws) with whom accommodation may be shared' (Greve 1964: 15).

He also maintained that 'domestic friction' could be exacerbated by lack of privacy and that 'a great deal of so-called domestic friction may be a consequence of poor housing' (ibid. 18). The research also illustrated how local government structures were not designed to deal adequately with the problem. Housing departments did not have responsibility for homeless families. Welfare departments which did have such responsibilities under part III of the 1948 National Assistance Act were oriented more towards providing support for elderly people. Welfare departments could pass the buck to children's departments however. Homeless families were not allowed to stay indefinitely in temporary accommodation and failure to find alternative accommodation in the private sector resulted in their children being taken into care. The LCC's children's department had 1,060 children in care in March 1960 because their parents had nowhere to live. Homeless children in care cost more than the average child because they were less likely to be fostered and twice as likely to be placed in a residential council or private nursery (which cost £12–£13 a week compared with an average £8.4). Altogether it was costing the LCC annually about £½ million to keep such children (enough to build 1,000 new homes). In other words, it was costing twice as much to keep a child in care for a year as for a council to build a home large enough to house a family (Greve 1964: 53).

Meanwhile, attention turned to the treatment of families once in the reception centres run by welfare departments and in particular the widespread policy of separating husbands and wives. In the LCC area at that time, for example, one in four husbands were excluded from accommodation for homeless families. They were expected to find lodgings. Audrey Harvey describes the experiences of such a family barely mentioning lone parents (Harvey 1960), although in a later pamphlet on poor tenants she does report that 'the Minister of Housing has to exhort local authorities, when choosing tenants, not to discriminate against "lone" mothers with children, particularly those who are homeless. This is the cruellest and most shameful of all forms of selectivity' (Harvey 1968: 73).

Jeremy Sandford, in the article already mentioned, also heavily criticized this policy specifically in relation to Newington Lodge in Southwark. Such was the public criticism of this separation of families that the LCC changed its policy and by the end of 1963 only one in forty husbands were excluded from temporary accommodation and they were always admitted to intermediate and short-stay accommodation (Greve 1964: 12). At King Hill, an ex-prisoner of war camp in Kent used to provide for homeless families, the policy of separating families was challenged by the excluded husbands. Together with local community activists they occupied the hostel. This resulted in the husbands being sent to prison (see Rose 1978). Nevertheless, as Hilary Rose later commented, 'the defence of the right of families to live together was successful in shifting central government policy even if many local authorities managed to drag their feet in practice' (Rose 1985: 246).

In 1966 the Ministry of Health, Home Office, and Ministry of Housing and Local Government issued a joint circular about arrangements in temporary accommodation (Circulars 20/66, 178/66, 58/66, respectively). The Seebohm Committee, set up in 1967 to review local authority and allied personal social services, drew attention to two points in this circular which were 'important for the preservation of families'. The first was that:

they should not, in any circumstances, be split up on reception into temporary accommodation. It is in just such predicaments that they need the mutual support of all their members. Domestic friction is an important factor in precipitating homelessness; we should not by public policy help to make this a permanent separation of husband and wife. (Cmnd. 3703 (1968): 127)

There was no suggestion that 'domestic friction' was a problem in itself. In emphasizing the importance of not allowing the state to disrupt normal family life and enabling those who wished to live as families to do so, as Hilary Rose pointed out, 'it carried with it the unseen consequence that homeless accommodation ceased to be a refuge for women from violent husbands' (Rose 1985: 247). In the 1960s it is therefore easy to see why homelessness was seen by many to cause family breakdown rather than the converse.

The treatment of families once they had become the responsibility of welfare departments did suggest that distinctions were made between two-parent and one-parent families. John Greve's 1961 study shows that lone parents were not moved on to short-stay housing and then into a local authority tenancy as quickly as two-parent families. He predicted:

'As time passes the unconventional, abnormal or unacceptable families will be left behind in larger numbers while conventional homeless families are rehoused. Already they create some of the most perplexing difficulties for welfare workers (Greve 1964: 46).

Homelessness remained a problem throughout the 1960s. In 1969 a total of 3,302 illegitimate children were in care because the mother was unable to provide. This was a 50 per cent increase on 1963 and no doubt part of this increase was due to the increasing difficulties in finding accommodation (Home Office 1969). The Finer Committee received evidence showing that 41 per cent of families admitted to temporary accommodation in eight London boroughs between 1966 and 1969 were lone mothers with children. Another study in South Wales where housing stress was less, found 30 per cent of such families had one parent only (Glastonbury 1971).

By the end of this decade lone parents were beginning to be named more explicitly. The Seebohm Committee described 'the very young family, the large family with the low-income or the fatherless family' (Cmnd. 3703 (1968): 125) as being at greatest risk of becoming home-less. Nevertheless they were 'not numerous . . . about 2 per cent of households comprise fatherless families and many of them, and many large families as well are already adequately housed' (ibid.). The Finer Committee appointed two years later took a rather less sanguine view. They received a mass of evidence on housing, only exceeded by the amount received on financial issues. They concluded that 'some of the most severe of the housing problems of one parent families arise from the breakdown of marriages' (Cmnd. 5629 (1974): 369). Drawing on Cullingworth's research, they stated that 'marital breakdown was the primary cause of temporary homelessness in thirty six per cent of the study sample and domestic violence in another 13 per cent' (ibid. 378). The terminology was changing from 'domestic friction' to 'domestic violence', nevertheless the Committee endorsed the Department of Environment, Department of Health and Social Security, and the Welsh Office's circular of February 1974 repeating the earlier view that accommodation for homeless families which excluded husbands was not acceptable (ibid. 379).

They also received evidence showing that local housing authorities were still distinguishing between deserving and undeserving house-holds in the allocation of council accommodation. The Cullingworth Committee had found that Ipswich, for example, did not define an unmarried mother and her child(ren) as a family' and Barking only did so if she was over 40 years of age. The Committee summed up the evidence as follows:

We were surprised to find some housing authorities who took up a moralistic attitude towards applicants: the underlying philosophy seemed to be that council tenancies were to be given only to those who 'deserved' them and that the 'most deserving' should get the best houses. Thus unmarried mothers, cohabitants, 'dirty' families and 'transients' tended to be grouped together as 'undesirable'. Moral rectitude, social conformity, clean living and a 'clean' rent book on occasion seemed to be essential qualifications for eligibility—at least for new houses. Some authorities may reflect public opinion in the same way that they have policies unfavourable to newcomers (white and non-white), but this is a case where local authorities must lead public opinion. (Central Housing Advisory Committee 1969: 32–3)

By the end of the 1960s the split between responsibilities for the *provision* of housing in general and the welfare of homeless families was becoming harder to sustain. The responsibilities of children's and welfare departments were put into one department in 1970 with the creation of social services departments following the recommendations of the Seebohm Committee. However, in the reorganization of local government and the redrawing of local authority boundaries which also occurred in the early 1970s, responsibilities for housing and the social services rested with different authorities (with the exception of the six new metropolitan areas). Housing went to the district authority and so remained at the lowest and therefore the weakest tier of local government. Social services, along with education, went with county authorities. This made the rationalization not only of policies towards homeless families but also of housing finance more difficult and therefore slower to achieve. Central government had to become more directive.

The 1970s

Priorities within housing policy changed during the 1970s as concentration on slum clearance and the preservation and modernization of the housing stock became less intense. Dwellings were built to add to rather than to replace existing stock. The systems of rent and rate rebates began to be rationalized and take into account family size and income. With these changes, the chances of lone parents being able to find and afford accommodation altered. New dwellings were built at a rate of over 300,000 a year and local authorities accounted for about half of these (just under half under the Heath Government, just over half under the Labour Government). Slum clearance was no longer such a priority. Losses due to conversion from multi-occupation to single household occupation fell (see Table 7.2).

The trend towards owner-occupation grew steadily in the 1970s, as Table 7.1 shows, and by 1981, 57 per cent of all dwellings in the UK were owner-occupied compared with 30 per cent in 1951. Local authority tenancies accounted for 29 per cent compared with 18 per cent, thirty years earlier. There was a dramatic fall during the same period in the proportion of dwellings rented from private owners from 53 per cent to 13 per cent. These changing patterns of tenure altered the opportunities for lone parents to acquire reasonable accommodation, and the routes into local authority housing changed (see Table 7.3).

Lone parents remained heavily dependent on the rented sector throughout the 1970s. Until the 1975 Sex Discrimination Act it was not easy for single women to get a mortgage in their own name (they had to provide a male guarantor) and certainly not if they had children. Their lower earnings in any case put them (and still does for a significant proportion of single women) at a disadvantage in the housing market. Family law changed, giving divorced or separated wives

TABLE 7.2. *Average annual change in dwelling stock (UK)*

New construction	Year				
	1961/70	1971/80	1981	1988	1990
Private enterprise	198	161	119	205	160
Housing association	4	16	19	13	17
Local authorities	152	111	58	21	17
New town corporations and government departments	14	14	11	—	1
TOTAL	368	302	207	239	195
Slum clearance	−65	−55	−30	−9	−8
Net gains for conversions and others	−44	−19	−9	−1	2
TOTAL NET GAIN	258	228	168	229	189

Source: CSO 1992: 146.

greater chances of continuing to occupy the matrimonial home and in some cases a share in the equity of the house once a marriage ended. As the number of divorces increased rapidly during the 1970s this was an issue of growing significance. Nevertheless the tenure patterns of lone parents remained significantly different from those of two-parent families. As the Finer Committee had commented, referring to 1970: 'A particularly disturbing feature of this situation is the concentration of one-parent families in furnished accommodation in the conurbations in England and Wales' (Cmnd. 5629 (1974): 363). They went on to say that although not all one-parent families suffer from a housing problem:

There is, however, an unmistakable and pronounced incidence of hardship and disadvantage in housing to be found in the group as a whole. Its members are more likely to be sharing accommodation with others. They are much less likely to be owner occupiers, and much more likely to be living in privately rented accommodation, especially in the furnished sector, and particularly in areas of housing stress, where lone parents live in low grade conditions at high rent. (ibid. 366)

Overall, as Table 5.4 in Chapter 5 shows, lone parents' access to local authority accommodation improved during the 1970s and in some ways this compensated for the contraction of the private sector. In general children coming into care because of homelessness fell by about two-thirds in the 1970s (compared with an overall fall of children coming into care of 30 per cent). The numbers coming into care because of the loss, death, or desertion of the mother also fell slightly. By the middle of the 1970s, lone parents were receiving more assistance with their housing costs so there was less excuse for local authorities to discriminate against lone parents on the grounds of incapacity to pay a higher rent for better quality accom- modation, there was evidence that lone parents were still being housed in the less desirable properties. The inconsistent systems of rent and rate rebates were subject to some rationalization during the 1970s although it was not until 1982 that a unified housing benefit was introduced. Some local authority rents were based on an assump- tion that tenants ought to pay a certain proportion of their income in rent, disregarding family size, others charged rents according to the type of accommodation provided. Other differential rent schemes were based on the assumption that families of different size required a certain minimum disposable income, and it was these schemes that eventually came to form the basis of housing benefit in the early 1980s.

In 1972 the Conservative Government passed the Housing Finance Act which required local authorities to introduce rent rebate schemes for their tenants by October 1972 and schemes for private tenants by the beginning of 1973. In its original form the Bill did provide a lower 'needs' allowance for lone parents so that they would then have received a lower rebate compared with a two-parent family on the same income. As the Finer Committee said, this was inconsistent with the central policy of the scheme 'to relieve need'.

This was out of line with the provisions of schemes such as family income supplements, which from the outset has treated one-parent and two-parent families alike. By this time we had ourselves come to the conclusion . . . that although there are some savings, such as food and clothing, when one partner is absent from home, these may be offset to some extent against the additional expenditure one-parent families face for items like child care and in paying for work actually done by the missing parent, while housing costs were often greater. (Cmnd. 5629 (1974): 390)

They successfully made representations to the Secretary of State for the Environment and the rent rebate schemes contained in the 1972 Housing Finance Act followed the Family Income Support model and equated the needs of one- and two-parent families.

Another aspect of the 1972 Housing Finance Act began by focusing on widows but was later extended to divorced and separated mothers. Section 66 of the Act provided that on the death or desertion of a spouse which resulted in a change or transfer of tenancy, the rent should not be increased. The Finer Committee wanted the provision extended when a tenancy was granted or transferred following divorce or separation, not just following desertion.

The debates about homelessness during the 1970s were different from the 1960s, for they took place against the background of the rediscovery of domestic violence as well as growing official recognition that lone parents were discriminated against in the local authority sector. In 1974 a joint Department of Environment and DHSS circular was issued attempting to clarify the role of local authorities and in particular identified groups who should be given priority in the allocation of housing. Meanwhile the second wave women's movement was taking the issue of violence against women as one of their central concerns (for a detailed account, see Rose 1978, and Hague and Malos

1993). When Chiswick Women's Aid was opened as a general house in 1971, the numbers of women who just turned up at its doorstep attempting to escape violence in their homes was unexpected. This received a lot of publicity. Erin Pizzey, who championed Chiswick Women's Aid and attracted a lot of media attention, quickly separated herself from the women's movement, although she continued to fight on behalf of 'battered women'. However, other women's groups established refuges and by 1975 there were 28 centres open and a total of 83 attempting to open Women's Aid centres. National Women's Aid held its first conference in 1974 and attracted representatives from all over the United Kingdom. Most centres were run as communities where any rules made were made collectively. Those who succeeded in getting money from their local councils could find they were expected to have a 'live-in' warden. A few became just like another hostel and women were pressured to return to their husbands. Commenting on the latter, the authors of an article in *Spare Rib* wrote:

Holding a marriage together is seen as success, rather than the woman making an independent decision. This is in line with thinking within the Department of Health and Social Security who have been collecting statistics to prove that *marital breakdown is the chief cause of homelessness*. (April 1975, p. 11, emphasis added)

This reversed the causal relationship between family breakdown and homelessness as it was presented in the 1960s and was one which gained currency in government departments in the late 1980s.

The Government however could not ignore the growing concerns, evidence, and campaigns about domestic violence. A Select Committee to study violence in marriage was established, reporting in September 1975. Subsequently, there was a Select Committee on violence in the family which focused on children. The 1976 Domestic Violence and Matrimonial Proceedings Act established legal remedies to protect women from the violent men with whom they lived. As a result of this Act, they were given the right to obtain an injunction to prevent molestation or to oust the man from the house. These rights applied to cohabitants as well as wives and the women did not have to have a long-term interest in the home. It is applied even if the man was the sole owner. Nevertheless this Act did not interfere with long-term property rights and the powers were short term. (An ouster injunction was limited to three months.) Further changes in matrimonial property law and judges' interpretation of it were required to strengthen women's claims to occupy or have access to a share in the equity of the home.

The situation of lone parents and their access to housing continued to be a problem. By 1977 the issue was regarded as serious enough for the Department of Environment and the Welsh Office to produce a joint circular *Housing for One-Parent Families* which urged local authorities to review their policies to ensure any discrimination against lone parents ceased. However, the relationships of the social services departments now responsible for homeless people with housing departments was confused and practice throughout the country was inconsistent. Policies needed to be established at national level and responsibility for housing and homeless people needed to be with the same local government department. In 1977 the Housing (Homeless Persons) Act was passed with all-party support. It had started as a Private Members Bill (Stephen Ross, a Liberal MP) and was similar to a draft Department of Environment Bill. For the first time local authority housing departments became responsible for housing the homeless. This meant that public housing was not confined to those on the waiting list and on locally determined definitions of 'need' which, as already discussed, disadvantaged lone parents (and other households deemed to be unorthodox or undeserving) and gave priority to those who had been resident in the area for a long time. Instead, local housing departments had a duty to provide accommodation to an applicant who was unintentionally homeless, in priority need, and had a local connection.

The subsequent Code of Guidance made it clear that women who left home because they had experienced or were at risk of violence fell within the definition of unintended homelessness. It was left to the discretion of officials in the housing department to determine both the probability that remaining in the home would lead to violence from the other person and that threats of violence were likely to be carried out. (Attempts in both Houses to include all those where violence against them was probable had failed.) It was also made clear that cohabitants, carers for dependent children, and adults who were not necessarily related by blood or marriage were included. Case law subsequently clarified the situation of women living in refuges and they were included among those defined as homeless. (A leading case was *R v. London Borough of Ealing ex parte Sidhu* [1983] HLR 45.) The Act defined priority need as someone who 'had dependent children who are residing with him [sic]'. Pregnant women were also included but childless single women and young people were mostly excluded. As the legal officer of the National Council for One Parent Families subsequently commented: 'It is a continuation of the philosophy already observed in matrimonial law generally of creating a seeming priority for women while it is in fact a priority for the bearers and carers of children, and not for women themselves' (Logan 1986: 57). This was a continuation of the informal practice followed by local authorities in interpreting the 1948 National Assistance Act which had spoken of homeless persons as meaning homeless 'families'; moreover, as Hilary Rose had pointed out, with some families more deserving than others (Rose 1978). Nevertheless the Act did not distinguish between lone mothers on the basis of their marital status and during its passage through Parliament the unmarried mother did not preoccupy members in either House. Far more attention was paid to 'battered women' and the omission of young single people. (The television documentary *Johnny Come Home* had recently been shown and had provoked much debate.)

Important changes also occurred in private law which strengthened lone parents' ability to keep a roof over their head. These had begun in the late 1960s with the 1967 Matrimonial Homes Act. This offered some protection to the estranged spouse (usually the wife) who was not the owner or the tenant of the home by allowing her to continue to occupy the house. This meant she could not be forced to leave without a court order and with a court order if necessary she could exercise her right to enter the house. She could also pay the rent or mortgage in order to protect her right to stay in the house even though she was neither the owner nor the tenant. However, these provisions only applied as long as the marriage lasted; once the marriage had been dissolved these powers ended. Clearly this was of limited value to women whose marriages had ended and the 1970 Matrimonial Proceedings and Property Act had wider powers, enabling the courts to make decisions concerning the reordering and disposition of the property. It did not, as the Finer Committee pointed out (Cmnd. 5629 (1974): 374), deal directly with occupation. Instead, if the wife remained in the matrimonial home, this could be taken account of in determining the level of maintenance for example. Here it would seem is the beginning of the idea of the 'clean break' where the need for a roof over the mother and children's head was 'traded' for maintenance. (Until the 1963 Matrimonial Causes Act, there was no provision in the divorce courts for anything other than maintenance. Section

5 of this Act gave courts the power to pay a lump sum on divorce for the first time.)

The Act also allowed tenancies subject to the Rent Acts to be transferred between spouses. However, local authorities were not yet subject to the Rent Acts (which meant it was far easier for local authority housing departments to evict families for rent arrears than it was for private landlords, particularly as they were not responsible for rehousing homeless families at this time). The Finer Committee supported the Law Commission's recommendation that a wife who remains in occupation after the husband had left should be able to benefit from the transmission provisions of Schedule 1 of the 1968 Rent Act. In the early 1970s there was some discussion of the advantages of joint tenancies which, for example, the Labour Party favoured. The Finer Committee felt that joint tenancies were not necessarily advantageous to the wife because she would then legally be responsible for rent arrears. (Some local authorities threatened divorced or separated wives with eviction unless they cleared what were their former husband's arrears or refused to rehouse them. This was a practice the Finer Committee deplored, not least because it was illegal.) The issue of the transfer of tenancies attracted more attention in the 1970s as domestic violence became more visible as discussed above. Women needed not only to prevent their husbands from residing in the matrimonial home which the 1976 Act did, but also needed some security if he was the tenant. It was not until the 1980 Housing Act that tenants in the public sector had the same rights as those in the private sector. Paradoxically, by giving council tenants security of tenure they made it harder for sympathetic housing departments to resolve tenancy disputes in a relationship breakdown because if the husband was the tenant he had stronger rights against eviction. (See, for example, a GLC survey in which two-thirds of all London housing authorities confirmed that the 1980 Act had made more rather than fewer difficulties in these cases (cited by Logan 1986: 74).) The 1996 Housing Act, in giving powers to housing authorities to evict anti-social tenants including those perpetrating domestic violence, will reduce some of these difficulties.

The joint ownership of the matrimonial home became an issue with the growth in the numbers of divorces. English law, unlike Scottish and most Continental law, has no concept of community of property. Rather than introduce the concept of community of property, the courts began to recognize that non-monetary contributions to the family could be taken into account. The 1973 Matrimonial Causes Act consolidated the powers of the 1970 Matrimonial Proceedings and Property Act. Section 25 gave the courts guidelines to follow in each case. The courts therefore had to consider the spouse's financial needs, resources, and expectations as well as their ages and the duration of the marriage and their standard of living. Conduct could be taken into account and so too could the contribution a spouse had made in looking after the home and caring for any dependent members of the family. The courts were also required to put the parties in the financial position in which they would have been if the divorce had not taken place. This at least recognized that a spouse's contribution to the marriage did not have to take the form of a quantifiable financial share. Indirect contributions could count too.

In an early landmark case *Wachtel* v. *Wachtel* [1973] 1 A11 ER 829, Lord Denning emphasized that divorce was not a punishment for the guilty party but that it was a misfortune befalling both parties for which both parties may be responsible. Conduct was only to be taken into account if it was 'obvious and gross'. He also ruled that in reallocating resources on divorce the starting point should be one-third to the wife. He presumed that the husband would have greater expenses than his ex-wife because he would need to employ a house-keeper if he had custody of the children and should he remarry he would then have to maintain his second wife. Conversely, his ex-wife would not require a housekeeper even if she had the children and should she remarry her new husband would reduce not increase her expenses.

Section 24 allowed the title to the matrimonial home to be reallo-cated. In the early cases lump sum and a division of the proceeds of sale of the house giving both parties some capital were made. A general assumption is that the courts were first concerned to preserve a home for any dependent children. An example of this was *Mesher* v. *Mesher* [1980] 1 A11 ER 126 (CA), where the court deferred the sale of the matrimonial home until the children had finished their education. In subsequent cases the former wife had to agree not to cohabit, remarry, or even move, for once the house was sold the husband could exercise his right to claim his share. Moreover, repayment of legal aid became due. Following *Leate* v. *Leate* [1982] 12 Family Law 11, in 1982 in which the court cancelled the Mesher order, substituting a quarter charge on the house in the husband's favour which was not to be enforced until his wife's remarriage or death, these orders were discouraged.

By the end of the 1970s, matrimonial law had strengthened mothers' and their children's claims on the right to occupy the matrimonial home as well as their ability to prevent its disposal or sale. The claims of lone mothers on local authority accommodation were stronger, because of their greater experience of homelessness.

Cuts in public expenditure following the IMF crisis in 1976 had meant housing departments were never given the extra resources necessary to fulfil the duties conferred on them by the 1977 Housing (Homeless Persons) Act as fully as its supporters hoped. Nevertheless local authorities continued building more dwellings and those which did have policies enabling their tenants to purchase their dwellings used the money to replace the stock.

The 1980s

Priorities within housing policies in the 1980s were very different. The incoming Conservative Government forced local authorities to drastically reduce their building programmes. Council tenants were given 'the right to buy' at generously discounted prices, but housing authorities were not allowed to spend the capital released on new buildings. By 1981 only 40,000 dwellings were being built annually in the public sector compared with an annual average of 150,000 in the 1970s. The private sector did not make good the difference and the total number of new dwellings built overall was halved compared with the previous decade (see Table 7.2). By 1991 private enterprise was building eight out of ten dwellings and the local authorities only built 11,000 new dwellings. Slum clearance had become far less significant, falling from 17,000 annually on average in the early part of the decade to 9,000 by the end. Conversion of existing stock resulted in net gains rather than losses and the private sector continued to contract and the public and private rented sector lost nearly three million dwellings. The numbers of owner occupiers increased to 15 million, over double the number in 1961.

With the huge reduction of local authority building coupled with the loss of dwellings due to the 'right to buy' policy, housing departments found it increasingly hard to meet the needs of homeless people as well as to house local people off the waiting list. Some local authorities interpreted the Code of Guidance very narrowly. There was evidence that some would do so from the outset. For example, in 1979 a woman had fled to Bristol from a violent husband in Eire. She approached the council for accommodation because the Women's Aid refuge was full when she arrived. The council contacted a social worker in Eire who they alleged assured them that Mrs Browne and her children would be cared for if she returned. When the council's refusal to house her was challenged in the courts, the judge upheld Bristol City's decision on the grounds that they had fulfilled their duty under the Act by giving her 'such advice and assistance as will secure that s(he) obtains accommodation from some other person'. As Bristol Women's Aid commented at the time, this weakened the Act because it allowed a housing authority to 'discharge its duty under the Act by securing accommodation anywhere, even outside the country'. In addition it could 'simply refer homeless people to another agency even when it is not clear that the other agency will definitely provide housing' (*Spare Rib*, October 1979, p. 11). The question of which authority has responsibility for housing a homeless family remained a problem. By narrowing the definition of 'unintentionally homeless', it was raised in cases of homeless immigrant families. Other authorities insisted that a woman fleeing domestic violence take out a non-molestation or ouster order so that she could remain in her home. These are often ineffectual and provide no protection for the woman and her children (see Barron 1990; Malos and Hague 1993). Of families with children housed under the 1977 Housing (Homeless Persons) Act in the first two years of its operation, over half were single parents (Logan 1986: 22). By the end of the 1980s over 40 per cent of householders renting from local authorities were women compared with just over 30 per cent at the beginning of the decade. This is not surprising given that homelessness was becoming a more important route into public sector housing (see Table 7.3) and although the proportion of owner-occupiers among lone

TABLE 7.3. *Allocation of local authority housing to new tenants (UK) (%)*

Reason	Year			
	1974	1981/2	1990/1	1994/5
Slum clearance	21	5	1	na
Homeless	9	16	31	27
Waiting list	67	67	54	61
Key workers	3	9	5	na

Sources: CSO 1993: 114; ONS: 1997: 178.

mothers has grown (see Table 5.4, Chapter 5), it has remained at half that for other households which between 1980 and 1990 grew from 60 per cent to 76 per cent.

Homelessness grew in the 1980s as both the public and private rented sector declined (Table 7.4). The need for women's refuges remained. Five years after the passing of the 1977 Act there were 150 groups running refuges. Two-thirds belonged to the Women's Aid Federation of England and Wales and five out of six of the properties used as refuges were rented from the local authority. Ten years later there were 200 groups giving shelter to 20,000 women and children each year. This represented only one-eighth of the provision recommended by the Select Committee on Violence in Marriage in 1976.

There was a shift from subsidizing bricks and mortar as local authorities provided fewer subsidized dwellings to subsidizing individuals in particular through the means-tested housing benefit system. Tax relief on the interest element of mortgage repayments remained capped and by the end of the 1980s there were moves to reduce or even abolish it. Housing benefit was reformed in 1982 and its administration put in the hands of local authorities. Despite the attempts in the early 1970s to rationalize the local authority schemes, a great deal of complexity and duplication remained for the Supplementary Benefit Commission had retained responsibility for paying the housing costs of claimants whether tenants or owner-occupiers. Local authorities, using a different means test, administered the rent and rate rebate schemes for non-claimant tenants in both the public and private sectors.

Following the review of the social security system conducted prior to the 1986 Social Security Act, housing benefit was simplified and the income and capital assessment rules were brought into line with the rules of Income Support (IS) which was to replace Supplementary

TABLE 7.4. *Annual number of households who are homeless and living in bed and breakfast or temporary accommodation (Great Britain)*

Year	Number accepted as homeless	Number in bed and breakfast	Number in temporary accommodation
1978	53,110	1,260	2,400
1983	78,240	2,700	7,140
1989	126,680	11,480	28,420
1991	159,000	12,200	59,900

Sources: Cm. 1508 (1991): 94; CSO 1994: 114.

Benefits. This meant that lone parents were no longer treated on a par with two parents, although to some extent this was compensated for by an additional premium and higher earnings disregards for lone parents. There is no evidence of an intention to treat lone parents less favourably at this time, as is discussed more fully in Chapter 6. Overall the purpose of the new scheme was not only to make the system more comprehensible but also to save £500 million. The government had been alarmed at the increase in expenditure on housing benefit which in 1984/5 had 7.5 million claimants although, as the Social Security Advisory Committee pointed out, the level of assistance given to individual claimants in terms of the proportion of rent and rates met was actually less than in 1979/80 (SSAC 1985: 48). SSAC also argued that the increase in expenditure was 'principally the result of economic factors and of a conscious policy of transferring responsibility for costs within the housing system' (ibid.). There was considerable concern about the combined effect of housing benefit and Income Support and the new Family Credit on work incentives. Over the next few years this concern grew to encompass lone parent families as well as two-parent families, as already discussed in Chapter 6.

Meanwhile, changes in private law were also having an impact on public expenditure as lone parents became dependent on means-tested assistance to meet the costs of their housing as well as their maintenance. The 1984 Matrimonial and Family Proceedings Act, section 25(1) required the court to give first consideration to the welfare of any child under 18 years old. More important were the changes contained in the Act which were based on the assumption that wherever possible a wife should be expected to become financially independent on divorce. The Government had accepted the argument of those such as the pressure group Campaign for Justice in Divorce, that matrimonial legislation was penalizing husbands and that because women were no longer discriminated against in the ways they once were it was wrong and outdated to assume that women should be dependent on their former spouses. The self-sufficiency of both spouses was henceforth to be the desired aim, especially if there were no children. A 'clean break', was to be preferred to continuing periodical payments. In order to achieve a 'clean break' rights to occupy or to a share in the equity of the matrimonial home were subsequently offset against maintenance payments, although in principle a spouse could not divest himself (or herself) of the responsibility to maintain a former spouse and children should they become dependent on state benefits. What became known as 'clean-break' settlements were being used not just in the case of childless couples but also where there were children. The spouse with custody of the children remained in the matrimonial home because the courts accepted that s(he) needed it more and this was in the best interests of the child(ren). In return s(he) received lower or even no maintenance payments. Income Support paid any shortfall in maintenance and provided she stayed on Income Support, after the first sixteen weeks the interest element of the mortgage was paid through the housing benefit scheme.

The provisions of the 1977 Housing (Homeless Persons) Act were incorporated, with no significant amendments, in part III of the 1989 Housing Act. Single people were still largely excluded and the local authorities' responsibilities were still open to wide interpretations. Some local authorities interpreted it and the subsequent Codes of Guidance issued by government from time to time very narrowly, others as broadly as they could. However, as council stocks continued to be depleted and under-investment in social housing continued, local authorities were forced to operate the Act more and more stringently (see e.g. Hague and Malos 1993). In 1989 the Department of Environment completed its review of homelessness legislation and decided against further changes in the law. Chris Patten, the Secretary of State for the Environment, told the House of Commons that:

The present terms of the Act strike a reasonable balance between the interests of the genuinely homeless and others in housing need. . . . We have also concluded that local councils remain the right bodies to take the lead responsibility in helping homeless people. (Commons Debates, 15 November 1989, c. 243)

He also announced that resources for the Housing Corporation's programme would be doubled to £1,736 million in 1992/3 and that he expected local authorities and housing associations to manage their programme in order to 'make maximum impact on housing need, including homelessness' (ibid., c. 244). He drew attention to the need to avoid bed and breakfast accommodation which was undesirable for the families concerned as well as costly (the average annual cost per family for 1987/8 was £12,500).

The 1988 Housing Act deregulated private sector rents. By 1989 when this Act was implemented, the private rented sector's share of housing had fallen to 8 per cent and the intention was to reverse this decline and attract more property into the private rented sector. Rents increased significantly. In 1990 the average amount of the rent which remained regulated under the pre-1988 rules was £31 per week. The average for tenancies entered into since 1988 was double that amount (SSAC 1995: 11). Local authority and housing association rents were also required to rise by 5 per cent per year in order to bring them up to market levels. Thus, despite the cuts in entitlement to housing benefit since 1988, the cost of the scheme rose with the average allowance growing at a faster rate than the number of recipients (ibid. 9). Expenditure on rent allowances which are received by housing associations and private tenants increased by 22 per cent per annum in real terms between 1989/90 and 1992/3 compared with 3.5 per cent during the previous three years (DSS 1993a: 22).

The 1990s

By the beginning of the 1990s it was becoming very clear that the demographic, social, and economic changes in both the labour and housing markets were having an impact on the cost of means-tested benefits and on IS (see Chapter 6) and housing benefit in particular (see Table 7.5).

Lone mothers featured prominently in the housing policy debates both in the media and in Parliament. Margaret Thatcher was not only concerned about the impact of the benefit system on fathers' willingness to support their children, but also about 'the perverse incentives [which] were operating to encourage the break-up of large households and the formation of smaller ones, for instance in the

TABLE 7.5. *Housing Benefit expenditure (£ million at 1992/3 prices)*

Year	Rent allowance	Rent rebate	Rate rebate/community charge benefit[a]
1978/9	410	1,602	1,077
1983/4	882	3,257	2,004
1988/9	1,341	3,454	1,745
1992/3	2,903	4,445	1,538

[a] From April 1993 this became council tax benefit.

Source: DSS 1993a: table 9b, p. 21.

treatment of the housing needs of unmarried pregnant mothers'
(Thatcher, 1995: 604).

In the early 1980s Government policies had been more concerned
about young people who 'chose' to leave home and live on benefits. As
a result their benefits had been cut and in 1988, in the case of 16- and
17-year-olds, withdrawn. Despite the growing evidence as witnessed by
the growth in numbers of young people on the streets that not all
parents were either able or willing to support their teenage children,
these cuts remained in place. Early in 1990 attention was turned on
lone mothers and combining the continued antipathy towards unemployed young people with concern about the growing numbers of
never-married mothers, the stereotypical lone mother in the media
and the political debates became the teenager who had deliberately
become pregnant in order to jump the council housing queue and to
acquire an income from the state. This, together with growing
concerns in areas in which a significant number of black immigrant
families were living, that these recent arrivals were also queue-jumping
over the sons and daughters of residents who had been born and
brought up in the area, led to a reappraisal of the claims of homeless
families to permanent local authority housing.

The Department of Environment was preoccupied with the deeply
unpopular community charge (poll tax) in 1991 and 1992 but once this
had been abandoned and replaced with the council tax in 1993,
attention turned to the allocation of social housing. In January 1994,
the International Year of the Family, the consultation paper *Access to
Local Authority and Housing Association Tenancies* was published by the
DoE. In the interests of 'fairness', it was proposed that section III of the
1985 Housing Act should be repealed, ending the local authorities'
duty to provide homeless families with permanent housing. Instead,
they would be offered temporary accommodation for a limited period
in the private sector if no social housing was available. The definition of
'homelessness' was to be restricted to 'roofless' families. If a family was
living with relatives or friends and asked to leave this would not be
taken as genuine homelessness, unless they had been evicted following
a court order. If a family had left accommodation in another part of the
country or even abroad, then they may not be considered homeless. It
was suggested that single mothers might have 'hostel' accommodation
or share houses rather than have access to the same range of accommodation as everyone else. Mrs Thatcher herself had considered such a
proposal before she left office, in her concern, as she later wrote, to

reduce the positive incentives to irresponsible conduct. Young girls were tempted to become pregnant because that brought them a council flat and an income from the state. My advisers and I were considering whether there was some way of providing less attractive—but correspondingly more secure and supervised—housing for these young people. I had seen some excellent hostels of this sort run by the churches. (Thatcher 1995: 629)

Figures published by the National Housing and Town Planning Council in 1993 had shown that in fact only 0.3 per cent of local authority tenants were under 20 and in 1992 only 2.4 per cent of new local authority lettings went to lone parents under 19 (*Guardian*, 25 October 1993). Moreover, the DoE's own research showed that 74 per cent of homeless people were already on a waiting list (Prescott-Clark et al. 1994).

The response to these proposals was one of universal condemnation not only from the voluntary sector, the churches, and professionals working in health and social services but also from such bodies as the Council of Mortgage Lenders and the Royal Institute of Chartered Surveyors. Shelter published a collection of these in 1994 (*Home Truths: Responses to the Consultation Paper*). This showed deep concern about the threat to the welfare of families in general and about children and young people in particular. However, in June 1995 the Government published the White Paper *Our Future Homes: Opportunity, Choice and Responsibility.* The following month the Judicial Committee of the House of Lords ruled that long-term protection was not the purpose of the original homelessness legislation (*R v. Brent London Borough, ex parte Awua* [1996] 1 AC 55). In January 1996 the Government introduced a Housing Bill, part vii of which incorporated their proposals with very little amendment with respect to homeless persons apart from extending the period of temporary accommodation to be arranged by the local authority from one year to two years. The 1996 Housing Act completed its passage through Parliament in July 1996. The allocation of housing accommodation will in the future be through a single register and homeless people will not necessarily move immediately to the top of that register. As David Cowan, a housing lawyer, wrote in the preface to his guide to the Act:

Personally, I cannot think of a worse system of Parliamentary justice than the removal of long-term protection for homeless persons. . . . The Government's argument is that so many people have complained to them about homeless persons 'jumping the queue' that the legislation is necessary. It is yet another example of minority groups being prejudiced as a result of seemingly majority opinion. (Cowan 1996)

Similar minority groups had been very active around the passage of the 1996 Family Law Act. In the summer of 1995 the Government was forced to shelve the Family Homes and Domestic Violence Bill, assumed by the Government to be non-controversial, because it was thought by some MPs to threaten 'traditional' family values. The *Daily Mail* gave widespread and sustained coverage to their views. This Bill would have extended provisions already contained in the 1976 Domestic Violence Proceedings Act, the 1978 Domestic Proceedings and Magistrates Court Act, and the 1983 Matrimonial Homes Act. Former spouses or cohabitants, persons living in the same household as each other would have acquired a right to apply for non-molestation orders and occupation orders to protect themselves and any children. At that time these remedies were only available to spouses and cohabitants. It would also have strengthened the property rights of cohabitants and would have permitted the court to include an 'exclusion requirement' in an interim care or an emergency protection order under the 1989 Children Act 1989. These measures, enabling unmarried mothers to evict violent partners to protect their children, attracted particular criticism. The Government, and the Lord Chancellor in particular, was not to be deterred. Many of the measures in the 1995 Bill were incorporated either into the 1996 Family Law Act, as the critics turned their attention to protecting 'traditional' marriage, as already discussed in the introduction, or into part v of the 1996 Housing Act which altered traditional eviction procedures and introduced new discretionary grounds for eviction for secure tenancies and assured tenancies with social landlords. This includes cases where a violent partner (a spouse or cohabitant) has forced the other to leave the home and is unlikely to return.

While these measures are welcome, the underlying problem still facing lone mothers or any low-income person or family is the inadequate supply of affordable accommodation. It is unlikely that the 1996 Housing Act will have a significant impact on the supply of housing, particularly affordable accommodation. The system of protection and security for tenants (or short leaseholders) has been further deregulated and while the private rented sector has grown by 300,000 dwellings since the deregulation in 1989, it is very uncertain that this marks a reversal of the long-term decline of this sector which can be sustained when the housing market in general picks up. Meanwhile, the more market-oriented rents found in both the private and public sector (local authority rents rose by 36 per cent in real terms between 1988/9 and 1993/4 and all new housing association assured tenancies rose by 43 per cent over the same period (Ginsburg 1995: 8)) has resulted in escalating expenditure on housing benefit. The Government, therefore, sought direct ways of cutting the cost.

One such measure that will affect women in the aftermath of separation or divorce is the change, effective from April 1996, whereby owner-occupiers who become dependent on IS will get no help with their mortgage repayments for at least 26 weeks and in some cases 39 weeks. (Widows and those deserted by a partner will qualify in the shorter period.) Much concern was expressed in the press when this was announced, but this was focused on those who became unemployed or sick. They were urged to take out an insurance to cover mortgage repayments during this period. There has been little discussion about the impact of this change on lone parents, although the breakdown of a relationship is not an insurable risk. The extent to which matrimonial law favours the mother with the custody of her children in the allocation of rights to the matrimonial home is sometimes exaggerated (Bradshaw and Millar (1991), for example, found that 58 per cent of families had moved home following marital breakdown. This is a figure 10 per cent higher than that found in a smaller study conducted just prior to the 1984 Act (cited by Logan 1986: 30)). However, given the increasing difficulty in gaining access to the rented sector, any measure which makes it harder for women to remain in the matrimonial home must increase their risk of homelessness.

At the same time the 1991 Child Support Act may have affected the willingness of fathers to agree to the mother staying in the matrimonial home with the children because this cannot be offset against maintenance. On the other hand, the 1995 Pension Act which requires the value of pension rights to be taken into account in any divorce settlement and the 1996 Family Law Act which allows for pension splitting on divorce are likely to encourage women to trade the right to the matrimonial home against future pension provision as the DSS's own research has found (DSS 1996).

Housing policy in general and the cost of housing benefit in particular have become major policy issues in the 1990s. In this Britain is not alone and along with countries such as the Netherlands and Norway attempts have been made to contain the rising cost of benefit schemes (Kemp 1990). However, Britain is different from many other countries in that it has a housing benefit scheme in which every increase in rent is matched pound for pound by an increase in benefits (i.e. the marginal cost of housing is nil, provided the accommodation is not 'unreasonable' and until the 1990s this had been defined more broadly, especially for single people. The restrictions introduced in 1997 reversed this trend). As Peter Kemp, the Director of the Centre for Housing Policy at the University of York, concluded:

The move towards market rents subsidised by housing benefit is a crude and ineffective instrument for achieving choice and higher quality in rented housing. All the sectors require better subsidies for capital investment, i.e. bricks and mortar, alongside the subsidy to consumers through housing benefit, which itself needs progressive reform. The rising rents scenario of the past five years is yet another example of the ideology free markets applied with little regard for social consequences or value for taxpayers' money. (Kemp 1995: 10)

For lone mothers this is very serious for they are heavily dependent on the rented sector. However, the discourse of 'choice' in which debates about housing policy have taken place in the 1990s failed to take account of the interaction with, and implications for, health and social services, overall public expenditure, and public and private law. Another result of the housing benefit system in the 1990s is that moving off IS is associated with a sharp increase in housing costs. A study of lone mothers and employment in 20 countries found that in Britain, in addition to this impact of the housing benefit system, 'if a lone mother needs to purchase child care, her in-work income is then likely to exceed Income Support only if the lone mother's earnings are very high. This situation compares unfavourably with the other countries studied' (Bradshaw et al. 1996). As the following chapter will show, the pressure on lone mothers to move from 'welfare to work' has grown in recent years, but unless the interaction of housing policies with social security and employment policies is not better understood, this pressure cannot have the intended consequences.

8

Lone Mothers, Employment, and Childcare

Employment policies until the mid-1970s were informed by a commitment from governments of both political parties to maintain full employment—at least for men. Attitudes and policies affecting the employment of women were complex. On the one hand the post-war social insurance and social assistance schemes were based firmly on the model of the family which comprised a male breadwinner and a dependent wife. A woman's marital, rather than employment, status determined her eligibility to benefits. This model was not seriously challenged within the benefit system until the mid-1970s. Independent taxation was not introduced until 1990. On the other hand, the marriage bar in teaching was abolished in 1944 and in the civil service in 1946. There was a shortage of labour following the end of the war and there was evidence from the Government's own surveys that older married women wanted to stay in or return to paid employment (Thomas 1944). The Ministry of Labour's economic survey for 1947 was clear that 'women now form the only large reserve of labour left, and to them the government are accordingly making a special appeal' (Cmd. 7046 (1947): 183). The shortage included those services associated with the expansion of the welfare state. For example, the practice of firing nurses when they married was abandoned and the Ministry of Labour together with the Ministry of Health helped hospital authorities to organize recruitment drives for part-time workers, thus using 'a reserve of professional skill which would otherwise have been wasted' (Ministry of Health Report for 1946/47, quoted in Myrdal and Klein 1956: 112). Shortages of hospital and other institutional cleaners were so great that the Government launched recruitment campaigns in the British West Indies and in Europe. In other words, government departments involved with the development of the post-war welfare state did not have entirely consistent policies towards women's employment.

There was an additional source of ambivalence towards mothers taking paid employment, particularly outside the home. This arose from the harmful effects which such employment was alleged to have on the development of their children into healthy, normal, and law-abiding citizens. This debate in Britain goes back at least to the turn of the century when the focus was on the nutritional and physical state of the children of working mothers (see e.g. Lewis 1980; and Davin 1978). By the early 1950s, as a result of the writings of Bowlby (1951) and others (e.g. Winnicott and Britton 1947), the focus had shifted to include the impact on their psychological and educational development. Thus prevailing wisdom among health and welfare professionals was that young children fared best with mothers who remained at home full-time and did not take even part-time employment until the children were in school.

The 1944 Education Act gave authorities the power to make provision for nursery education. This was to be provided free of charge. However, under the 1946 National Health Service Act the Ministry of Health remained responsible for the provision of day nurseries, for which charges could be made. The division between the care and the education of young children was embodied in law. The coordination between the Health, Education, and Labour Ministries which existed during the war, ended. Moreover, the Ministry of Health was clear that day care in nurseries should only be provided for children in exceptional circumstances.

the right policy to pursue would be positively to discourage mothers of children under two from going out to work: to make provision for children between two and five by way of nursery schools and nursery classes; and to regard day nurseries and daily guardians as supplements to meet the special needs . . . of children whose mothers are constrained by individual circumstances to go out to work or whose home conditions are in themselves unsatisfactory from the health point of view or where mothers are incapable for some good reason of undertaking the full care of their children. (Circular 22/45)

Within a year of the end of the war the number of day nurseries in England and Wales had been reduced from 1,300 to 914 and by the mid-1950s there were little more than 20,000 places compared with over 70,000 at their peak. These attitudes and divided structures and funding have remained embedded in British policies for pre-school children ever since. The development of nursery education since the early 1960s has largely taken the form of part-time provision and foremost are the educational needs of the child. Responsibility for day nurseries moved from health and welfare departments to the new Social Services Departments in 1970. Day care provision continued to be seen, following the Seebohm Committee (Cmnd. 3703 (1968)) recommendations, as necessary mainly to replace inadequate, or possibly dangerous family care. Day care services to enable mothers to take up paid employment have therefore been left to family and friends and, increasingly since the 1980s, to the market.

This chapter will show that government departments at both central and local level have developed inconsistent and fragmented policies with respect to both the employment of mothers and the development of formal day care provision and pre-school education. The evidence examined also suggests that in some respects there has been less ambivalence towards lone mothers taking up paid employment than towards married mothers doing so. For example, Bowlby was of the opinion that 'day care as a means of helping the husbandless mother should be restricted to children over three who are able to adapt to nursery school. Until the child has reached this age, direct economic assistance should be given to the mother' (Bowlby 1951: 85). Married mothers needed a different pattern of support.

The mother of young children is far more tied than is the mother of school age children, for whom part-time work is quite possible. Since the mother of young children is not free, or at least should not be free, to earn, there is a strong argument for increased family allowances for children in these early years. (ibid. 91)

There are also other factors to consider. After all, if a married mother chooses to depend upon her husband for her maintenance that is a private matter between them, unless her skills are scarce and are needed in the labour market. In this case employment must be offered in ways which interfere least with her 'domestic duties', which include providing services for her husband as well as looking after her children. (Viola Klein's study of married women workers in 1957 found that one-third of men interviewed disapproved of married women working outside the home and the majority disapproved of married mothers taking paid work (Klein 1960). Nearly ten years later, a national survey found that one in six married full-time housewives were not in employment because their husbands would not allow it (Hunt 1968).) However, if a lone mother chooses not to seek employment as the benefit system has allowed since 1948, then this is a public matter. However, as long as the numbers and proportions doing so remained small and the cost to the public purse was low in proportion to the overall social security budget, this attracted little attention beyond that of individual benefit officers. Lone mothers featured more prominently in the debates about mothers' employment and the need for day care services once their numbers and demands on the social security budget became more visible. More recently, debates about the impact of social security benefit levels on claimants' incentives to take up paid employment have begun to encompass lone mothers as well as fathers.

The 1950s

The shortage of labour was not temporary as was thought at first (see Cmd, 7046 (1947)). By 1951 there were one and a quarter million people employed in education, health, welfare, and charitable services compared with three-quarters of a million in 1931 (Rosenbaum 1970: 6). Four out of five of these workers, ranging from professional to manual workers, were women and the demand for their labour as the welfare state became established continued to grow. The raising of the school-leaving age in 1947 had removed 380,000 boys and girls from the labour market at the same time as increasing the demand for teachers. In 1951 there were 1.2 million more children under the age of 15 years than there had been in 1941. The British involvement in the Korean War, rearmament policies, and the introduction of national service for all young men made women's labour rather less disposable than Beveridge had envisaged. In April 1951 the Ministry of Labour forecast that the number of men and women in the Armed Forces would increase from 713,000 in 1950 to 860,000 in 1952. It was recommended therefore 'that something can be done to encourage more people to go to work, by the adjustment of working hours to allow more women with domestic duties to work in industry and by specific arrangement to retain the services of the elderly and disabled' (Ministry of Labour 1951: 142).

By 1951 one in four of married women were economically active, double the proportion Beveridge had assumed in his Report (Cmd. 6404 (1942): para. 108). According to the 1951 Census, there were over 7 million women in the working population, 3.2 million of them married. Altogether there were 830,000 part-time workers (defined as working less than normal hours in their particular occupation), all but 47,000 of them women. (Eighty per cent of the women part-time workers were married. Viola Klein and other social researchers have argued that this is almost certainly an underestimate, for she had found part-time and full-time workers in equal numbers in her survey (see Klein 1960).)

The number of people of working age remained nearly static during the 1950s. Women continued to be drawn into the labour market and by 1961 there were 4.4 million married women in paid work. Altogether 1.5 million married women and mothers had part-time employment. It is interesting to note that despite these trends, visible from the beginning of the decade, the Government Actuary in his first Quinquennial Review of the National Insurance system for married women 'saw no good reason to allow either for an increase or decrease in the proportion employed at each age and the proportions at 31st March 1954 were therefore assumed to apply in future years' (Government Actuary 1954: 42). In other words, by the end of the decade there were a million more married women in employment than predicted by those responsible for overseeing the finances of the National Insurance scheme. As Table 8.1 shows, the proportion of mothers combining full-time paid employment with responsibility for pre-school children declined slightly during the 1950s in contrast to the growth in those working part-time.

No national surveys of women's employment were conducted until

TABLE 8.1. *Proportion of mothers in paid work by age of youngest child, 1949–1995*

Age of youngest child	Work status	Date (end December)					
		1949	1959	1969	1979	1990	1995
0–4	Full-time	9	8	8	7	13	17
	Part-time	5	7	14	19	28	31
	All	14	15	22	26	41	48
5–10	Full-time	—	20	23	18	19	22
	Part-time	—	24	33	45	47	43
	All	—	44	56	63	66	67
11–15	Full-time	—	36	31	31	32	34
	Part-time	—	30	29	47	46	41
	All	—	66	60	78	78	75

Sources: EOC 1986: 87; CSO 1997.

1965, so apart from the Censuses the only evidence of the extent of lone mothers' employment during this period comes from a number of smaller surveys. In 1963 a study of working mothers and their children based on surveys undertaken in various parts of the country, together with a review of previous studies, was published (Yudkin and Holme 1969). The authors found that one in ten of the respondents in their surveys were 'fatherless' families. In contrast to the married working mothers of whom just under half were employed full-time, 80 per cent of 'fatherless' families were employed full-time (ibid. 41). Half of the pre-school children were looked after by grandmother or another relative and one-third were in day nurseries. Grandmother was much more likely to be involved in looking after children of lone mothers both after school and in the school holidays (22 per cent and 42 per cent, respectively, compared with 9 per cent and 32 per cent for children living with both parents) (ibid. 78). The authors concluded: 'This great reliance on the grandmother suggests that a large proportion of the sole supporters were living in their parents' home, as was found to be the case also in Douglas and Blomfield's survey' (ibid.).

Their survey of earlier studies also found evidence that National Assistance Board (NAB) officers were putting pressure on lone mothers on benefit to take up paid employment. For example, they described a mother on benefit who refused to go to work because she did not want her young children returning to the empty house. Once they reached the age of 8 and 9 years she was brought before the local sub-committee of the advisory committee who 'told her she was battening on the state and molly-coddling her children. She was extremely distressed but held out' (ibid. 77)

Evidence of attitudes and practices towards lone mothers claiming National Assistance during this period can be found in the annual reports of the NAB. These illustrate the lengths to which officers and the lay members of the local sub-committees of the advisory committee went to assist lone mothers with employment. The report for 1950 describes a young unmarried mother who had previously had a good employment record but who was destitute, as she could not live with her mother because her stepfather would not allow it. 'The sub-committee felt she had still a measure of self-respect. . . . They encouraged her with kindly words to get back to work and to make arrangements for some friend to look after her child. . . . A woman member arranged to supply additional clothing' (Cmd. 0276 (1951): 48)

The report for 1952 describes how active a sub-committee member had been in negotiating with an employer to keep a vacancy open for a young unmarried mother until there was a place at a nursery for her 2-year-old child. In another example the NAB officer both found the young mother a job and arranged a place in a day nursery (Cmd. 8900 (1953): 49). The following year included a report on the case of a nurse with an 8-month-old baby who refused to return to work. 'A woman member of the sub-committee after interviewing her privately in the office of a voluntary organization, was able to change her mind and the young woman was seeking residential work where she could take her child' (Cmd. 9210 (1954): 48).

At the end of the 1950s, members of the local sub-committees were still very active and the example given in the 1959 report was of a young mother with an illegitimate child who was not only found a job by a member of the committee but was given a grant to cover the deposit on a bicycle to overcome transport difficulties. How typical of the treatment of lone mothers claiming assistance during this period is impossible to tell from these examples and whether or not these young women experienced this as unwelcome pressure to move off benefit cannot be known. What is interesting is that all the examples are of unmarried mothers. Dennis Marsden's study of lone mothers on National Assistance, conducted in the mid-1960s, reported that 'in particular, some of the younger unmarried mothers said they had been under considerable pressure to work full-time' (Marsden 1969: 183). Some had been given a certain length of time to find a job, others had been told they had to go out to work once their children were at school. Marsden comments that perhaps the greater pressure brought to bear on unmarried mothers might have been because they were young, fit, and most only had one or two children. They were therefore more likely to be able to become independent. He notes that all the unmarried mothers with three or four children in his study had worked full-time when their families were smaller. However, as Chapter 6 has shown, there was a growing preoccupation with cohabitation by the mid-1960s. It may also have been therefore that:

Their way of life tended to be less settled, and investigations of their resources presented greater problems. These were members of the underclass, and the suspicion that they were likely to have a man-friend somewhere and even to be earning from prostitution, lay behind some of the NAB's nervousness. (ibid. 184)

There is evidence then that throughout the period from 1948 to 1966 when the NAB was responsible for means-tested benefits, different categories of lone mothers were treated differently and that the view that full-time employment was incompatible with the care of young children could be considerably modified for this group in practice. It is also clear that there was heavy reliance on informal childcare from family and friends. This, together with the priority lone mothers had in what day nursery provision there was, was taken for granted. It was therefore feasible and acceptable for lone mothers with young children to work full-time.

The 1960s

There is today no discernible policy concerning the employment of married women with children; there is only a jumble of *ad hoc* adjustments to special needs and situations. Employers react according to special circumstances; some . . . have built policy and organization on a recognition of the defined needs of this type of worker; others differently situated, avoid these issues and rely on other categories of labour. Trade unions maintain their traditional avoidance of the difficulties associated with married women workers. At a conference of representatives of trade unions catering for women working, held in April 1960, neither working mothers nor indeed married women workers were discussed. Similarly the government is either ambivalent or without policy. One minister may denounce working mothers as contributors to juvenile delinquency at a time when another department is seeking to attract them into teaching or into hospitals. (Yudkin and Holme 1969: 33).

This summed up the situation at the beginning of the decade but by the end issues concerning women's employment, pay, and opportunities had moved up the political agenda. The labour market was undergoing structural change as the service sector, including public services, continued to grow, accounting for 26 per cent of all employees in 1961 and 51 per cent (11.6 million employees) at the end of the decade. Nevertheless, altogether one-third of all women employees in 1961 were still found in the manufacturing sector. Health, education, and welfare services expanded and the rising number of births, which peaked at nearly a million in 1964, guaranteed that demands for these services would continue. In particular there was concern about shortages in nursing and teaching. While Minister of Health, Enoch Powell, at the end of the 1950s was responsible for recruitment campaigns in the

British West Indies. By the early 1960s the Ministry of Education was also becoming more concerned about the supply of teachers. The *Daily Telegraph*, 20 January 1961, quoted a Ministry official as saying: 'Our only reserve is married teachers. If we don't get them we are absolutely sunk' (cited by Yudkin and Holme 1969: 31).

Teachers were given priority in the allocation of nursery places as a condition for allowing local health and welfare authorities, for the first time since the end of the war, to increase day nursery provision. However, in 1960 the Ministry of Education had told local education authorities that for reasons of economy there could be no expansion of nursery school provision. Instead, the practice of offering children half-day places, thus spreading the resource over a larger number of children, was encouraged. In 1964 the Ministry of Education explained that the lack of progress in expanding nursery education was because 'it was felt that worthwhile provision was bound to absorb teachers badly needed in the primary schools' (cited by TUC Working Party 1976: 51). As Table 8.2 shows, only a minority of children were being provided with either pre-school education or a day nursery place in the mid-1960s when the Advisory Council for Education, appointed by Edward Boyle in 1963, was considering the whole subject of primary education. They reported in 1966 (the Plowden Report).

The discussion of pre-school provision in the Plowden Report reveals that attitudes towards mothers of pre-school children taking employment outside the home were still ambivalent and distinctions between married and lone mothers still prevailed. They recommended full-time attendance at nursery for only 15 per cent of 3- and 4-year-olds. The rest should be able to attend part-time if their parents so wished. They wanted priority given to children living in socially deprived areas for opinion that pre-school education could compensate for social and economic disadvantage was growing. (This view had been strengthened by schemes developed in the United States as part of the War on Poverty). Apart from the 10 per cent of mothers 'identified as being unable to care properly for their children' there were:

an identified number of children [who] ought to attend full-time because home circumstances are poor. The children of very large families, those from overcrowded homes, homes with only one parent or with sick mothers will have claims on full-time places. (Central Advisory Council for Education 1966: 127).

TABLE 8.2. *Provision for children under 5 in day nurseries and nursery schools and classes (England in 1965)*

	Nursery schools		Nursery classes children including Rising 5s	Day nurseries		Total children <5 in school and nurseries	
	Number	Places	Number	Number	Places	Number	%
Public	420	21,849	174,939	448	21,396	283,000	6.9
Private/voluntary	219	6,060	3,735	2,164	53,048[a]		

[a] Includes playgroups.

Source: Central Advisory Council for Education 1966: table 4, p. 108.

However, the majority of the council did not believe that the mothers of young children should be encouraged by the provision of full-time nursery places to go out to work. Such a policy raised 'a question of principle'.

Some mothers must work because they need the money. The government, for reasons of economic policy, wish to see more women working. . . . Our evidence is, however, that it is generally undesirable, except to prevent a greater evil, to separate mother and child for a whole day in the nursery. We do not believe that full-time nursery places should be provided even for children who might tolerate separation without harm, except for exceptionally good reasons. (ibid.)

The year before the Plowden Committee reported, the Ministry of Labour had asked Government Social Survey to find out why married women did or did not enter the labour market, what might affect their decision and whether or not they were employed 'to their full capacity, with regard both to the hours worked and to their qualifications and training potential' (Hunt 1968: 1). The study found that whereas 90 per cent of women believed a married woman had a right to go out to work if she did not have children, under 40 per cent thought married women with school-age children had the right to do so but for those with pre-school children the figure was only 5 per cent. The views expressed in the Plowden Report were not therefore out of line with general attitudes in the middle of the 1960s.

There is virtually no analysis in the employment survey which distinguishes lone mothers from married mothers, an indication that they were of no particular concern to the policy-makers involved with employment policies in the mid-1960s. Altogether 45 per cent of married women were working, 21 per cent full-time. Over half of widowed and 70 per cent of divorced women were economically active but this included those with and without children (ibid. 25). Hunt drew attention to the heavy reliance of working mothers on relatives for the care of their children. Moreover, this care was 'free'. The evidence showed that fathers looked after children while their mothers worked part-time. 'It appears therefore that an appreciable proportion of mothers of young children choose part-time work to fit in with their husbands' working hours' (ibid. 94). Grandmothers were more likely to provide care for children of mothers working full-time. Hunt concluded: 'The ability to obtain free care for children depended on relatives willing to undertake the care', but she warns that this source of care was likely to diminish in the future:

With the steadily increasing proportion of women who continue to work after marriage or return after a few years, the reserve of women available for caring for children in the family is diminishing. The process is likely to be hastened by the tendency for the members of families to live at a greater distance from each other than was formerly the case. (ibid.)

Women's employment continued to be widely debated in the latter half of the 1960s. Equal pay was firmly on the agenda. The Labour Party had come to power in 1964 with a promise of equal pay and by 1968 this issue was arousing more public interest, not least because women sewing machinists at the Ford Motor Company's Rover plant at Dagenham went on strike over a question of grading. This became 'enshrined in folk memory as the spark that fired the introduction of equal pay in the private sector of industry' (Pinder 1969: 524). In 1970 the Equal Pay Act reached the statute book. The Government contin- ued to exhort employers, particularly in the public sector, to increase the number of part-time jobs to attract married women. Primary schools were given quotas to fill with part-time teachers for example. The National Board for Prices and Incomes, in a report in 1967, criticized the NHS for not doing as much as some private-sector employers to develop working patterns suitable for married women workers to enable them to stay in, or return to employment (Cmnd. 8585 (1968)). The committee on senior nursing staff structures (the Salmon Committee) had put forward similar arguments (Ministry of Health and Scottish Home and Health Department 1966). By the end of the 1960s, half of all women employed in the NHS worked part-time. Altogether there were 2 million (full-time equivalents) workers in the health, welfare, and education services and still over four out of five were women (Rosenbaum 1970: 6). The private sector was indirectly encouraged to employ part-time rather than full-time workers by the operation of the selective employment tax introduced in 1967 to encourage more productive use of labour and to penalize its wasteful use. The following year employers in the service sector attracting the highest levy were refunded half the tax for every part-time worker and a year later in 1969 the refund was increased to two-thirds. The ratio of part-time to full-time workers fell during the 1960s from ten to one to under six to one (see Table 8.3).

Provision for the under-5s remained controversial following the

TABLE 8.3. *Historical trends in the number of part-time and full-time employees in employment (Great Britain)*

Year	Full-time (000s)	Part-time[a] (000s)		Ratio of full-time to part-time
		Total	Female	
1951	19,239	832	779	231:10
1961	19,794	1,999	1,851	99:10
1971	18,308	3,341	2,757	55:10
1981	16,407	4,442	3,789	37:10
1991	16,817	4,615	4,114	36:10
1996	16,301	5,181	4,393	31:10

[a] Except for 1951, part-time work is defined as working less than 30 hours per week.
Sources: HL 216 (1981/2); HC 122–ii (1990/1); *Labour Market Trends*, March 1997, p. 109.

publication of the Plowden Report. The General Council of the TUC urged the Government to expand nursery education, although some committees argued that they showed 'less concern when it is the convenience of working mothers rather than opportunities for children that are at stake' (Pinder 1969: 604). The 'new' occupation of child minding as the Plowden Committee called it, was more tightly regulated following the 1968 Health Services and Public Health Act (s. 60) which amended the 1948 Nurseries and Childminders Regulation Act. This obliged local authorities to register childminders and inspect their homes or premises in which they looked after children. It allowed local authorities to set a maximum on the number of under-5s, including the minder's own children, who could be looked after at the same time. The DHSS Circular 37/68 suggested three should be the maximum. The same circular reiterated the view on which Circular 212/45 had been based over twenty years earlier, that: 'wherever possible the younger pre-school child should be at home with his mother, and that the needs of older pre-school children should be met by part-time attendance at nursery schools or classes' (Ministry of Health 1968 cited in Cmnd. 5629 (1974): i. 468).

However the circular also made it clear that 'priority will normally need to be given to children with only one parent (e.g. the unsupported mother living with her child) who has no option but to go out to work and who cannot arrange for the child to be looked after satisfactorily' (ibid.).

The Government had given further recognition of the particular difficulties facing lone parents who were combining paid employment with responsibility for the care of children through the system of tax reliefs. In 1960 a new tax allowance was introduced for those taxpayers who were bringing up a child(ren) on their own (or in the case of a married man, had a disabled wife) which was an extension of the housekeeper's allowance introduced in 1918. Initially for widowers with children and with respect only of female relatives acting as resident housekeepers, the housekeeper's allowance had been expanded during the Second World War to include all lone parents (the condition that the housekeeper was a relative was relaxed). After 1960 taxpayers who employed non-resident help for their children could also claim an additional personal allowance (APA). In his budget in 1967, the Chancellor of the Exchequer (Jim Callaghan) had not made general tax reductions but 'there are two groups of people where I can take action at once. I refer to widows with children and single women with dependants' (Commons Debates, 11 April 1967, c. 1009). He increased the APA from £40 to £75 to bring it into line with the housekeeper allowance. The increase benefited 'widows, widowers and certain other taxpayers who have single handed responsibility for children' (ibid.). Widows were also exempted from 'claw back' when family allowances were increased in 1967 as described in Chapter 6. The following year the APA was increased again to £100 (Commons Debates, 19 March 1968, c. 294). These changes only helped those lone parents with earnings high enough to pay tax.

By the end of the decade the labour market had changed to some extent in ways which allowed married women to combine their 'domestic duties' with paid work more easily than hitherto. Unemployment rates were still low and it was expected that the demand for women's labour would continue to grow. Questions about women's pay and opportunities were coming to the fore and women were making their presence felt and their voices heard on these issues both inside and outside the trade union movement. However, change was uneven over the country and as the sociologist Pauline Pinder wrote: 'This is not to say that every employer goes out of his way to make things easier for married women, in areas where labour is plentiful it is she who will have to make the adjustments if she wants to work' (Pinder 1969. 582)

At the same time, variations in the level of day nursery and nursery education provisions were still very wide, as had been noted by Yudkin and Holme in the early 1960s, and the Plowden Committee in the mid-1960s, with rural areas on the whole being badly served and some metropolitan areas among the best. The provision of full-time day care and education for pre-school children was still controversial. Overall the development of more opportunities for part-time employment and a commitment to expand part-time day care and education provision for the under-5s took for granted that women's earnings were supplementing another wage or, in the case of widows, a national insurance benefit. (The earnings rule for widowed mothers had been abolished in 1964.) It was also assumed that childcare could be shared within the family and with growing numbers of fathers in particular, provided mothers were able to choose their working hours accordingly. Employment opportunities had therefore improved for married mothers but only for lone mothers either receiving adequate maintenance or who were living in households with adults able and willing to share the housekeeping and childcare. Lone mothers who were indeed living alone could not take advantage of these changes and their numbers were growing. By the end of the decade the proportion dependent on means-tested benefits had doubled to 40 per cent.

The 1970s

The debates about women's employment in the 1950s and 1960s had focused mainly on married women, i.e. working wives. Throughout the 1970s the debates were rather different as working mothers, including lone as well as married mothers, moved more firmly into focus. The decade had started with the Equal Pay Act which was phased in over a period of five years between 1970 and 1975. The 1975 Sex Discrimination Act, while leaving untouched discrimination against women in the social security and taxation systems and in family law, did tackle discrimination against girls and women in education and training. The Equal Opportunities Commission was established. Maternity leave and pay were introduced in the Employment Protection Act which was passed in 1975 and gave certain maternity leave entitlements for the first time. A pregnant woman was given the right not to be unfairly dismissed—pregnancy itself was no longer a valid reason for dismissal. She had the right to six weeks' maternity pay of 90 per cent of her normal weekly earnings and the right to return to her job after her baby was born for up to 29 weeks after the birth. No distinction was made on the basis of her national insurance record or her marital status but women working fewer than 16 hours a week or those who had not been employed by the same employer continuously for at least two years (or five years if she worked between 8 and 16 hours) before the beginning of the eleventh week before the baby was due, were excluded from the provisions of the Act. These were modest reforms compared with many of the UK's European partners. Nevertheless, they represented some progress.

Maternity allowances and grants under the national insurance scheme also remained modest. The maternity grant had been introduced under the 1911 National Health Insurance Act and from the outset no distinction was made between married and unmarried contributors (except that for the two years following the Act the grant was paid to a woman's husband even if she was the contributor). In the post-Second World War national insurance scheme, in addition to a maternity grant payable either on the woman's or her husband's contributions, a weekly maternity allowance was introduced payable to a woman on the basis of her own contributions, provided as a married woman she had not exercised her option to pay a lower contribution. Initially it was paid at a higher rate than sickness or unemployment benefit, symbolic of the government's perception of married women as primarily wives and mothers rather than as workers (at least from the point of view of the Ministry of National Insurance). It was paid for 13 weeks. In 1951 the rate was reduced to the same level as other short-term benefits and the period payable extended to 18 weeks. The birth rate was no longer a cause for concern and evidence suggested women wanted the benefit spread over a longer period. Married and unmarried contributors were eligible on the same basis. In 1966 an earnings-related supplement was introduced into all short-term benefits when contributions became partially earnings-related. This could increase the value of the benefit paid by a maximum of one-third. The maternity grant had been increased to £25 in 1969 but remained frozen throughout the 1970s (it became non-contributory between 1982 and 1987) but was not increased again until 1988 when it became a means-tested grant of £100 (maximum) administered by the Social Fund.

The majority of married mothers who combined paid employment with the care of young children did so on a part-time basis. Day care provision and full-time nursery education for pre-school children grew very slowly, although the subject was much more widely debated throughout the 1970s than in previous decades. It was also a controversial topic.

The related questions of women's employment and child care facilities raises strong emotions and it is clear that while social attitudes are changing, there is still widespread disagreement in society at large and an ambivalence in Government circles as to whether it is desirable for the mothers of young children to work outside the home. (TUC Working Party 1976: 6)

The attitudes and priorities underlying the Plowden Report's recommendations for the expansion of nursery education were shared by the Conservative Government in the early 1970s. In 1972 the White Paper, *Education: A Framework for Expansion* (Cmnd. 5174) was published. Over the next ten years it was planned to provide part-time nursery places for 75 per cent of all 4-year-olds and 35 per cent per cent of 3-year-olds. Full-time education would only be available to 15 per cent of the 3- to 4-year-old age group. These would all be socially disadvantaged children, including the children of lone parents who needed to work. The Plowden Committee had discussed nursery education in the context of compensating for disadvantaged circumstances. In the early 1970s there was a debate, stimulated in particular by Keith Joseph, then Secretary of State for Social Services, about 'the cycle of deprivation' and the need to break into this cycle (see e.g. his speech to the Pre-School Playgroup Association, 29 June 1972). That year, OPCS on behalf of the DHSS conducted a survey, the purpose of which was 'to investigate the circumstances and needs of one-parent families and to compare them with families having two parents' (Hunt, Fox, and Morgan 1973: 1). Their findings lent some support to the view, to which Keith Joseph subscribed, that the deprivation of children of lone mothers as well as of poor large families was likely to be self-perpetuating. 'Parents whose own environment is unsatisfactory may be more likely to have broken marriages and thus produce an unsatisfactory environment for their children with the possibility of deprivation for the succeeding generation' (ibid. 64).

The study had found that the average educational level of lone mothers was lower than that of married mothers. The educational level of former husbands of lone mothers and particularly lone fathers was lower than the average level of education of married fathers. The authors concluded that:

It seems possible that single motherhood and broken marriages may be more likely to occur among the educationally deprived. The survey indicates that the educational attainment of children in single-parent families are likely to be lower than those of children with two parents. Lone parents' hopes for their children's education are lower. (ibid.)

Some used these findings as a justification for blaming lone mothers for their own poverty, others as a reason for improving the social conditions in which lone mothers and their children lived. Day care and nursery education could therefore be presented both as a means of compensating for inadequate parenting and as a way of enabling lone mothers and fathers to take full-time employment.

The Finer Committee had welcomed Sir Keith Joseph's interest in 'the cycle of transmitted deprivation' for they too had been concerned about evidence that 'among children in one-parent families there may be more who show signs of disturbed or delinquent behaviour than among children in two-parent families' (Cmnd. 5629 (1974): 429). They were 'in no doubt that there has to be a much larger provision, through public or publicly assisted means, of adequate and suitable arrangements for the children of working lone parents' (ibid. 463). However, they did not believe this should be provided in the form of local authority day nurseries or that their provision should be available on demand. First, this would be very costly and resources were unlikely to be forthcoming. Second, part-time day care was preferable to full-time day care and even full-time care should be provided on a non-institutional basis. 'We believe that for children of working mothers, and particularly where the mother works full-time, local authorities should be encouraged to develop comprehensive day fostering or family day care services' (ibid. 467). (Day fostering would be provided by childminders directly employed by local authorities. This would have been rather similar to the French 'crèches familiales'. Like many others at the time they were concerned about the extent of unregistered childminding (see TUC Working Party 1976).) Their views were therefore entirely consistent with those Bowlby had expressed 20 years earlier as well as with the more recent Plowden and Seebohm Committees. The committees laid much emphasis on 'the philosophy of maximising freedom of choice' which they believed their proposed guaranteed maintenance allowance would provide because it would: 'both make better provision for the lone mother who stays home, and provide more extensive and flexible opportunities for those who wished to combine part-time or full-time work with responsibility for the care of children' (ibid. 456).

However, the committee was clear that the mother's 'choice' should be balanced by 'another principle written into much of our legislation, that in matters concerning children their welfare should be regarded as paramount' (ibid.).

The Labour Government elected in 1974 was committed to developing 'the social wage' in return for wage constraint—the Social Contract. This included improved benefits and services for families and children. Taking a very different perspective on day care from the Finer Committee, the TUC at this time was arguing for a national and universal programme for under-5 because they were:

convinced that in order to meet the needs of young children and to cater for the growing number of women with children under five who are now at work, we require a comprehensive service for the under-fives which combines both welfare and education and which is freely available for all. (TUC Working Party 1976: 15)

This was one of the fourteen objectives of the TUC Charter for Women at Work which had already been adopted and around which the wider and growing women's movement was also campaigning. They were concerned about the quality of care provided by many childminders. However, the Social Contract was not kept by the Government in the aftermath of the shock to the economy following the big oil price increases in the early 1970s and cuts in public expenditure followed the acceptance of a loan from the IMF in 1976. The DHSS held a conference in Sunningdale on *Low Cost Day Care* in 1976. Attempts were made to coordinate policies within local authorities but local education authorities were not obliged by law to provide any education for pre-school children, and social service departments, while responsible for the care of children without adequate family care, did not have to make day care provision in the form of day nurseries. The DHSS and DES issued joint circulars in 1976 and 1978 urging cooperation at the local level and at the national level an interdepartmental consultative group on day care services for under-5s was established. Without earmarked resources, local authorities were unlikely to expand discretionary services when they were having to make savings on their mainstream services. Publicly funded provision for pre-school children grew unevenly and slowly (see Table 8.4).

With the rediscovery of abuse within families in the early 1970s, day

TABLE 8.4. *Provision for pre-school children (England)*

Type of provision	Number of places	
	1975	1985
Nursery school/class		
Full-time	14,000	42,363
Part-time	168,000	224,573
Primary school[a]		
Full-time	240,717	226,936
Part-time	19,251	18,695
Registered playgroups	327,961	393,840
Registered childminders	85,616	126,847
Day nurseries		
Local authority	25,992	28,904
Private	26,893	25,886

[a] Includes 'rising 5s'.

Source: Cohen 1988: tables 5.6, 5.7, 5.10, 5.12, 5.13.

nursery places were taken increasingly by children deemed to be 'at risk'. In 1973 only 44 per cent of the children in day nurseries had been referred by a health visitor or social worker. Ten years later a study found the proportion had increased to three-quarters (Van der Eyken 1984: 67). Publicly funded day care for lone parents who needed to work full-time was becoming a scarcer resource and in some local authorities non-existent. This was important for lone mothers in some parts of the country who still depended on the priority they had for such provision at the beginning of the 1970s (Table 8.5).

A national study of lone mothers claiming Family Income Supplement (FIS) conducted by the DHSS in the middle of the 1970s and published in 1979 also found that they were heavily dependent on either relatives or local authority provision for the care of their children while they worked. Altogether 30 per cent used a local authority day nursery and 43 per cent depended on grandmother with a further 11 per cent depending on other relatives. Unmarried mothers were particularly dependent on grandmothers (51 per cent) which is not surprising as 54 per cent of them were living in the same household. FIS claimants also relied heavily on relatives for after-school care and care in the school holidays. Over 40 per cent of mothers with primary school children relied on grandmother or a relative at these times

TABLE 8.5. *Lone mothers' use of various forms of pre-school care provision (1970)*

Area	Pre-school			School				% working	
	Relative	LA nursery	Neighbour	After		Holidays		Full-time	Part-time
				Relative	Neighbour	Relative	Neighbour		
Dorset	(17)	—	(2)	26	4	34	9	24	26
Dundee	36	42	—	51	6	64	6	30	14
Glamorgan	(24)	—	(1)	38	7	52	3	16	12
Halifax	51	25	4	28	3	43	1	22	23
Haringey	31	22	3	32	12	49	15	26	17

Source: Hunt, Fox, and Morgan 1973: table 11, p. 75, and table 15, p. 79.

(Nixon 1979: 95). More FIS mothers would have chosen local authority day nursery care for their pre-school children if it had been available. The author concluded that 'it is regrettable therefore that this important area of local authority provision has been seriously affected by the current cuts in expenditure' (ibid. 155). Reflecting on her findings overall, she wrote:

There is still considerable debate about whether the welfare of both mother and children is better served by the mother working or staying at home. Perhaps the major difference between this country and other European countries is that in the latter lone mothers are generally *expected* to work, and as a consequence, much more effort is made to ensure that all lone mothers are given the opportunity both to seek and to obtain suitable employment. Here in Britain the emphasis is much more on providing lone mothers with a *choice* between working and staying at home and it may be argued that whilst this emphasis persists, there will be less effective effort to make provision for lone working mothers. (ibid. 152, emphasis in the original)

The number of FIS claimants grew throughout the 1970s, although the numbers fluctuated from year to year (Table 8.6). There was a big increase in lone parents claiming after 1979 when they were allowed to claim if they worked 24 hours rather than 30 hours a week. The FIS scheme attracted much attention and criticism throughout this period mainly because of low take-up rates (initially about half) and because, combined with a range of other means-tested benefits and services, FIS recipients faced a deep poverty trap if they wished to reduce or end their dependence on this benefit by earning more. Concern about this was focused mainly on two-parent families, i.e. low-paid fathers.

The Finer Committee had also commented on the low standard of living lone parents on supplementary benefit faced and were concerned that they could do so little while on benefit to improve their situation. The earnings disregard which from 1948 had always been higher for those not required to register for employment, came in for much

TABLE 8.6. *Number of FIS recipients, 1971–1980 (Great Britain)*

Year	All recipients	One-parent families	% of all families on FIS
1971	71	24	34
1976	77	35	45
1980	97	53	55

Source: Brown 1983. table 4 7, p. 62, and table 6.1, p. 92.

criticism. The disregard had been increased from £1 in 1948 when it was worth as much as the non-householder's allowance, to £1.50, plus half the next 50p in 1959 and to £2 in 1966. Neither of these increases restored its value either in relation to the allowance or to average earnings. 'This disregard helps parents who can do the occasional or small job while spending most of their time looking after their family, and who may thereby obtain some personal satisfaction and increased social contacts as well as a little extra income' (Cmnd. 5629 (1974): 337).

Marsden had found evidence that lone mothers felt penalized by the low level of disregard in the mid-1960s and the Child Poverty Action Group also reported such criticisms in the 1970s (Lister 1972). Earnings disregards were increased for those not required to register for employment to £4 in 1975 and to £6 from 1976, remaining at £2 for unemployed claimants and £4 for their wives, thus differentiating between lone and married mothers for the first time. There was some evidence that lone mothers were being pressured to take paid employment and move off benefit altogether but most of the criticisms of harassment arose from the application of the cohabitation rule (Streather and Weir 1974: 25–7).

The numbers of lone mothers claiming Supplementary Benefit grew but grew unevenly during the 1970s despite the introduction of FIS. An examination of the factors underlying this growth by the SBC's Economic Advisers Office in 1976 concluded that they were different from those underlying the growth in the 1960s. The Finer Committee had concluded that demographic trends had had little impact on the increased numbers claiming NA/SB but rather that the increased value of benefit relative to earnings accounted for the growth. This was challenged on three grounds. Between 1966 and 1971 lone mothers tended to be younger and to have more and younger children; the higher level of unemployment in 1971 compared with 1966 discouraged women from looking for jobs as well as forcing them out of employment; and there was evidence that women were not, as was assumed, as sensitive to relative financial awards (even supposing they were fully informed of the way in which the benefit system operated). The Economic Advisers Office concluded that 'the unemployment level and the ratio of scale rates plus average housing costs to average earnings were important determinants of fluctuations over the years 1966 to 1971' (Hamill 1976: 16). Taking these factors into account it was predicted for the remainder of the 1970s that while demographic changes were likely to lead to an increase of mothers on benefit, if unemployment rates fell the rate of increase of lone mothers on benefit would also fall.

At the end of the 1970s the SBC were able to report that 'after the gradual rise in the number of one-parent families from 125,000 in 1966 to 322,000 in 1978, it came as rather an agreeable surprise that during 1979 their numbers fell to 306,000' (Cmnd. 8033 (1980): 67). They attributed this in part to the fall in unemployment during 1979 and noted that the rise in unemployment early in 1980 had resulted in an increase in the numbers of lone parents claiming benefit. The SBC's attitude towards lone mothers' employment was similar to that of the Finer Committee:

We stress that our support for better working opportunities for lone parents is not based on the view that they *ought* to be supporting themselves. Many lone parents believe that it is better to concentrate their efforts exclusively on the difficult and important task of bringing up children single-handed, and they are entitled to do that. Thus it is important to raise benefits to a level at which lone parents do not feel compelled to take a job to support their families. Freedom of choice should be the aim. (Cmnd. 8033 (1980) 12, emphasis in the original)

The 1980s

At the beginning of the 1980s the median income of lone parent families was 79 per cent of that of couples with children. By the end of the decade it had fallen to 68 per cent. In 1980 it was estimated that 42 per cent of lone mothers were claiming SB, a lower proportion than in the first half of the 1970s (Weale et al. 1984: 33). By the end of the decade the majority of lone mothers were dependent on means-tested benefits. They attracted little attention from the policy-makers in the early years and a great deal in the latter years as the discussion in Chapter 6 has shown. Changes to lone parent benefits were therefore modest initially. Lone mothers were still seen primarily as a group struggling to do their best for themselves and their children. In the 1980 Social Security Act a more complicated earnings disregard was introduced along the lines discussed by the SBC in their major review of SB in 1978 (DHSS 1978: 65). The Secretary of State for Social Services, Patrick Jenkin, explained why he wanted to change the flat rate disregard.

I have for a long time felt that this was an awful obstacle to a single parent trying to help support herself and her children. We are therefore introducing a tapered earnings disregard for single parents. . . . This change should on balance give encouragement to more lone parents who want to become self-supporting. (Commons Debates, 20 December 1979, c. 909/10)

Instead of losing benefit £ for £ once earnings had reached £6, the first £4 of earnings were wholly disregarded and half of the following £16. This meant a lone parent could earn up to £12 net of work expenses including childcare costs. A study of the operation of the disregard subsequently found considerable ignorance about the workings of the disregard and in any case whether or not a lone mother worked depended on 'a complex interaction of preferences, child care constraints, job opportunities and financial returns' (Weale et al. 1984: 190). There was a suggestion in the SBC review that the wives of unemployed and sick claimants should also have a tapered disregard: 'It is already accepted that lone parents should be encouraged by a higher disregard to maintain a link with the employment field, to which they will eventually return.' They also believed that: 'a higher disregard for claimants' wives can be justified in order to encourage them to continue in employment, to raise the family's living standards, to maintain their link with the employment field and to encourage their self reliance' (DHSS 1978: 64–5). However, this was ignored in the legislation. The different approach to lone and married mothers' relationship to paid work was evident also in the proposals for reforming the income tax system.

The Labour Government had been in the process of producing a Green Paper called 'Tax and the Family', but they left office before it was published. The new Conservative Government produced a modified version called *The Taxation of Husband and Wife* (Cmnd. 8093 (1980)). The central issues of women's presumed dependence on their husbands and the aggregation of husband and wife's income was discussed. The authors of the new Green Paper clearly favoured replacing the married man's tax allowance with a system which would allow non-earning spouses to transfer their tax allowances either fully or partially to their spouses. That such a change 'could well discourage married women from taking up work in the first place . . . [and] would be particularly true when she was contemplating part-time work' (ibid. 24) was not presented as a problem. The possibility of abolishing the married man's tax allowance (MMA) and using the £3 billion additional tax revenue to double child benefit, extend the invalid care allowance to married women, or to pay a special home responsibility payment, was given scant attention. In contrast, the possibility of changing the APA for single parents, which had been increased and aligned with the MMA in the mid-1970s following the Finer Committee's recommendations, and replacing it with an addition to the already enhanced child benefit for one-parent families, was regarded positively. This was 'because it would concentrate help for lone parents in the single form of a cash benefit, low paid working lone mothers whose earnings are below the tax threshold would gain financially and their incentive to work would be improved' (ibid. 27).

All these arguments could equally be applied to married mothers in the event of increasing child benefit with the revenue raised from abolishing the MMA but if such a change were made 'married men might be even more inclined to regard themselves as losers'. The unpopularity among many men of the switch from 'the wallet to the purse' when the child benefit was introduced in 1978 replacing the child tax allowance (affecting fathers' take-home pay) and cash family allowances was still fresh in their memories. What this Green Paper does show is that attitudes towards mothers taking up paid employment were still influenced by their marital status.

The proposals in this Green Paper were not well received, although there was agreement that the status quo was unacceptable and a further Green Paper was produced in 1986 (Cmnd. 9756), *The Reform of Personal Taxation*. It was proposed to introduce a system of independent taxation with transferable tax allowances between spouses. As well as giving married women 'a fair deal by the tax system' (N. Lawson 1992: 886) it 'would also end the present discrimination against the family when the wife feels it right to stay at home, which increasingly nowadays means discrimination against the family with children' (ibid. 885). Nigel Lawson, the then Chancellor of the Exchequer, was totally opposed to the integration of tax and benefit systems and did not accept the equivalence of tax allowances and cash benefits, however changing the APA into a cash benefit was still suggested. In addition to the reasons given in 1980, a fourth reason was added. Such a change 'would reduce the tax penalty on marriage' (Cmnd. 9756 (1986): 23). At that time 450,000 single parents, including 100,000 widows were claiming APA (ibid. 22). As the MCA declined in value between 1987 and 1995 as successive Chancellors failed first to raise it in line with prices and then to restrict it to the lower tax bands, so too has the APA.

Concern that parity between one- and two-married-parent families had gone too far in the tax and benefit system, resulted in the MCA being increased in the 1996 Budget. The APA, however, was increased in line with it, perhaps because it benefits mainly lone fathers and absent fathers paying maintenance. The CSA had already provoked the anger of the latter.

There was little evidence of government concern with day care provision in the 1980s. Childcare provision was viewed as a private matter and government had a limited role. What responsibilities it did have were for local authorities, not central government, and they were expected to look to the voluntary sector for additional support. As the Under-Secretary of State at the DHSS told Parliament, 'day care will continue to be primarily a matter of private arrangements between parents and private and voluntary resources except where there are special needs' (Commons Debates, 18 February 1985, c. 397). There continued to be an emphasis on part-time education for under-5s. In a report for the European Commission's Childcare Network, Bronwen Cohen cites a DHSS Draft Guidance on Day Care Provision for Under-Fives in 1985 which recommended that 'Children under the age of 2 years are not placed in large institutional nurseries offering group-based care since their ability to cope with the number of different contacts with staff and other children inevitable in such nurseries will be limited'. It had also urged local authorities to 'consider using forms of provision with low unit costs such as childminding, which when properly supported can provide an excellent level of care, and which can be readily tailored to suit the needs of individual families' (cited in Cohen 1988: 18).

The numbers of places with childminders doubled between 1984 and 1991 to over a quarter of a million compared with 96,000 in 1980 (HC 227–ii (1995): 549) but, beyond registration, local authorities have not given them the support of the kind recommended by the Finer Committee and found, for example, in Australia and in France.

The review of the social security system in the mid-1980s did not single out lone parents for particular attention, as already discussed. The change from FIS to Family Credit (FC) meant that lone parents were still treated on a par with married couples who would also qualify if they worked 24 hours a week. The White Paper claimed that the new FC would 'significantly improve incentives to work' (Cmnd. 9691 (1985): 32). However, families moving from the new Income Support (IS) which replaced SB faced the loss of free school meals and a reduction in housing benefit. Owner-occupiers lost all their help with mortgage interest repayments. FC was based on earnings net of tax and national insurance but took no account of any expenses associated with working, for example travel or childcare costs. While many lone mothers in employment still relied heavily on relatives and friends to provide childcare, which for most was inexpensive or 'free', those who had to pay were penalized. When FC was introduced in 1988 a lone mother with two children received benefit to bring her income up to £143 a week. At that time half of women in full-time employment were earning less than £145 a week. For women manual workers the proportion earning less than £145 was three-quarters (J. Brown 1989: 35). Those on IS also faced disincentives if they wished to take some part-time work for while the earnings disregard was increased to £15 from 1988, it was based on gross earnings, taking no account of expenses associated with work as the previous disregard had done. Overall, these changes had decreased incentives for lone mothers either to combine IS with a little part-time employment or to move on to FC. As a group of lone mothers at an inner-city school in Bristol said when these changes were made known to them, 'They don't want us to work' (personal communication) (Table 8.7).

The Social Security Act 1986 also changed maternity benefits. Maternity pay became statutory maternity pay (SMP) and like statutory sick pay was administered by employers. It also became taxable and a contribution condition was introduced. Maternity allowance remained for those unable to satisfy the length of service conditions in SMP provided they satisfied the contribution condition (which was different from that for SMP!). Mothers for the first time were given some choice of when to claim their benefit. Previously, women had to give up

TABLE 8.7. *Numbers of two-parent and lone parent families claiming FIS/FC, 1980–1995 (UK) (000s)*

Year	One-parent	Two-parent	Total
1980	54	51	105
1983	83	133	216
1986	90	128	218
1989	122	190	312
1992	154	250	404
1995	298	371	670

Sources: CSO 1990: table 3.22, p. 60, CSO 1996: table 3.22, p. 62.

employment 11 weeks before the baby's due date and could claim benefit for a maximum of 7 weeks following the birth.

These proposals for maternity allowance will lead to a better targeted and more flexible benefit, administered as part of ordinary payroll arrangements for employees. The allowance will go only to women who can demonstrate a recent attachment to the labour market and will give those women more choice about when to give up work, depending on their individual circumstances, job and health. (Cmnd. 9691 (1985): 48).

This meant, however, that women employed part-time but earning less than the lower earnings limit (LEL) for national insurance contributions could not qualify either for SMP or for the maternity allowance. As a result of the EC Pregnant Workers Directive (92/ 85/EC), maternity leave has been extended from 6 to 14 weeks, although the payment of the maternity allowance remained at 18 weeks. The number of women earning less than the limit increased from 1.88 million in 1988 to 2.3 million in 1993 (HC 227–iii (1995): 345). In 1993, 20 per cent of pregnant women failed to qualify for SMP or maternity allowances (HC 227–ii (1995): 81). Throughout the 1980s the Government had resisted pressure from the EU to improve maternity provisions and opposed legislation for parental leave. They were concerned about the costs to employers and the damage these increased costs would allegedly do to their competitiveness (Cohen 1988: 15).

Meanwhile the numbers of lone mothers dependent on IS and FC grew and the gap between the employment rates of lone mothers and married mothers widened. It was the increase in IS claimant numbers which alarmed the Government in general and the then Prime Minister, Margaret Thatcher, in particular as previously discussed. Despite the evidence that over half of lone mothers wanted to move off benefit and into paid employment if childcare was available (Bradshaw and Millar 1991), policies initially focused on what the Secretary of State for Social Security, Peter Lilley, called 'reversing the inadvertent nationalization of fatherhood' (BBC, Radio 4, World at One, 6 March 1993). It was only when it became clear that many fathers were unable or unwilling to pay more for their children that more attention was paid to improving lone mothers' work incentives and their need for childcare.

The 1990s

In the second half of the 1980s the UK had had one of the fastest rates of growth in economic activity rates among women with children under 10 years old in the EU. By 1991 over half were in paid employment but as Table 8.3 shows, it was part-time employment which had continued to increase. Moreover, in contrast to the 1950s and 1960s, part-time jobs were structured more with the employers' than the employees' needs in mind. There had been a shift in the occupational structure of the employed population towards highly paid non-manual occupations and away from low-paid manual occupations. The 1992 General Household Survey showed that between 1981 and 1992 while the proportion of people in semi-skilled and unskilled manual occupations fell from 32 per cent to 26 per cent, the proportion in professional and managerial occupations rose from 11 per cent to 18 per cent. Among employed women, 83 per cent were in the service sector and 13 per cent in the manufacturing sector by 1990. Inequalities between the highly paid and low paid grew (the ratio of the lowest decile to the highest decile of gross hourly earnings for women changed from 2.6 to 3.2 between 1983 and 1993). Mothers in professional or managerial occupations were more likely to be in paid employment than mothers in unskilled manual occupations and for the first time more likely to be employed full-time when their children were under 5 years old. For example, in the period 1990 and 1992 nearly one-third worked full-time and over one-quarter part-time. The comparable proportions for mothers in unskilled manual occupations were 1 per cent and nearly half (Holterman 1995: 26). More children were growing up in a family where no one was in paid employment. Between 1979 and 1990/1 the proportion of children living in a family with no one in full-time employment had risen from 18 per cent to 26 per cent (DSS 1993b). On the other hand, more children in two-parent families were growing up with both parents in paid employment. The increase was particularly noticeable among couples with pre-school children: from 29 per cent in 1980 to 44 per cent in 1991 (Holterman 1995: 37). These families could afford to pay for childcare and day care provision in the private sector grew dramatically (see Table 8.8). Day nursery provision in the public sector declined and lone mothers, increasingly dependent on the social housing sector for accommodation, as shown in previous chapters, had little choice over where they lived and those

TABLE 8.8. *Daycare in the public and voluntary/private sectors, 1987–1992*

	Total children		1987–92 percentage change
	1987	1992	
Public sector			
Day nurseries	34,709	28,400	−18.2
Playgroups	3,370	1,600	−52.5
Childminders	1,798	2,200	+22.4
Private/voluntary sectors			
Day nurseries	30,687	91,600	+333.5
Playgroups	404,681	409,800	+11.8
Childminders	148,845	252,100	+162.3
Total of children (000s)			
under 5	3,005	3,236	+14.2
ages 3–4	1,182	1,286	+19.3

Source: HC 227–ii (1994/5): table 8, p. 581.

who did not live near relatives or friends who could provide childcare 'free' or at a low cost, had little option but to stay on benefit. One study found that 27 per cent of lone parents and one-third of couples were spending between one-quarter and one-half of the mother's take-home pay on childcare. Moreover, the cash volume of paid-for childcare had increased over fourfold among mothers of pre-school children between 1980 and 1990 (Marsh and McKay 1993b) (Table 8.8).

The 1991 Child Support Act, as discussed in an earlier chapter, focused on increasing the numbers of absent fathers who paid maintenance as well as increasing the amount each paid. Bradshaw and Millar (1991) had found that lone mothers in receipt of maintenance were more likely to be in paid employment.

Receiving maintenance in itself makes it easier to go to work. Maintenance payments are income which the caring parent receives in any circumstances. So it is 'portable income'. It is additional to earnings. Receiving maintenance can also help to make the transition from Income Support into work easier. (Cm. 1264 (1990): 41).

Child benefit and one-parent benefit are also 'portable' elements of income but the Government had failed to maintain the value of child benefit in the 1980s and had no plans to increase it substantially.

Instead, the Government also announced that the number of hours which qualify for FC would be reduced from 24 hours to 16 hours from April 1992 for all claimants. Maintenance payments would be disregarded in FC but not in IS.

The formula for calculating the amount of maintenance the absent parent should pay included an element for the caring parent as well as for the children. Absent fathers are not only obliged under the Child Support Act 1991 to maintain their children—an obligation firmly rooted in the centuries-old common law—but also their mothers, as carers of their children, irrespective of their marital status. The Government denied that this represented a major break with the past but the father of a child born outside marriage had not previously been under any direct duty to support the mother.

It is difficult to see in practice what the difference is between paying maintenance to a mother and paying her for caring. The Lord Chancellor attempted to explain the difference to the House of Lords like this:

I should also make it clear that, although the formula contains an element to take account of the costs of looking after a child, this in no way represents spousal maintenance. A child, particularly a young one, needs to be looked after, either by the lone parent herself or by someone else. That care costs money, either directly to the paid carer or by the caring parent. It is absolutely right that those costs should be taken into account since they are directly caused by the existence of the child. In no way can they be considered to be spousal maintenance. (Lords Debates, 14 March 1991, c. 343)

The Child Support Agency had far more difficulty in improving the amount of maintenance paid by absent fathers than the government envisaged. Sufficient numbers of absent fathers were not going to pay the costs of childcare particularly in the form of paying what in effect is maintenance to the mother. As this became clearer the problem of the lack of childcare had to be addressed. However, given the ideological aversion to giving local authorities responsibilities in this area, except for children 'in need' as defined in the 1989 Children Act, and a determination to make further cuts in public expenditure, the scope for improving a lone mother's chance of moving off benefit into paid employment (or at least from IS to FC) investing in affordable childcare provision was limited.

In October 1994 a childcare disregard was introduced into FC so that up to £40 of childcare costs (which must be incurred with a registered childminder or day nursery) can be offset against benefit before FC is reduced. In the first six months 15,000 families were receiving help with childcare charges compared with the 150,000 expected. This was 'rather less than anticipated' (DSS 1996: 31). Nevertheless, in November 1995 an increase in the disregard to £60 was announced. However, if parents are already receiving the maximum FC the disregard makes little difference. After-school provision has been encouraged by a Department of Health initiative, starting in 1991 with a grant of £1.5 million, expanded in 1993 with a grant of £45 million. It is estimated that this will provide 50,000 additional after-school places in the first three years with a further 18,000 from another grant announced in 1996. The voluntary sector is responsible for overseeing these developments and schemes will have to be self-financing after twelve months which means parents will have to pay the full costs. The 1990 Finance Act reintroduced tax relief on workplace nurseries to encourage employers to make more provision. Two years later there were 425 workplace nurseries providing 12,000 places for children under 5 years. In 1992 the DH and DEE jointly funded playgroups to the sum of £6 million a year. Small wonder the House of Commons Employment Committee in 1995 described the childcare system as 'a mixed bag of provision'. They were very clear that 'Professional child care is not an option for most women with dependent children because even where suitable care is available its cost, compared with wages, makes it completely unrealistic' (HC 227-i (1995) p. ix). They avoided explicitly recommending additional resources, rather there should be 'a national strategy for child care', the aim being to increase the availability of childcare and to reduce its cost. It was not clear how this was to be achieved.

The Government continued to resist pressure from the EU to introduce either parental or family leave. A nursery education voucher scheme was piloted in 1995 and extended nationally in 1996. This has had the result of increasing pressure on places in nursery and infant schools in the state sector, and in some areas private provision has had to close. The aim of the scheme was more to reallocate, rather than substantially increase, nursery provision and was not primarily concerned to facilitate mothers' employment. In 1996 the DSS announced a new incentive to assist lone mothers into paid employment. The scheme, piloted in 1997, is to 'provide individual help with job search and assistance with training for work, to enable lone parents to take up the opportunities already available' (Cm. 3213 (1996): 31).

Funds are available for the private and voluntary sectors to develop 'innovative schemes' and it is estimated that the scheme will cost £14 million over the three years and should reach 25,000. It would seem that the DSS had discovered what the former NAB understood: the mentoring role of the NA officer and lay members of the local advisory committees was an important and time-consuming part of the benefit officers' work with lone mothers claiming benefit. Moreover, it was work done, however imperfectly, out of a sense of public service. The private employment agencies who succeed in finding lone mothers employment will be paid what the *Daily Mail*, 5 February 1997, called 'bounties' for doing so. The more important difference is that in the 1950s there were jobs and childcare which lone mothers could afford, because it was either subsidized by the local authority health department or because friends and relatives provided it 'free'. Without both of these from the Parent-Plus scheme, advice can only make limited improvements in the situation of lone mothers on benefit and there is a risk that the 'advice' may be experienced as harassment. In February 1997 the DSS sent out letters personally signed by Peter Lilley to all lone mothers with school-age children on IS, reminding them of their eligibility for FC. 'Single mothers' jobs drive' reported the *Daily Mail*, 5 February 1997. Prior to the election, the Labour Party had already endorsed 'welfare to work' programmes and while the need for childcare is recognized it is not clear how affordable and high quality care will be made available without additional resources. There is evidence that the cost of childcare increased in the 1990s, and faster than the rate of inflation. Lone parents working part-time had experienced a doubling of childcare costs between 1992 and 1994. Those with primary school-age children had experienced the sharpest increase (Finlayson, Ford, and Marsh 1996: 299). The same study found that in 1992 one in four of lone parents were paying for childcare and by 1994 this had increased to one in three (ibid. 301). At the same time there was evidence of heavier reliance on partners, grandparents, and relatives. In other words, childcare in the market does not replace informal childcare in a simple way.

Will pressure on lone mothers with school-age children to find employment grow so that their eligibility for IS will depend on a willingness to register for employment? Speeches of Ministers in the new Labour Government made it clear within days of the election that lone mothers will be expected to move from 'welfare to work' once their children are in school. The childcare disregard on FC is already limited to those with children under 11 years old and the Social Security Committee has considered the possibility of making distinctions in the maintenance formula between mothers with children of primary school age and younger, and those with older children. If curbing the cost of the social security budget overrides all other considerations and the rising numbers on IS are not understood in the context of changing employment and wage structures together with the consequences of shifting more childcare provision from the informal to the formal market place, then this may seem the next logical step. However, it may not increase the well-being of either lone mothers or their children. The Employment Committee, in their recent consideration of mothers in employment cited above, deliberately avoided pronouncing on the desirability of mothers taking paid work or not. 'That,' they said, 'is a choice for women with dependent children and their families' (HC 227-i (1995) p. vi). In the childcare and employment markets of the 1990s the choice for most lone mothers is a hollow one and whatever they 'choose' they are likely to remain poor. This will remain the case until social security and childcare policies are debated and determined within the broader context of employment and housing policies, and until the structural factors driving the growing inequalities within both these markets are addressed.

9

Conclusion

As we said at the end of Chapter 1, the major division among policy-makers in regard to lone motherhood is whether or not the clock can be put back and 'the traditional' two-parent family restored. In terms of demographic and behavioural change, our findings make this seem unlikely. The changes have been dramatic and rapid, but to date they have been all in one direction: the numbers of lone mothers have increased. Indeed, the immediate post-war years, which were characterized by the prevalence of male breadwinner families and full employment, may increasingly appear the 'odd years out' as our historical perspective increases. Similarly, in terms of the behaviour of lone mothers themselves, a much higher proportion of lone mothers lived with their families of origin and went out to work in the 1950s and 1960s, but this was at a time when their visibility was low and they were highly stigmatized, matters that changed rapidly thereafter.

In contrast, perceptions of the problem have swung back and forth, especially in respect of never-married mothers. Policy-makers have been more or less inclined to treat lone mother families like two-parent families, more or less inclined to single out never-married mothers, and more or less punitive in their approach. There has been no linearity in the shifts in attitudes and policy towards lone mother families. Conservative opinion in the 1990s has been as hostile towards unmarried mothers as was poor law policy in the nineteenth century, and for not dissimilar reasons. But in between, these women have been regarded (briefly) as doing their duty as citizens in the First World War and as unfortunate victims in the immediate post-Second World War years.

Notwithstanding these shifts, the state has become more and more important as a source of financial support to lone mother families during the twentieth century. Moreover responsibility for the benefits and services they needed have significantly shifted from local to central government. Absent fathers have never been especially important and the part played by the labour market actually diminished after 1970 until very recently. Thus state policy towards lone mothers has been impossible to characterize in simple terms. It has been Janus-faced in often condemning lone motherhood and yet giving lone mothers the means to subsistence. As long as only a minority of lone mothers availed themselves of the benefit system, governments were not particularly concerned. But governments have also sought to encourage a particular family form. Married couples have historically been given more consideration than cohabiting couples, particularly in respect of taxation. Furthermore, something like the 'cohabitation rule' that exercised so much feminist protest in the 1970s (see Chapter 6) showed that government had a very clear picture of how two-parent families should divide responsibilities for the maintenance and care of each other and their children. However, the 'considerations' attendant upon marriage have dwindled steadily in the late twentieth century, even under successive Conservative Governments. Public law has increasingly treated the individual rather than the family. This trend has been evident even in social security law, although a means-tested system such as that in the UK will always require that the needs of the household be assessed. In the post-war period, lone mothers gained the right, as mothers, to state benefits. While no government ever gave its stamp of approval to lone mother families, in the post-war years and particularly from the 1970s social security and housing benefits were sufficient to facilitate their autonomous existence, albeit at a low level.

The Conservative Government elected at the beginning of the 1970s had attempted to challenge the consensus about the welfare state in the manner that has become established fact since 1979, and especially since 1990. For example, the 1972 Housing Finance Act, which among other things introduced some order into the chaotic rent structures existing at the time in the public sector, as discussed in Chapter 7, could have had far-reaching consequences if a Labour Government with a strong commitment to the welfare state and to the reduction of inequality had not come to power soon afterwards. As Roy Parker wrote at the time, the Act

is not just a matter of correcting balance; it is an incisive and far-reaching attempt to alter attitudes and policies towards public housing . . . it is a question of whether housing is to be treated like most other consumer goods or whether we regard it as a social service and develop it as such. If we accept the residual view of public housing, what will it become? And what will become of those who, by force of circumstances, or preference, are housed in that sector? (Parker 1971: 12)

Twenty-five years later these are pressing questions and of particular concern to lone mothers and other poor families and pensioners. The Family Income Supplement (FIS) also introduced in the early 1970s has survived. This means-tested supplement to the low waged was presented as a short-term measure until a fully fledged tax credit scheme could be fashioned. Child benefit was the only survivor of the tax credit proposals but has never been large enough to remove the need for FIS (now Family Credit (FC)). Since 1992 FC has been used to supplement not only those in full-time employment but those working part-time. There are proposals to extend it to childless claimants. The existence of FC makes it easier for a government to resist any form of wage regulation including the introduction of a minimum wage. Employers dependent on cheap labour are subsidized by taxpayers who, in the absence of a progressive tax system, are not the better off. At the same time the state acquires greater access to the details of poorer people's lives as well as possibilities of greater control over those lives. It is not only lone mothers on Income Support (IS) who must name the father of their child(ren) but also those claiming FC. The benefit penalty for not doing so without 'good cause' is the same for each group of claimants and its application is growing.

It was no accident that Margaret Thatcher waited until her third term to tackle the welfare state, for she understood very well that she first had to weaken the trade union movement and the professions as well as local government (H. Young 1989). It was against this background that the family in general, and lone mothers and fathers in particular, were put under a much harsher spotlight in the early 1990s than in the early 1980s. John Major's administration in the 1990s, as far as social provision is concerned, built on both the ideological and economic foundations established by his predecessor in the 1980s. It was therefore, possible to take the deregulation of both the housing and employment markets further. Rents have risen in every sector and earnings are less secure and often lower for a significant minority of those in employment. Unemployment remains at a level which would have been politically unacceptable in the 1950s and 1960s. Expenditure on means-tested benefits has therefore increased but the claimants are held responsible. In the case of unmarried mothers, today they are more likely to be viewed as coldly rational and calculating, determined to live a life of 'idleness' on state benefits. Behind this lies the firm conviction that lone motherhood causes poverty. While this certainly tends to be true of the consequences for divorced women, in the case of the group considered the most morally reprehensible—unmarried mothers—there is copious evidence that a majority are poor before they become pregnant. The focus is no longer on structural economic changes and the objective of policy is not, among other things to reduce inequalities. Instead individual 'choice' and 'responsibility' is emphasized and the reaction to the young unmarried mother, for example, is either to change what Margaret Thatcher called the 'perverse incentives' which resulted from inappropriate or over-generous welfare provision or to hold the individual responsible for that 'choice' and let them—and their children—take the consequences. For example, priority access to permanent social housing was no longer justified on the grounds of homelessness because 'A major cause [of homelessness] has been the increase in the number of households *wanting* to live separately due to relationship breakdown and the younger age at which people *choose* to leave home' (Cm. 1508 (1991): 93, emphases added). Margaret Thatcher 'firmly resisted the argument that poverty was the basic cause—rather than the result—of their [homeless young people's] plight' (Thatcher 1995: 629).

From this it followed that state dependency had to be discouraged and 'a new ethos for welfare policy' developed which had 'most controversially, built in incentives towards decent and responsible behaviour' (ibid.). However, this analysis underplays both the extent to which social policies interact with each other as well as with economic policies. By reversing the causal link, unexpected or, to use Peter Lilley's word, 'inadvertent' consequences may follow. The swing of the pendulum of government opinion firmly against lone mothers since the late 1980s has translated into a desire to put the clock back in two senses: first, to reduce the level of public expenditure on lone mothers; and second, to reduce the number of lone mothers. There is the additional hope, here as in the United States, that the first will serve to promote the second. The result of this very different perception of the responsibilities and legitimate sphere of action of governments places social policy debates in a different framework from that of twenty years ago.

Putting the Genie Back in the Bottle I: Reducing Public Expenditure

Since 1990, lone mothers have seen an erosion of their entitlements to income support and to housing benefit. In the 1990s there has been a new determination to make sure that they are 'less eligible' than married couple families, to use the language of the nineteenth-century poor law. Any attempt to secure neutrality in respect of family form in accordance with the policy prescriptions of the 1970s has been abandoned. At the same time there has been a strong effort to increase the other two possible sources of support for lone mothers: men and employment. As Goodin (1997) has suggested, this amounts to an argument that it is better morally to depend on the market and the family than on collective provision via the state. Given the Conservative Party's traditional equivocation in encouraging the mothers of small children to go out to work, more emphasis was put initially on securing maintenance payments from biological fathers via the 1991 Child Support Act. More recently, and in part because of the severe problems experienced in implementing the CSA, attention has focused more firmly on the only remaining major source of support for lone mother families, the labour market.

The cross-national figures on lone mothers' employment would suggest that state policies play a large part in encouraging or discouraging their employment rates. It is unlikely that choice on the part of lone mothers themselves is sufficient to explain the huge variation in their labour-market participation rates (41 per cent for the UK; 70 per cent for Sweden; 82 per cent for France; 60 per cent for the USA, and 40 per cent for Germany). While, as the last chapter showed, the changes to the thresholds for family credit and national insurance entitlements have resulted in an increase in employment rates for some lone mothers during the 1990s, the lack of affordable childcare remains a major stumbling block. However, given women's low pay and low occupational status, it is highly unlikely that lone mothers (or indeed all married mothers) could ever rely solely on earnings as a means of support, as statements from both main political parties seem increasingly to indicate they should. In these circumstances, and given the lack of any significant improvement in the level of contributions from fathers, it is likely that lone mothers will become poorer in the future as the state reduces its support.

Childcare provision, in contrast to most of the UK's European partners has never been extensively organized or funded by government. In the late 1980s middle-class women remained in the labour market even when they became mothers, partly because the housing market of the late 1980s required high mortgage repayments from those who wished to stay in that market in order to keep a roof over their heads. They purchased the childcare they needed. The private market expanded rapidly but there has been little discussion of the quality of the care provided or of the pay or conditions of the growing number of childcare workers. Conversely, those without either the educational qualifications or experience to command a job, let alone a job with higher than average earnings, stayed on benefit because the cost (in foregone benefits, including housing benefit) of moving from IS to FC, or even off FC altogether, became too high.

The absence of affordable childcare whether provided by the market or by family and friends, further reduced their chances of fitting the image of lone parents 'single-handedly' supporting their children. They became welfare mothers and the fathers of their children became 'feckless fathers'. Men, particularly unskilled men, had even less chance to earn 'a family wage' or even to have a job. (Of course, nobody cares for children and has a job outside the home 'single-handed'. That such a description is used is an example of how invisible women's caring within the family is.) However, these generalizations do not fit women from all minority ethnic groups. Lone mothers particularly from Afro-Caribbean or Asian communities are more likely to have full-time employment while their children are young.

European comparisons show clearly that lone mothers do best where they are able to package income from a variety of sources. Running down one source—the state—when improvement in the other two is likely to be only marginal is thus likely to have serious implications for the welfare of lone mothers and their children. Whether it will also discourage the formation of lone mother families is more difficult to predict. It may do so in the medium to long term. As we pointed out in Chapter 1, there is no evidence that state benefits cause lone motherhood, but they have certainly facilitated autonomous living. There is little possibility in the circumstances of the late 1990s of lone mothers returning once more to their families of origin. But it will take some time for women to realize the implications of the new policies. In the meantime, the children in those families are paying the price. The result of the more draconian American 1996 Personal Responsibility and Work Opportunity Act, which cuts off all benefits to lone mothers after five years is as yet unclear. But even if the number of lone mothers is reduced by such a policy, there will always be some and always, therefore, some children to be written off.

Putting the Genie Back in the Bottle II:
Reducing the Numbers of Lone Mothers

It is much harder for government to try to put the clock back in the second sense, by implementing policies intended directly to reduce the numbers of lone mother families.

The number of lone mothers has been increasing rapidly since the mid-1980s fuelled by the tendency for divorce to occur sooner in marriage; and a rise in never-married motherhood emanating from the break-up of cohabiting unions and to a lesser extent solo motherhood. It is clear from our analyses that lone mothers are not a single homogeneous group and consequently a combination of policies targeted at the different sub-groups of this population may be more effective than blanket policies. Policies aimed at reducing the economic vulnerability of lone mothers are likely to be more effective than those aimed at reducing the number of lone mothers, although the first may lead to the second. The prevention and amelioration of poverty amongst lone mothers requires both short- and long-term strategies to temper the legacy for the women and children involved.

Post-marital lone mothers compared with never-married lone mothers tend to have older children but the trend to earlier divorce has meant that recent cohorts of post-marital lone mothers are more likely to have young children than earlier cohorts. These mothers of young children are less likely to be in employment and thus have to rely on maintenance or state benefits or a combination to support themselves and their children. Since the 1980s, we have also had a growth in unemployment and there is evidence that unemployed men run a higher risk of divorce (Haskey 1984) and unemployed fathers who are separated and divorced are also the least likely to be able to provide financial assistance for their wives and children. Such trends, together with the tendency for lone mothers to have accumulated less human capital on their passage to adulthood, are in part likely to account for the low incomes of divorced and separated mothers.

Our demographic analyses showed that, contrary to popular belief, there has not been a dramatic increase in women having children on their own in recent decades. The proportion of pregnant women having a baby on their own has been remarkably constant which suggests that there may be a solid core of women who either through choice, constraint, or by mistake have a baby on their own. The important engine behind the growth in never-married motherhood is the rise of cohabitation, which has escalated since the mid-1980s. These unions tend to be short lived; they either convert into marriages or they break up. The rise in the joint registration of babies born outside marriage parallels almost exactly the decline in bridal pregnancies. This suggests that cohabiting unions have replaced the hastily contracted marriages so common in the recent past. These marriages were amongst the most fragile of marriages, with relatively high levels of divorce and lone motherhood. With the rise of cohabitation, mothers in these vulnerable partnerships have been re-labelled never-married lone mothers rather than post-marital lone mothers. Moreover, when this group of mothers were included in the post-marital set they were likely to have been amongst the poorest lone mothers as they were younger when they formed their families and both partners were more likely to be drawn from less advantaged social and economic back-grounds. Cohabiting couple families are also amongst the poorest two-parent families in Britain (Kiernan and Estaugh 1993) so it is not surprising when these partnerships dissolve that such families are precipitated into poverty. Lone mothers are a diverse group, but never-married mothers are likely to be a more homogeneous set than post-marital lone mothers.

As the 1974 Finer Report on One-Parent Families pointed out, in a liberal democratic society it is extraordinarily difficult to control marital and reproductive behaviour. In other words, it is virtually impossible for the state fundamentally to change the marriage system which has redefined the nature of lone motherhood in the late twentieth century. If the child support legislation had been pushed to its logical conclusion, it may have had this effect. The goal of the policy was to get men to support their biological children, which in turn required men to have only as many children as they could financially support. If the Child Support Agency's powers had been fully exercised in respect of imprisoning defaulting fathers en masse, then logically men may not have felt free both to re-partner and have more children. Whether this would have been desirable is another question. The fact is that it did not happen because of the huge public outcry against the legislation which, perhaps serves to prove the Finer Committee's point.

The other major piece of family legislation in the 1990s, the 1996 Family Law Act, has also sought to influence behaviour directly by promoting marriage saving and making divorce a more long drawn-out process. The Lord Chancellor, Lord Mackay started out, some twenty years after the publication of the Finer Report, by wishing to make divorce more difficult. However, his 1995 White Paper sought only further to reform the grounds for divorce—by finally abolishing fault — and to introduce more mediation into the divorce process. But during the course of the parliamentary debates on the legislation, there was a concerted effort on the part of politicians to have it do more to promote marriage. In the House of Lords, Baroness Young said that 'for one party simply to decide to go off with another person . . . reflects the growing self-first disease which is debasing our society'. Indeed, she argued strongly that fault should be retained in divorce law because 'law influences behaviour' (Lords Debates, 29 February 1996, c. 1638). Not all were as convinced of the power of the law in this respect, Bishop Habgood, for example, denied that the reform of the divorce law had resulted in an increase in divorce rates, blaming instead the increased economic independence of women, the 'culture of immediacy', and high expectations of personal gratification (ibid.: c. 1645). The precise causal relationship between divorce law and divorce behaviour is as difficult to ascertain as it is for any other aspect of law and family change. However, from the historical evidence we know that marriage and divorce law cannot stop married people separating and living with other people, or from cohabiting rather than marrying. If divorce is perceived to have been made more difficult, then the legislation may have the unintended outcome of discouraging people from marrying in the first place. Making the divorce process more protracted may also, on the one hand, prolong the conflict for children which is known to be damaging, and, on the other hand, may have the intended or unintended consequence of children being older at the point of divorce which in turn may mean that the mothers are more likely to be available for employment.

However, again, it is not easy to characterize the role of the state as seeking to exercise more control over marriage and reproduction. In the case of both major pieces of 1990s family legislation, the state has sought to play down its own part in favour of promoting the responsibility of men and women as fathers and mothers. Admittedly, in the case of the child support legislation, it required a monumental effort to set up a completely new administrative agency in order to secure the obligation of fathers to maintain, but the idea in this and the Family Law Act has been to provide a framework in which couples will recognize their obligations to one another and to their children. Of course parental responsibility has assumed the dual meaning of responsibility towards children, on the one hand, and a preference for parental responsibility over state responsibility on the other. Arguably, the second has predominated.

What seems to be happening is first, that the boundary between the private sphere of family responsibility and that of state responsibility is being more tightly drawn, and second that the responsibilities traditionally associated with the male breadwinner model of marriage are being extended both beyond the life of a marriage and to cohabiting relationships in which marriage has never figured. In other words, the responsibility of men to maintain and women to care is being reinforced. This is of course also in line with the aim of reducing the role of the state and the level of public expenditure. Thus while the evidence (mainly American) as to how much men tend to gain financially on divorce and women lose was important in promoting the idea of getting absent fathers to pay more, in practice government hoped that a combination of more money from fathers and from the labour market would replace dependence on state benefits.

However, the desire of government to set up frameworks within which mothers and fathers work out their salvation raises difficult issues in respect of the state's responsibility to secure greater justice in the treatment of different family members. In the case of the Family Law Act, the support given to mediation (a cheaper alternative than recourse to solicitors and the courts) assumes a model of the family which is neutral in respect of power and resources and open in terms of communication. The sociological research of the 1980s and 1990s shows that this is far from being the actual case. At the extreme, as many as one in five of lone mothers gave violence as a reason for separating from, or not living with an absent parent (Bradshaw and Millar 1991: 11). What is evident in all this is that more recent policy towards lone mothers in Britain has focused exclusively on the parents, traditionally on the mothers themselves, and also in the 1990s on the fathers. Children, the main justification for the anxiety about lone motherhood, have figured but little.

Defining the Problem as One of Mothers and Fathers

Behind the anxiety about lone mother families in the English-speaking world is the fear that increasing individualism is eroding all notion of obligation one to another, particularly between parent and child. This is what Baroness Young was referring to when she talked about the perils of the 'self-first disease'. Commentators on the political Left and Right in both this country and the United States have linked growing individualization to greater selfishness and concomitant diswelfares for children (Bellah et al. 1985; Dennis and Erdos 1992; Lasch 1977; Popenoe 1993). This elision between greater individualism, lack of investment in family, and greater selfishness is relatively new. Observers of change in the gender division of labour in the 1970s, and in particular the growth in the dual-earner family, were relatively optimistic about the future, as they were about the future of the family in general (Rapoport and Rapoport 1971; M. Young and Wilmott 1973). However, commentators who are today prepared to argue that greater individualism is compatible with interdependence rather than with the pursuit of independence are in a distinct minority on both sides of the Atlantic (Cancian 1987; Smart 1995).

The reaction of government has been to try to seek the means by which men and women's traditional obligations to maintain and to care will be secured. However, it is unlikely that this rather unimaginative and highly private solution to the issues raised by lone motherhood will ever be enough. In the case of men, commentators worry most about the creation of what Dennis and Erdos (1992: p. x) called 'the obnoxious Englishman'. The anxiety about young men who are not tied into families is stronger than at any time since the beginning of this century, when observers pointed out the importance of the men's obligation to provide for wives and children in securing their work incentives (e.g. Bosanquet 1906). This is not so far away from Gilder's (1981) comments in the United States, or Dench's (1994) in this country, that families serve to make men socially useful. Absent fathers, particularly unmarried, young absent fathers, have therefore become the objects of policy-makers' attention and the solution has been to force them into their traditional role of breadwinners via the child support legislation.

Making men take financial responsibility for their children, if not the mothers of their children, has broad popular support. Nevertheless, making the child support legislation retrospective was always likely to be problematic in the case of men who had formed second families, while arguably doing little to address the more fundamental issues to do with masculinity that underlie the often irresponsible behaviour of young men. As Stacey (1990) discovered in her ethnographic study of American working-class families, young men were no longer sure whether a male breadwinner was to be regarded as a hero or a chump. Luker's (1996) study of American teenage mothers began with the tale of an unmarried father whose wage for full-time work at MacDonald's gave him a mere $684 a month take-home pay and no medical benefits. Luker is not alone in pointing out that in the flexible, low-wage labour market of the 1990s (which prevails in both the USA and Britain) young men often do not earn enough to support families even if they wished to do so. More fragile still is male involvement in family life. Male working hours in Britain are the longest in Europe. Whether or not the proceeds go towards the maintenance of women and children, such trends do little to promote male involvement in families. Policies to encourage male caring and interdependence in families may be as important to securing the quality of family life in the long term as the pursuit of absent fathers for maintenance.

Lone mothers are expected to care, although increasingly they are also expected to take paid work. The policy prescription for lone mothers has swung from treating them primarily as workers (at the turn of the century), to primarily as mothers (at mid-century), and now threatens to swing again. Staying at home to look after children, which is often lauded as responsible behaviour on the part of married women is increasingly being condemned as irresponsible in the case of lone mothers. And yet maternity leave and maternity pay in the UK are not generous by European standards and one-fifth of pregnant women do not qualify for either. Regardless of the extraordinarily confused nature of the debate about mothers' employment in Britain, there is little chance of stopping the increasing trend towards labour-market parti-cipation. Evidence as to what lone mothers themselves want is sparse. However, it seems that about the same proportion of lone mothers as married mothers want to work (Bradshaw and Millar 1991), but given that there is only one parent to work and care, and given the cost of childcare, it is not surprising that lone mothers express a preference for part-time work. Policies that recognize the reality of lone mothers' need to package income from a variety of sources would better meet the reality of their need to work and care than policies premissed on defining them as either workers or mothers.

The current debate about family credit and its impact on mothers' work incentives however is also an example where by framing the debate too narrowly, important relationships between housing and employment policies maybe missed and therefore the incentive effects of changing benefit levels misread. The Supplementary Benefit

Commission at the end of the 1970s, understood perhaps better than
the Finer Committee that movements on and off Supplementary Benefit for lone mothers, as well as for other claimants, were affected by
housing costs as well as by the prevailing level of unemployment. A
recent study of lone mothers and employment in 20 countries found
that 'in the UK, housing costs increase comparatively sharply for lone
mothers if they move into work from Income Support' (Bradshaw et al.
1996). As long as childcare was provided 'free' by friends and relatives,
its availability was taken for granted, and in the 1980s inappropriate
changes in the earnings' disregards were made just at the time when,
because the housing market had changed, lone mothers were becoming less likely to be living with or near friends and relatives able and
willing to provide childcare. Lone mothers have always received mixed
messages about whether or not they should take paid employment
when their children are young, but on balance throughout the period
examined public expenditure considerations have won out, particularly
as far as the unmarried mother is concerned. In some respects this
made the decision about whether or not to take paid work clearer for
lone mothers than married mothers.

The position of lone mothers raises in its most acute form the
problem of valuing unpaid work in our society. It is the fact that raising
children is not considered to be a positive and productive contribution
to society that makes it possible to levy the charge of welfare dependency against lone mothers. The whole idea of promoting 'active' as
opposed to 'passive' benefits and of forcing welfare recipients to take a
job ignores the possibility that childcare is work and essential work.
The American literature has openly declared for a decade now that it is
better for a child to have one employed parent to act as a role model
than none (Novak and Cogan 1987). The right to package income
requires that greater recognition be accorded unpaid work. There is
no reason why such recognition should be confined to lone mothers.
Feminists in the years before and after the First World War campaigned
strongly for 'mothers' endowment' in the form of cash assistance for all
mothers; it was hoped that widows' pensions (granted in 1925) would be
the first step along this path (Lewis 1995). In the Scandinavian countries
in particular, no firm boundary is drawn between lone mothers and
married mothers, rather it is assumed that adult women have different
needs—for childcare and replacement income—at different points in
the life course. The caring work that women do in Britain has been
little recognized. Widows gained their entitlements by virtue of having

been wives, not mothers, and on the basis of their husbands contributions. As carers, women have only ever qualified for lower level social assistance benefits, whether as mothers or as carers for dependent adults. There are a number of different ways forward. In-work benefits, such as family credit, are particularly important for lone mothers because they do enable a degree of income packaging, but their possible effect in terms of depressing wages is a source of concern. Certainly in principle they are a wage supplement and not a reward for caring work. The idea of a cash benefit for mothers with a child under 5, irrespective of marital status or of a basic, 'citizens' income (Atkinson 1995) is crucial not only for addressing the issue of poverty but for recognizing the value of caring work. Universal rather than categorical or means-tested benefits have the advantage of not trapping individuals in a particular household, employment, or marital status, thus recognizing the fluidity of both employment and family circumstances. Until some progress is made on this score the prospects for lone mothers being able successfully to package income are slim. Modern income maintenance systems were designed to secure citizens a measure of autonomy during periods when they are unable to engage in the labour market. Governments in the 1990s have argued that social services provided by the state should be replaced by cash or vouchers, thus giving elderly people or parents more 'choice'. Yet in the case of social security payments themselves, it seems that the receipt of cash now stands condemned for it is believed to sap the motivation to take a job and to cause dependency.

But more than cash is needed. As Barbara Castle wrote, reflecting on the period in the 1970s, when as Secretary of State for the Social Services, she fought for improving the social wage: 'What matters to women even more than the cash wage increase they or their husbands get is the standard of publicly provided services which mean so much to the family—health care, education, housing and a good environment. In other words the social wage' (Castle 1981: 21). Childcare policies however have been fragmented in the UK ever since the end of the Second World War. As Chapter 8 showed, the division between the care of pre-school children and their education has been perpetuated in different funding and administrative structures.

Housing policies, by shifting subsidies from 'bricks and mortar' to individuals have not produced sufficient affordable accommodation in either the social (formerly called public) or the private sectors. Houses are allocated in the social sector with little regard to the need for families, especially lone mothers, to be near informal sources of support. As social sector tenants become poorer on average, material resources within the whole community diminish. Transport policies with the emphasis on the 'private' car have produced an environment which make simple everyday activities such as going to school dangerous for children unless escorted by an adult. Twenty-five years ago, four out of five primary school children went to school unescorted, by the 1990s fewer than one in six could do so. This structures parents', particularly mothers', days which in turn constrains their employment choices. The lack of co-ordination between housing, transport, and employment policies has meant that the price poorer families pay for finding and keeping a roof over their heads is that they are disconnected from a variety of resources both formal and informal. The childcare provided in the 1950s and 1960s by family and neighbours and on which, as Chapter 8, showed, lone mothers in particular depended, has literally become out of reach and only the well-paid working mothers can afford to replace it by purchasing care in the unsubsidized market. Employers are exhorted to develop 'family, friendly' practices but what is needed is a 'family friendly' environment, which neither 'the market' nor residual welfare state can provide. As Tawney wrote half a century ago:

No individual can create by his isolated action a healthy environment, or establish an educational system with a wide range of facilities, or organize an industry in such a manner as to diminish economic insecurity, or eliminate the causes of accidents in factories or streets. Yet these are the conditions which value the difference between happiness and misery, and sometimes, indeed, between life and death. In so far as they exist they are the source of a social income, received in the form not of money, but of increased well-being. (Tawney 1964: 127)

The ideologically driven policies of the past seventeen years have been subject to far less informed scrutiny than was the case in the previous twenty years. Changes in the structure of government, both local and central, and changes in the policy-making process also reduced government's and Parliament's ability to contribute in an informed way to some of the key debates. Complex legislation was put before Parliament without the detail necessary for MPs to scrutinize and fully understand the implications of a Bill before them. Too much was left to be settled by Ministers subsequently by regulation.

The 1991 Child Support Act is a prime example of Parliament, and the House of Commons in particular, failing to grasp what impact it would have on lone mothers and absent fathers and their second families. It never occurred to many of the male MPs that they might be affected. While such legislative skeletons may have an easier passage through Parliament, they may come to haunt Ministers once they are implemented. The UK has a highly centralized social security system—perhaps even one of the most centralized in the world—but in the past this was balanced a little by the continuation until the early 1970s of local advisory committees with a lay membership as well as by the nature of the career structure within the Ministries and the National Assistance Board and Supplementary Benefit Commission. Many senior civil servants in the Ministry of Pensions and National Insurance (followed by the Department of Health and Social Security) had at earlier stages in their careers worked in local or regional offices. They knew claimants' lives could be far more complex than any regulations could encompass and that employers and landlords could behave as unreasonably or irresponsibly as claimants could.

The former liable relative officers would not have been surprised at the difficulties the CSA has had in trying to establish the identity of, and to extract maintenance from, absent fathers, although new technology has made it easier to ascertain biological fatherhood. Conversely, the discretion the law gave them allowed them to exercise their prejudices. Similarly when local government had more responsibilities and control over the resources necessary to exercise them, on the one hand, they could be more responsive to the needs of their localities, but, on the other, they could behave in a discriminatory and prejudiced way. Housing departments could turn their backs on groups of which they did not approve. Lone mothers had less chance of access to public housing and having gained access were likely to be allocated poorer housing. If they were also newcomers or members of a minority ethnic group they fared even worse. This study has looked at policy responses largely at the national level and has therefore not addressed the question of the considerable variation in the circumstance of lone mothers as well as in the level of provision between local authorities. It would be easy to recommend that more responsibility be devolved to local government again but the story of housing or childcare policies shows that this results in uneven and inequitable policies across the country, unless adequate standards are set by central government and the local authorities have the resources to meet them.

The Need to Focus on Children and Supporting Parents

Between 1979 and 1991 the number of children living in households with below 50 per cent of average income trebled to 3.9 million. The numbers of children living in families with two parents and dependent wholly on means-tested benefits increased threefold: the same change in magnitude as the numbers of children in lone parent families dependent on Income Support. This means that in the early 1990s one child in three was growing up in a poor household compared with one in ten in the late 1970s. An important feature of the context in which lone mothers have been considered to be 'a problem' is this dramatic growth in child poverty. While there is merit in insisting on the parental responsibility to care for and maintain children, the evidence suggests that this alone is not enough. Significant numbers of lone mothers were poor before they became pregnant and would have been poor if they had married. One of Phoenix's (1991) most striking findings from her qualitative evidence was that the material position of her teenage interviewees was unlikely to have been improved by waiting a few years before having a child. When both gender roles in the family and in the workplace and the structure of personal relationships are changing rapidly, an attempt to solve the problems that are posed for children by seeking to impose the terms of the traditional marriage contract looks rather dubious. It does nothing to recognize the problem that women have in combining paid and unpaid work; it does little to encourage men to share the unpaid work of caring, despite the evidence regarding the importance of this to children; and it does nothing to redress the profound growth in inequalities that has taken place since 1980 (Hills 1995, 1996). Indeed, in seeking to reduce the amount paid in benefits to lone mothers Government seems prepared to see innocent children suffer also, just as at the beginning of the nineteenth century Thomas Malthus (1803) contemplated the abolition of the poor law and starving children in order to shame their fathers into feeding them and thus to enforce personal responsibility.

There are limits as to what individual parental responsibility can achieve. Early twentieth-century policy-makers eventually recognized that collective support for parents—through the provision of school meals and medical inspection in the first instance—was likely to elicit more parental care for children, rather than substituting for it. There is no more need for a choice to be made between collective and individual responsibility in respect of children, than there is for one to be made between work and motherhood in respect of lone mothers. Indeed the problem of lone motherhood is intimately linked to investment in children, something that is conspicuously missing from the way in which the problem has been defined in the UK in the 1990s despite the concern that has been expressed about lone motherhood in terms of the negative outcomes for children.

Never-married mothers are typically younger, poorer, less likely to be in employment, more likely to be in receipt of income support and less likely to be in receipt of maintenance than post-marital lone mothers. Young never-married mothers in particular are more prevalent in Britain than in any other EU Member State. This is a by-product of our high rates of teenage childbearing. The UK rate is around three times that in France and Sweden, over twice that in West Germany, almost four times that of Italy, six times that of the Netherlands, and ten times the rate in Switzerland. The USA is one of the few Western nations that has a rate higher than that in the United Kingdom. In 1989 the UK contributed 37 per cent of all teenage births occurring in European Community but less than 20 per cent of all the births. The UK compared with other European nations also has a relatively high rate of childbearing in the early twenties.

Post-marital lone mothers are also disproportionately drawn from women who become mothers at a young age. Women who become mothers at a young age compared with those who delay motherhood tend to come from less advantaged social and economic backgrounds and, perhaps most critically, are educationally disadvantaged, with all that implies for work careers and levels of remuneration. Young parents tend to have accumulated less human and social capital on their way to adulthood and in adulthood are likely to have fewer resources than older parents to invest in themselves and their children. If parents separate, women who become mothers at young ages are less likely to possess the skills and qualifications necessary for obtaining jobs which would enable them to support themselves and their children. Their ex-partners are also the least likely to be able to make a substantial contribution to the support of their children. This suggests that the children of young parents are themselves disproportionately likely to suffer from the same disadvantages as their parents. Young parenthood poses other risks to people's life chances, with drawbacks including poor housing, homelessness, unemployment, and reliance on state benefits. Moreover,

as Rowlingson and McKay (1997) have shown the local employment
rate has a big impact on the prevalence of never-married motherhood,
in that the higher the rate of unemployment in an area the greater the
level of unmarried motherhood. This study as well as our analysis of
the National Sexual Attitudes and Lifestyle Survey highlighted that
unplanned and mistimed pregnancies still occur despite the advent of
effective contraception and legal abortion. A particularly vulnerable
time is first and subsequent acts of intercourse where around one in
four women, even in the 1990s, did not use contraception. Being in
education or fulfilling work are probably amongst the most effective
bars to early pregnancy. Many other European countries have education systems with either a later school-leaving age or more intensive
post-school vocational training schemes than has been the case in
Britain, these may have dampened the possibilities for or created a
culture antithetical to early family formation.

Undoubtedly, there will always be men and women who want and
have children at a young age and many will be satisfied and successful
parents: the issues are more to do with choice and opportunity. With
the currently evolving labour market it is more important than in
earlier decades, when there was full employment and an economy
that provided relatively well-paid manual and unskilled jobs to under-
pin and support family life, to provide and encourage young men and
women to equip themselves with the qualifications and skills needed for
satisfactory work within and without the labour market. Such changes
suggest that education and training may have a central position in
current and future strategic policies aimed at reducing lone parenthood
or at least tempering the poverty which is an all too frequent accom-
paniment. Educated lone mothers are more likely to be employed than
less educated lone mothers but still have lower participation rates than
similarly qualified married mothers which speaks to the importance of
childcare in facilitating labour-market participation.

Childcare is not just a service for enabling mothers to take paid
employment but neither is it solely about compensating for inadequate
parenting however defined. Similarly a cash benefit to mothers of small
children could serve as some recognition of caring work rather than as
an invitation to welfare dependency. These distinctions are ideological
and are not necessary if the welfare of children is considered in the
broadest sense. The focus of the policy debates about lone mothers
should return to their children, and their needs, not only in relation to

childcare, and should encompass all children. After all as John Bowlby wrote nearly fifty years ago:

just as children are absolutely dependent on their parents for sustenance, so in all but the most primitive communities are their parents, especially their mothers, dependent on a greater society for economic provision. If a community values its children it must cherish their parents. (Bowlby 1951: 84)

BIBLIOGRAPHY

Abel-Smith, B., and Townsend, P. (1965), *The Poor and the Poorest* (Occasional Papers in Social Administration, No. 12; London: G. Bell and Sons).

Acland, Hon. Lady (1902), *Marriage as the Foundation of the Home* (Oxford: A. R. Mowbray).

Acton, W. (1875), *The Functions and Disorders of the Reproductive Organs* (1st edn. 1857; London: John Churchill).

Allen, G. (1895), *The Woman Who Did* (London: John Lane).

Amato, P. R., and Keith, B. (1991*a*), 'Parental Divorce and the Well-Being of Children: A Meta-analysis', *Psychological Bulletin*, 110: 26–46.

—— —— (1991*b*), 'Parental Divorce and Adult Well-Being: A Meta-analysis', *Journal of Marriage and the Family*, 53: 43–58.

Analytical Services Division (1996), *The Requirement to Co-operate: A Report on the Operation of the Good Causes Provision* (in House Report No. 14; London: DSS).

Anderson, M. (1983), 'What is New about the Modern Family: A Historical Perspective', in *British Society for Population Studies: The Family* (London: Office of Population and Census Statistics) 36–59.

Archbishop of Canterbury's Group on the Divorce Law (1966), *Putting Asunder: A Divorce Law for Contemporary Society* (London: SPCK).

Archbishop of Canterbury (1971), *Marriage, Divorce and the Church*, A Report of a Commission Appointed by the Archbishop of Canterbury to Prepare a Statement on the Christian Doctrine of Marriage (London: SPCK).

Arden, A. (1978), *Housing: Security and Rent Control* (London: Sweet and Maxwell).

Arney, W. R., and Bergen, B. J. (1984), 'Power and Visibility: The Invention of Teenage Pregnancy', *Social Science and Medicine*, 18 (1): 11–19.

Arnot, M. (1994), 'Infant Death, Child Care and the State: The Baby-Farming Scandal and the First Infant Life Protection Legislation of 1872', *Continuity and Change*, 9 (2): 271–311.

Askham, J. (1984), *Identity and Stability in Marriage* (Cambridge: Cambridge University Press).

Atkinson, A. B. (1995), *Public Economics in Action: The Basic Income/Flat Tax Proposal* (Oxford: Oxford University Press).

Atkinson, R. (1965), *Sexual Morality* (London: Hutchinson).

Bailey, D. S. (1957), 'Marriage and the Family: Some Theological Considerations', in C. H. Rolph (ed.), *The Human Sum* (London: Heineman).

Bainham, A. (1991), 'The Privatisation of the Public Interest in Children', *Modern Law Review*, 53 (2): 208–21.

Bane, M. J., and Ellwood, D. T. (1994), *Welfare Realities from Rhetoric to Reform* (Cambridge, Mass.: Harvard University Press).

—— and Jargowsky, P. A. (1988), 'The Links between Government Policy and Family Structure: What Matters and What Doesn't', in A. Cherlin (ed.), *The Changing American Family and Public Policy* (Washington, DC: Urban Institute Press).

Barnes, K. C. (1958), *He and She* (London: Darwen Finlayson).

Barron, J. (1990), *Not Worth the Paper? The Effectiveness of Legal Protection for Women and Children Experiencing Domestic Violence* (Bristol: WAFE).

BBC (1993), 'Panorama: "Babies on Benefit"', 20 Sept.

Beck, U., and Beck-Gernscheim, E. (1995), *The Normal Chaos of Love* (Cambridge: Polity Press).

Becker, G. (1981), *A Treatise on the Family* (Cambridge, Mass.: Harvard University Press).

Behlmer, G. (1994), 'Summary Justice and Working-Class Marriage in England, 1870–1940', *Law and History Review*, 12 (2): 229–75.

Bellah, R., Madsen, R., Sullivan, W., Swidler, A., and Tipton, S. M. (1985), *Habits of the Heart: Middle America Observed* (London: Hutchinson).

Bennett, N., Blanc, A., and Bloom, D. (1988), 'Commitment and the Modern Union: Assessing the Link between Premarital Cohabitation and Subsequent Marital Stability', *American Sociological Review*, 53: 127–38.

Bernstein, R. (1966), 'Are We Still Stereotyping the Unmarried Mother', in R. W. Roberts (ed.), *The Unwed Mother* (New York: Harper and Row).

Bird, R. (1995), 'Child Support: Reform or Tinkering?', *Family Law*, March: 1112–14.

Bland, L. (1986), 'Marriage Laid Bare: Middle Class Woman and Marital Sex c.1880–1914', in J. Lewis (ed.), *Labour and Love: Woman's Experience of Home and Family* (Oxford: Blackwell)

—— (1995), *Banishing the Beast: English Feminism and Sexual Morality, 1885–1914* (London: Penguin).

Blankenhorn, D. (1995), *Fatherless America: Confronting our Most Urgent Social Problem* (New York: Basic Books).

Bone, M. (1979), *The Family Planning Services: Changes and Effects* (London: HMSO).

—— (1985), *Family Planning in Scotland in 1982* (London: HMSO).

Bosanquet, H. (1906), *The Family* (London: Macmillan).

Bott, E. (1971), *Family and Social Network: Roles, Norms and External Relations in Ordinary Urban Families* (1st edn. 1957; London: Tavistock).

Bowlby, J. (1951), *Maternal Care and Mental Health* (Geneva: WHO).

—— (1977), *Child Care and the Growth of Love* (1st edn. 1953; Harmondsworth: Penguin).

Bracher, M., Santow, G., Morgan, S. P., and Trussell, J. (1993), 'Marriage

Dissolution in Australia: Models and Explanations', *Population Studies*, 47: 403–25.

Bradshaw, J. (1989), *Lone Parents: Policy in the Doldrums* (Occasional Paper, No. 9; London: Family Policy Studies Centre).

—— (1990), *Child Poverty and Deprivation in the UK* (London: National Children's Bureau).

—— (1996), *Lone Mothers and Work* (Findings, No. 96; York: Joseph Rowntree Foundation).

—— and Millar, J. (1991), *Lone-Parent Families in the UK* (Department of Social Security Research Report, No. 6; London: HMSO).

—— Kennedy, S., Kilkey, M., Hutton, S., Corden, A., Eardley, T., Holmes, H., and Neale, J. (1996), *The Employment of Lone Parents: A Comparison of Policy in Twenty Countries* (London: Family Policy Studies Centre/Joseph Rowntree Foundation).

Bromley, P., and Lowe, N. (1987), *Bromley's Family Law,* (7th edn. London: Butterworth).

Brophy, J. (1985), 'Law, State and the Family: the Politics of Child Custody', Ph.D. thesis (Sheffield University).

Brown, A., and Kiernan, K. (1981), 'Cohabitation in Great Britain: Evidence from the General Household Survey', *Population Trends*, 25: 4–10.

Brown, J. (1983), *Family Income Support* (London: PSI).

—— (1989), *Why Don't They Go to Work? Mothers on Benefits* (SSAC Research Paper, No. 2; London: HMSO).

Buchanan, C., Maccoby, E. E., and Dornbusch, S. M. (1996), *Adolescents After Divorce* (London: Harvard University Press).

Burgess, E. W., and Locke, H. J. (1945), *The Family: From Institution to Companionship* (New York: American Book Company).

Burghes, L. (1987), *Made in the USA: A Review of Workfare, the Compulsory Work-for-Benefits Regime* (London: Employment Unit).

—— (1993), *One Parent Families: Policy Options for the 1990s* (York: Family Policy Studies Centre/Joseph Rowntree Foundation).

—— and Brown, M. (1995), *Single Lone Mothers: Problems, Prospects and Policies* (London: Family Policy Studies Centre).

Burgoyne, J., Ormerod, R., and Richards, M. (1987), *Divorce Matters* (Harmondsworth: Penguin).

Burkhauser, R. V., Duncan, G. J., Hauser, R., and Berntsen, R. (1991), 'Wife or Frau, Women Do Worse: A Comparison of Men and Women in the United States and Germany following Marital Dissolution', *Demography*, 28: 353–60.

Burns, A., and Scott, C. (1994), *Mother-Headed Families and Why They have Increased* (Hillsdale, N J: Lawrence Erlbaum).

Bury, J. (1984), *Teenage Pregnancy in Britain* (London: Birth Control Trust).

Caird, M. (1894), *The Daughters of Danaus* (London: Bliss Sands and Foster).

—— (1897), *The Morality of Marriage and Other Essays* (London: George Redway).

Cancian, F. M. (1987), *Love in America: Gender and Self-Development* (Cambridge: Cambridge University Press).

Carlson, A. C. (1987), 'Family Realities', *Public Interest*, No. 89 (Fall): 32–5.

Carpenter, E. (1894), *Marriage in a Free Society* (Manchester: NP).

Carstairs, G. M. (1962), *This Island Now* (London: Hogarth Press).

Castle, B. (1980), *Diaries 1974–1976* (London: Macmillan).

—— (1981), 'Sex and the Social Wage', *Over 21*, Apr.:21.

—— (1993), *Fighting All the Way* (London: Macmillan).

Cd. 6478 (1912), *Report of the Royal Commission on Divorce and Matrimonial Causes* (London: HMSO).

Cd. 6480 (1912), *Minutes of Evidence of the Royal Commission on Divorce and Matrimonial Causes* (London: HMSO).

Cd. 6481 (1912), Royal Commision on Divorce and Matrimonial Causes, *Minutes of Evidence* (London: HMSO).

Cmd. 6404 (1942), *Report of the Committee on Social Insurance and Allied Services,* The Beveridge Report (London: HMSO).

Cmd. 6922 (1946), *Report of the Care of Children Committee* (London: HMSO).

Cmd. 7046 (1947), *Economic Survey for 1947* (London: HMSO).

Cmd. 7225 (1947), Ministry of Labour, *Report for the Years 1939/46* (London: HMSO).

Cmd. 7695 (1949), *Royal Commission on Population Report* (London: HMSO).

Cmd. 8030 (1950), Ministry of National Insurance, *Report of the National Assistance Board for the Year ended December 1949* (London: HMSO).

Cmd. 8276 (1951), Ministry of National Insurance, *Report of the National Assistance Board for the Year ended December 1950* (London: HMSO).

Cmd. 8900 (1953), Ministry of National Insurance, *Report of the National Assistance Board for the Year ended December 1952* (London: HMSO).

Cmd. 9210 (1954), Ministry of National Insurance, *Report of the National Assistance Board for the Year ended December 1953* (London: HMSO).

Cmd. 9248 (1954), *Report of the Department Committee on the Adoption of Children* (London: HMSO).

Cmd. 9530 (1955), Ministry of National Insurance, *Report of the National Assistance Board for the Year ended December 1954* (London: HMSO).

Cmd. 9678 (1956), *Report of the Royal Commission on Marriage and Divorce* (London: HMSO).

Cmd. 9684 (1956), *Report of NIAC on Widows Benefits* (London: HMSO).

Cmd. 9752 (1956), Ministry of Pensions and National Insurance, Report of the National Insurance Advisory Committee, *Question of Earnings Limits for Benefits* (London: HMSO).

Cmd. 9781 (1956), Ministry of National Insurance, *Report of the National Assistance Board for the Year ended December 1955* (London: HMSO).

Cmd. 9855 (1956), *Report of NIAC on the Question of Dependency* (London: HMSO).

Cmnd. 1085 (1960), Ministry of National Insurance and Pensions, *Report of the National Assistance Board for the Year ended December 1959* (London: HMSO).

Cmnd. 1191 (1960), *Report on Children and Young Persons* (London: HMSO).

Cmnd. 1410 (1961), Ministry of Pensions and National Insurance, *Report of the National Assistance Board for the Year ended December 1960* (London: HMSO).

Cmnd. 1730 (1962), Ministry of National Insurance and Pensions, *Report of the National Assistance Board for the Year ended December 1961* (London: HMSO).

Cmnd. 2386 (1964), Ministry of National Insurance and Pensions, *Report of the National Assistance Board for the Year ended December 1963* (London: HMSO).

Cmnd. 2582 (1965), *Committee of Inquiry into the Impact of Rates on Households* (London: HMSO).

Cmnd. 2605 (1965), Committee on Housing in Greater London, *Report,* The Milner Holland Report (London: HMSO).

Cmnd. 2674 (1965), Ministry of National Insurance and Pensions, *Report of the National Assistance Board for the Year ended December 1964* (London: HMSO).

Cmnd. 2997 (1966), Ministry of National Insurance and Pensions, *Explanatory Memorandum, Ministry of Social Security Bill* (London: HMSO).

Cmnd. 3042 (1966), Ministry of National Insurance and Pensions, *Report of the National Assistance Board for the Year ended December 1965* (London: HMSO).

Cmnd. 3123 (1966), *Reform of the Grounds of Divorce: The Field of Choice* (London: HMSO).

Cmnd. 3585 (1968), National Board for Prices and Incomes, *Report No. 60 Pay of Nurses and Midwives in the NHS* (London: HMSO).

Cmnd. 3604 (1968), *Report No. 62: Increases in Rents of Local Authorities* (National Board for Prices and Incomes; London: HMSO).

Cmnd. 3693 (1968), Department of Health and Social Security, *Annual Report 1967* (London: HMSO).

Cmnd. 3703 (1968), Committee on Local Authority and Allied Personal Services, *Report,* The Seebohm Report (London: HMSO).

Cmnd. 3883 (1969), Department of Social Security, *National Superannuation and Social Insurance: Proposals for Earnings-Related Social Security* (London: HMSO).

Cmnd. 4462 (1970), Department of Health and Social Security, *Annual Report 1969* (London: HMSO).

Cmnd. 4714 (1971), *Annual Report 1970, Department of Health and Social Security* (London: HMSO).

Cmnd. 5019 (1972), Department of Health and Social Security, *Annual Report 1971* (London: HMSO).

Cmnd. 5107 (1972), *Report of the Department Committee on the Adoption of Children* (London: HMSO).

Cmnd. 5116 (1973), Green Paper, *Proposals for a Tax-Credit System* (London: HMSO).

Cmnd. 5174 (1972), *Education: A Framework for Expansion* (London: HMSO).

Cmnd. 5629 (1974), Department of Health and Social Security, *Report of the Committee on One-Parent Families*, i and ii, The Finer Report (London: HMSO).

Cmnd. 5700 (1974), Department of Health and Social Security, *Annual Report 1973* (London: HMSO).

Cmnd. 6910 (1977), Supplementary Benefit Commission, *Annual Report 1976* (London: HMSO).

Cmnd. 7725 (1979), Supplementary Benefit Commision, *Annual Report 1978* (London: HMSO).

Cmnd. 8033 (1980), *Report of the Supplementary Benefit Commission for the Year ended 1979* (London: HMSO).

Cmnd. 8093 (1980), *Taxation of Husband and Wife* (London: HMSO).

Cmnd. 9517–19 (1985), *Reform of Social Security, i, ii, iii* (London: HMSO).

Cmnd. 9691 (1985), *Reform of Social Security: Programme for Action* (London: HMSO).

Cmnd. 9756 (1986), *The Reform of Personal Taxation* (London: HMSO).

Cm. 1264 (1990), *Children Come First: The Government's Proposals on the Maintenance of Children* (London: HMSO).

Cm. 1508 (1991), *Department of Environment Annual Report 1991. The Government's Expenditure Plans 1991/2 to 1993/4* (London: HMSO).

Cm. 1514 (1991), *Department of Environment, Annual Report 1991, The Government's Expenditure Plans 1991–92 to 1993–94* (London: HMSO).

Cm. 2207 (1993), *Department of Environment Annual Report 1993. The Government's Expenditure Plans 1993/4 to 1996/7* (London: HMSO).

Cm. 2743 (1995), *Child Support: Reply by the Government to the Fifth Report from the Select Committee on Social Security* (London: HMSO).

Cm. 2799 (1995), *Looking to the Future: Mediation and the Ground for Divorce: The Government's Proposals* (London: HMSO).

Cm. 3213 (1996), *Social Security Department's Report. The Government's Expenditure Plans 1996/7 to 1998/9* (London: HMSO).

Cm. 3296 (1996), *The Draft Child Benefit, Child Support and Social Security (Miscellaneous Amendments) Regulations 1996* (London: HMSO).

—— *The Government's Expenditure Plans 1996–97 to 1998–99* (London: HMSO).

Central Advisory Council for Education (England) (1966), *Children and their Primary Schools*, i (London: HMSO).

CSO (1970), *Social Trends 1970*, (No. 1; London: HMSO).

Central Housing Advisory Committee (1955), *Unsatisfactory Tennants* (London: Ministry of Housing).

—— Central Housing Management Sub-Committee (1969), *Council Housing*

Purposes, Procedures and Priorities, The Cullingworth Report (London: HMSO).

Central Statistical Office (CSO) (1972), *Social Trends 3* (London: HMSO).

—— (1976), *Annual Abstract of Statistics 1975* (London: HMSO).

—— (1990), *Annual Abstract of Statistics* (London: HMSO).

—— (1992), *Social Trends 22* (London: HMSO).

—— (1993), *Social Trends 23* (London: HMSO).

—— (1994), *Social Trends 24* (London: HMSO).

—— (1995), *Social Trends 25* (London: HMSO).

—— (1996), *Annual Abstract of Statistics* (London: HMSO).

Chapman, E. R. (1897), *Marriage Questions in Modern Fiction* (London: John Lane).

Chase-Lansdale, P. L., and Hetherington, E. M. (1990), 'The Impact of Divorce on Life-Span Development: Short and Long Term Effects', in P. B. Baltes, D. L. Featherman, and R. M. Lerner (eds.), *Life-Span Development and Behavior,* (Hillsdale, N.J.: Lawrence Earlbaum Associates), 105–50.

—— Cherlin, A. J., and Kiernan, K. E. (1995), 'The Long-Term Effects of Parental Divorce on the Mental Health of Young Adults: A Development Perspective', *Child Development,* 66: 1614–34.

Cheetham, J. (1977), *Unwanted Pregnancy and Counselling* (London: Routledge and Kegan Paul).

Cherlin, A., Kiernan, K. E., and Chase-Lansdale, P. L. (1995), 'Parental Divorce in Childhood and Demographic Outcomes in Young Adulthood', *Demography,* 32: 299–318.

—— Furstenberg, F. F., Chase-Lansdale, P. L., Kiernan, K. E., Robins, P. K., Morrison, D. R., and Teitler, J. O. (1991), 'Longitudinal Studies of Effects of Divorce on Children in Great Britain and the United States', *Science,* 252: 1386–9.

Chesser, E. (1950), 'The Law of Abortion', *Medical World,* 72: 495.

—— (1952), *Marriage and Freedom,* (1st edn. 1946; London: Rich and Cowan).

—— (1960), *Is Chastity Outmoded?* (London: British Medical Association).

—— (1964), *Love Without Fear: A Plain Guide to Sex Technique for Every Married Adult* (1st edn. 1941; London: Arrow Books).

—— Davey, C., Gorer, G., Maclure, S., Nicholls, J., Watson, W. (1961), *Teenage Morals* (London: Councils and Education Press).

Chester, R. (1971), 'Contemporary Trends in the Stability of English Marriage', *Journal of Biosocial Science,* 3: 389–402.

Child Poverty Action Group (1971), *Poverty,* Nos. 20–1: 6–7.

—— (1976), *Poverty,* No. 35: 20–6.

—— (1993), *Child Support Handbook,* 1st edn. (London: CPAG).

Child Support Agency, The (1994), *The First Two Years,* Annual Report 1993/4 and Business Plan 1994/5 (London: HMSO).

Clark, D. (1991) (ed.), *Marriage, Domestic Life and Social Change: Writings for Jacqueline Burgoyne, 1944–1988* (London: Routledge).

Cockett, M., and Tripp, J. (1994), *The Exeter Family Study: Family Breakdown and its Impact on Children* (Exeter: University of Exeter Press).

Cohen, B. (1988), *Caring for Children*, Report for the European Commission's Childcare Network (London: Family Policy Studies Centre).

Cole, M. (1949), *Growing up into Revolution* (London: Longman).

Coleman, D. (1989), 'The Contemporary Pattern of Remarriage in England and Wales', in E. Grebenik, C. Hohn, and R. Mackensen (eds.), *The Later Phases of the Family Cycle: Demographic Aspects* (Oxford: Clarendon Press).

Collier, R. (1995), *Masculinity, Law and the Family* (London: Routledge).

Collini, S. (1979), *Liberalism and Sociology: L. T. Hobhouse and Political Argument in England, 1880–1914* (Cambridge: Cambridge University Press).

—— (1991), *Public Moralists: Political Thought and Intellectual Life in Britain, 1850–1930* (Oxford: Clarendon Press).

Comfort, A. (1963), *Sex in Society* (London: Gerald Duckworth).

Convocations of Canterbury and York (1935), *The Church and Marriage*, Report of the Joint Committees of the Convocations of Canterbury and York (London: SPCK).

Cotter, E. H. J. (1967), 'Compulsive Desire for Pregnancy', letter to *British Medical Journal*, II (15 Apr.): 177.

Council of Europe (1996), *Recent Demographic Developments in Europe, 1996* (Strasbourg: Council of Europe Press).

Cowan, D. (1996), *The Housing Act 1996: A Practical Guide* (Bristol: Jordans).

CPAG, *see* Child Poverty Action Group.

Crellin, E., Kellmer Pringle, M., and West, P. (1971), *Born Illegitimate: Social and Educational Implications* (London: National Children's Bureau).

Cretney, S. (1985), 'Money after Divorce—The Mistakes We Have Made?', in M. D. A. Freeman (ed.), *Essays in Family Law* (London: Stevens and Sons).

—— (1996), "What Will the Women Want Next?" The Struggle for Power within the Family, 1925–75' ', *Law Quarterly Review*, 112: 110–37.

CSO, *see* Central Statistical Office.

Davidoff, L., and Hall, C. (1987), *Family Fortunes: Men and Women of the English Middle Class 1780–1850* (London: Hutchinson).

Davin, A. (1978), 'Imperialism and Motherhood', *History Workshop Journal*, Spring: 9–65.

Davis, G., and Murch, M. (1988), *Grounds for Divorce* (Oxford: Clarendon Press).

Demant, V. A. (1963), *Christian Ethics: An Exposition* (London: Hodder and Stoughton).

Dench, G. (1994), *The Frog, the Prince and the Problem of Men* (London: Neanderthal Book).

Dennis, N., and Erdos, G. (1992), *Families without Fatherhood* (Choice in Welfare Series, No. 12; London: Institute for Economic Affairs).

Department of Health (1943), 'The Care of Illegitimate Children', Circular 2866, 16 Nov.

Department of Health (1996), *Adoption: A Service for Children* (London: Department of Health).

Department of Health and Social Security (1969), *Extract from the Annual Report 1968, Department of Health and Social Security, Part II. Social Security Services* (London: HMSO).

—— (1978), *Social Assistance: A Review of the Supplementary Benefit Scheme in Great Britain* (London: DHSS).

—— (1981), *Social Security Statistics for 1980* (London: HMSO).

—— (1987), *Social Security Statistics for 1986* (London: HMSO).

—— (1988), *Social Security Statistics for 1987* (London: HMSO).

—— (1989), *Social Security Statistics for 1988* (London: HMSO).

—— (1990), *Social Security Statistics for 1989* (London: HMSO).

Department of Social Security (1993a), *The Growth of Social Security* (London: HMSO).

—— (1993b), *Households Below Average Income: A Statistical Analysis 1979–1990/91* (London: HMSO).

—— (1994), *Social Security Statistics 1993* (London: HMSO).

—— (1995), Analytical Services Division, *The Requirement to Co-operate: A Report on the Operation of the 'Good Cause' Provisions* (London: DSS).

—— (1996), *Pensions and Divorce* (Social Security Research Report, No. 50; London: HMSO).

Devlin, P. (1965), *The Enforcement of Morals* (Oxford: Oxford University Press).

Donnison, D., and Chapman, V. (1965), *Social Policy and Administration* (London: Allen and Unwin).

Dronkers, J. (1995), 'The Changing Effects of Lone Parent Families on the Educational Attainment of their Children in a European State', *Sociology*, 28: 171–91.

DSS, *see* Department of Social Security.

Duncan, G. J., and Rodgers, W. R. (1987), 'Lone Parents and their Economic Problems: Transitory or Persistent?', in *Lone-Parent Families* (Social Policy Studies, No. 8; Paris: OECD).

Duncan, G. R., Gustafsson, B., Hauser, R., Schnaus, G., Jenkins, S., Messinger, H., Miffels, R., Nolan, B., Ray, J.-C., and Voges, W. (1995), 'Poverty and Social Assistance Dynamics in the US, Canada and Europe', in K. McFate, R. Lawson, and W. Julius Wilson (eds.), *Poverty, Inequality and the Future of Social Policy* (New York: Russell Sage Foundation).

Dunnell, K. (1979), *Family Formation 1976*, OPCS Social Survey (London: HMSO).

Edwards, R., and Duncan, S. (1995), 'Rational Economic Man or Women in

Social Context?', in E. Bortolaia Silva (ed.), *Good Enough Mothering? Feminist Perspectives on Lone Motherhood* (New York: Routledge).

Eekalaar, J. (1978), *Family Law and Social Policy* (London: Weidenfeld and Nicolson).

—— (1991*a*), *Regulating Divorce* (Oxford: Clarendon)

—— (1991*b*), 'Parental Responsibility: State of Nature or Nature of the State?', *Journal of Social Welfare and Family Law,* 37 (1): 37–50.

—— and Maclean, M. (1986), *Maintenance after Divorce* (Oxford: Clarendon).

Ehrenreich, B. (1983), *The Hearts of Men: American Dreams and the Flight from Commitment* (London: Pluto Press).

Elliott, B. J., and Richards, M. P. M. (1991), 'Children and Divorce: Educational Performance, and Behaviour, Before and After Parental Separation', *International Journal of Law and the Family,* 5: 258–76.

Ellis, H. (1910), *Studies in the Psychology of Sex,* vi. *Sex in Relation to Society* (Philadelphia: F. A. Davis Co.).

—— (1912), *The Task of Social Hygiene* (London: Constable).

Ellwood, D. T., and Bane, M. J. (1985), 'The Impact of AFDC on Family Structure and Living Arrangements', in R. G. Ehrenberg (ed.), *Research in Labor Economics,* vii (Greenwich, Conn.: JAI Press).

EOC (1986), *Childcare and Equal Opportunities: Some Policy Perspectives* (London: HMSO).

—— (1995), *Life Cycle and Inequality in Britain: Women and Men in Britain* (Manchester: Equal Opportunities Commission).

Eppel, E. M., and Eppel, M. (1966), *Adolescents and Morality* (London: Routledge and Kegan Paul).

Ermisch, J. (1989), 'Divorce: Economic Antecedents and Aftermath', in H. Joshi (ed.), *The Changing Population of Britain* (Oxford: Basil Blackwell).

—— (1995), *Pre-Marital Cohabitation, Childbearing and the Creation of One Parent Families* (Working Papers of the ESRC Research Centre on Micro-social Change, Paper 95–17; Colchester: University of Essex).

—— and Francesconi, M. (1996), *The Increasing Complexity of Family Relationships: Lifetime Experience of Single Motherhood and Stepfamilies in Great Britain* (Working Papers of the ESRC Research Centre on Micro-social Change, Paper 96–11; Colchester: University of Essex).

Eurostat (1994), *Social Europe: The European Union and the Family* (Luxembourg: Eurostat).

Fawcett, M. G. (1894), *Home and Politics* (London: Women's Printing Society).

—— (1895), 'The Woman Who Did', *Contemporary Review,* LXVII (May).

Ferguson, J., and Fitzgerald, H. (1954), *Studies in the Social Services* (London: HMSO).

Ferri, E. (1976), *Growing up in a One-Parent Family: A Long-Term Study of Child Development* (London: National Foundation for Educational Research).

Field, F. (1974), *Unequal Britain: A Report on the Cycle of Inequality* (London: Arrow Books).

—— (1975), 'How Good a Model is FIS for a Means-Tested GMA?', *Poverty*, 31: 17–22.

Finch, J. (1989), 'Social Policy, Social Engineering and the Family in the 90s', in M. Bulmer, J. Lewis, and D. Piachaud (eds.), *The Goals of Social Policy* (London: Unwin Hyman).

—— and Mason, J. (1993), *Negotiating Family Responsibilities* (London: Routledge).

Finer, M., and Macgregor, O. (1974), *The History of the Obligation to Maintain*, Cmnd. 5629, Vol. 2, Appendix v.

Fink, J. (1997), 'Condemned or Condoned? Investigating the Problem of Unmarried Motherhood in England, 1945–60', Ph.D thesis (University of Essex).

Finlayson, L., Ford, R., and Marsh, A. (1996), 'Paying for Child Care', *Labour Market Gazette*, July: 295–303.

Fisher Committee (1973), *Report of the Committee on Abuses of Social Security Benefits* (London: HMSO).

Flemming, S. (1986), 'Introduction', in E. Rathbone (ed.), *The Disinherited Family* (first published 1924, Bristol: Falling Wall Press).

Fletcher, R. (1966), *The Family and Marriage in Britain* (1st edn. 1962; Harmondsworth: Penguin).

Folbre, N. (1994), *Who Pays for the Kids?* (London: Routledge).

Ford, R., Marsh, A., and McKay, S. (1995), *Changes in Lone Parenthood* (Department of Social Security Research Report, No. 40; London: HMSO).

—— —— and Finlayson, L. (1996), *What Happens to Lone Parents: A Cohort Study 1991–1995* (London: Policy Studies Institute).

Franklin, A. W. (1966), 'Leontine Young and "Tess of the d'Urbervilles"— Some Thoughts on Illegitimacy', *British Medical Journal*, I (26 March): 789–91.

French, E., and Beer, J. (1972), *Voluntary Welfare Associations and Unmarried Mothers in Greater London* (Department of Planning and Transportation Intelligence Unit Research, Memo 345, London: Greater London Council).

Furstenberg, F. F., Jr., and Cherlin, A. J. (1991), *Divided Families: What Happens to Children When Parents Part* (Cambridge, Mass.: Harvard University Press).

Garfinkel, I., and McLanahan, S. S. (1986), *Single Mothers and their Children: A New American Dilemma* (Washington, DC: Urban Institute).

Garnham, A., and Knights, E. (1994a), *Putting the Treasury First: The Truth about Child Support* (London: Child Poverty Action Group).

—— —— (1994b), *Child Support Handbook*, 1st edn. (London: CPAG).

Gay, P. (1984), *Education of the Senses: The Bourgeois Experience Victoria to Freud*, i (New York: Oxford University Press).

General Household Survey (1996), *Living in Britain 1996*.

General Register Office (GRO) (1964), *Registrar General's Statistical Review 1964*, Part iii *Commentary* (London: HMSO).

—— (annual), *Registrar General's Statistical Reviews* (London: HMSO).

Gibson, C. (1994), *Dissolving Wedlock* (London: Routledge).

Giddens, A. (1992), *The Transformation of Intimacy: Sexuality, Love and Eroticism in Modern Societies* (Cambridge: Polity Press).

Gilder, G. (1981), *Wealth and Poverty* (New York: Basic Books).

—— (1987), 'The Collapse of the American Family', *Public Interest*, 89 (Fall): 20–5.

Gill, D. (1977), *Illegitimacy, Sexuality and the Status of Women* (Oxford: Blackwell).

Gillis, J. (1979), 'Servants, Sexual Relations and the Risks of Illegitimacy in London, 1801–1900', *Feminist Studies*, 5 (Spring): 142–73.

—— (1985), *For Better, For Worse: British Marriages, 1600 to the Present* (Oxford: Oxford University Press).

Ginsburg, N. (1995), 'The Impact of Rising Rents on Housing Benefit and Rented Housing', *Benefits*, Issue 14, (Sept./Oct.): 6–10.

Glastonbury, B. (1971), *Homeless Near a Thousand Homes* (London: Allen and Unwin).

Glenn, N. D., and Kramer, K. B. (1987), 'The Marriages and Divorces of Children who Divorce', *Journal of Marriage and the Family*, 49: 811–25.

Goldstein, J., Freud, A., and Solnit, A. (1973), *Beyond the Best Interests of the Child* (New York: Free Press).

Goldthorpe, J. H., Lockwood, D., Beckhofer, F., and Platt, J. (1968), *The Affluent Worker: Industrial Attitudes and Behaviour* (Cambridge: Cambridge University Press).

Goode, W. J. (1959), 'The Theoretical Importance of Love', *American Sociological Review*, 24 (1): 38–47.

Goodhart, C. B. (1973), 'On the Incidence of Illegal Abortion', *Population Studies*, 27 (2): 207.

Goodin, R. (1997), 'Social Welfare as a Collective Social Responsibility', in D. Schmidtz and R. E. Goodin (eds.), *Social Welfare as an Individual Responsibility: For and Against* (New York: Cambridge University Press).

Gorer, G. (1971), *Sex and Marriage in England Today: A Study of the Views and Experience of the under-45s* (London: Nelson).

Gough, D. (1961), 'Work with Unmarried Mothers', *Almoner*, 12 (13 Mar.): 490–7.

—— (1966), *Understanding Unmarried Mothers* (London: NCUMC).

—— (1971), 'Adoption and the Unmarried Mother', in R. Tod (ed.), *Social Work in Adoption: Collected Papers* (London: Longman).

Government Actuary (1954), *First Quinquennial Review* (London: HMSO).

Graham, H. (1987), 'Being Poor: Perceptions and Coping Strategies for Lone

Mothers', in J. Brannen and G. Wilson (eds.), *Give and Take in Families* (London: Allen and Unwin).

Grand, S. (1888), *Ideala: A Study from Life* (London: E. W. Allen).

—— (1893), *The Heavenly Twins* (London: Heinemann).

Gray, A. H. (1923), *Men, Women and God: A Discussion of Sex Questions from the Christian Point of View* (London: Student Christian Movement).

Greenberg, D., and Wolf, D. W. (1982), 'The Economic Consequences of Experiencing Parental Marital Disruption', *Children and Youth Services Review*, 4: 141–62.

Greenland, C. (1957), 'Unmarried Parenthood: Ecological Aspects', *Lancet*, 19 January: 148–51.

—— (1958), 'Unmarried Parenthood', *Medical Officer*, XCIX: 265–86.

Greve, J. (1964), *London's Homeless* (London: Bell).

—— Pope, D., and Greve, S. (1971), *Homelessness in London* (Edinburgh: Scottish Academic Press).

Griffith, E. F. (1941), *Sex and Citizenship* (London: Gollancz).

—— (1948), *Morals in the Melting Pot* (London: Methuen).

GRO, *see* General Register Office.

Grosskurth, P. (1980), *Havelock Ellis: A Biography* (London: Allen Lane).

Grundy, E. M. D. (1989), *Women's Migration: Marriage, Fertility and Divorce* (OPCS Series LS, No. 4; London: HMSO).

Hague, G., and Malos, E. (1993), *Domestic Violence: Action for Change* (Cheltenham: Clarion Press).

Hair, P. (1966), 'Bridal Pregnancy in Rural England in Earlier Centuries', *Population Studies*, 20 (2): 233.

Haire, N. (1927), *Hymen or the Future of Marriage* (London: Kegan, Paul, Trench and Trubner).

Hall, P. M. (1959), *The Social Services of Modern England*, 4th edn. (London: Routledge and Kegan Paul).

—— and Howes, I. V. (1965), *The Church in Social Work: A Study of Moral Welfare Work Undertaken by the Church of England* (London: Routledge and Kegan Paul).

Hamill, L. (1976), 'The Increase in Female One-Parent Families Receiving Supplementary Benefit', unpublished seminar paper, SBC, 7 Sept.

Hamilton, C. (1981), *Marriage as a Trade* (1st edn. 1909; London: Women's Press).

Hamilton, M. W. (1962), 'Extra-Marital Conception in Adolescence', *British Journal of Psychiatric Social Work*, 6 (3): 114–21.

Hantrais, L., and Letablier, M.-T. (1996), *Families and Family Policy in Europe* (London: Longman).

Hardy, M., and Crow, G. (1991), *Lone Mothers: Coping with Constraints and Making Opportunities* (Brighton: Harvester Wheatsheaf).

Harkness, S., Machin, S., and Waldfogel, J. (1996), 'Women's Pay and Family

Incomes in Britain, 1979–1991', in J. Hills (ed.), *New Inequalities: The Changing Distribution of Income and Wealth in the UK* (Cambridge: Cambridge University Press).

Harris, J. (1993), *Private Lives, Public Spirit: A Social History of Britain, 1870–1914* (Oxford: Oxford University Press).

Hart, H. L. A. (1963), *Law, Liberty and Morality* (Oxford: Oxford University Press).

Hart, N. (1976), *When Marriage Ends: A Study in Marriage Status Passage* (London: Tavistock).

Hartley, S. F. (1966), 'The Amazing Rise of Illegitimacy in Great Britain', *Social Forces*, 44 (4): 533–45.

—— (1975), *Illegitimacy* (Berkeley: University of California Press).

Harvey, A. (1960), *Casualties of the Welfare State* (Fabian Tract No. 321; London: Fabian Society).

—— (1968), 'What Help for Poor Tenants?', in *Social Services for All? Part Three* (Fabian Tract, No. 384; London: Fabian Society).

Haskey, J. (1983a), 'Remarriage of the Divorced in England and Wales: A Contemporary Phenomenon', *Journal of Biosocial Science*, 15: 253–71.

—— (1983b), 'Marital Status before Marriage and Age at Marriage: Their Influence on the Chance of Divorce', *Population Trends*, 32: 4–14 (London: HMSO).

—— (1984), 'Social Class and Socio-Economic Differentials in Divorce in England and Wales', *Population Studies*, 38 (3): 419–38.

—— (1991), 'Lone Parenthood and Demographic Change', in M. Hardy and G. Crow (eds.), *Lone Parenthood: Coping with Constraints and Making Opportunities* (London: Harvester Wheatsheaf).

—— (1992), 'Pre-Marital Cohabitation and the Probability of Subsequent Divorce', *Population Trends*, 68: 5–15 (London: HMSO).

—— (1993), 'Trends in the Numbers of One-Parent Families in Great Britain', *Population Trends*, 71 (Spring): 26–33 (London: HMSO).

—— (1995), 'Trends in Marriage and Cohabitation: The Decline in Marriage and the Changing Pattern of Living in Partnerships', *Population Trends*, 80: 5–15 (London: HMSO).

—— (1996), 'The Proportion of Married Couples who Divorce: Past Patterns and Current Prospects', *Population Trends*, 83: 25–36 (London: HMSO).

Hauser, R., and Fischer, I. (1990), 'Economic Well-Being among One-Parent Families', in T. M. Smeeding, M. O'Higgins, and L. Rainwater (eds.), *Poverty Inequality and Income Distribution in Comparative Perspective* (Brighton: Harvester Wheatsheaf).

HC (1996), *Sixth Standing Committee on Delegated Legislation*, 10 July (London: HMSO).

HC 69 (1993/4), *First Report of the Social Security Committee: The Operation of the Child Support Act* (London: HMSO).

HC 98 (1982), Law Commision, *Family Law: Illegitimacy* (Report No. 118; London: HMSO).

HC 122-ii (1990/1), Employment Committee, *Part-time Work Vol 2* (London: HMSO).

HC 153 (1990/1), National Audit Office, *Department of Social Security Support for Lone Parent Families* (London: HMSO).

HC 199 (1994/5), Third Report from the Parliamentary Commissioner for Administration, *Investigation of Complaints Against the Child Support Agency* (London: HMSO).

HC 227, i, ii, and iii (1994/5), Employment Committee, First Report 1994/5, *Mothers in Employment*, i, ii, and iii (London: HMSO).

HC 303 (1994/5), Social Security Committee, *The Operation of the Child Support Act. Memorandum from the Chief Executive* (London: HMSO).

HC 307 (1994/5), *Parlimentary Commissioner for Administration Annual Report for 1994* (London: HMSO).

HC 341-ii (1972/3), Inland Revenue Staff Federation, *Memorandum of Evidence to the Select Committee on Tax Credit System* (London: HMSO).

HC 382 (1994/5), Fifth Report of the Social Security Committee, *The Work of the DSS and its Agencies* (London: HMSO).

HC 429 (1990/1), *38th Report of the Committee of Public Accounts: Department of Social Security: Support for Lone Parent Families* (London: HMSO).

HC 440 (1995/6), Fourth Report from the Social Security Committee, *Child Support: Good Cause and the Benefit Penalty* (London: HMSO).

HC 470 (1993/4), Fifth Report from the Social Security Committee, *The Operation of the Child Support Act: Proposals for Change* (London: HMSO).

HC 479 (1988), Law Commission, *Facing the Future: A Discussion Paper on the Ground for Divorce* (London: HMSO).

HC 596 (1994/5), *Child Support Agency Annual Report and Account* (London: HMSO).

Herbert, A. P. (1934), *Holy Deadlock* (London: Methuen).

Heron, A. (1963) (ed.), *An Essay by a Group of Friends: Towards a Quaker View of Sex* (London: Friends Home Service Committee).

Hetherington, E., Cox, M., and Cox, R. (1978), 'The Aftermath of Divorce', in J. Stevens and M. Matthews (eds.), *Mother–Child, Father–Child Relations* (Washington, DC: National Association for the Education of Young Children).

Higgenbotham, A. (1989), '"Sign of the Age": Infanticide and Illegitimacy in Victorian London', *Victorian Studies*, 32 (Spring): 319–37.

Hills, J. (1995), *Income and Wealth*, ii (York: Joseph Rowntree Foundation).

—— (1996) (ed.), *New Inequalities: The Changing Distribution of Income and Wealth in the UK* (Cambridge: Cambridge University Press).

Himmelfarb, G. (1986), *Marriage and Morals among the Victorians* (London: Faber and Faber).

HL 216 (1981/2), Select Committee on the European Communities, *Voluntary Part-time Work* (London: HMSO).

Hobhouse, L. T. (1906), *Morals in Evolution* (London: Chapman Hall).

Hochschild, A. (1989), *The Second Shift: Working Parents and the Revolution at Home* (New York: Piatkus).

Hoem, J. (1991), *Trends and Patterns in Swedish Divorce Risks 1971–1989* (Stockholm University Research Reports in Demography, No. 64; Stockholm: University of Stockholm).

Hoffman, S. D., and Duncan, G. (1988), 'What Are the Economic Consequences of Divorce?', *Demography*, 25 (4): 302–6

Holroyd, M. (1989), *Bernard Shaw*, ii. *1898–1918: The Pursuit of Power* (London: Chatto and Windus).

Holterman, S. (1995), *All our Futures* (Ilford: Barnardo's).

Home Office (1961), *Eighth Report on the Work of the Children's Department* (London: HMSO).

—— (1969), *Sixteenth Report on the Work of the Children's Department* (London: HMSO).

Hopflinger, F. (1990), 'The Future of Household and Family Structures in Europe', Council of Europe Seminar on Present Demographic Trends and Lifestyles in Europe (Strasbourg: Council of Europe Press).

Howard, M. (1993), 'Picking up the Pieces', mimeo, Conservative Political Centre Fringe Meeting, Blackpool, 5 Oct.

Hunt, A. (1968), *A Survey of Women's Employment*, i, Report (London: HMSO).

—— Fox, J., and Morgan, N. (1973), *Families and their Needs* (London: HMSO).

Irvine, E. E. (1954), 'Research into Problem Families: Theoretical Questions Arising from Dr. Blacker's Investigations', *British Journal of Psychiatric Social Work*, 9 (May): 24–33

Izzard, E. A. (1969), 'Accomodation for Unmarried Mothers', *Case Conference*, 16 (8): 315–17

Jalland, P. (1986), *Women, Marriage and Politics, 1860–1914* (Oxford: Oxford University Press).

Joad, C. E. M. (1946), *The Future of Morals* (1st edn. 1924; London: John Westhouse).

Johnson, A. M., Wadsworth, J., Wellings, K., and Field, J. (1994), *Sexual Attitudes and Lifestyles* (Oxford: Blackwell Scientific Publications).

Jones, W. C., Meyer, H. J., Borgatta, E. F. (1966), 'Social and Psychological Factors in Status Decisions of Unmarried Mothers', in R. W. Roberts (ed.), *The Unwed Mother* (New York: Harper and Row).

Kemp, P. (1990), 'Income Related Assistance with Housing Costs: A Cross-National Comparison', *Urban Studies*, 27 (6).

—— (1995), 'Housing Benefits: Some Peculiarities of the British', *Benefits*, Sept./Oct.: 1–10.

Key, E. (1914), *The Renaissance of Motherhood* (London: G. P. Putnams Sons).

Kiernan, K. E. (1971), 'The Illegitimacy Phenomenon of England and Wales in the 1950s and 1960s', unpublished paper.

—— (1983), 'The Structure of Families Today: Continuity or Change?', in *The Family* (OPCS Occasional Paper, 31.17; London: HMSO).

—— (1986), 'Teenage Marriage and Marital Breakdown: A Longitudinal Study', *Population Studies*, 1 (40): 35–54.

—— (1992*a*), 'Men and Women at Work and Home', in R. Jowell, L. Brook, and G. Prior (eds.), *The British Social Attitudes Survey*, 9th Report (Aldershot: Dartmouth).

—— (1992*b*), 'The Impact of Family Disruption in Childhood on Transitions made in Young Adult Life', *Population Studies*, 46: 213–34.

—— (1994), 'The Changing Demography of Partnership', Witness Briefing Paper, in *Report of the All Party Parliamentary Group on Parenting* and the International Year of the Family UK. Parliamentary Hearings, London.

—— (1995), *Transition to Parenthood: Young Mothers, Young Fathers: Associated Factors and Later Life Experiences*, (London: LSE, STICERD Discussion Paper No. 113), 54 pages.

—— (1996*a*), 'Partnership Behaviour in Europe: Recent Trends and Issues', in D. Coleman (ed.), *Europe's Population* (Oxford: Oxford University Press).

—— (1996*b*), 'Lone Motherhood, Employment and Outcomes for Children', *International Journal of Family Policy and Law* 3 (3): 233–49.

—— (1997*a*), 'Becoming a Young Parent: A Longitudinal Study of Associated Factors, *British Journal of Sociology*, 48 (3): 406–28.

—— (1997*b*), *The Legacy of Parental Divorce: Social, Economic and Demographic Experiences in Adulthood* (London: STICERD, LSE, ESRC Centre for the analysis of Social Exclusion, CASE Paper No.1).

—— and Eldridge, S. M. (1987), 'Inter and Intra Cohort Variation in the Timing of First Marriage', *British Journal of Sociology*, 38 (1): 44–65.

—— and Estaugh, V. (1993), *Cohabitation: Extra-Marital Childbearing and Social Policy* (Occasional Paper, 17; London: Family Policy Studies Centre).

King, D. (1987), *The New Right: Politics, Markets and Citizenship* (Basingstoke: Macmillan).

Klein, V. (1960), *Working Wives* (Occasional Paper, No. 5; London: Institute of Personnel Management).

Kravdal, O. (1988), 'The Impact of First-Birth Timing on Divorce: New Evidence from Longitudinal Analysis Based on the Central Population Register of Norway', *European Journal of Population*, 4: 247–69.

Kronick, J. C. (1966), 'An Assessment of Research Knowledge concerning the Unmarried Mother', in R. W. Roberts (ed.), *The Unwed Mother* (New York: Harper and Row).

Lamb, M. E. (1981), *The Role of the Father in Child Development*, 2nd edn. (New York. Wiley).

Lambert, L., and Streather, J. (1980), *Children in Changing Families: A Study of Adoption and Illegitimacy* (London: Macmillan).

Land, H. (1977), 'The Child Benefit Fiasco', in K. Jones (ed.), *The Yearbook of Social Policy 1976* (London: Routledge).

—— (1980), 'The Family Wage', *Feminist Review*, 6: 55-77.

—— (1986), 'Women and Children Last: Reform of Social Security?', in M. Brenton and C. Ungerson (eds.), *The Yearbook of Social Policy 1986* (London: Routledge).

—— and Parker, R. (1978), 'Family Policy in Britain: The Hidden Dimensions', in A. Kahn and S. Kamerman (eds.), *Family Policy in Fourteen Countries* (New York: Columbia University Press).

Langford, C. (1976), *Birth Control Practice and Marital Fertility in Great Britain* (London: Population Investigation Committee).

Lasch, C. (1977), *Haven in a Heartless World* (New York: Basic Books).

Laslett, P. (1977), *Family Life and Illicit Love in Earlier Generations* (Cambridge: Cambridge University Press).

—— Oosterveen, K., and Smith, R. M. (1980) (eds.), *Bastardy and its Comparative History* (London: Edward Arnold).

Law Commision (1979), 'Family Law: Illegitimacy' Working Paper No. 74.

—— (1988), *Facing the Future: A Discussion Paper on the Ground for Divorce* (London: HMSO).

—— (1990), *Family Law: The Ground for Divorce* (London: HMSO).

Lawson, A. (1993), 'Multiple Fractures: The Cultural Construction of Teenage Sexuality and Pregnancy', in A. Lawson and D. L. Rhode (eds.), *The Politics of Pregnancy* (New Haven: Yale University Press).

Lawson, N. (1992), *The View from No. 11* (London: Bantam Press).

Layard, R., Piachand, D., and Stewart, M. (1978), *The Causes of Poverty* (Background Paper No. 5 to Royal Commission on the Distribution of Income and Wealth; London: HMSO).

Leathard, A. (1980), *The Fight for Family Planning* (London: Macmillan).

Lecky, W. E. H. (1884), *History of European Morals*, ii (1st edn. 1869; London: Longman).

Leete, R. (1978), 'Adoption Trends and Illegitimate Births 1951-77', *Population Trends*, 14 (OPCS, London: HMSO).

Lefaucheur, N. (1993), 'French Policies towards Lone Parents: Social Categories and Social Policies', in K. McFate, R. Lawson, and W. Julius Wilson (eds.), *Poverty, Inequality and the Future of Social Policy* (New York: Russell Sage Foundation).

—— and Martin, C. (1993), 'Lone Parent Families in France: Situation and Research', in J. Hudson and B. Galaway (eds.), *Single Parent Families: Perspective on Research and Policy* (Toronto: Thompson Educational Publishing Inc.).

Lesthaeghe, R. (1995), 'The Second Demographic Transition in Western

Countries: An Interpretation', in K. O. Mason and A.-M. Jensen (eds.), *Gender and Family Change in Industrialized Countries* (Oxford: Clarendon Press).

Lewis, J. (1980), *The Politics of Motherhood: Child and Maternal Welfare in England 1900–1939* (Beckenham: Croom Helm).

—— (1986), *What Price Community Medicine?* (Brighton: Harvester Wheatsheaf).

—— (1991), *Women and Social Action in Victorian and Edwardian England* (Aldershot: Edward Elgar).

—— (1992), 'Gender and the Development of Welfare Regimes', *Journal of European Social Policy*, 3: 159–73.

—— (1995), *The Voluntary Sector: The State and Social Work in Britain* (Aldershot: Edward Elgar).

—— and Maclean, M. (1997), 'Recent Developments in Family Policy in the UK: The Case of the Family Law Act', in *Social Policy Review*, 9 (London: Social Policy Association), 87–104.

—— Clark, D., and Morgan, D. (1992), *'Whom God Hath Joined Together': The Work of Marriage Guidance* (London: Routledge).

Lewis Fanning, E. (1949), 'Report of an Inquiry into Family Limitation', *Papers of the Royal Commission of the Population* i (London: HMSO).

Lindsey, B., and Evans, W. (1929), *The Companionate Marriage* (London: Brentano's Ltd).

Lippmann, W. A. (1929), *Preface to Morals* (London: Allen and Unwin).

Lister, R. (1972), 'The Earnings Rule', *Poverty* 24 (Autumn/Winter): 18–24.

—— (1973), *As Man and Wife? A Study of the Cohabitation Rule* (London: CPAG).

—— (1995), 'Dilemmas in Engendering Citizenship', *Economy and Society*, 24 (1): 1–40.

Logan, R. (1986), *Homelessness and Relationship Breakdown* (London: National Council for One Parent Families).

Luker, K. (1996), *Dubious Conceptions: The Politics of Teenage Pregnancy* (Cambridge, Mass.: Harvard University Press).

Macdonald, E. K. (1956), 'Follow-up of Illegitimate Children', *Medical Officer*, 14 Dec.: 361–5

McDonald, P., and Weston, R. (1986), 'The Data Base for Child Support Reform', in *Child Support*, Social Justice Project (Canberra: Australian National University).

McDougall, W. (1908), *An Introduction to Social Psychology* (London: Methuen and Co.).

Mace, D. R. (1943), *Does Sex Morality Matter?* (London: Rich and Cowan).

—— (1945), *The Outlook for Marriage* (London: Marriage Guidance Council).

—— (1948), *Marriage Crisis* (London: Delisle).

Macintyre, S. (1977), *Single and Pregnant* (London: Croom Helm).

McKay, S., and Marsh, A. (1994), *Lone Parents and Work* (DSS Research Report No. 25; London: HMSO).

McLanahan, S., and Booth, K. (1989), 'Mother-Only Families: Problems, Prospects, and Politics', *Journal of Marriage and the Family,* 51 (Aug.): 557–80.

—— and Bumpass, L. (1988), 'Intergenerational Consequences of Marital Disruption', *American Journal of Sociology,* 94: 130–52.

—— and Sandefur, G. (1994), *Growing up with a Single Parent* (London: Harvard University Press).

McLaren, A. (1990), *A History of Contraception: From Antiquity to the Present Day* (Oxford: Blackwell).

Maclean, M. (1991), *Surviving Divorce: Women's Resources after Separation* (London: Macmillan).

—— (1994*a*), 'The Making of the Child Support Act of 1991: Policy Making at the Intersection of Law and Social Policy', *Journal of Law and Society,* 21 (4): 505–19.

—— (1994*b*), 'Delegalising Child Support', in M. Maclean and J. Kurazewski (eds.), *Families, Politics and the Law* (Oxford: Clarendon Press).

—— and Wadsworth, M. E. J. (1988), 'The Interests of Children after Parental Divorce: A Long Term Perspective', *International Journal of Law and the Family,* 2: 155–66.

MacMurray, J. (1935), *Reason and Emotion* (London: Faber and Faber).

McWhinnie, A. (1956), "Out of wedlock", *Case Conference,* 3 (1): 20–2.

Maidment, S. (1984), *Child Custody and Divorce* (London: Croom Helm).

Malthus, T. R. (1803), *Essay on the Principle of Population,* 2nd edn. (London).

Mansfield, P., and Collard, J. (1988), *The Beginning of the Rest of your Life: A Portrait of Newly-Wed Marriage* (London: Macmillan).

Marris, P. (1958), *Widows and their Families* (London: Routledge and Kegan Paul).

Marsden, D. (1969), *Mothers Alone* (London: Allen Lane, Penguin Press).

Marsh, A., and McKay, S. (1993*a*), *Families, Work and Benefits* (London: Policy Studies Institute).

—— —— (1993*b*), 'Families, Work and the Use of Child Care', *Employment Gazette,* August: 381–90.

—— Ford, R., and Finlayson, L. (1997), *First Effects of the Child Support Agency* (DSS Research Report; London: HMSO).

Marshall, R. (1972), *Families Receiving Supplementary Benefit* (Statistical and Research Report Series, No. 1; London: HMSO)

Martin, J., and Roberts, C. (1984), *Women and Employment: A Lifetime Perspective* (London: HMSO).

Martin, T. C., and Bumpass, L. L. (1989), 'Recent Trends in Marital Disruption', *Demography,* 26: 37–51.

Maslow, A. (1968), *Towards a Psychology of Being* (New York: Van Nostrand).

Mason, K. O., and Jensen, A.-M. (1995) (eds.), *Gender and Family Change in Industrialized Countries* (Oxford: Clarendon Press).

Mayall, B., and Petrie, P. (1983), *Childminding and Day Nurseries: What Kind of Care?* (London: Heinemann Educational Books).

Mayes, J., Forder, A., and Keedan, O. (1975), *Penelope Hall's Social Services of Modern England*, 9th edn. (London: Routledge and Kegan Paul).

Mead, L. (1986), *Beyond Entitlement: The Social Obligations of Citizenship* (New York: Free Press).

Meikle, W. (1916), *Towards a Sane Feminism* (London: Grant Richards).

Meltzer, H. (1994), *Day Care Services for Children* (OPCS; London: HMSO).

Meulders-Klein, M.-T. (1990), 'The Position of the Father in European Legislation', *International Journal of Law and the Family,* 4: 131–53.

Millar, J. (1989), *Poverty and the Lone-Parent Family: The Challenge to Social Policy* (Avebury: Aldershot).

—— (1996), 'Mothers, Workers, Wives: Policy Approaches to Supporting Lone Mothers in Comparative Perspective', in E. Bortolia Silva (ed.), *Good Enough Mothering?* (Brighton: Harvester Wheatsheaf).

Ministry of Health and Department of Health for Scotland (1959), *Report of the Working Party on Social Workers in Local Authority Health and Welfare Services* (London: HMSO).

Ministry of Health and Scottish Home and Health Department (1966), *Report of the Committee on Senior Nursing Staff Structures* (London: HMSO).

Ministry of Housing and Local Government, Welsh Office (1969), *Council Housing, Purposes, Procedures and Policies,* The Cullingworth Report (London: HMSO).

Ministry of Labour (1951), *Gazette*, June (London: HMSO).

Ministry of Social Security (1967), *Circumstances of Families* (London: HMSO).

Moore, G. E. (1968), *Principia Ethica* (1st edn. 1903; Cambridge: Cambridge University Press).

Moral Welfare (1960), 'A Final Study of Unmarried Mothers and their Children', May: 79–87.

Morgan, D. H. J. (1985), *The Family, Politics and Theory* (London: Routledge and Kegan Paul).

—— (1991), 'The Ideology of Marriage and Family Life', in D. Clark (ed.), *Marriage, Domestic Life and Social Change* (London: Routledge).

Morgan, P. (1995), *Farewell to the Family: Public Policy and Family Breakdown in Britain and the USA* (Choice in Welfare Series, No. 21; London: IEA).

Morris, C. (1954) (ed.), *Social Casework in Great Britain*, 2nd edn. (London: Faber and Faber).

Morris, D. (1971), *The End of Marriage* (London: Cassell).

MSS, *see* Ministry of Social Security.

Mueller, C. W., and Pope, H. (1977), *Marital Instability: A Study of its*

Transmission between Generations', *Journal of Marriage and the Family*, 39: 83–93.

Muller-Lyer, F. C. (1931), *The Family* (London: Allen and Unwin).

Murch, M. (1980), *Justice and Welfare in Divorce* (London: Sweet and Maxwell).

Murphy, M. J. (1985), 'Demographic and Socio-Economic Influences on Recent British Marital Breakdown Patterns', *Population Studies*, 39 (3): 441–60.

Murray, C. (1984), *Losing Ground: American Social Policy, 1950–1980* (New York: Basic Books).

Myrdal, A., and Klein, V. (1956), *Women's Two Roles: Home and Work* (London: Routledge and Kegan Paul).

NACAB (1994), *Child Support One Year On* (London: NACAB).

National Council for One Parent Families (1980), *An Accident of Birth: A Response to the Law Commission's Working Paper on Illegitimacy* (London: NCOPF).

—— (1994), *The Child Support Agency's First Year: The Lone Parent Case* (London: NCOPF).

National Council for the Unmarried Mother and her Child (1968), The Human Rights of those Born Out-of-Wedlock (London: NCUMC).

National Labour Women's Advisory Committee (1967), *Labour Women's National Survey into Care of Children* (London: Twentieth Century Press).

NCOPF, *see* National Council for One Parent Families.

NCUMC, *see* National Council for the Unmarried Mother and her Child.

Nevitt, A. (1967), *Fair Deal for Householders* (Research Series, No. 279; London: Fabian Society).

New Society (1976), 'Killing a Commitment: The Cabinet v the Children', 36 (715): 630–2.

Newsom, G. E. (1932), *The New Morality* (London: Ivor Nicholson and Watson).

Nicholson, J. (1968), *Mother and Baby Homes* (London: NCUMC).

Nissel, M. (1987), *People Count: A History of the General Register Office* (London: HMSO).

Nixon, J. (1979), *Fatherless Families on FIS* (DHSS Research Report, No. 4; London: HMSO).

Novak, M. and Cogan, J. (1987), The New Consensus on Family and Welfare: *A Community of Self-Reliance* (Marquette University, Milwaukee: American Enterprise Institute).

O'Donovan, K. (1993), *Family Law Matters* (London: Pluto Press).

ONS (Office for National Statistics) (1997), *Social Trends 27* (London: HMSO).

OPCS (Office of Population Censuses and Surveys) (1983), *Fertility Report from the 1971 Census Series DS* (London: HMSO).

—— (1984), *Marriage and Divorce Statistics 1981* (Series FM2; London: HMSO).

—— (1987), *Birth Statistics: Historical Series 1837—1983* (London: HMSO).

OPCS (Office of Population Censuses and Surveys) (1990), *Marriage and Divorce Statistics 1837–1983: Historical Series* (FM2, No. 16; London: HMSO).
—— (1993a), *Marriage and Divorce Statistics 1991* (Series FM2; London: HMSO).
—— (1993b), *General Household Survey Report 1991* (London: HMSO).
—— (1994), *Birth Statistics 1992* (Series FM1; London: HMSO).
—— (1995a), *Population Trends* (No. 79; London: HMSO).
—— (1995b), *General Household Survey Report 1993* (London: HMSO).
—— (1995c), *Marriage and Divorce Statistics 1993* (Series FM2; London: HMSO).
—— (1996a), *Living in Britain* (London: HMSO).
—— (1996b), *Population Trends* (No. 84; London: HMSO).
—— (1996c), *Population Trends* (No. 85; London: HMSO).
—— (1996d), *Population Trends* (No. 86; London: HMSO).
—— (annual), *Abortion Statistics* (Series AB; London: HMSO).
—— (annual), *Birth Statistics* (Series FM1; London: HMSO).
—— (annual), *Marriage and Divorce Statistics* (Series FM2; London: HMSO).
—— (annual), *Mortality Statistics* (Series DH1; London: HMSO).
OPCS/GRO Scotland (1993), *1991 Census Historical Tables Great Britain* (London: HMSO).
Oppenheimer, H. (1966), 'Moral Voice and Divine Authority', in I. R. Ramsey (ed.), *Christian Ethics and Contemporary Philosophy* (London: SCM Press).
Oppenheimer, V. K. (1994), 'Women's Rising Employment and the Future of the Family in Industrialised Societies', *Population and Development*, Review 20 (2) (June): 293–342.
Page, R. (1984), *Stigma: Concepts in Social Policy Two* (London: Routledge and Kegan Paul).
Pankhurst, C. (1913), *The Great Scourge and How to End it* (London: E. Pankhurst).
Parker, R. (1971), *The Housing Finance Bill and Council Tenants* (Pamphlet Nine; London: CPAG).
Parker, S. (1990), *Informal Marriage, Cohabitation and the Law, 1750–1989* (London: Macmillan).
Parsons, R. J. S. (1983), 'Social Work with Single Parent Families: Consumer Views', *British Journal of Social Work*, 13: 539–58.
Phizacklea, A. (1982), *One Way Ticket* (London: Routledge and Kegan Paul).
Phoenix, A. (1991), *Young Mothers* (Cambridge: Polity Press).
Pierson, P. (1994), *Dismantling the Welfare State? Reagan, Thatcher and the Politics of Retrenchment* (Cambridge: Cambridge University Press).
Pinder, P. (1969), *Women at Work*, vol. xxxv, broadsheet 512 (London: PEP).
Pochin, J. (1969), *Without a Wedding-Ring: Casework with Unmarried Parents* (London: Constable).

Politics, Economics, and Planning (PEP) (1946), 'The Unmarried Mother', *Planning*, No. 255 (Sept. 13).

Popenoe, D. (1988), *Disturbing the Nest: Family Change and Decline in Modern Societies* (New York: Aldine de Gruyter).

—— (1993), 'American Family Decline, 1960–1990: A Review and Appraisal', *Journal of Marriage and the Family*, 55 (August): 527–55.

Prescott-Clark et al. (1994), *Routes into Local Authority Housing* (London: HMSO).

Prinz, C. (1995), *Cohabitation or Marriage? New Living Arrangements in the Changing Societies of Europe* (Aldershot: Avebury Press).

Quilter, H. (1888) (ed.), *Is Marriage a Failure?* (London: Swan Sonenschein).

Rainwater, L., Rein, M., and Schwartz, J. (1986), *Income Packaging in the Welfare State* (Oxford: Clarendon Press).

Rapoport, R., and Rapoport, R. N. (1971), *Dual-Career Families* (Harmondsworth: Penguin).

Re-Bartlett, L. (1911), *The Coming Order* (London: Longman).

—— (1912), *Sex and Sanctity* (London: Longman).

Reid, J. H. (1971), 'Principles, Values and Assumptions underlying Adoption Practice', in R. Tod (ed.), *Social Work in Adoption: Collected Papers* (London: Longman).

Renvoize, J. (1985), *Going Solo: Single Mothers by Choice* (London: Routledge).

Rhymes, D. (1964), *No New Morality* (London: Constable).

Richards, M. P. M. (1982), 'Post-Divorce Arrangements for Children: A Psychological Perspective', *Journal of Social Welfare Law*, May: 133–51.

—— (1993), 'Children and Parents and Divorce', in J. Eekelaar and P. Saricevic (eds.), *Parenthood in Modern Society: Legal and Social Issues for the Twenty First Centure* (Dordrech: Martinus Nijhoff).

—— and Elliott, B. J. (1991), 'Sex and Marriage in the 1960s and 1970s', in D. Clark (ed.), *Marriage, Domestic Life and Social Change: Writings for Jacqueline Burgoyne, 1944–1988* (London: Routledge).

Rights of Women (1980), *Illegitimacy: ROW Evidence to the Law Commission* (London: ROW).

Riley, D. (1983), *War in the Nursery: Theories of the Child and the Mother* (London: Virago).

Roberts, R. W. (1966) (ed.), *The Unwed Mother* (New York: Harper and Row).

Robinson, J. A. T. (1963), *Honest to God* (London: SCM Press).

Rogers, B. (1994), 'Pathways between Parental Divorce and Adult Depression', *Journal of Child Psychology and Psychiatry*, 8: 1–11.

Roll, J. (1992), *Lone Parent Families in the European Community: A Report to the European Commission* (London: Family Policy Studies Centre).

Rose, H. (1978), 'In Practice Supported, in Theory Denied: An Account of an Invisible Urban Movement', *International Journal of Urban and Regional Research*, 2: 521–37.

Rose, H. (1985), 'Women's Refuges: Creating New Forms of Welfare', in C. Ungerson (ed.), *Women and Social Policy* (London: Macmillan).

Rosenbaum, M. (1970), 'Social Services Manpower', *Social Trends 1970* (No.1; London: HMSO).

Rosenbaum, S. (1972), 'Social Services Manpower', *Social Trends 1971* (No. 2; London: HMSO).

Ross, E. (1993), *Love and Toil* (Oxford: Oxford University Press).

Roussel, L. (1978), 'La Cohabitation Juvenile en France', *Population*, 33 (1): 15–42.

Rowe, J. (1966), *Parents, Children and Adoption: A Handbook for Adoption Workers* (London: Routledge and Kegan Paul).

Rowlingson K., and McKay, S. (1997), *The Growth of Lone Motherhood: the Pursuit of Economic Independence and Individual Happiness* (London: Policy Studies Institute).

Rowntree, G., and Carrier, N. (1958), 'The Resort to Divorce in England and Wales, 1838–1957', *Population Studies*, 11 (3): 188–233.

Royal Commission on Marriage and Divorce (1956), *Minutes of Evidence* (London: HMSO).

Royden, M. (1922), *Sex and Commonsense* (London: Hurst and Blackett).

—— (1925), *The Moral Standards of the New Age* (London: League of the Church Militant).

Rubinstein, D. (1991), *A Different World for Women: The Life of Millicent Garrett Fawcett* (Hemel Hempstead: Harvester Wheatsheaf).

Russell, B. (1916), *Principles of Social Reconstruction* (London: Allen and Unwin).

—— (1985), *Marriage and Morals* (1st edn. 1929; London: Unwin Paperbacks).

Rutter, M. (1981), *Maternal Deprivation Reassessed*, 2nd edn. London: Penguin.

SBC, *see* Supplementary Benefit Commission.

Schofield, M. (1965), *The Sexual Behaviour of Young People* (Harmondsworth: Penguin).

—— (1973), *The Sexual Behaviour of Young Adults: A Follow Up Study to 'The Sexual Behaviour of Young People'* (London: Allen Lane).

Seccombe, W. (1993), *Weathering the Storm: Working-Class Families from the Industrial Revolution to the Fertility Decline* (London: Verso).

Selman, P. F. (1988), *Family Planning* (London: Chapman and Hall).

—— and Glendinning, C. (1996), 'Teenage Pregnancies: Do Social Policies Make a Difference?', in J. Brannen and M. O'Brien (eds.), *Children in Families: Research and Policy* (London: Falmer Press).

Shaw, G. B. (1913), *Getting Married: A Disquisitory Play,* 'Preface', (London: Constable).

Shelter (1994), *Home Truths: Responses to the Consultation Paper* (London: Shelter).

Shorter, E. (1975), *The Making of the Modern Family* (New York: Fontana).

Simms, M. (1971), 'The Abortion Act after Three Years', *Political Quarterly*, 42 (3): 269–86.

Smart, C. (1984), *The Ties that Bind: Law, Marriage and the Reproduction of Patriarchal Relations* (London: Routledge, Kegan Paul).

—— (1989), 'Securing the Family? Rhetoric and Policy in the Field of Social Security', in M. Loney et al. (eds.), *The State or the Market: Politics and Welfare in Contemporary Britain* (London: Sage).

—— (1991), 'The Legal and Moral Ordering of Child Custody', *Journal of Law and Society*, 18 (4): 485–500.

—— (1995), 'The Family and Social Change: Some Problems of Analysis and Intervention', in B. Neale and C. Smart (eds.), *The New Parenthood? Discussions from the ESRC Project 'The Legal and Moral Ordering of Households in Transition'* (GAPU Research Working Paper, 13; Leeds: Leeds University), 32–43.

Social Security Advisory Committee (1985), *Fourth Report* (London: HMSO).

—— (1995), *Housing Benefit: The Review of Social Security* (Paper 3; Leeds: BA Publishing Services Ltd).

Soloway, R. A. (1982), *Birth Control and the Population Question in England 1877–1930* (Chapel Hill: University of North Carolina Press).

Sorensen, A. (1990), *Single Mothers, Low Income and Women's Economic Risks: The Cases of Sweden, West Germany and the United States* (Working Paper, No. 60; Luxembourg: Luxembourg Income Study).

Sparks, J. (1986), 'Marital Condition Estimates 1971–85: A New Series', *Population Trends* (No. 45; London: HMSO).

Spence, J. C. (1946), *The Purpose of the Family* (London: Convocation Lecture for the National Children's Home).

Spencer, H. (1892), *The Principles of Ethics* (London: Williams and Norgate).

—— (1969), *Man versus the State* (1st edn. 1884; Harmondsworth: Penguin).

SSAC, *see* Social Security Advisory Committee.

Stacey, J. (1990), *Brave New Families: Stories of Domestic Upheaval in Late Twentieth Century America* (New York: Basic Books).

Stevenson, O. (1973), *Claimant or Client?* (London: Allen and Unwin).

Stone, L. (1995), *The Road to Divorce: England 1530–1987* (Oxford: Oxford University Press).

Stopes, M. (1918), *Married Love* (New York: Critic and Guide Co.).

Strachey, St Loe (1909), 'A Poisonous Book', *Spectator*, 20 Nov.: 846–7.

Streather, J., and Weir, S. (1974), *Social Insecurity: Single Mothers on Benefit* (Poverty Pamphlet, 16; London: CPAG).

Streeter, B. H. (1927), 'Moral Adventure', in B. H. Streeter, C. M. Chilcott, and J. Macmurray (eds.), *Adventures in the Faith of Science and the Science of Faith* (London: Macmillan).

Supplementary Benefit Commission (1971), *Cohabitation* (London: HMSO).

Supplementary Benefit Commission (1976), *Living Together as Husband and Wife* (London: HMSO).

—— (1979), Response of the Supplementary Benefit Commission to *Social Assistance: A Review of the Supplementary Benefits Scheme in Great Britain* (London: SBC).

Swanwick, H. (1935), *I Have Been Young* (London: Victor Gollancz).

Swiney, F. (1908), *The Awakening of Women or Women's Part in Evolution* (1st edn. 1899; London: Willian Reeves).

Symon, P. (1990) (ed.), *Housing and Divorce: Studies in Housing* (No. 4; Glasgow: University of Glasgow Centre for Housing Research).

Szreter, S. (1996), *Fertility, Class and Gender in Britain, 1860–1940* (Cambridge: Cambridge University Press).

Tawney, R. (1964), *Equality*, 5th edn. (London: Allen and Unwin).

Taylor, M., Keen, M., Buck, N., and Corti, L. (1994), 'Income Welfare and Consumption', in N. Buck, J. Gershuny, D. Rose, and J. Scott (eds.), *Changing Households: The British Household Panel Survey 1990–1992* (Colchester: University of Essex ESRC Research Centre on Micro-Social Change).

Teichman, J. (1978), *The Meaning of Illegitimacy* (Cambridge: Englehardt Books).

Thane, P. (1978), 'Women and the Poor Law in Victorian and Edwardian England', *History Workshop Journal*, 6: 29–51.

—— (1991), 'Towards Equal Opportunities? Women in Britain since 1945', in T. Gourvish and A. O'Day (eds.), *Britain since 1945* (London: Macmillan).

Thatcher, M. (1995), *The Downing Street Years* (London: Harper Collins).

Thomas, G. (1944), *Women at Work: The Attitudes of Working Women towards Post-war Employment and Related Matters* (London: Wartime Social Survey).

Thompson, B. (1956), 'Social Study of Illegitimate Maternities', *British Journal of Preventative Social Medicine*, 10: 75–87.

Thorburn, J. (1980), *Single Parent Families: Some Social Work Responses* (Occasional Paper, 6; Norwich: University of East Anglia).

Titmuss, R. M. (1962), *Income Distribution and Social Change* (London: Allen and Unwin).

Tizzard, B. (1977), *Adoption: A Second Chance* (London: Open Books).

Tod, R. (1971) (ed.), *Social Work in Adoption: Collected Papers* (London: Longman).

Townsend, P. (1975), 'Problem of Introducing a Guaranteed Maintenance Allowance for One-Parent Families', *Poverty*, 31: 29–39.

Triseliotis, J. P. (1970), *Evaluation of Adoption Policy and Practice* (Edinburgh: Edinburgh University, Department of Social Administration).

TUC Working Party (1976), *The Under Fives* (London: TUC).

United Nations *Demographic Year Book 1965* (New York: United Nations).

van da Kaa, D. J. (1987), *Europe's Second Demographic Transition, Population Bulletin*, (Washington, DC: Population Reference Bureau).

Van der Eyken, W. (1984), *Day Nurseries in Action: A Report from the Child Health Research Unit* (Bristol: University of Bristol).

Vicinus, M. (1985), *Independent Women: Work and Community for Single Women, 1850–1920* (London: Virago).

Vincent, C. E. (1961), *Unmarried Mothers* (New York: Free Press of Glencoe).

—— (1971), 'The Unwed Mother and Sampling Bias', in R. Tod (ed.), *Social Work in Adoption: Collected Papers* (London: Longman).

Wadsworth, M., and Maclean, M. (1986), 'Parents' Divorce and Children's Life Chances', *Youth Services Review*, 8: 145–99.

Waldfogel, J. (1996), *What do we Expect Lone Mothers to do? Competing Agendas for Welfare Reform in the United States* (STICERD Discussion Paper, WSP/124; London: London School of Economics).

Walker, K. (1940), *The Physiology of Sex and its Social Implications* (Harmondsworth: Penguin).

—— (1957), *Love, Marriage and the Family* (London: Odhams).

Wallerstein, J. S., and Kelly, J. B. (1980), *Surviving the Breakup: How Children and Parents Cope with Divorce* (London: Grant McIntyre).

Walley, J. (1972), *Social Security: Another British Failure* (London: Charles Knight).

Ward, M. (1894), 'The Strike of a Sex', *Quarterly Review*, 179 (Oct.): 289–317.

—— (1909), *Daphne, or Marriage a la Mode* (London: Cassell).

Weale, A., Bradshaw, B., Maynard, A., Piachand, D. (1984), *Lone Mothers, Paid Work and Social Security* (London: Bedford Square Press).

Weeks, J. (1981), *Sex, Politics and Society* (London: Longman).

Weitzman, L. (1985), *The Divorce Revolution: The Unexpected Social and Economic Consequences for Women and their Children in America* (New York: Free Press).

Wells, H. G. (1906a), *Socialism and the Family* (London: A. C. Fifield).

—— (1906b), *The Comet* (London: Macmillan).

—— (1911), 'Mr. Asquith will die', *Freewoman*, 7 Dec.: 47.

—— (1980), *Ann Veronica* (1st edn. 1909; London: Virago).

Westermarck, E. (1908), *The Origin and Development of Moral Ideas* (London: Macmillan).

White, L. (1990), 'Determinants of Divorce: A Review of Research in the Eighties', *Journal of Marriage and the Family*, 52 (4): 904–12.

—— and Booth, A. (1985), 'The Transition to Parenthood and Marital Quality', *Journal of Family Issues*, 6: 435–49

Williams, G. (1945), *Women and Work* (London: Nicholson and Watson).

Wilson, W. J. (1987), *The Truly Disadvantaged* (Chicago: Chicago University Press).

Wimperis, V. (1960), *The Unmarried Mother and her Child* (London: Allen and Unwin).

Winnett, A. R. (1968), *The Church and Divorce* (London: A. R. Mowbray).

Winnicott, D. W. (1958), *Collected Papers* (London: Tavistock Institute).

—— and Britton, C. (1947), *Human Relations*.

Wong, I. Y.-L., Garfinkel, I., and McLanahan, S. (1993), 'Single-Mother Families in Eight Countries: Economic Status and Social Policy', *Social Service Review*, 67 (June): 177–97.

Woolf, M. (1971), *Family Intentions* (OPCS; London: HMSO).

Wootton, B. (1959), *Social Science and Social Pathology* (London: Allen and Unwin).

Wright, H. (1968), *Sex and Birth Control* (London: Allen and Unwin).

Wright, T. R. (1986), *The Religion of Humanity: The Impact of Comtean Positivism on Victorian Britain* (Cambridge: Cambridge University Press).

Wynn, M. (1968), *Fatherless Families* (London: Michael Joseph).

Yarrow, A. (1964), 'Illegitimacy in South-East Essex', *Medical Officer*, 24 Jan.: 47–8.

Yelloly, M. A. (1964), 'Social Casework with Unmarried Parents', MA thesis (University of Liverpool).

—— (1965), 'Factors Relating to an Adoption Decision by Mothers of Illegitimate Infants', *Sociological Review*, 13 (1): 5–14.

—— (1980), *Social Work Theory and Psychoanalysis* (New York: Van Nostrand Reinhold).

Young, H. (1989), 'One of Us, but Different', *The Guardian*, 8 Apr.

Young, L. (1954), *Out of Wedlock* (New York: McGraw-Hill Book Co.)

Young, M., and Willmott, P. (1973), *The Symmetrical Family: A Study of Work and Leisure in the London Region* (London: Routledge and Kegan Paul).

Younghusband, E. (1964), *Social Work and Social Change* (London: Allen and Unwin).

Yudkin, S., and Holme, A. (1969), *Working Mothers and their Children* (1st edn. 1963; London: Sphere Books).

INDEX